'This new book will become a classi~ ~ ~~~ ~nd a very pleasant one at that. Shippey ta~ ~nd thought of
the Vikings. Along with ex~ ~echnology, he
asks: "what gave them their ~ ~with it for so
long?" His answers often focu~ ~~~ amusements of Old
Norse heroes . . . a fine read v~ ~~y someone who understands Old Norse
sagas, myths and legends.'

> – Jesse Byock, Professor at the Cotsen Institute of Archaeology at UCLA
> and author of *Viking Age Iceland* and *Viking Language: Learn Old Norse*

'As tough and uncompromising as the Viking heroes whose lives and deaths it
recounts, Tom Shippey's book also shares their dark sense of humour . . . Shippey
upsets entrenched positions, dissects legend from history, and reveals how the
Vikings were able to dominate in the North for more than three centuries.'

> – Carolyne Larrington, Professor of Medieval European Literature,
> University of Oxford

'With his usual erudition and insight, Tom Shippey has shed some light on an
always interesting question: how different from us can a strange people (the
Vikings) be and still be considered human? Put another way: what does the
difference between how those people see themselves and how we see them say
about our capacity for sympathy and understanding? In Shippey's hands the
Vikings are a challenging subject, but an illuminating one.'

> – Stephen R. Donaldson, author of *The Chronicles of Thomas Covenant*

'Shippey's account of the mindset and motives of Vikings offers a judicious
challenge to scholarly orthodoxies, while reaching out to a much broader
readership. The horned helmets may have been banished, but the tough-minded
and rapacious marauder now reappears in ways that deserve serious attention
. . . a tour de force. Its author has done Viking studies a memorable service.'

> – Andrew Wawn, Emeritus Professor of Anglo-Icelandic Studies,
> University of Leeds

TOM SHIPPEY

LAUGHING
SHALL I DIE

LIVES AND DEATHS
OF THE
GREAT VIKINGS

REAKTION BOOKS

In memory of
Ernest Shippey
(1904–1962)

Í austrvegi lét hann raisa brýr

In the east, he built bridges

Published by
REAKTION BOOKS LTD
Unit 32, Waterside
44–48 Wharf Road
London N1 7UX, UK

www.reaktionbooks.co.uk

First published 2018, reprinted 2018 (three times), 2019
Paperback edition first published 2020
Copyright © Tom Shippey 2018

Printed and bound in Great Britain by TJ Books Ltd, Padstow, Cornwall

A catalogue record for this book is available from the British Library

ISBN 978 1 78914 217 4

Contents

Scandinavia.

Britain and the Irish Sea.

France and Spain.

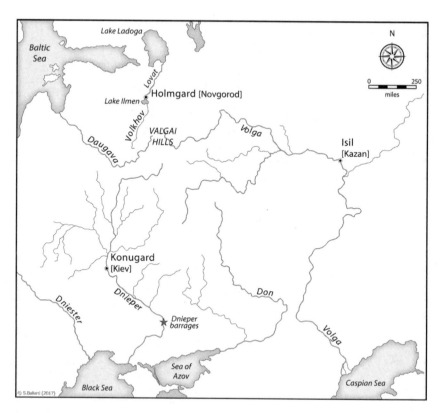

Waterways in the East.

PREFACE

This book is about the lives, and especially the deaths, of the great heroes and heroines of the Viking Age, as revealed in Old Norse poems and sagas, the greatest body of vernacular literature surviving from early Europe. It does not try to be a narrative history, though it takes in chronicles and accounts from several other languages. Nor is it a study of Norse mythology, another area well served already. It is about individual people, individual poems, and most of all about collective psychology: what made the Vikings so different and so distinctive.

Since the book is meant for the reading public I have made every effort to keep it reader-friendly. Notes and references, if useful, are at the end. Special letters and diacritics are not used except in quotations, and some modern place- and personal names. I write Ragnarok, not Ragnarǫk (scholarly convention) or Ragnarök (modern Icelandic convention).[1] The same goes for Volsung, Hogni, Volund and other names. Similarly, I have rendered the Old Norse letters Ð/ð as D/d, and Þ/þ as Th/th;[2] I have not marked vowel length; and I have deleted the last letter (which is actually a grammatical ending) in names like Ragnarr or Sveinn. The result is, for instance, the familiar Odin for Old Norse *Óðinn*. I keep the old letters and accent marks for the names of modern Icelandic scholars, and spell them as they do.

Vikings also readily used nicknames, sometimes rude, like Ketil Flatnose, sometimes respectful, like Killer-Glum, sometimes descriptive, like Thorkel the Tall, and frequently obscure, like Ragnar Hairy-breeches and his alleged son Ivar the Boneless. I use them without scare quotes, but sometimes give the original form where we aren't sure what it means. As a general but not inflexible rule I use the Old Norse/Icelandic title the first time a poem or saga is mentioned (such as *Atlakviða* or *Völsunga saga*) with the modern English translation ('The Lay of Atli'; 'The Saga of the Volsungs'), and thereafter use the English form – unless the relationship is obvious, as with *Njáls saga* and 'Njal's Saga'. Every now and then I quote a phrase or some lines from a poem in their original form as well as in translation, but this is either to show that Old Norse and modern English are not so very different (especially vulgar modern English), or else to show the Viking love of enigmatic language, a major feature of the art of the skald.

Finally, it wasn't just Vikings who caused problems over names. Anglo-Saxons regularly wrote Æthelstan and Æthelred, but modern historical convention (for no known reason) writes Athelstan but Ethelred. I have opted to follow convention in this area, as it is not worth the trouble of challenging.

That is not the case in other areas. Academics have laboured to create a comfort-zone in which Vikings can be massaged into respectability. But the Vikings and the Viking mindset deserve respect and understanding in their own terms – while no one benefits from staying inside their comfort zone, not even academics. This book accordingly offers a guiding hand into a somewhat, but in the end not-so-very, alien world.

Disturbing though it may be.

INTRODUCTION

Wwe all know what Vikings are. We even know what they looked like. Their bearded faces, often with horned or winged helmets on top, stare out from book covers and T-shirts and sardine tins. There are movies about them, and television series. The gods of their pantheon, Odin and Thor, Balder and Loki, are well-known names. Everyone has at least heard about Ragnarok and Valhalla. Vikings have become part of the modern world's cultural wallpaper.

Of course, a good deal of what we think we know is just plain wrong, starting with those horned helmets, completely impractical in any kind of close combat. But more important than what's wrong is what's missing. There's a question that has to be asked. How did the Vikings get away with it for so long? Or, putting it another way, what gave them their edge? An edge they maintained for almost three centuries, during which they became the scourge of Europe, from Ireland to Ukraine, from Hamburg to Gibraltar, and beyond in both directions.

It certainly wasn't logistical superiority. The small and scattered populations of Scandinavia, with its short growing season and often stony soil, were far inferior in manpower and resources to the Anglo-Saxon kingdoms, the Frankish empire, the Moorish realms of Spain, let alone the Byzantine Empire and the Muslim caliphate beyond it. Was it technological, then? Often put forward as an explanation are the Vikings' magnificent longships, about which we now know a lot more than we did. These certainly gave Vikings the advantages of surprise and mobility, vital for hit-and-run raids, the old habit of seaborne marauding. But Vikings soon took to marauding on land, and while they did not mind hit-and-run, they were also ready to stand and fight. And in stand-up fights they were hard to defeat. Even harder to daunt. If you beat them, they just came back again.

Nor were they opposed by mere pacifists. Especially in Western Europe, the native populations of Irish and English, Franks and Frisians and Germans were endemically warlike, in societies controlled by warrior elites and kings whose major business had always been war. Vikings, some-how, when it came to organized violence, managed to raise the bar. Though often mentioned, the weakness and disorganization of their enemies is not a full explanation either. Vikings were surely quick to take advantage, but not notably well-organized themselves. Western kings soon learned you could always pay one set of Vikings to fight another.

No, what gave them their edge was something psychological: I call it the Viking mindset. To put it bluntly, it's a kind of death cult. Explaining that mindset is the purpose of this book.

Not just Valhalla ...

In a way, the death cult answer just given has been obvious ever since the literature of the Old North started to be rediscovered centuries ago. As awareness of Old Norse poems, sagas and especially myths began to dawn again, what hit the learned men of Europe right between the eyes was Viking attitudes to death. People noticed immediately that this long-forgotten literature, preserved only in remote Iceland, centred far more than anything else they were used to on scenes of death, of grim defiance, on famous last stands and famous last words. The hero's death song was an artform in itself, with many examples recorded. This was so obvious that as early as 1689 someone tried to make sense of it.

He was a Dane called Thomas Bartholinus. (His real name was Bertelsen; he came from a medical family and his father, also Thomas Bartholinus, was the man who first described the human lymphatic system.) In 1689, though, the younger Bartholinus published a work, all of it in Latin, whose title translates as *Three Books, Digested from Old Books and Documents Until-now Unedited, on the Causes of the Contempt for Death among the Still Pagan Danes*. It was a kind of 'Reader's Digest' of all the big death scenes then known from Old Norse literature, and it took the learned world by storm – Walter Scott was still reading it with fascination, and using it, 150 years later.

Bartholinus's answer to the question he implied in his title was a mythological one. He thought that the 'contempt for death' so obvious in his sources was a result of the Norse belief that those who died in battle, sword in hand, would go to Odin's great hall Valhalla, the 'Halls of the Slain', there to spend their afterlife in feasting and fighting, up to the day of Ragnarok, the final combat.

The idea has been popular ever since. It dominates the action of the Kirk Douglas movie *The Vikings* (1958). But now we're not so sure. Back in the seventeenth century, in a completely Christian Europe securely anchored in religious belief, a mythological explanation looked natural. The whole idea, however, is largely drawn from just one passage in Snorri Sturluson's thirteenth-century handbook of myth and legend,[1] and it's not likely that religious belief and practice were anything like as generally accepted or all-encompassing in the Viking Age as they were in long-Christian Europe.

Bartholinus posed a good question, but it demands more than a single-explanation answer. What's needed is a closer look at Viking psychology, as revealed in the literature they and their descendants left behind and as expressed in individual stories, sagas, legends. That is, once again, what this book is about. What is revealed is often varied, dealing with people in different places, at different times, facing different conditions. But beneath it all there is a kind of consistency, a particular attitude, which – to get ahead of myself – I do not think could have been faked.

The trouble with 'Vikings'

If you say a question has an obvious answer, it's only fair to say why the answer hasn't been given already – especially after many decades of scholarly study. It's because there's a problem with terminology, and a problem with cultural attitudes, especially in the world of modern scholarship. To put it bluntly (again), most scholarly books with 'Viking' in the title turn out not to be about Vikings, because Vikings aren't popular among scholars. This book is different: it really is about Vikings.

The fact is that in the Vikings' own language, Old Norse, *víkingr* just meant pirate, marauder. It wasn't an ethnic label, it was a job description. And what this means for us is that if you come across headlines – as these days you very often do – which say something like 'Vikings! Not just raiders and looters any more!' then the headlines are wrong. If people weren't raiding and looting (and land-grabbing, and collecting protection money), then they had stopped being Vikings. They were just Scandinavians. But while most Vikings were Scandinavians, most Scandinavians definitely weren't Vikings, not even part-time. The two groups should not be confused, not even with the aim of making 'the history of the Vikings' look nicer.

The trouble is that raiding and looting, pirating and marauding, are (and this is, for once, putting it very mildly) not congenial topics in the modern academic world. So academics make a quiet shift. The trend was started in 1970 by a book called *The Viking Achievement*, with chapters on 'Trade and Towns', 'Transport', 'Art and Ornament' and so on.[2] These weren't

Viking achievements at all, they were Scandinavian achievements, created by – this is a later book's more honest title – *The Norsemen in the Viking Age*.[3] But Vikings make modern academics uneasy.

Sometimes uneasiness shows itself not in the titles (which publishers insist on; they know what sells) but in the subtitles. The British Museum exhibition of 2014, with its accompanying and very impressively illustrated book, was called *Vikings: Life and Legend*. 'Life' got a lot more space than 'legend', and there was some silent censorship. Jonathan Clements's *Brief History of the Vikings* (2005) asks whether they were 'The Last Pagans or the First Modern Europeans'. The latter option is preferred: Vikings, we're told, promoted European integration. Anders Winroth's *The Age of the Vikings* (2014) 'looks at Viking endeavors in commerce, politics, discovery, and colonization'.[4] One can see the sidestep there: all those were *Scandinavian* endeavours, not Viking ones at all, but they are much more acceptable as topics than piracy and marauding. In short, many books proclaimed as being about Vikings actually *back away from* real Vikings, the pirates and marauders, retreating to the scholarly comfort-zones of exploration, trade, urban development and distanced narrative history. All of which is admittedly part of the story. Just not the only part, and very much *not* the part that has, ever since the seventeenth century, catapulted Vikings into the forefront of popular imagination.

The result is that Viking studies have long been polarized. From the start there was the romantic or what one might call the comic-book approach, full of clichés, often mistaken. The movie *Eric the Viking* of 1989 is a reliable source for most of them: berserkers, skulls, horned helmets, valkyries, Valhalla and a great deal of 'quaffing'; to which *The Vikings* added spaewives, invocations of Odin, dying sword in hand, and the popular sport of severing blonde ladies' plaits by competitive axe-throwing.

In their embarrassed flight from this – and it is certainly founded often enough on straight misunderstanding, not to mention straight invention – modern scholars have created a minimalist school of Viking studies. One can imagine the way their view might be put in the civilized surroundings of the faculty club:

> Pagan marauders, permanently drunk on mead, constantly raping and massacring? Not at *all*, terribly overstated. There may have been a little trouble with the locals, as there always is with groups of young men away from home, but you can't believe what monkish chroniclers say, all their numbers must be wrong, that would be like believing people's insurance claims, and as for sagas . . .

I exaggerate the scholarly attitude, but not much.[5] It deals with the literary evidence in particular – of which we have a great deal – by turning a blind eye and arguing about dates.

Dates are of course important and are discussed later on. Nevertheless, the 'faculty club' view, as I call it, misses out a great deal, including the vital question of Viking mindset, or even Viking ideology. It is at least as one-sided as the comic-book images. The evidence of English, Irish, Frankish, Greek and even Arabic sources, as well as the native Scandinavian ones, is thoroughly consistent, as some have started to concede. In recent years it has been remarked by two or three professors – and as something of a corrective to the general academic consensus – that we should not forget that Vikings were under no obligation to observe the Geneva Convention; that while Vikings were not mad, they were often bad and always dangerous to know; even that there was something 'psychopathic' about Viking culture.[6]

To which one need only add that twenty-first-century 'psychopathic' could be ninth-century 'well-adjusted'.

Viking Age fact or medieval fiction?

What follows in this book is not quite a list of 'top ten Vikings'. Sometimes characters come in pairs, linked by alliance, as in the case of Ganger-Hrolf of Normandy and his shadowy mentor Hastein, or by deadly enmity, like Egil Skallagrimsson the skald and King Eirik Blood-axe of York. Sometimes names and careers have to be extricated with difficulty from scattered sources. Dramatic female characters are also part of the story: not themselves Vikings by trade, but often the most determined instigators and proponents of the heroic mindset. Not only are there more than ten Vikings to consider, there are even different kinds of Viking. The 'Viking Age' spanned three centuries, and Vikings were nothing if not adaptable when it came to searching out new sources of profit. But whether they were raiding monasteries, organizing slave markets, grabbing land to settle or engaging in something very like a 'game of thrones', what they did was based on violence. That is what Vikings were good at: especially good at, spectacularly good at.

Going back to the question of why that should be, this book opens with a consideration of the 'Viking mindset'. And it comes up with an answer that is – this is what universities these days call a 'trigger warning' – uncomfortable, uncongenial and probably to many unwelcome. (So it goes, to borrow a phrase from Kurt Vonnegut.)

I go on to give an overview of the death cult, as revealed in one scene after another, and in particular the 'die laughing' enigma. This central literary preoccupation, so prominent in Old Norse, is surrounded and supported by historical evidence from many directions in many languages. Some of the most powerful corroboration comes from archaeology, which in recent years has repeatedly changed opinions, and just as repeatedly confirmed what sagas say – and which tender hearts again did not want to believe, such as the mechanics of organizing mass beheadings. (Though what recent archaeology has revealed is people doing this *to* Vikings, not the other way round. The Vikings and their enemies learned from each other.)

The book as a whole also takes us from prehistory, myth and heroic legend into well-documented eras where we have information coming from all sides. The general trend is from darkness into the light, but it's not a smooth progression. The earliest event mentioned, well before the Viking Age got started, is surprisingly well corroborated by several sources, one of them written down within living memory. By contrast, events that occurred hundreds of years later in Iceland were not recorded in writing until centuries after they happened. They were recorded, however, by people who believed themselves, no doubt correctly, to be the descendants of the old heroes and who knew to the inch where everything took place: not first-hand evidence, then, but very good evidence just the same. In the end, every case has to be judged for reliability on its own merits. I will forbear from trying to prejudge them collectively here.

Having been tough on the sidesteps and evasions of others, however, I have to face up to a question which those others would certainly put. How far can the kind of literary evidence used in what follows be trusted? Just to begin with, much of it is evidently fantastic. Were-bears, swan maidens, elf women, spaewives, valkyries and murderous goddesses all turn up repeatedly in sagas of all kinds. Egil Skallagrimsson, a great Viking and certainly a historical character, is alleged to have been descended from trolls – but then in modern times a rather convincing medical explanation has been given for this. Interventions by Odin are almost routine, reflecting the great contest in the north between pagan and Christian, maybe closer-run than later hindsight made out. There are hints of deeper mythic structures, too embedded in belief as well as story to be winkled out.

Fantasy, however, is easily detected and allowed for. A more serious criticism comes from the fact that much of the material used here, especially the kings' sagas, and the 'sagas of old times' or *fornaldarsögur*, was written hundreds of years after the events, by people who weren't Vikings at all, only their descendants. Isn't it naive to take them as reliable accounts of anything?

Most of them were at least *thought* to be true records. Snorri Sturluson (1179–1241), the Icelandic politician and author of many such sagas, famously protested that his stories must be true because they were based on poems 'that were recited before the rulers themselves or their sons' and then memorized and passed on orally until a time came when they could be written down by people like Snorri. While skalds might be thought to flatter, he insisted, 'no one would dare to tell [a chieftain] to his face about deeds of his which all who listened, as well as the man himself, knew were falsehoods and fictions. That would be mockery and not praise.'[7]

Snorri may have ruined himself as an authority on heroic death by his own death – and *his* death was recorded early and probably from eyewitness accounts. When his enemies caught him hiding in his own cellar on 22 September 1241, too slow to get to the secret escape tunnel only rediscovered recently, all he said was, desperately but unheroically, 'Mustn't strike, mustn't strike'.[8] He should have known this never worked with Vikings or their descendants. They just cut him down. But sometimes we have the early poems he based his sagas on, and can check him, and he comes out of such cross-checking surprisingly well. There are other sources of information as well as the poems and sagas, often coming from the Vikings' enemies, while sometimes there is also the grim, mute, inarguable but often incomprehensible evidence of archaeology.

For all that, saga evidence is generally written off by historians as 'not reliable', which by modern historical standards is true: few or no dates, for one thing. Ray Page, a Cambridge professor (and this author's tutor, though he would never have thanked anyone for reminding him), wrote repeatedly in his excellent *Chronicles of the Vikings* that 'the rigorous historian must look at [sagas] with suspicion', that the sagas of Icelanders in particular 'are not commonly cited as historical sources save by those who have failed to keep up with the scholarly times'.[9]

One might remark that 'the scholarly times' are not infallible and are indeed very much subject to fashion. But one can certainly agree with Page's insistence that '[sagas'] authenticity must be continually questioned' – though one should also add that sometimes the questioning comes out positive, saga narrative being confirmed by archaeology.[10] Moreover, even Page concedes that poems like the lays of Volund and Atli, which I discuss later on, 'give some clues to the values [their authors and audiences] accepted'.[11] There is an impressive consistency, and an often underrated complexity, in just what is revealed about those values in Eddic poems, kings' sagas, sagas of old times, sagas of Icelanders and much else, including skaldic poems and runestones.

Uncovering those values is, then, just as reasonable a goal as writing (another) 'rigorous' narrative history, dates and all! Though the fiction demands, of course, to be set against what we can uncover of the facts.

Evaluating 'imaginaries'

Maybe the fiction/fact dichotomy does not, in any case, represent the true situation – which, as it happens, we are rather well placed to understand. One of the useful words introduced by modern literary theory is the idea of 'an imaginary' (adjective used as noun), by which I mean 'a collective picture of an era derived from books, films, television, and so on'. The obvious example in the modern world is the 'imaginary' of 'the Wild West', made up, as we all know, of gunslingers, wagon trains, rustlers, the u.s. cavalry and, of course, cowboys and Indians.

How true to fact was this? Obviously, many of the characters in it, from Billy the Kid to Crazy Horse, were real people with real biographies. Equally obviously, many of the familiar scenarios – shoot-outs in Main Street, circled wagon trains, stagecoaches pursued by yelling braves – became clichés very much more common in fiction than in fact. One feature of the Wild West imaginary is that it has no sense of time: things had changed a lot in the 1870s from the 1830s, but this is rarely indicated in the B-movies and cheap TV series.

There is nowadays a 'Viking imaginary' as well, composed of berserkers, valkyries, horned helmets and so on; this is what modern scholars complain about and have set themselves to combat. The point they are trying to make – though they don't put it like this – is that the modern Viking imaginary is based not on reality but on an early medieval Viking imaginary. In other words, the poems and sagas (and with them the mindset this book sets itself to discuss) were all or mostly created two or three centuries later than the real Viking Age, and so they are not a good representation of it.

Before considering how true that is, we might consider further the situation of our nineteenth-, twentieth- and twenty-first-century 'Wild West', about which we have a lot more data. How good is our representation of the Wild West? The creation of this imaginary overlapped in time with the real situation – dime novels about gunfighters were being written in the East while the gunfighters themselves were still alive in the West, a situation dramatized comically in Clint Eastwood's *Unforgiven* (1992). The case of the Vikings and the 'early medieval Viking imaginary' is certainly similar, but in critical respects not the same.

The Viking Age lasted much longer than the era of the Wild West: three hundred years as opposed to sixty or seventy. It ended dramatically, with the defeat and death of giant King Harald of Norway in 1066, but without the immense social, technological and political changes of the late nineteenth century. The living conditions of most Scandinavians did not change at all, and in Iceland people probably did not even notice the 'end of an age'.

As regards literature, skaldic verse continued to be composed for generations after 1066, as well as before, and Eddic verse continued at least to be copied, or else we wouldn't have any. The development of saga writing is certainly post-Viking (as was writing of any kind in the early Scandinavian world, runes apart), but the legends on which some of the sagas were based were circulating by the end of the Viking Age, if not earlier: Adam of Bremen had heard about Ragnar 'Lodbrog' by 1070, and a hundred years later Saxo Grammaticus knew forms of many of the legends, which were already old enough for them to have got confused. It is significant that in the 1220s Snorri Sturluson wrote his account of the Norse myths in his *Prose Edda* because he thought that they were *beginning* to be forgotten, but also that they needed to be remembered, for the use of practising poets. The myths were from the pagan era, officially terminated more than two hundred years before when Iceland became by agreement Christian. But they were still known, and in a way they were still vital.

There was, then, a much longer twilight for the Viking Age in literature and a much greater continuity, in social conditions and cultural attitudes, than there was for the Wild West. Quite how great that continuity was we don't know, it's true. Quite how reliable are the literary representations of the Viking Age in the 'early medieval imaginary' of the sagas, again, we don't know. But then we cannot be sure how reliable modern representations of 'the Wild West imaginary' are either. Some more than others, no doubt. It seems obvious that *Lonesome Dove*, for instance, is much truer to life than the stereotyped adventures of 'The Lone Ranger'; where John Wayne and Clint Eastwood stand in this spectrum is not so clear.

One therefore has to decide about the poems and the sagas in much the same way as one may want to decide about *The Searchers* or *Pale Rider*: case by case, and remembering the much greater continuity of the post-Viking era. One last and important difference between the two situations is this. Much of the Wild West imaginary was created by people in close touch with each other, in Hollywood scriptwriter conferences or the dime novel mills of New York. They all copied from each other. The Viking imaginary of the early medieval period (if that is what it was) was put together – scores of sagas, hundreds of poems – by people without modern communications, scattered across the Northern world, rarely in touch with each other, and over a period of several centuries. Even a saga writer in Akureyri (say) may have had little idea of what was being written and copied elsewhere in Iceland. Yet what was produced was strikingly similar – and strikingly distinctive – when it comes to that characteristic mindset, as I keep calling it.

Was this the product of collusion, and so as phony as the Hollywood West? That is what is implied by the minimalist or 'faculty club' school of commentary. But once the question is framed, rather than assumed or hinted at, the implied answer – 'well of course it is!' – looks unlikely. How did all those scattered writers collude? And how strange it is that they managed to produce so many – and such distinctive – patterns of behaviour and speech with so few traces of deliberate copying. And then there are the cross-checks which this book continues to search out, from the accounts of the victims, from the reports of the archaeologists. I think, in brief, that the post-Viking writers understood their ancestors pretty well. They certainly thought they did.

So, step outside the faculty club! Forget the horned helmets as well! It's the mindset, pragmatic, fatalistic, egalitarian, ironic and full of (apparent) contradictions, which should take the eye. It takes working out, and it needs discrimination as well, which I hope this book will provide. But that's what made the Vikings great – in fiction, and quite likely in fact as well.

This book, then, uses all available sources, in several languages and from several disciplines, to probe what can be ascertained about the values of the Viking Age – with decent scepticism, it is hoped, and definitely with as much cross-referencing as possible. But its intention is to let the Vikings and their descendants speak for themselves. Their many voices express a spirit which is like no other on earth. They deserve not to be silenced or toned down into acceptability.

Though there's a mean streak there, as this book will show.

PART I

Dying Hard

ONE

The Viking Mindset:
Three Case Studies

I think the greatest collection of poetry in the whole world is contained in the manuscript known as the Codex Regius, the 'King's Book'. It was a king's book only temporarily and accidentally. It's really a farmer's book, and we don't even know who the farmer was, who the poets were, who deserves the credit for copying and preserving the whole set of 29 poems. The manuscript is now probably the greatest treasure of the Icelandic state, but there ought to be a memorial in Reykjavik as well, to 'the Unknown Farmer'.

What happened is that during the Middle Ages the literature of the old North, and most of its history and mythology, became completely forgotten. Except in far-off Iceland, that is, where the Icelanders, scratching a living from their poor soil and rich fishing grounds, continued to remember old traditions, old poems, old stories; and, once they had been converted to Christianity and taught the art of writing by clerics from the south, to write them down. They wrote and wrote and wrote: sagas of old times, kings' sagas, sagas of their own ancestors, sagas about skalds, and skaldic poems. Quite why this became a national activity, no one knows. They had plenty of sheepskins to make vellum as writing material, and in the long winter nights near the Arctic circle there may have been little else to do, but by the same token writing by candlelight during the long nights must have been both difficult and expensive. Still, write they did. But for centuries no one noticed.

Then, as the Middle Ages drew to a close, the kings of Scandinavia started to take an interest in their own ancestry, and they – or more likely their librarians – realized that here the Icelanders were the authorities on the subject. It became known that information was valuable and that old manuscripts would make acceptable gifts. Accordingly, early in the 1640s Bishop Brynjólfur Sveinsson of Skálholt in Iceland acquired a manuscript, from some farmstead in his diocese, and sent it to King Christian IV of Denmark, Iceland then being a Danish possession.

Twenty years later a Danish scholar, Peder Resen, brought out an edition of the two major mythological poems in the manuscript, *Hávamál* and *Vǫluspá*, respectively 'The Words of the High One' (that is, Odin) and 'The Prophecy of the Seeress'. With it he added a version of the *Prose Edda*, a mythological handbook written in the 1220s in Iceland by Snorri Sturluson. Since Snorri quoted extensively from the poems of the Codex Regius, the whole set of 29, plus a few others found elsewhere, became known as the *Poetic Edda* or the *Elder Edda*.[1]

Resen and his successors (such as Thomas Bartholinus) created a major literary shock for the learned world of Europe as word of this forgotten tradition of myth and poetry, legend and history began to leak out. This operated on several levels, but perhaps the first shocking element was mythological. Old Norse myth, unlike the Christian myth, was rootedly pessimistic. It was not a 'divine comedy' that would end happily, but just the opposite, a 'divine tragedy', in which even the gods would die. Or, putting it another way, and once again putting it bluntly, the myths and legends of the old northern world seemed to be all about losers. This is something perhaps even stranger to the twenty-first-century world than it was to the seventeenth and eighteenth.

Winning and losing: a different attitude

Losing is a vital part of the Norse belief structure, expressed in the myth of Ragnarok, preserved both in the poem *Vǫluspá* and in Snorri's expansion of it in his *Prose Edda*. Ragnarok is like Armageddon, the battle at the end of the world. In it the gods and their human allies will march out to fight against the frost giants and the fire giants, the trolls and the monsters. And in that battle – and this is not at all like Armageddon – our side, the good guys, will *lose*. Thor will kill the Midgard Serpent, the great snake that coils round the world, and then drop dead from its poison. Odin will be swallowed by the wolf Fenrir. Heimdal and the traitor god Loki, Tyr and the great hound Garm: both pairs will kill each other, but Frey, left swordless, will fall before the fire giant Surt, who will then set the world ablaze.[2]

The gods know this is going to happen. That is why Odin habitually betrays his own chosen heroes to death, and this is where the myth of Valhalla comes in. Odin wants his best heroes dead so he can collect them in his own Halls of the Slain (Valhalla), where they will fight each other every day, for practice, and come back to life-in-death at the end of every day, to feast.[3] Odin knows Ragnarok is coming, but since he does not know when, he wants his team to be at all times as strong as possible, even though the result is foreordained. Even the gods will die, and their side will lose as well, and they know they will. But this does not make them want to negotiate, still less change sides. *Refusal to give in is what's important.* It's only in ultimate defeat that you can show what you're really made of.

All this shows an attitude to winning and losing markedly different from ours. To us, calling someone 'a loser' is seriously insulting. This must be the result of 150 years of competitive sport. All modern games start off by imposing fair conditions. Same numbers on each side, level pitch, no ground advantage, toss a coin at the start for choice of ends in case there *is* some advantage, change ends halfway through to cancel any such advantage, umpires and referees to see fair play – all the rules are there to see that the better team wins. So if you lose, you must have been inferior in some way, strength or speed or skill, and if you lose consistently, then there's something wrong with you: no excuses.

Vikings were wiser. They knew that in the real world, conditions aren't fair. Heroes may be outnumbered, betrayed, trapped, caught off guard or just plain run out of luck. That doesn't make you what we call 'a loser'. To their way of thinking, the only thing that would make you a loser would be giving up. And there's another factor, perhaps the most distinctive thing about the Viking mindset. It too caught the attention of the learned world of Europe very early on, and created a strange mix of surprise, disapproval and, eventually, guarded respect. This was that the heroes of the Viking Age, both gods and men, fixated as they seemed to be on death and defeat, *just did not seem able to take death and defeat seriously.* Unlike the ponderous heroes of the classical world, with whom every educated person was then familiar, they kept on making jokes, coming out with wisecracks. To them, the throwaway line was another artform. They had no sense of their own dignity. Or maybe, they had such a *strong* sense of their own dignity that they felt no need to stand on it. Whatever the reason, this attitude was something entirely new and intriguing: a new literary flavour.

Finally, and combining the attitude to losing with the attitude to joking, what was especially relished in story after story was the stroke that showed that the hero *hadn't* given up, even in an impossible situation. What was best was showing you could turn the tables, spoil your enemy's victory, make a joke out of death, die laughing.

People who think like that, one may well conclude, can be beaten by superior force, but though they can be killed like anyone else, they are (once again) impossible to daunt. If they're alive they'll come back at you, they're not done until they're stone dead; even if they're dying or helpless they will try to think of some trick, and if you fall for it, then the joke's on you.

Viking humour. Their secret weapon. Part of their mindset. Take warning, though, once again! There's a mean streak running all the way through it.

Viking sense of humour, 1: cutting out hearts

My first example comes from the Codex Regius, which contains mythological poems about gods and legendary poems about heroes in an approximately 50/50 mix. One of the best of the legendary poems is *Atlakviða*, 'The Lay of Atli'. Atli is the historical figure Attila the Hun (d. AD 453), and his enemy Gunnar is a historical figure too, based on the Burgundian king Gundaharius, who ruled a kingdom on the Rhine about twenty years earlier.[4] (The Burgundians came originally from *Borgundar-holm*, now Danish Bornholm, but had migrated south in the upheavals after the Fall of Rome.) In legend, though, Gunnar is one of the famous family of the Nibelungs, and the vital fact about them is that, at the time when 'The Lay of Atli' is set, they had murdered Sigurd the Dragon-slayer and seized the fabulous hoard he took from the dragon Fafnir. In legend again, they were the richest people in the world.

Also according to 'The Lay of Atli', what Atli/Attila wants is the treasure of the Nibelungs, and Gunnar and his brother Hogni are the only men who know where it is hidden. Atli is married to their sister Gudrun, and he invites them to visit him; it's a trap. They accept the invitation and walk into the trap.

The first strange thing in the situation is that they did so with their eyes wide open. They knew it was a trap. The next and even stranger thing is Gunnar's demand. When the Huns take him prisoner and ask him whether he will buy his life with the treasure, he says he will not reply until he has his brother Hogni's heart in his hand. The Huns, very reasonably, sense something is up, take a kitchen slave called Hjalli, cut out his heart and bring it to Gunnar. He rejects it contemptuously:

> Here I have the heart   of Hjalli the coward,
> Not like the heart   of Hogni the brave.
> Much does it tremble   as it lies on the plate,
> It trembled more by half   when it lay in his breast.[5]

It is in fact a large, soft, flabby, wobbly heart and could never have come out of a hero. So the Huns try again, this time on the proper target, Hogni; this time I give the original as well as my translation, to show the underlying similarity between Norse and English:

Hló þá Hǫgni,	Hogni laughed then,
er til hiarta scáro	when they cut to the heart
qviqvan kumblasmið,	the living scar-smith,
klecqva hann sizt hugði . . .	he had no mind to whine . . .[6]

Hogni is a smith-of-scars: he has dealt out many wounds, now he shows how to take one.

His heart is taken to Gunnar, who regards this one with approval:

> Here I have the heart   of Hogni the bold,
> Not like the heart   of Hjalli the coward.
> Little does it tremble   as it lies on the plate.
> Much less did it tremble   when it lay in his breast.[7]

And then Gunnar says he won't talk:

> Always I had a doubt,   while we two lived,
> Now it's only me,   now I alone am alive.[8]

It's a great scene, and great poetry (which my translation cannot capture), but one has to admit, the whole sequence is both enigmatic and challenging. Working out the enigmas, and noting the challenge, tells us a lot about the Viking mindset.

For us the challenge lies in the image of the ideal heart. Our compliments go 'big-hearted', 'warm-hearted'. The Norse ideal, in marked contrast, is a small heart, a hard heart, one without generosity, contracted to essentials. The vital thing is that it *shall not tremble*, will remain unmoved. As for the enigmas, there are four. Why did Gunnar and Hogni walk knowingly into a trap? Why doesn't Gunnar resist like his brother? Why does Gunnar ask for his brother's heart? And what makes Hogni laugh as they cut his heart out? It's the first that is maybe the trickiest.

The strange thing is that what made Gunnar and Hogni walk into the trap was precisely the fact that they had been warned. Their sister Gudrun knew her husband's treacherous plan and sent her brothers a coded warning: a ring with a wolf's hair twisted round it. The brothers listen to Atli's invitation, with its promises of many gifts, horses and weapons, slaves and land. The promises don't interest them: they are already the richest men in the world. But the ring with the wolf's hair? What does that mean? It's easy to decode. Hogni comments (and here I use the translation by the poet W. H. Auden):

> Why did our sister send us a ring
> Woven with wolf's wool? A warning, I think.
> A wolf's hair was wound in the ring.
> Wolfish our road if we ride this errand.[9]

With warning received and understood, Gunnar then *changes his mind*. They will accept the invitation after all.

This seemed enigmatic even to Norsemen, and another Norse poem, *Atlamál*, or 'The Greenlandic Lay of Atli', also in the Codex Regius but allegedly composed in the tiny Icelandic colony of Greenland, did its best to improve the story. It tells a tale of a message from Gudrun in runes, which had been altered by Atli's messenger so it was no longer a warning. But the original logic of the earlier poem is clear enough – if you think like a hero.

Everyone knows the schoolyard tactic where A says to B, 'Is that a threat?' and B says to A, 'No, it's a warning.' You cannot honourably back down from a threat, but you can save face by taking a warning. B is offering A a way out. The strategy rarely works even in the schoolyard, and it doesn't work at all with Old Norse heroes. This is because, however you quibble with words, a warning is *close* to a threat, and if you accept a warning, someone might possibly *think* you were frightened. So a warning comes close to being a dare, and with heroes, especially Viking heroes, dares have to be accepted. So sending a warning of any kind was exactly the wrong thing to do. It meant the Nibelung brothers had to take the dare.

The Burgundians ride from the Rhine across Mirkwood into the land of the Huns, and there they are betrayed and taken alive. Hogni cuts down seven men before he is taken, and throws another into the fire, but Gunnar is bound without resistance. We then come to the second question: why doesn't he fight like his brother? The answer to that is easy: because he can see ahead, and his resistance will not be physical. What it will be is final, completely decisive.

The next enigma is why Gunnar demands his brother's heart. Did he not trust his brother? Did he think Hogni would crack under torture? Surely not. But who knows – maybe if the Huns had offered to torture Gunnar, Hogni would have done a deal. The very characteristic logic of the situation, as Gunnar says, is that the only person you can really trust all the way is yourself – as long as you are quite sure your own will is unbreakable, which Gunnar's is.

Finally, why does Hogni laugh when they cut out his living heart? It's much better than whining; it shows contempt for pain. But perhaps also we are meant to think that he knows what his brother is up to and appreciates the joke that's coming.

Anyway, the Huns fall for the trick and now the laugh is on them. The only person who now knows where the treasure is is Gunnar, and he won't talk. One may conclude that it's no use trying to play 'prisoner's dilemma' with Viking heroes. You have no leverage on them. Once they realize he's not going to talk, the Huns take Gunnar and put him in the snakepit, to be stung to death by adders. He plays the harp defiantly as he dies. (The Greenlandic poem, over-egging the pudding as usual, says his hands were tied so he played the harp with his toes.) 'The Lay of Atli', the shorter and better poem, just says approvingly, 'That's how a bold ring-giver must guard his gold from men'.[10] Now, says Gunnar, the great treasure will lie forever in the Rhine.

So, if you cannot win, make certain your enemy cannot win either – and the story does not end there. The whole sequence of thought is nevertheless, considered dispassionately, close to crazy. Couldn't Gunnar have won the game just by refusing the invitation and staying at home? No, because then there would have been no confrontation; a challenge would have been ducked. Should he have fought, like his brother? No, because killing a few enemies would make no difference long-term. The joke in the final situation is that Gunnar makes his captors destroy their own last hope, by reducing the number of men who know the secret to one. They underestimated him.

The scene and the poem bring out recurrent features of Old Norse literature, the literature of the Vikings. It's enigmatic: you have to decode it. It's cruel: Hjalli the kitchen slave is 'collateral damage', but he has to be there for his unheroic heart to be recognized and rejected, and for the contrast to be made with a real hero's heart. The scene shows values very different from ours: for heroes, hard-heartedness is a virtue. Most surprising of all, the end of the story is (kind of) funny. The laugh is on the Huns. By cutting out Hogni's heart they lost their last bargaining point.

Vikings, we can see, very much appreciated a Good Sense of Humour.

Viking sense of humour, 2: forging the cunning thing

It has to be admitted right away that it was not the GSOH (Good Sense of Humour) regularly advertised on modern dating sites. In fact by modern standards it is a thoroughly BSOH, Bad Sense of Humour, and it has certainly drawn frequent expressions of disapproval from modern scholars: distasteful, morally uncomfortable, far from attractive, and so on.[11] It's too violent and too aggressive for liberal moderns, and, one could add, remembering Gunnar and his brother, too cruel and too hard-hearted.

It gets worse, and here I need to give what is called in liberal modern colleges a 'trigger warning'. The story of Volund the smith – Weyland in modern English – is about as 'distasteful' as it gets. But it was famous all across the northern world, and it makes a point that needs to be faced. The best version of it comes in *Vǫlundarkviða*, 'The Lay of Volund', another poem from the Codex Regius; this time it is a mythical rather than a legendary story, for Volund is a semi-supernatural figure with no historical connections at all. It goes like this.

Volund is one of three brothers. All married swan maidens. The wives stayed for seven years, but then flew away. Two of the brothers went off to seek for them, but Volund, the great smith, stayed behind, forging gold rings, waiting and hoping for his wife to return. King Nidud of Sweden, 'Lord of the Njars', hears that Volund is alone with his wealth and sends men to take him. When they arrive at Volund's hall, Volund is out bear-hunting, but they find seven hundred gold rings threaded on ropes. They take just one of them before concealing themselves, but when Volund returns, he notices. (He's like a dragon: he knows know exactly how many rings he's got.) He thinks his wife must have come back and taken it. He falls asleep waiting for her, and when he wakes up, he's in chains. Nidud gives his daughter Bodvild the ring Volund had meant for his wife, and he himself takes Volund's sword.

Volund says nothing – naturally, heroes don't whine – but his looks betray him. Nidud's queen sees his reaction (this again is how I translate her words):

> His teeth gnash   when his sword is taken,
> And when he sees   the ring of Bodvild.
> His eyes are like   the glittering snake.[12]

Clearly, Volund means revenge. It would be safest to kill him while he is helpless, but he is a famous smith – valuable property. How can one keep his services while rendering him harmless? The queen knows the answer to that, too:

> Cut away from him   his strength,
> Then set him down   on Sævarstod.[13]

Put him on Sævarstod, a prison island. But before that, hamstring him, cut the big tendons that run behind the knee. These never grow back. So although Volund can still hobble round his workshop, on crutches or holding on to the furniture, running is out of the question; and since he is entirely in Nidud's power, marooned on an island without hope even of rescue, he has to work for Nidud or starve, and any attempted revenge can be cruelly punished. His position seems totally hopeless. The poem goes on. Volund, now a slave:

> Sat, he did not sleep,   always he struck with his hammer,
> Busily he crafted   cunning things for Nidud.[14]

There is a terrible pun in the last line, or a concealed meaning. The word for 'cunning thing' is *vél*, which is also part of Volund's name: he is the 'cunning man'. But the cunning thing, or things, that Volund is forging are (a) the jewels and smithwork he has been set to make for his master, King Nidud (surface meaning); (b) his secret plan for revenge (hidden meaning); and (c) the means he is forging to carry out that revenge (even more hidden meaning).

All plans laid, Volund first entices Nidud's sons to his forge to see the treasures he is making. He then kills them and buries them under his forge. From their skulls he makes silver-inlaid goblets, from their eyes he makes jewels for Nidud's queen, from their teeth he makes a brooch for their daughter Bodvild. He hands them all over. They are 'cunning things' in every sense: beautiful works of art, concealed objects of horror, part of the hidden plan of revenge. Bodvild then comes to him in secret to have him mend her broken ring. He gives her ale to drink and then – the Norse poem skips over this, but the story is hinted at elsewhere[15] – he rapes her while she is stupefied and gets her pregnant.

Isn't this just suicidal, given Volund's situation? Haven't King Nidud and his queen taken the necessary steps to ensure that Volund, crippled and marooned, has no chance whatsoever of getting away with anything like that? No, because, as everyone has forgotten, Volund is a famous smith, married to a swan maiden, with powers verging on the supernatural. He has made himself wings in secret. When Nidud comes to ask where his boys are, Volund first demands a promise that Bodvild and her child will not be harmed, then tells Nidud what he has done . . . and then he flies away.

Nidud laments, as Volund hangs tauntingly in the sky:

> No one is so mighty   he can shoot you down,
> There where you sweep   up in the sky.[16]

The last words of the poem are Bodvild's, confessing to her father:

I did not know   how to resist him.
I had no strength   to resist him.[17]

There is of course plenty in this story to regard as 'morally distasteful'. Volund is a rapist and child-murderer. To us, the fact that this is retaliation for robbery, slavery, torture and mutilation is no excuse. But then, we live in a world that has police forces to punish law-breaking; Volund does not. What he does is furthermore and obviously not aimed at the immediate victims, the sons and daughter, but at their parents, the robber king and mutilator queen: the best way to hurt them is through their children. Volund even takes care to protect Bodvild, with a kind of success, for their child will become in time the famous hero Widia. What is macabre is the pun on *vél*, the rings and the jewels, but also the skull-goblets, the eyeball-gems, the brooch of teeth: horror made beautiful, by skill. As defeat is made victory, by cunning.

What is admirable, meanwhile – to the Viking mentality, anyway, which is not ours – is the way Volund hides his feelings. Not fully, of course, for Nidud's queen saw the warning signs, the teeth gnashing, the eyes flashing. It's a motif that comes up several times in this book. Norse heroes are supposed to look completely impassive, no matter what the shock or the pain; to look as if they have no feelings, to maintain a 'poker face'. But if they really didn't have any feelings, there would be no virtue in looking impassive. So the inner shock and resentment is revealed by signs that no one can control, the responses of the autonomic nervous system: flushing, sweating, taking a deep breath.

In the myth of Thor's visit to Utgard-Loki, someone cracks a bone in the leg of one of Thor's magic chariot-pulling goats to get out the marrow, so that when the goats are brought back to life next morning, one of them is lame. Thor says nothing, but people see how his 'knuckles went white'[18] – because he is clenching the haft of his hammer. This is a bad sign, and everyone apologizes until Thor calms down. So Volund's momentary self-betrayal is all in order, not unheroic. After that he bears robbery and loss, pain and mutilation, humiliation and shame, without apparent reaction. He lets people think he is beat, subservient, a good slave, hammering out cunning things for Nidud. He was – but he was working out more than one 'cunning thing'.

What Volund is really demonstrating is the truth of the Icelandic proverb 'A thrall takes vengeance at once, a coward never.' Just lashing out immediately is low-class behaviour, while forgiving and forgetting is of course unthinkable. A real hero bides his time, waits, as we would say, until he has all his ducks in a row. Because – and this time it is one of our proverbs – 'He who laughs last laughs longest.' Volund's victory is sealed when he hangs in the sky above Nidud, gloating over him. 'Gloat' is an Old Norse word borrowed into English: not a coincidence.

Viking sense of humour, 3: the hero and the piggies

Volund is a semi-mythical being with near-supernatural powers, so he can escape what looks like terminal defeat (though he will never get his hamstrings back). Ordinary mortals cannot escape, but they can still show Good Sense of Humour in extremity. King Gunnar did, defying Atli from the snakepit, back in the fifth century, and he set a model, to be followed by a hero who lived some four centuries later.

The hero of this story is Ragnar Hairy-breeches (one of many strange nicknames in the northern world), and he has a whole saga devoted to him. If he was a historical character, and he may have been, he lived in the first half of the ninth century, four hundred years after Atli and Gunnar. But according to the saga he died in York (which he almost certainly didn't), thrown like King Gunnar into a snakepit by King Ella of Northumbria. The tale of his death nevertheless exemplifies one of those things that shocked the bewigged scholars of the eighteenth century: Norsemen did not think you had to be grave and serious to keep your dignity. Their heroes were so securely self-assured that they did not need marks of status, and they could afford to crack jokes – even, or especially, against themselves.

The classic example for this kind of humour, for many eighteenth- and nineteenth-century admirers and imitators, was the death of Ragnar, and the defining poem was the one he was supposed to have sung while being put to death in King Ella's snakepit, 'Ragnar's Death Song' or 'The Song of the Crow' (*Krákumál*). Like Gunnar's brother Hogni, Ragnar dies laughing: the last half-line of his death song is *lœjandi skalk deyja*: word-for-word, 'laughing shall I die'.[19]

What, however, did Ragnar find so particularly funny as he died? 'The Song of the Crow' is not the only surviving poem ascribed to him, nor the only account of his death. Indeed, the editors of the *Corpus Poeticum Boreale*, the first nineteenth-century attempt to collect the complete 'poetry of the North', made it clear that they much preferred another, untitled set of verses about Ragnar's death, which they found 'more simple and genuine'.[20] Perhaps the most striking thing about this second compilation, however (which for convenience I call 'The Kraka Dialogues'), is the mordant comment in it given to Ragnar which shows the most characteristic qualities of the Norse throwaway line: concision, obscurity, vulgarity, threat.

What Ragnar is supposed to have said as he died in King Ella's snakepit, according to this second version, is: *Gnyðja mundu grísir, ef galtar hag vissi.*[21] One of the things that has always struck English translators of Norse is that it seems on the surface really rather easy to translate, with words which are unexpectedly familiar. But then one isn't quite sure what they mean. In this case *grísir* means greasies, little pigs, piggies, while *gnyðja* is clearly onomatopoeic and means grunt, or even, arguably, 'go oink oink'. And what Ragnar is saying – grimly, roguishly, perhaps with a nod and a wink – is, 'the piggies would grunt if they knew of the old boar's death'. He, of course, is the 'old boar', and the 'piggies' are his sons.

His sons, however, were in legend – and some of them also all too probably in history too – among the worst terrors of the Viking world, notably Sigurd Snake-eye and Ivar the Boneless. So what are we meant to think Ragnar meant by the 'grunting'? The story and the poem were clearly well known, for more than three hundred years after the event is supposed to have taken place, the learned Saxo Grammaticus knew all about it. Saxo was a Danish historian who wrote his Latin *Gesta Danorum*, 'The Deeds of the Danes', in sixteen books round about the year 1200. He clearly knew a great deal of old legend and old poetry, but to everyone's annoyance ever since, he insisted on rephrasing it all in his own verbose, high-flown and horribly confused style. Not only did he know about Ragnar, but he knew about the piggies as well, though the way he puts it is this: 'if the young pigs only knew the distress of their boar, they would certainly break into the sty and release him from his suffering without delay.'[22]

Saxo expanded the enigmatic remark about piggies grunting in an attempt to make sense of it. But his expansion shows complete misunderstanding of 'the Viking mindset'. We are not meant to think of Ragnar hoping for rescue, of which there is absolutely no chance at all. What he is hoping for and confidently expecting is *vengeance*. And the joke lies in the difference between the barnyard image of little piggies grunting (which you would never get in a proper classical epic) and the turmoil of blood and violence that Ragnar, but not King Ella, can foresee. Which would include the macabre death by torture of King Ella (probably only in legend); but in historical reality, whether or not it was motivated the way the legend has it, would include the Viking conquest of Northumbria and much of the rest of England, by the alleged Ragnarssons, the 'little piggies' themselves, in the 860s and 870s.

To sum up: in the Viking mindset, cruel jokes against other people are funny, and cruel jokes against yourself are even funnier, but the funniest joke of all is the one that is both at once – especially if the other people the joke is on do not immediately see it. But they will – when it's too late. Now that will be really funny . . .

With Ragnar, as with Gunnar and Hogni, and with Volund, Good Sense of Humour wins again.

Cruel, yes. But what links all these characters is that they are alone, surrounded by their enemies, without hope of rescue and to all appearance completely helpless. Now *that* is the time to show what you're made of. When you've lost. When you've nothing left but yourself. Die laughing, and die laughing because in one way or another you've still managed to turn the tables.

Die like a Viking: fact or ambition?

Are the stories above really about Vikings? Ragnar was a Viking, certainly, but Gunnar and Hogni weren't, and neither was Volund. Were they composed by Vikings, then? 'The Lay of Volund' is thought to have been written in England some time after the Vikings began to settle there in the later ninth century, after the Ragnarsson conquests.[23] The Ragnar legend probably came from the same area, so it too is the work of the Vikings' immediate descendants.[24] The Gunnar story, though, is very old in its origin. 'The Lay of Atli' is in Old Norse and must have been composed by a Norseman, but for all we know he may have been a stay-at-home who never had anything to do with actual Vikings.

This raises a question, one which in this book keeps on recurring: how far *can* one believe literary evidence? All three of the stories detailed above must be fiction. The story of Volund is a myth. Atli was a historical character, and so was Gunnar, but they probably never met each other. The legend has them dying at almost the same time, but in reality we know their death dates were sixteen years apart. Gunnar almost certainly died in battle, in his own kingdom, centred around Worms on the Rhine, not in a Hunnish snakepit out on the steppe.

Ragnar Hairy-breeches may also have been a historical character, but if he was, he too almost certainly did not die in a Northumbrian snakepit as a captive of King Ella. For one thing, one can't help wondering where Ella would have got the adders from and how long it would have taken Ragnar to die, for English adders are not usually lethal. Much more likely is that the old story of King Gunnar and Atli the Hun was adapted for a later hero, and the poems about his death made up to fit.

This kind of thing probably happened more than once. In *Jomsvíkinga saga*, 'The Saga of the Jomsvikings', the hero Bui gets a slash across the face that takes off his lower jaw. He strikes back, remarks stoically, 'The

Danish woman in Bornholm won't think it so pleasant to kiss me now', and, knowing the battle is lost, seizes his treasure chests and jumps overboard, never to be seen again. (We say, 'you can't take it with you'. Yes you can. Bui just has.) His wisecrack is repeated in *Droplaugarsona saga*, 'The Saga of Droplaug's Sons', of an event that took place many years later. In an Icelandic skirmish, Helgi Droplaugarson also takes a blow in the face and remarks, like Bui, 'I was never beautiful, but you've made little improvement.'[25] Neither story sounds very plausible. It's hard to see how Bui could do more than mutter without a lower jaw, while if Helgi had to bite his beard to hold his jaw up, as the saga declares, it's hard to see how he could say anything at all. So, was Helgi imitating a famous saying from the past? Or, more likely, was the saga's author imitating a saying already famous, to spice up his story?

Whether true or false, what is shown by the stories about Gunnar and Ragnar, and Bui and Helgi, is a kind of ambition. That's the way to go. That's the way to die, or to bear pain. Spoil your enemy's victory, like Gunnar. Anticipate a time when your enemy will get what he's not expecting, like Ragnar. Deny your enemy the spoils of victory, like Bui. If nothing else, make a joke about your own situation, like Helgi and the other three as well.

Summing up, then, humour is a vital part of the whole Viking mindset, as recorded in their own legends and in the legends and stories about them and their successors. It goes along with the death cult. A hero is defined not by victory but by defeat. Only in defeat can you show what you're really made of. Only in final defeat can you show that you will never give in. That's why the gods have to die as well. If they did not die, how could they show true courage? If they were really immortal and invulnerable, who would respect them?

TWO

Hygelac and Hrolf:
False Dawn for the Vikings

The Viking Age is normally reckoned to have begun on 8 June 793, when the longships came out of the North to strike the rich, famous, isolated and defenceless monastery of St Cuthbert on Lindisfarne island, off the northeast coast of England. 'The raiding of heathen men miserably devastated God's church by looting and slaughter,' says the *Anglo-Saxon Chronicle*.[1] At the time, no one could understand how such a thing could happen. Alcuin, the Yorkshire deacon headhunted by Charlemagne to join the royal scriptorium in France, wrote in horror to King Ethelred of Northumbria:

> It is some three hundred and fifty years that we and our forefathers have inhabited this lovely land, and never before in Britain has such a terror appeared as this we have now suffered at the hands of the heathen. Nor was it thought possible that such an inroad from the sea could be made.[2]

It was the Pearl Harbor of the Dark Ages. Something completely unexpected, unpredictable, only made possible (it is often claimed) by a sudden development in technology, the famous Viking longship.

So the story goes – and it was repeated once again at the start of the *Vikings* TV series (2013–) – but it cannot be true. Leaving the question of ships aside for the moment, the Vikings did not arrive at Lindisfarne by accident: they knew it was there, they knew the raid was worth assembling a fleet; this means that someone had made a reconnaissance. They also at some point must have made a long open-sea crossing with perfect confidence, cruising in 'with the favouring north-east breeze and settled weather conditions of an early summer anti-cyclone over the northern North Sea'.[3] They must have been sniffing round the shores of Britain for some time, maybe in the far north for as long as a generation. Just four years before the attack on Lindisfarne, the *Anglo-Saxon Chronicle* records, there occurred a series of events that might have been taken as a warning sign:

> In his days [the reign of King Beorhtric of Wessex] three ships of Northmen first came from Hordaland. The king's reeve rode there and wanted to compel them to go to the king's town because he did not know what they were, and they killed him. These were the first ships of the Danish men which sought out the land of the English.[4]

Once again, the last sentence is not credible. A later account of the same incident specifies that the reeve's name was Beaduheard (it was clearly well remembered) and that it all took place at Portland, halfway along the south coast of England.[5] Meanwhile, though the *Chronicle* says vaguely that these were ships of the Danes, it also specifies that they came from Hordaland, on the Atlantic coast of Norway. Portland is a very long way from Hordaland, much further than Lindisfarne from Denmark. To reach it the Vikings must have had to go either all the way down the North Sea and through the English Channel, or else circumnavigate Britain to the west, down past Scotland and Wales and round the long promontory of Cornwall. This must have involved halts for water, if nothing else. The Norwegians knew their way and had some purpose in mind, whatever that may have been.

It is worth noting too that the people who reported the raid knew where the raiders came from: there had been a conversation of some sort before or after the confrontation with Beaduheard. In fact, the later account adds that Beaduheard thought the new arrivals were just traders and rode to collect the harbour tax from them, another incident remembered by the TV series *Vikings*. Finally, the Old English *sohton to*, translated above as 'sought out', can mean 'attacked'. Maybe what the chronicler was trying to say was not that these were the first ships from the North that had ever been seen, but that this was the first time they had come with hostile intentions – which is why Beaduheard was taken unawares.

In any case, and going back to the question of ships, Deacon Alcuin should have remembered a bit more of his own history. Three hundred and fifty years before, his English ancestors had been heathen pirates, just like the Vikings. Roman chroniclers and poets, long before Alcuin, repeatedly mention the assaults on France and Britain of seaborne raiders from the North, grudgingly conceding their ability to master wind and weather. The Imperial Roman government built forts and signal stations all along the Yorkshire coastline and further south, and set up a new military appointment to take charge of the defences, the *comes litoris Saxonici*, the Count of the Saxon Shore. No doubt many of the pirates really were Saxons from north Germany, the men of the *seax*, the short, curved chopping sword, but, just like the later English calling Norwegians 'Danes', the Romans called all northern pirates 'Saxons', even if they were Angles, or Jutes, or some other group of dangerous barbarians; the Celts have kept up the habit, calling the English *Saes* or *Sassenach* to this day. But whoever they were, they had no more trouble than the later wave of Scandinavian Vikings in crossing the North Sea and raiding down-Channel.

Had Alcuin and the Anglo-Saxon chronicler just *forgotten* about all this? There is no denying their shock and horror, much increased in subsequent years as one monastery after another was devastated like Lindisfarne. But really, in normal northern circumstances everyone would have known better than to put large amounts of valuable property on the coast, or worse still just *off* the coast, and leave it completely unguarded. The truly surprising thing about 8 June 793 is not the sudden attack but the centuries of invulnerability before it. The peaceful centuries are the anomaly, not the centuries of war and pillage that preceded and followed them.

There was a Viking Age before the Viking Age. And the question that really needs to be asked is what stopped it? What gave Britain and the North security, at least from the sea, for Alcuin's 'three hundred and fifty years'? (Or anyway 250 years, for he overestimated.)

The fall of King Hygelac

What the legendary history of the North suggests, some of it corroborated by documents and by archaeology, is that there was some great turmoil up there in the Scandinavian heartland that first drove the Angles and the Saxons and the Jutes overseas to Britain and ended in a catastrophe so complete that it gave Western Europe peace from the North for ten generations. The catastrophe turns on the fate of two men, the two great proto-Vikings who probably called themselves *Hugilaikaz and *Hrothuwulfaz. (The asterisks before their names indicate that they were never recorded in that exact form. The form is a guess, though a very well-informed guess based on a great deal of evidence, as to what the names were in the men's own lifetimes.)

Ironically, both *Hugilaikaz and *Hrothuwulfaz were contemporaries of 'King Arthur'. He has been remembered; they have been almost forgotten. But while there are grave doubts about the 'historical King Arthur', of whom we know effectively nothing, their stories can be recovered.

The existence of *Hugilaikaz is so well recorded as to be beyond question. In the fifth and sixth centuries, which is when he lived and died, the Germanic languages, such as modern English, Danish, German and Dutch, had not significantly separated from each other, and the northern populations all spoke what is now called Primitive or Proto-Germanic. We have several hundred inscriptions in that language, all short, almost all of them from the Scandinavian area and written in the earliest pre-Viking form of the runic alphabet. Very soon the language separations would start (one might well wonder what caused them), and by the time of Alcuin Old English and Old Norse would be markedly different from each other, though still maybe just about mutually comprehensible. This means that *Hugilaikaz turns up in Old English as Hygelac or Hyglac and in Old Norse as Hugleikr. But Latin writers closer to his own time have his name – though it didn't mean anything to them – pretty much in its original form.

The most famous account of his death comes from a Frankish historian, Gregory of Tours, writing in Latin not long after the year 574, within living memory of the event itself. In his *Historia Francorum* (Book 3, Ch. 3), Gregory says this:

> The Danes sent a fleet under their King Chlochilaichus and invaded Gaul from the sea. They came ashore, laid waste one of the regions ruled by Theuderic and captured some of the inhabitants. They loaded their ships with what they had stolen and the men they had seized, and then they set sail for home. Their King remained on the shore, waiting until the boats should have gained the open sea, when he planned to go on board. When Theuderic learned that the land had been invaded by foreigners, he sent his son Theudebert with a powerful army and all the necessary equipment. The Danish King was killed, the enemy fleet was beaten in a naval battle, and all the booty was brought back on shore once more.[6]

Gregory does not give an exact date, but it must have been in the reign of King Theuderic I (511–533) and before the next event he mentions, which takes place about 525. His version of the name is 'Chlochilaichus' – note that, as with 'Alcuin' (whose real name must have been Alhwini), the Latin alphabet was not good at handling the Germanic sounds *w* and (as in Scottish 'loch') *ch*.[7]

However, there is another Frankish account of the raid, written about 160 years later, by someone who had read Gregory but knew a few things that Gregory didn't. This one, the anonymous *Liber historiae Francorum*, calls the 'Danish' king 'Chochilaicus'.[8] (This chronicler has got the name down rather better than Gregory, or Gregory's copyists, without the intrusive *l*.) Just as with the detail about the Norwegians from Hordaland above, the name must have come from some kind of conversation with, perhaps interrogation of, a surviving raider. This later author also knows that the 'region laid waste' was that of the 'Attoarii' (and remember what was said just above about Latin not being good at handling the Germanic *w*). It's also clear from this account that King Chochilaicus got quite a long way upriver, maybe as far as the River Waal, into the area of modern Nijmegen. But for him as for the British paratroopers of 1944, that was 'a bridge too far'.

One might leave the whole incident there – big raid, got caught, didn't try it again – but for two further accounts, both of them English. These add yet more information, but the most important thing they tell us is that the failed raid made a serious impact and that it was even better remembered by the losers than by the winners. One of these is the 'Book of Monsters', the *Liber monstrorum*, thought to have been written maybe in Malmesbury about the same time as the second Frankish account given above. It is not interested in the raid so much as in *Hugilaikaz himself, partially Anglicized in the *Liber* as Huiglacus. What it says, naturally enough given the book's subject, is that he was a monster – not morally, but in size. He was a giant, so big that the victorious Franks kept his skeleton and put it on show as an exhibit:

> And there are monsters of an amazing size, like King Hygelac, who ruled the Geats and was killed by the Franks, whom no horse could carry from the age of twelve. His bones are preserved on an island in the river Rhine, where it breaks into the ocean, and they are shown as a wonder to travellers from afar.[9]

Significantly, this author thinks that 'Huiglacus' was a king not of the Danes but of the 'Getae', convincingly identified with the *Gautar* of south Sweden and the *Geatas* or 'Geats' of *Beowulf*. And – remember that Gregory thought he had remained on shore to cover the departure of his fleet – he seems to have been killed not upriver by Nijmegen but somewhere on the many mouths of the Rhine delta, perhaps on Walcheren, scene of another major battle of 1944.

But the last account is the most famous, the most detailed and the most unexpected. This comes from the Old English epic *Beowulf*, surviving in one manuscript alone (unlike all the other works mentioned so far). That manuscript dates from close to the year 1000, centuries after *Hugilaikaz was killed, but there are strong indications that our one manuscript is a copy of a poem written long before, at much the same date as the last two sources mentioned, 700–725.[10]

The hero of the poem, Beowulf himself, talks about Hygelac (as the name is usually spelled in the poem) freely and frequently. The first time Beowulf is mentioned he is called simply 'Hygelac's thane'. When he is asked who he and his men are, he doesn't give his own name, instead replying, 'We are Hygelac's hearth-companions.' Hygelac is in fact Beowulf's uncle, and the poet also knows the names of Hygelac's father, his two elder brothers, his son, his wife, and even his father-in-law and son-in-law – most of whom, like Hygelac, died violent deaths, killed by enemies or by each other.

In the poem, Beowulf indeed seems emotionally dependent on his uncle – which is unfortunate for him, as the poet knows very well how Hygelac died. In four separate passages he mentions the disastrous raid, in ways independent from but strongly corroborating the accounts given by the other side, the victorious Franks. He is quite sure that Hygelac is king not of the Danes, nor the Getae, but of the Geatas, who in Old Norse would be the *Gautar*, inhabiting what are now the south Swedish provinces centred on Gothenburg. He knows nothing about Theuderic or Theudebert, but he does give the name of the Frankish standard-bearer 'Dayraven', and it is a Frankish name, not an English one. He also identifies the enemy not just as Franks but as Frisians, and twice as the 'Hetware', a name in Germanic form which is probably what the Latin author above was trying to render as 'Attoarii'. And the poet's assertion that Beowulf was at the last battle but escaped by swimming home – with, he says, thirty suits of armour on his back, rescued from the battlefield – reminds one of Gregory's statement that King Ch(l)ochilaicus had remained on shore to cover the embarkation.

There is, of course, a very strong element of pure fantasy in everything connected with Beowulf himself. His name (a rare one) has long been understood as 'wolf of the bees', and as every reader of Winnie the Pooh will realize, this would be a reference to a honey-eating bear. Beowulf in fact shows strong signs of being a were-bear disguised as a hero. Reminiscing proudly about former triumphs before he goes on to fight his dragon, Beowulf says of Dayraven the Frank, 'the edge did not kill him, but my wargrip broke his bone-house and the pulses of his heart' – in other words, I bear-hugged him until his ribs broke and his heart stopped.[11] Beowulf prefers to fight barehanded (no pun intended) and has little luck with swords: two named swords, Hrunting and Nægling, let him down, and he breaks Nægling on the dragon that kills him. 'His hand was too strong,' says the poet by way of explanation.[12] He is a famous swimmer, too. It's true that no one in modern times has ever been able to believe the story about him swimming back from the Rhine mouth to Sweden carrying some half a ton of metal, for Beowulf himself is a figure from fairy tale. But his uncle Hygelac, oversized though he may have been, demonstrably was not.

The poem in any case knows a lot more about Hygelac, and his disastrous raid is arguably the geopolitical centre of what is a uniquely geopolitical epic. The picture given by the poem is this. The Geats in south Sweden have formed a rather uneasy back-to-back alliance with the Danes, whose capital, according to their own legends, was on the Danish island of Sjaelland, not far from modern Copenhagen. The Danes are looking west and south, and their enemies are the Jutes on the Jutland peninsula, the Frisians along what is now the Dutch coast, and the Bards (now vanished), somewhere on the Baltic coast of north Germany. The Geats are looking north and east, and their enemies are the Swedes. But the conflicts are seen not so much as tribal or national ones as personal feuds between royal families, usually related to each other. For the poet, Hygelac is famous above all for avenging the death of his brother, in a battle – narrated with special gusto – with the king of the Swedes, the old, cruel, formidable grandfather Ongentheow, at a place called Ravenswood or Ravensholt – of which, however, there is no trace in any other account. But then, who would wish to remember the battle? Not the Swedes, who lost. And the Geatish royal house, with its skalds and its praise-poets, would soon be extinct and forgotten, except for some reason in England, far away.

After Hygelac's death, the story is protracted by the poet's need to find room for a heroic career for Beowulf himself, but if he is left out the story becomes plausible, if unconfirmed. With King Hygelac dead, his son Heardred supports one side in a Swedish civil war to destabilize the Swedish kingdom. But he picks the wrong side and is himself killed, and even when the Geatish candidate does fight his way to rule over the Swedes, he shows no gratitude and is just as threatening as his relatives. Near the end of the poem, with Beowulf dead from a dragon bite, an unnamed Geat says gloomily:

So many a spear will be held cold at dawn, gripped in hand, nor will harpsong waken the warriors, instead the black raven will croak to the eagle, eagerly say much over the corpses of how well he ate, while with the wolf he robbed the dead.[13]

Death for the men, slavery for the women: that's what's coming. The poet adds, *he ne leag fela*, 'he did not lie much'; that is, 'he was not far wrong' or, allowing for English understatement, 'he was dead right about that.'

Beowulf himself, great warrior and monster-fighter though he is, seems unable to protect his uncle, his cousin or his people and is notably absent, or only improbably present, at all major battles – but then, he is a figure from fairy tale, not from real politics. It looks very much as if Hygelac's death at the mouth of the Rhine – which we know actually happened – also led to the wipeout of his dynasty and (though the *Gautar* of course stayed on the map) his people's loss of independence. One piece in the chess game of sixth-century Scandinavian politics was off the board, a major discouragement for any further Viking activity.

King Hrolf, the Danish King Arthur, only much more likely

The other half of this story centres on *Hrothuwulfaz, in Old English *Hrothulf*, in Old Norse *Hrólfr*, anglicized here as Hrolf. He is the close Scandinavian equivalent of 'King Arthur'. They must have been near-contemporaries, both active in the early to mid-sixth century. Both became famous not just in their own right but also through the tales of the knights, or champions, who came to their court. Both eventually became national heroes, for Britain and for Denmark. The evidence we have for both of them comes from centuries after their own time, but it has to be said that the evidence for King Hrolf is a whole lot better, even archaeologically, than it is for King Arthur.

Since Scandinavia was late in developing literacy, except for the runic inscriptions carved on stone, wood and bone, most of the Danish and Icelandic accounts of Hrolf come from six or seven hundred years after his time, approximately 1140–1225 – though they include two poems that may be much older.[14] All of them must derive at some stage from stories passed on orally: there were no war reporters in the Dark Ages creating an immediate 'paper trail'. The fullest account of him is from even later: *Hrólfs saga kraka*, 'The Saga of Hrolf *kraki*', was composed perhaps as late as 1400 or 1450, and like *Beowulf* it is very strongly infiltrated by fairy tale.[15] (One of the strangest things about the two works, so far apart in place and time, is that it looks like the *same* fairy tale. Professor Tolkien was so struck by this that he decided to write the fairy tale as it should have been, first in modern English and then with a sample in Old English, now published as *Sellic Spell*, Old English for 'wonder tale'.[16])

Oral tradition, of course, is not so much intrinsically unreliable as generally unstable. Several of the chroniclers earnestly trying to compose accounts of Danish or Swedish or Norwegian history in the later Middle Ages seem to have been working off not much more than famous names, nicknames or scraps of information, which they felt they had to work into a connected story. This seems to have been the case with *Hugilaikaz, the king from a wiped-out dynasty. The only trace of him in Scandinavian legend is a king called Hugleikr – the Old Norse form of his name – in Snorri's *Ynglinga saga* ('The Saga of the Ynglings'). Snorri says of this king, however, that he 'was no warrior, and he stayed peaceably on his estates',[17] amusing himself with musicians and jugglers – the exact opposite of the historical raider-king. Probably Snorri knew only the name, decoded it (correctly) as *hugi*, meaning 'mind', and *leikr*, 'play', understood it as 'the playful mind' and concocted a story of a frivolous layabout king to match. But *leikr* or *lác* can also mean 'play' as in swordplay or (as with the Anglo-Saxon St Guthlac) war-play, a much more likely meaning for a name chosen by a Dark Age parent: 'the warlike mind'. There are other cases where we can trace this kind of antiquarian invention and no doubt more where we cannot.[18]

The accounts of Hrolf and his family accordingly often contradict each other. *Hrólfs saga* starts off by saying there were two brothers called Frodi and Halfdan and that Halfdan was the father of Hroar and Helgi. Snorri Sturluson says Frodi was Halfdan's father, not his brother. Saxo Grammaticus, the most detailed of the Danish chroniclers, writing about 1200, agrees with *Hrólfs saga* except that Hroar has dwindled to being King Roe. The *Lejre Chronicle*, sixty years before Saxo, has inverted the genealogy, so that Ro is now the father, and Haldan and Helgi are his sons. Interestingly, the man who translated some of that chronicle from Latin into Danish reverted to the more popular story, so that Haldan, as in Saxo and *Hrólfs saga*, goes back to being the father of both Helgi and Ro. So it wasn't all just free invention: there were people who felt mistakes could and should be corrected.

And in the whole whirlwind of stories there are some strong consistencies. The same names keep coming up, if often garbled by the inadequacies of Latin spelling: Halfdan, Hroar, Helgi, Hrolf, Yrsa, all from the same family, and, associated with them one way or another, Frodi, Skuld, Hjorvarth and Adils. Not to mention spaewives and elf-women and (again) a were-bear, a character who can take bear as well as human shape – just like Beorn in Tolkien's *The Hobbit*, which of course is no coincidence. There are furthermore three anchor points in the whole story.

Everyone agrees, first, that Hrolf's birth was incestuous. His father, unanimously agreed to be King Helgi, raped a queen of Germany who is given various names, as if no one was quite sure. She bore a girl child, whom she hated and gave a dog's name, agreed to be Yrsa, sometimes Latinized as Ursula. The child grew up to be amazingly beautiful, and by accident or design she fell or was put into Helgi's path. He carried her off, married her and had a son with her, Hrolf – whose mother was accordingly also his sister, while his father was his grandfather, and his mother was at once granddaughter and daughter-in-law of Helgi's father, Halfdan.

Yrsa's mother – showing a characteristically Norse feeling for delayed and, if possible, ironically appropriate revenge – then passed on the news about Yrsa's birth, and there is a fairly general agreement that Yrsa was then married off to King Adils of Sweden (though Snorri, making nonsense of the story, thinks she was married to Adils first). No one seems very certain about what happened to Helgi. Two sources suggest, though not with much conviction, that he committed suicide out of shame.

Everyone also agrees, even more firmly than they do about the incest, that Hrolf is the great hero-king of the Danish Dark Ages, the pre-Viking Age. But in Scandinavian tradition at least, no very great exploit or victory is attributed to him: he is famous for gathering mighty champions about him, but with one exception he does not seem to use them for anything much during the main part of his career. The one exception is his raid on King Adils of Sweden, his father-in-law/brother-in-law. Danish tradition, virulently anti-Swedish, makes this into a story of a friendly visit that is turned into a string of murder traps by the Swedish sorcerer-king, from which Hrolf and his champions fight their way clear, assisted (in *Hrólfs saga*) by the advice of a one-eyed farmer whom anyone but an idiot would recognize as the god Odin in disguise.

The big scene, related five times by four different early Scandinavian chroniclers, comes as Hrolf and his twelve champions flee across the Fyrisvellir, the Plains of Fyrir, pursued by Adils and an army of angry Swedes. Hrolf escapes by sowing his gold plunder across their tracks, at which the Swedes – unheroically concerned with profit, not revenge – stop to pick it up. In the end even King Adils disgraces himself, by stopping for the ring *Svíagríss*, the 'piglet of the Swedes'. First, he tries to pick it up from horseback on the point of his spear, but when that fails he dismounts and stoops for it, whereupon Hrolf says memorably, 'I have made the greatest of the Swedes stoop like a swine.' (The word he uses in *Hrólfs saga* is *svínbeygða*, 'swine-bowed' or 'swine-bent', and Snorri uses the same word in one of his two accounts of the event, written two hundred years before *Hrólfs saga*: an indication of how single words can fix scenes in the mind for centuries.)[19]

Hrolf's great exploit, though, and the first detailed example of the tradition of heroic death scenes that this book follows, is being killed.

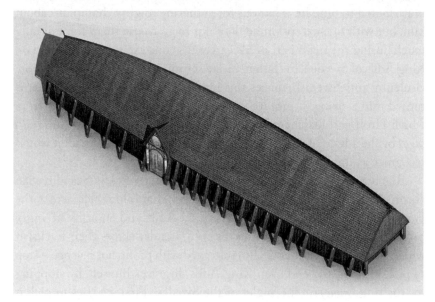

Virtual images of one of the great Viking Age halls discovered at Lejre.

There is general agreement that this took place at Lethra, or Hledro, or *Hleiðargarðr*, which is the modern village of Gamle Lejre, not far from Roskilde on the north coast of the Danish island Sjaelland. This is also the traditional home of the Skjoldung dynasty, the Shieldings, the men of the shield. As recently as the 1970s Gwyn Jones's *History of the Vikings* lamented that there is now no trace in this small and peaceful village of the great hall where the Skjoldungs feasted, writing that it is sad 'to think of those high lords without a roof to their heads, but in respect of Lejre that is the case, and likely to remain so'.[20]

Great scholar though he was, Professor Jones's prediction was soon proved wrong. Beginning in 1984, archaeologists found the traces of not one, not two, but so far as many as six enormous halls at Lejre, the biggest of them 60 metres (200 ft) long. All are too late to be Hrolf's, and they do not show the signs of burning that one would expect from some parts of the story. However, only a fraction of the site has been excavated, and the earliest of the halls was built in the mid-sixth century, which is to say, just after the date of Hrolf's last stand, if one bases one's chronology on the single secure date we have from *Beowulf.*

There is further general agreement (in Scandinavian tradition only) that it was all the fault of a witch woman called Skuld. This is suspicious in several respects. Skuld is the name of one of the three Fates of Norse mythology, so suitably ominous and threatening to Christian writers. *Hrólfs saga* says she was the child of Helgi and an elf-woman, whom Helgi annoyed by not acknowledging the birth. The *Lejre Chronicle* (guessing wildly, one feels, for a place where she might fit in) makes her the child of Ursula and Adils. Again, though, there is general agreement that her husband was someone called Hjorvard, or Hiarwardus, who succeeded Hrolf. But only for a few minutes. He too saw a joke too late.

The fall of the House of the Skjoldungs

A string of stories clusters around the death of King Hrolf and his champions. They exemplify vital elements of the Viking ethic and the unexpectedly complex Viking psychology. Once again, though, they are anything but 'heart-warming'. Bad Sense of Humour all over again.

The main story outline is simple enough. Hrolf and his champions are caught off-guard at Lejre by an overwhelming force led by Skuld and Hjorvard. They refuse to flee or surrender and are wiped out to the last man. Or last but one, for one member of the retinue survives, a spindly youth called Vogg, weakest of the company. Long before, on seeing the great Hrolf, he had laughed, and when asked 'why are you laughing?' had answered cheekily (referring to Hrolf's height and thinness) that he had expected to see a great warrior, but what he saw was a pole-ladder, a *kraki.* Hrolf took the word as his nickname and rewarded Vogg with a gold arm ring. When he saw Vogg's delight, he commented, punningly: *Litlu verðr Vöggr feginn*, which means 'Vogg rejoices in little,' or 'it doesn't take much to please Vogg.' However, since *vöggr* was also a dialect word for 'child',

Hrolf was also perhaps quoting a proverb similar to our 'little things please little minds.' Vogg nevertheless went through a further pantomime – told in different ways by different writers – until he got a second ring to balance the first. And then he swore that if Hrolf died by violence, he, Vogg, would avenge him.[21]

With Hrolf surrounded by berserkers and mighty champions, in contrast to the puny Vogg, it seemed a pointless boast at the time, but it came true. *Hrólfs saga* at this culminating point garbles the story badly, but according to Saxo, writing centuries before the saga, Vogg (Saxo calls him Viggi) lived when all his comrades died. In the heroic world this was utterly disgraceful, and feeble Viggi, as the last survivor of Hrolf's bodyguard, even offered to swear allegiance to the new king – even more disgraceful. Hjorvard carelessly accepted, maybe hoping for a kind of legitimation, and passed Viggi his own sword to swear allegiance on – only to be promptly run through, dying in the hour of victory.[22] Vogg/Viggi shows the Viking admiration for cunning, resource, cheek and wit, along with or instead of raw strength.

The refusal to survive, the insistence on fighting to the last man, is one of the most familiar motifs of Old Norse (and Old English) story, and it is what caught the eye of classically educated scholars as the Old Norse tradition began once again to become familiar in the early modern period – as most notably in Thomas Bartholinus the Younger's compilation about 'the causes of the contempt for death among the still pagan Danes' (1689). The question he raised remains a good one, and Hrolf's champions at least provide the suggestion of an answer.

The most famous of the champions looks, it must be confessed, like Beowulf in his fairy-tale form once again. His name is Bodvar, a name that survives in the Yorkshire village of Battersby (and more ignominiously in Len Battersby, once the village idiot of the popular soap opera *Coronation Street*). However, his nickname is Bjarki, and this is easy to understand, given that his father's name is Bjorn (which means 'bear') and his mother's Bera (or 'she-bear'). Bjarki means 'little bear', and he is, even more obviously than Beowulf, a were-bear.

In Hrolf's last battle the other champions miss him, though they do see a great bear fighting furiously in their own front ranks. The one who is sent back to get Bjarki finds him sitting by himself, upbraids him and brings him out to the battle, but as he does so, the great bear disappears, for it has been a 'sending' by Bjarki, who must take one form or the other, not both. (All of which Tolkien remembered in his portrayal of the were-bear Beorn in *The Hobbit*.) Bodvar, however, is a raw-strength hero: not too complicated.

More interesting is his close companion Hjalti. His name was originally Hott, and he was a coward, kept for the amusement of the warriors, who whiled away mealtimes by throwing bones at him – a common practice, specifically mentioned as a penalty by Sven Aggesen in his twelfth-century *Law of the Retainers*. (The *Anglo-Saxon Chronicle* further records that on 19 April 1012, Archbishop Ælfheah of Canterbury, also known as St Alphege, was pelted by his Viking captors 'with bones and the heads of cattle' and eventually finished off with the back of an axe.)[23] Briefly: Bodvar rescues Hott, makes a man of him with a drink of dragon's blood, and gains him new status and the name of Hjalti, meaning 'hilt', from the sword he is given, Gullinhjalti, or Golden-hilt. He is known further as Hjalti the Magnanimous, for forbearing to take revenge on the bone-throwers.

His magnanimity, however, takes strange form before the famous last battle when the king and all his champions are killed except (for a few minutes) for Vogg. As the saga tells it, in chapter 32, when Skuld and Hjorvard launch their attack on King Hrolf, Hjalti is not in Hrolf's hall with the other retainers, having been given permission to sleep out. In fact he is lying with his *frilla*, or girlfriend, when he realizes that Skuld and Hjorvard are about to attack. He asks his *frilla* suddenly whether she would prefer two 22-year-old men or an eighty-year-old. She replies, 'I think two 22-year-olds better than men of eighty.' Hjalti calls her a whore, *hóra*, bites her nose off and says few will find her a treasure from now on. When she says she didn't deserve this, he replies *Ekki verðr við öllu sét* and goes off to his death. Hjalti's reply is so laconic as to be almost impenetrable, and it has been translated in quite different ways: 'stuff happens' catches the general tone of it.[24] As for the emotions it conveys, what are they: resentment, jealousy, even despair?

It is, to say the least, an oddly unprovoked scene and of course a cruel one. Yet it's not inexplicable, and there is even something of a modern parallel. In 1917 the British officer Siegfried Sassoon was on leave from the Western Front and found himself in a London music hall. It must have been some time after the British had introduced their new invention, the tank, to the fighting, for the chorus girls were singing a derisive song mocking the Germans, and glorying in what the tanks had done to them. Sassoon was so enraged he wrote a short eight-line poem about it, 'Blighters'. The title itself is ironic. In old-fashioned British English, 'blighter' is a word of mild condemnation. But it carries a secondary meaning, from the word 'Blighty', old-fashioned British soldiers' English for 'Britain': so it can mean 'people back home', and here, 'people far away from the fighting'. The chorus girls were kicking their legs, the audience was laughing. They'd all soon stop, Sassoon snarled in his poem, if they ever saw a tank. He wishes one could show up. That would soon cut out the mirth and the mocking, directed at the 'riddled corpses round Bapaume'.[25]

Sassoon disliked the audience laughing; he disliked the chorus girls, whom he describes as 'harlots' (Hjalti too thinks his girlfriend is a whore); he seems to have disliked them all mocking the Germans, whom he had been fighting, for the 'riddled corpses round Bapaume' could as easily be Germans machine-gunned by tanks as British soldiers machine-gunned by Germans. And while he doesn't bite anyone's nose off, he would clearly like to see the girls and the audience seriously frightened, to say the least.

Men who have to risk their lives, one may conclude, *don't like spectators*, people who can look on unmoved, or worse, entertained.[26] Hjalti, meanwhile, is thinking forward to his own death, which he knows is certain. Will his *frilla* miss him? From her answer he deduces: not much; she will find easy consolation and not worry about where it comes from. The scene shows the resentment of those trapped by the code of honour against those who are free of it. Not, of course, that honourable men *want* to be free of it, whether Hjalti or Sassoon, but they resent those who can be free of it, at the same time as they despise them.

The same feeling can be detected in the words given to Hjalti in what was once perhaps the most famous and long-admired of Norse heroic poems, *Bjarkamál in fornu*, 'The Old Lay of Bjarki'. We have only a few lines of this in the original Old Norse, and the only ones with any narrative content were preserved only because Snorri Sturluson put them in the mouth of a famous Icelandic poet of a much later time, Thormod Dark-Brow's Skald, on a similarly suicidal occasion on 29 July 1030 (see Chapter Ten). Despite the poem's traditional title, 'The Lay of Bjarki', the surviving lines of it come from Hjalti as he tries to wake his comrades for battle. They go, in Old Norse and English once again:

Dagr es upp kominn,	The day has come up,
dynja hana fjaðrar.	the roosters clap their wings.
Mál es vilmögum	Time for the wretched serfs
at vinna erfiði.	to do the heavy labour.
Vaki æ ok vaki	Wake now, wake,
vína höfuð,	company of friends,
allir inir œztu	all you best ones
Adils of sínnar.	of Adils' people.
Hár inn harðgreipi,	Har the hard-grip,
Hrólfr skjótandi,	Hrolf the shooter,

ættum góðir menn,	men of good birth,
þeir es ekki flygja.	they who do not flee.
Vekka yðr at víni,	I do not wake you to wine
né at vífs runum,	not the whispers of women,
vekk yðr hörðum	I wake you to the hard
Hildar at leiki.	sport of Hild.[27]

Whatever one thinks of this, it is very far removed from modern cultural preferences. One aspect of it is misogyny – the poem rejects women and their 'whispers'. Another is birth pride: the companions are 'men of good birth', and that is the same thing as 'those who do not flee'. Courage in war, the poem seems to be saying, is of men only, and is hereditary, too.

But at the same time there is a kind of wry joke in it, and Hjalti knows this time that the joke is on him and on the other aristocratic males. Normally, dawn – and this is clearly a dawn poem, a poem about awakening, as it will be also on 29 July 1030 – is the time when the 'wretched serfs' go to work, lighting the fires and grinding at the everlasting querns, while the pampered fighting-men drowse on in their blankets. But today is the day the fighting-men do their work, and it will be *erfiði, Arbeit*, 'heavy labour' indeed. Implied is the thought that today the roles are reversed, and it is the warriors who are the wretched ones being woken.

Hjalti does not say that today he would willingly swap places with one of the serfs, any more than he says he wishes he could view the battle from safety like his *frilla*, but the irony is there. It's a mix of pride, self-congratulation, rueful acceptance and, as said above, the fighting-man's bitter resentment not at enemies but at spectators – and holding it all together, amusement at the way things turn out.

It's fiction, of course, like the nose-biting, but it's fiction that embodies a mindset, and that mindset is not a simple one, not just masculine chest-beating. Being able to laugh at one's own death, to make jokes (preferably cruel ones, of course) as one sees one's fate: as said in Chapter One, that is a large part of the Viking ethic – or if one prefers to think so, the Viking 'imaginary' – and it goes back (at least in legend) to the pre-Viking ethic, too, to the time of kings *Hugilaikaz and *Hrothuwulfaz. One might suggest to Bartholinus that it wasn't contempt for death so much as acceptance that death was part of the deal. 'You have to take the rough with the smooth,' to quote another proverb. Modern soldiers say, with exactly the same mordant humour, 'if you can't take a joke, why did you sign up?'

Geopolitics in the storm centre

Did these men really exist, and what do their stories tell us, geopolitically and prehistorically? There is no doubt at least about *Hugilaikaz/Hygelac. The oddest thing about *Hrothuwulfaz/Hrolf is that he too turns up in *Beowulf*, a source maybe four hundred years older than any of the Danish versions and only a few generations removed from the events themselves. There he is called Hrothulf. But there are three odd things: he never says anything, never does anything, and the poet never bothers to say who he is – he is just *there*; most people think, as a dark shadow, an ominous presence. With him are most of the characters from the later Danish legends, but linked together with a new plausibility.

Hrothulf appears in the great hall of Heorot, 'Hart Hall' or 'Stag Hall', only after Beowulf has killed the monster Grendel and during the celebrations. He is sitting by his uncle King Hrothgar (the Ro or Hroar of later story), from which one can deduce, though the poet never says this, that he is the son of Hrothgar's brother Halga (or Helgi), who seems by this time to be dead. Nothing is said about his birth, but it looks as if a reference to the notorious Yrsa has been deleted – the poet, or maybe the monastic copyist, is squeamish elsewhere about incest.

At the peak of the celebrations, though, the Danish queen Wealhtheow (a name that, on the face of it, means 'foreign slave') comes out and unexpectedly, if obliquely, tells her husband off. She has, we learn, two sons by Hrothgar, Hrethric and Hrothmund, and what has alarmed her is that her husband appears, in the joy of his heart at having got rid of Grendel, to have adopted Beowulf as a son. But she doesn't want any more 'sons' competing with hers for the throne, when (she says this very carefully) her much older husband shall in the course of nature pass on to see destiny, or in plain English, die. And having dealt with the Beowulf issue – she also does her best to make a friend of him by the gift of an enormous golden torque or neck ring, which will eventually be stripped from Hygelac's body by the Franks – she says, twice, that she is sure she can also count on Hrothulf to see to the interests of her sons, his cousins.[28] It seems clear that the poet thinks she can't and expects his Anglo-Saxon audience to know already that she couldn't.

The poet knows another thing, too, that the later Norse saga tradition did not, and that is where Hjorvard Hrolf's-bane fits in. He's another member of the family, Hrolf's first cousin, son of Hrolf's father's elder brother, and so would be by modern reckoning the rightful king of Denmark. It is Beowulf himself who mentions 'Heoroweard' and briefly notes who he is. He remarks also that Heoroweard did not inherit his father Heorogar's weapons, a marked sign of disfavour, nor was he present in his uncle Hrothgar's hall. The unstated gist of this is that Healfdene, or Halvdan, had *three* sons – not two as Danish tradition has it – Heorogar, Hrothgar and Halga, who shared power peacefully. But they had *four* sons between them – respectively Heoroweard, Hrethric and Hrothmund, and Hrothulf. In this generation, family loyalty broke down. Wealhtheow and her sons Hrethric and Hrothmund have almost disappeared from legend, but Hrethric might lurk behind the Rœrik Ring-stingy of Danish royal genealogies – being stingy with rewards was not a survival quality in a Dark Age throne-contender. If Hrothulf killed Hrethric, and Heoroweard the disinherited killed Hrothulf, then we have a tale of civil war, of cousins killing each other to become kings of Denmark. In this view, Skuld the sorcerer woman, about whose origins no one seems very sure, becomes a 'bolt-on' Danish addition to the tale, to take the blame of what was a discreditable story – which in *Beowulf* alone has very clear motivation, a royal cousin's resentment at being excluded from the throne. (It has a real-life parallel in the events after the death of King Alfred the Great in 899, when his son Edward and his elder brother's son Æthelwold competed for the throne.)

Old English tradition, furthermore, has a place for Frodi, or Froda, who according to *Hrólfs saga* killed his brother Halvdan, and who according to Sven Aggesen was killed *by* his brother Halvdan. *Beowulf* does not think they were brothers at all. Froda instead was king of the Heathobards, or Battle-Bards, defeated by the Danes, but the father of the famous hero Ingeld, or Ingjald or Ingellus, famous for rejecting peace-marriage and trying honourably if disastrously to take revenge. The Old English poem *Widsith* says laconically:

> Hrothwulf and Hrothgar held peace together
> for a very long time, uncle and nephew,
> after they destroyed the race of the Vikings,
> and beat down the point of Ingeld,
> cut down at Heorot the power of the Heathobards.[29]

Apart from anything else, this suggests that Hrolf *did* have a major victory to his credit: he destroyed the Bards, once aggressive and formidable but who have vanished even more completely than Hygelac's Geats. The 'Hothbrodd' who according to Saxo killed King Ro looks like another garbled memory of this half-forgotten feud. Maybe Ro (or Hroar, or Hrothgar) was killed by 'the Heathobeardan', and someone thought this was a personal name, not a tribal one.

The geopolitical point is that if we can trust *Beowulf* – and its story does hang together very consistently, and the more convincingly because it is told so casually, as if everyone knew it already – then what happened in central Scandinavia is that three royal families out of four – the Geats, the Danes, the Bards – wiped each other out, or wiped themselves out. At the end of the poem the only king left standing is the Swede Eadgils, who must be the treacherous, undignified sorcerer-king Adils about whom Danish tradition is so scornful. Even he is the last survivor of a family all of whose other members (grandfather, father, uncle, brother) have been killed in battle, usually by each other.

And it may well be significant that memory was kept best not in Scandinavia, but in England. There is a Hrothmund in the early genealogy of the kings of East Anglia (known from archaeology to have very strong Scandinavian connections). There are several historical Hygelacs, mostly in the northeast of England, where the name seems to have remained popular, and the only recorded real-life Beowulf is the 'Biu-uulf' in the list, ironically, of pre-Viking benefactors of the monks of Lindisfarne.[30]

Possibly, and understandably, many emigrants to England were drawn not from the winners but from the losers in the bitter dynastic and tribal warfare that engulfed and then destroyed the sixth-century North: defeated Geats fleeing from the Swedes to north Yorkshire, to Gillingshire by the Tees, the home of the 'Geatlings', as the Venerable Bede records.[31] Defeated Danes fleeing from their own relatives to Suffolk. And (though he does not come into this story-complex) defeated Jutes like Hengest, fleeing to Kent along with his brother Horsa. Scandinavians might not want to remember the discreditable parts of the story, constructing their own suitably boastful versions, Danish or Norwegian as the case might be; forgetting the names of vanished tribes; inventing characters to take the blame; and adding heavy doses of sorcery and fairy tale. But if any peace did follow the wars of *Hugilaikaz and *Hrothuwulfaz, it was the peace of exhaustion. One Danish archaeologist, Frands Herschend, has remarked that in the mid-millennium, AD 500 and after, Scandinavia 'went down to hell'.[32]

Weapons, ships and gold

What has archaeology got to tell us about this place and time? The recent and unexpected discovery of the great halls at Lejre has already been noted. There are three other archaeological indications that deserve comment: weapon deposits, ships and gold hoards.

First, the weapon deposits. At some eight known sites, those of Torsbjerg, Nydam, Ejsbol, Kragehul, Vimose, Illerup, Hjortspring and

Krogsbolle, all in Jutland or on the islands close by, archaeologists have found piles of weapons, sometimes accompanied by whole ships, sometimes with other objects mixed in, all of them thrown into or placed on the surface of what was once (or still is) a peat bog. The amount of material is surprising, even shocking. At Nydam, not only were there two boats (one of them destroyed in the Dano-Prussian War of 1864, which broke out a few months after the first discovery was made), and local legend of a third, but the archaeologists found a hundred swords and 552 spearheads, along with bows and arrows, axes, shield bosses and horse trappings.

At Hjortspring on the island of Als close by, besides another very well-preserved boat, there were eleven single-edged swords, 169 spearheads of different types, fragments of ten mail-coats, and 64 wooden shields, along with other items. All these seem furthermore to have been deposited in the bog at the same time, which is not the case with some of the other sites, such as Torsbjerg, used over a period of some centuries. The excavators at Hjortspring suggest that what we are looking at is the spoils from a defeated raiding force. The boat they found would have had a crew of about 22, so the number of weapons would match a force of three or four boats, each ordinary warrior carrying a heavy and a light spear, commanders or nobles wearing mail-coats and carrying a sword and heavy lance apiece. But since the find was disturbed before excavation and is certainly not complete, there might have been as many as eight boats involved. The excavators at Illerup in north Denmark reckon they are looking at the spoils of a thousand-man expedition from Norway around the year AD 300.[33]

One strange and ominous fact about these finds is that much of the equipment has been deliberately smashed. The spearheads have been bent, the shields and armour broken, the sword blades in some cases heated and then carefully rolled up into coils, making them completely unusable. Another detail is that in some cases, surviving bits of wood show that they have been attacked by insects and aerobic bacteria: they did not sink into the bog immediately but lay on the surface, in some cases for years. But no one touched them or tried to salvage them. Looting the dead was normal Dark Age custom, and carrying weapons taken in battle has remained a mark of honour to this day. But deliberately breaking valuable equipment or throwing it away? No one has offered any explanation for these finds other than a religious one: the sites are sacrifices to the gods, presumably to a war god.

And just as the first-century Roman historian Tacitus noted the no-survivors ethic, as practised by Hrolf and his champions four centuries later, among the early Germans,[34] so other classical historians noted, with horror and alarm, the kind of rite that would explain Nydam, Hjortspring or Illerup. The fifth-century Spanish historian Orosius thus commented of the Cimbri – probably a tribe from what is now Himmerland in north Jutland – that

> After capturing the two Roman camps and a vast amount of booty, the enemy destroyed everything that they had laid their hands on in some new, unexpected form of curse. Clothing was ripped up and discarded, gold and silver thrown into the river, the men's armour was torn apart, the horses' harness scattered and the horses themselves drowned in the river, while the men had nooses tied round their necks and were hanged from trees. In this way the victor knew no booty nor the vanquished any mercy.[35]

Other passages in much later sagas confirm a custom by which an enemy army was dedicated to Odin by having a spear thrown over it.[36] After which the rule is, as Orosius says: no loot, and of course, no prisoners. One might not wish to believe in such clearly non-productive behaviour, but the weapon dumps of Jutland, with their piles of untouched and rendered-unserviceable gear, await any other explanation.

One may wonder what happened to the sixty-odd men who provided the arms found at Hjortspring, the four hundred-odd who manned the ships at Nydam. It is unlikely that they became prisoners of war. The silver bowl of Gundestrup, found indeed in Himmerland, shows men having their throats cut over a cauldron like the silver bowl itself.[37] Nothing could look much more peaceful nowadays than the pastoral landscapes of south Denmark and north Germany – the latter including the traditional home of the Angles, and the largest of the weapon deposits, at Torsbjerg – but for many centuries it seems to have been a crucible of war, and war of an unusually fierce and unrelenting kind, tribe against tribe. Maybe in the end it seemed, to the Angles and the Jutes and the other groups losing out, a good place to get away from.

Had they the technology to escape? The sudden arrival of the Vikings on British shores in the late eighth century is often put down to the development of the Viking longship, and many eulogies have been written about these beautiful boats, so well preserved in the barrows of Gokstad and Oseberg and now even better understood as the result of other finds, like the ones at Skuldelev by Roskilde, very near Hrolf Kraki's Lejre. They deserve the praise that has been given. But were they really a whole order of magnitude better than what went before?

A number of well-dated finds enable one to see what kind of progression there was in ship technology, and the answer is that while there was a major jump during the Roman period, after that what one sees is just steady improvement rather than radical change. In his study of *Dark Age Naval Power,* John Haywood remarks that 'the ships used by Saxons, Angles and Heruls in the fourth and fifth centuries had a performance which was not greatly inferior to those used by the Vikings.'[38] The three most interesting finds in this context come from Hjortspring, Nydam and Sutton Hoo.

The Hjortspring boat comes from long before even the pre-Viking Age being considered here. It is in effect a war canoe, almost 18 metres (60 ft) long, with a prow at both bow and stern – like all northern ships, as Tacitus remarks, and like the others controlled by steering oar. Unlike them, however, and like Roman galleys, it had a projecting double beak like a ram, and it was built without the use of iron. The striking fact about it, however, is that it was neither rowed nor sailed but paddled, by some eighteen paddlers. Paddling has some advantages, allowing boats to reach a respectable speed, as one sees from Chinese dragon boats or Pacific war canoes. Even the assault boats of the Second World War armies were paddled: if you are paddling, one major advantage in a war situation is that you are looking where you are going and facing the likely enemy. But it is much more tiring than rowing. It might be all right for short fair-weather passages from island to island in the relatively sheltered waters of the Baltic, but it is not a possible method of propulsion for open-sea journeys across the North Sea or out into the Atlantic.

Neither rowing nor sailing is in principle a complex technology, as Haywood remarks, and the Germanic tribes must very soon have learned both, if they did not invent them spontaneously, from the expanding Roman Empire. Scholars have often been reluctant to believe in Dark Age Germanic sailing ships, but classical writers were quite clear that the Saxons, and others, were sailors. The Heruls who raided northern Spain in the mid-fifth century are unlikely to have got there if they had had to row all the way from Denmark, either with long rest breaks or else rowing in shifts, which would only have doubled their water consumption; it's still less likely that they paddled.

Nevertheless, the Nydam ship, now on display in the museum at Schleswig, has often been regarded disparagingly. Its construction has been dated definitively by the tree rings in its wood to AD 310–20, though it is thought to have had maybe fifty years of use before its final capture and dedication. It is some 21 metres (70 ft) long, with rowlocks for fifteen pairs of oars. Its planking is bigger, heavier, less carefully fitted than that of the later Viking boats, and some have said that as a result it must have been 'crank', relatively unstable, without the spreading lines that made a Viking boat sit on rather than in the water. Others, however, say that it is made of different kinds of wood, which over 1,500 years in saturated earth have shrunk at different rates. It may have looked and handled better originally. But if this is the kind of boat in which we are to imagine the Angles, not many years later, emigrating to Britain from almost exactly where it was found, was it capable of sail? A simple common-sense point is that it is very hard to shift many people in a rowing boat, because the same number of people are needed to row it back. But a sailing boat as big as the Nydam one could transport maybe thirty people with their gear from Jutland to East Anglia, say, for a small crew of half-a-dozen to take it back for another load – in effect a shuttle service. It is hard to see how Britain turned into England any other way.

And then there is the boat found, with all its burial treasures, in the 1930s at Sutton Hoo in Suffolk. The long argument as to whether this was a sailer or not – it was found without a keel-block in which to step a mast, though this may be because it had been removed to allow the burial chamber for the dead man to be constructed – was settled eventually by having a half-size replica built, by Edwin and Joyce Gifford. They are quite sure that the Sutton Hoo boat was built for sail, pointing to a number of technical features, including its midship section, its waterline shape, its leaf-shaped plan form, the additional frames to take heavier rudder loads, the projecting stem and stern posts which cut leeway, and the fact that though it has oar-tholes, these are not in the midship area, which argues that rowing was only an auxiliary method of propulsion – as it continued to be for sailing ships right up to the coming of steam.[39]

In any case, the replica, called *Sæ-Wylfin*, 'She-wolf of the Sea', showed remarkable qualities when fitted with mast and sail. On its first trial on the estuary of the River Deben, running under sail, it overtook the modern motor ferry. One member of the crew remarked, 'Well, that settles that,' and so it does. The Giffords insist that ships like this, more than 27 metres (90 ft) long, with room for forty oars as well as mast and sail, 'were fully resolved designs, difficult to improve upon even with today's knowledge'.[40] They are unconvinced by the argument that the ship lacks a keel: a keel is there to help you sail to windward, and early seafarers avoided trying to do this. Ships like this would have been perfectly adequate, with the right wind, for a voyage from south Sweden round the Skaw and down the coasts of Denmark, Germany and Holland to the Zuyder Zee, where *Hugilaikaz began his raid inland, and they would have been close to ideal for penetration up the broad rivers of the Rhine and Waal to Nijmegen. The Franks had ships too, and maybe bigger, coastal defence types: massive figureheads have been found in the Scheldt near Antwerp, not far from where King Hygelac's bones were exhibited.[41]

The final issue is gold: hoards and wealth. On the archaeological evidence, the Roman Iron Age must have been a time of extraordinary wealth for the southern Scandinavian peoples, in contact – friendly or hostile – with the Roman Empire, but well out of its military reach. Some of the finds have again been deliberately smashed or broken, like the fairly small collection of silver jewellery found close to the main Nydam site. But others remain mysterious. The most famous Danish archaeological objects must be the two massive gold horns found, only a few yards apart but one many years after the other, at Gallehus, close to the modern Danish–German border and again only a few miles from Nydam. The larger of them – both were stolen and destroyed in the nineteenth century, but copies have been made from drawings – is covered in images of animals and dancing armoured warriors, and also has a famous runic inscription in Proto-Germanic: **ek hlewagastiz holtijaz horna tawido**, 'I, Hlewagast the Holting, made the horn'. Nationalistic argument has raged as to whether the inscription is proto-Danish, proto-German or even proto-English. But what were the horns doing in the ground? Were they lost accidentally? Surely not: they're too big. Buried for safe-keeping? Part of a lost burial, like Sutton Hoo? Sacrificed like the weapon dumps? The horns make the point that archaeology can tell us 'what' very accurately, but not, or rarely, 'why'.[42]

The fact remains that the record is one of unusual wealth in the whole Roman period, shown by many finds of gold rings, bars, brooches, bracteates (gold ornaments that imitate coins) and 'hackgold' (gold items cut up without regard for their nature, as if in a process of division by weight). The last suggests strongly what some archaeologists have said: that the whole area was living quite successfully off a so-called 'plunder economy' – just as the literary record indicates. But at the end of the Roman period, in the fifth century, things started to change. There are fewer and eventually no rich burials. More of the finds look like hoards, that is, people's savings buried to hide them; it is of course a bad sign to find one of these, for it indicates that the hider and owner never came back. The Danish archaeologist Lotte Hedeager has characterized the Late Germanic Iron Age (just after the period of Hygelac and Hrolf, mid-sixth century and later) as one of 'persistently sparing investment' – which we might less cautiously call poverty.[43]

Other indications suggest that the end of the Roman period was also a time of major social reorganization, and one imposed rather than developed by consent. In his book *Mead-halls of the Eastern Geats* (2011) the Swedish archaeologist Martin Rundkvist suggests, in careful academic language, that the mid-sixth-century transfer of power of which he sees the signs in Ostergotland is unlikely to have taken place 'in an undramatic fashion'.[44] *Beowulf* puts it more strongly, but they are talking about the same thing. Using modern terms, the story is one of centralizing power, professionalization of the military, disappearance of local groups and tribal names, and wars – so Hedeager suggests – to control strategic resources including land and access to bog iron.

The last is a modern view, by a modern scholar who characteristically prefers sensible economic motives for war. Our ancient texts, like *Beowulf* and *Hrólfs saga*, suggest just as plausibly that the wars were undertaken for glory, for revenge, to expand power. But the results are the same either way. And where glory is displayed by the possession of precious objects, like the great neck ring given to Beowulf by Wealhtheow and lost by Hygelac 'on his last expedition', the economic motive and the glory motive may come out to much the same thing.

Archaeological evidence, then, almost always admits multiple explanations and multiple causes. Factors for the sixth-century slump could include climate change, plague and soil exhaustion, while there is good evidence for a major volcanic explosion in the mid-530s that threw so much dust into the air as to cause short summers and poor harvests worldwide. But a slump there was. Professor Herschend has already been quoted on the results. Martin Rundkvist says more temperately that for Scandinavia, the storm centre of north European geopolitics, it was 'a highly stressful time'.[45] They may have had the ships, but they no longer had the men, the money or the confidence.

The royal families, says *Beowulf*, had fought each other to extinction. With the fall of Hygelac in Holland, and Hrolf *kraki* at Lejre not long afterwards, the First Viking Age came to an end. Oddly, the great trauma was remembered best in England, maybe by the refugees. Like deacon Alcuin, they thought that was the end of it.

THREE

Volsungs and Nibelungs:
Avenging Female Furies

So far in this book women have figured primarily as victims: Nidud's daughter Bodvild, Hjalti's nameless girlfriend. This is not typical. The sagas of Icelanders especially are full of dominating and aggressive women, from Hallgerd 'Long-legs' in *Njáls saga* to Gisli's loaded-purse-swinging wife Aud in *Gísla saga*, 'The Saga of Gisli'.[1] Women also play prominent and even dominant roles in the greatest legend of the ancient North, the story of two linked families, the Volsungs and the Nibelungs.

This contains everything that people think of when they think of Norse myth: dragons, valkyries, werewolves, treasure-hoarding dwarfs, the one-eyed god Odin and the trickster god Loki, strange fertility rites, the 'helm of terror' which Fafnir the dragon wears, and, above all, Andvaranaut, the cursed ring of power. Historical human characters drawn into the story include Attila the Hun and the two great kings of the Goths, the doomed Ermanaric (Iormunrekk in Norse) and Thidrek, or Theodoric, conqueror of Italy. The legend was responsible for the greatest medievalizing work of the nineteenth century, Richard Wagner's *The Ring of the Nibelung*, and influenced also the greatest medievalizing work of the twentieth century, J.R.R. Tolkien's *The Lord of the Rings*.

Its main hero is generally taken to be Sigurd, whom the Germans call Siegfried. He is the son of Sigmund, son of Volsung, founder of the Volsung dynasty. He marries into the family of the Nibelungs and is then murdered by them, so that he is the hinge, the connector of the two family stories. But the legend contains also three powerful female characters, who between them show that there was a role for women as well as men in the hero(in)ic ethic of the old North.

They are Signy the Volsung, Sigmund's sister, who sacrifices her sons, and her husband, and herself, for vengeance; Brynhild, the disobedient valkyrie who has her lover Sigurd killed to avenge her shame and then kills herself from grief; and Gudrun the Nibelung, who in one version or another kills or sends to their deaths two sets of sons, as well as two husbands, several brothers and a stepson. Nor do they go to their deaths alone. Brynhild takes thirteen slaves with her, a reminder that human sacrifice, perhaps especially of women, was a part of some Viking funerals. This chapter centres on these three women and their part in the Viking drama of 'contempt for death'.

Legend, history and the 'king problem'

There are five ancient written versions of the Volsung/Nibelung story,[2] but it survives graphically as well. Wood and stone carvings from Scandinavia, Britain, the Isle of Man and, very surprisingly, northern Spain (see Chapter Seven) show the manacled Sigmund preparing to kill the witch-wolf, Sigurd stabbing the dragon from beneath, Sigurd roasting the dragon's heart with the nuthatches twittering advice behind him, and other scenes.[3] Turning to the written versions, the oldest is the poems of the *Poetic Edda*, some 35 of them, depending on what one counts, of which about half (seventeen, all of them among the 29 in the Codex Regius) deal with some aspect of the Volsungs and the Nibelungs. Most unfortunately, some early vandal tore a 'gathering' of eight pages out of this manuscript before it was discovered, and those eight pages contained what was probably the core of what would have been the 'Great Lay of Sigurd', about whose contents there has ever since been doubt: a bonus for Tolkien, as it happens, who set himself to write the missing poem and the legend as it should have been, in his *The Legend of Sigurd and Gudrún* (not published until 2009).

Two thirteenth-century Icelandic writers, however, wrote versions of the whole story, and both men had probably seen complete versions of the poetic cycle, which they retell in prose. Unfortunately again, they seem to have understood it in different ways, or misunderstood it, and they tell different stories. These are once again Snorri Sturluson, whose *Prose Edda* was designed as a handbook for future poets and contains an abbreviated version of the whole; and the anonymous author of the much longer *Völsunga saga*, or 'The Saga of the Volsungs'.

The story was famous outside Iceland and outside Scandinavia, for we also have a long poem in Middle High German, the *Nibelungenlied*, 'Song of the Nibelungs', probably written rather earlier than the two Old Norse prose versions. This centres on the Nibelungs, not the Volsungs, though a major part of it is the relationship between the Nibelungs and Siegfried. The *Nibelungenlied* knows nothing of Siegfried's father Sigmund, his grandfather Volsung or his half-brother Sinfjotli, though these may have been even more important in the earliest versions of the story, of which we have some hints. Nor does it introduce the pagan gods, and it does not know quite what to do with the fatal ring, though the poet seems to feel that a ring ought to be in the story somewhere.

Finally, there is a long catch-all saga, *Þiðreks saga af Bern*, 'The Saga of Thidrek of Verona', which centres on the historical Gothic king Theodoric but brings in Volsungs and Nibelungs as well. This is written in Old Norse, but scholars are increasingly sure that it is a translation, not from the High German of the *Nibelungenlied* but from Low German, a language like Dutch that was of special importance in the Middle Ages as being the language of the powerful Hanseatic League of trading cities.

Working out how these legends relate to each other has long been recognized as the *Königsproblem*, the 'king problem', of Germanic philology, much confused by strong nationalistic feeling – whose story is it, the Germans or the Icelanders or the Danes or the Norwegians? No one has ever solved the problem to general satisfaction, though there have been many efforts (not only Professor Tolkien's). But is it all just a legend or a myth? Is there any truth in it?

It was realized a long time ago that, as noted in Chapter One, the Nibelungs, at least, were real people. The central figure of that family is Gunnar, his father is Gjuki, his sister is Gudrun and he has brothers who names, in Norse, are Giselher and Guthorm, or Guttorm. These correspond very well to the family of the Burgundian kings of Worms-am-Rhein, whose names are given in the Latin *Lex Burgundionum* as Gibica, Gundaharius, Gislaharius and Gundomaris.[4] To pick just one of them, Proto-Germanic *Gunda-hari, 'battle warrior', would regularly become not only Gunnar in Old Norse, but Gunther in High German and Guth-here in Old English – and indeed Guthere does figure along with his famous brother Hagena, or Hogni, in the Old English poem *Waldere*. The *Nibelungenlied*'s Giselher must have been Gislaharius; Gundomaris may well reappear as Guttorm in 'The Saga of the Volsungs', and although the *Lex Burgundionum* mentions no female members of the family, Gudrun, originally *Gunda-runo, fits too well to be an accident. The family got into Latin historical record because, as said above, it was wiped out about the year 437 in an attack by the Huns, though not, as it happens, by Attila. The Burgundians recovered as a tribe from the disaster – though their ruling family didn't – and settled in France, in what is now the wine country of Bourgogne.

How about the Volsungs? Surrounded as they are by gods and dwarfs and dragons, they look suspiciously mythical. In 'The Saga of the Volsungs', the founder of their line is indeed called Volsung, but this does not sound right. The *-ung* ending nearly always means 'descendant of', as if the original name should have been Volsi. *Beowulf* in fact knows the name as Wæls, and refers to Sigmund, Sigurd's father, as 'the Wælsing', the 'son of Wæls',[5] which *does* sound right. However, the original and correct name for the founder of the dynasty may have been censored out by later Christian writers, for in Old Norse *völsi* is a word for 'horse penis'. (There is an Old Norse short story incorporated into 'The Saga of St Olaf' that accuses the pagan Swedes, possibly unfairly but possibly not, of worshipping a horse penis in winter fertility rites.) 'The Saga of the Volsungs' as we have it starts off with an involved story about an apple sent by Odin to ensure conception, and a sword which only the hero Sigmund can draw, planted by Odin in a huge tree called Barnstock. This clearly means 'bairn stock', 'child stock', so once again there is some kind of story of miraculous conception lurking in there. Possibly the original founder of the dynasty was once thought to be a fertility god.

None of this looks very historical at all – though one should remember that we are fairly sure there was a real king *Hugilaikaz of the Geats, but if you believe 'The Saga of King Hrolf', the Geats chose their kings by seeing whose behind was big enough to fill their enormous throne by sitting on it; and Hygelac does get a listing in the *Liber monstrorum*. History and legend can get seriously mixed.

Meanwhile, the most famous of the Volsungs, Sigurd (or Siegfried), has often been identified as a historical character, but the argument is not convincing. German scholars of the nineteenth century saw the origin of their nation and its freedom in the great defeat and annihilation of three Roman legions in AD 9 (the site of the disaster, at Kalkriese in east Germany, has incidentally only recently been identified from archaeological finds).[6] They very much wanted to find a native account of it, and by tortuous reasoning equated the German leader Arminius with Siegfried. The theory has convinced no one except German nationalists looking for a hero.

In any case, Sigurd looks suspicious in other respects. In Norse and in German he gets the credit for killing the dragon Fafnir, but not in *Beowulf* – and *Beowulf*, it should be remembered, may well be two or three hundred years older than the oldest Old Norse version. *Beowulf* knows of a dragon slayer, but gives the credit to Sigemund, who 'ventured alone beneath the grey stone',[7] and Sigmund is in all Norse versions Sigurd's father. They are clearly the same person, because the *Beowulf* poet mentions that Sigemund was alone, 'Fitela was not with him',[8] and Fitela must be Sinfjotli, Sigmund's incestuously conceived son from 'The Saga of the Volsungs'. The pair are prominent in other early poems. In the poem *Eiríksmál*, 'The Lay of Eirik', the two heroes who stand by Odin in Valhalla are Sigmund and Sinfjotli: it is a sign of Eirik Blood-axe's greatness that Sigmund is prepared to challenge his entry and then welcome him as an equal.[9] One might well think that the Sigmund–Sigurd relationship is rather like the Lancelot–Galahad one in the Arthurian cycle: the original hero was the father, Lancelot or Sigmund. Poets and storytellers feeling a need for a sequel, or a hero who better fitted their ideas, managed it by saying in effect, 'yes, the father was very famous, but if you want a story about the *real* hero, you want the one about his son, and I'm the only one who knows it!'

Sigurd is also the hinge or pivot character in the whole cycle of poems and legends. He rounds off the story of the Volsungs, in which he functions mainly as dragon slayer. He starts the story of the Nibelungs, in which his main role is to free, but then to betray, the lapsed valkyrie Brynhild. One might wonder whether he was perhaps grafted in to do exactly that job, of joining two stories, with the dragon slayer role borrowed from his father Sigmund and the valkyrie-lover role implicit in a story that was originally female-centred. Professor Theodore M. Andersson, latest to consider the *Königsproblem* at length, notably decided to call his study of 1980 not 'The Sigurd Legend' but *The Legend of Brynhild*, and that looks right.

As for Brynhild, she has several possible historical originals, the name Brunhilda being fairly common. A Gothic princess of that name married the Frankish king Sigibert, who was murdered in 575, and his widow – who lived on for almost forty years – made a name for herself by her determined and savage attempts at vengeance. However, murder, betrayal and savage revenge were so normal in the seriously dysfunctional Merovingian dynasty (the descendants of *Mero-wech) that it is hard to see why she would have had any special priority.[10]

None of this gives any definite solution to the notorious *Königsproblem*, but one may say, first, that there was clearly a story about the wipeout of the Burgundian dynasty by the Huns in the earlier fifth century. There was also clearly a story about the Wælsings, or Volsungs – that is to say, the descendants of Wæls or Volsi – circulating in Scandinavia and England. No date is fixable for this, but one or two of the minor characters in it – like Hothbrodd, killed by Helgi Hundingsbana – look like escapes from the story of the Skjoldungs covered in the previous chapter, so one might look to the early sixth century. At some point, a heavy dose of myth and folklore was added – dragon, valkyrie, dwarfs and dwarfish treasure – and perhaps the treasure (and the ring) were also pivotal.

Gunnar's family, meanwhile, is called the Nibelungs, or Niflungar, or in Latin Nebulones, but it is hard to see why, since there is no ancestral *Nibel or *Nifl. *Nifl* means 'mist', as in the modern German *Nebel*, and Niflheim or Niflhel, 'land of mist', is where the dwarfs live. It's possible that there was a story about the Volsungs killing a dragon and taking its dwarf-made treasure, and that someone put this together with the fabulous treasure of the Burgundians, hidden from the Huns and never found, and decided that the two treasures were one and the same, the treasure in fact of the Nibelungs, the dwarfs, the children of mist and darkness. And so the stage would be set for also calling the last owners of the treasure 'the Nibelungs' and telling a story to explain how they got it from the hero Sigurd, who took it from the dragon Fafnir, who took it from the god Loki, who took it from the dwarf Andvari.[11]

All one needs then is a provocation, and that provocation is Brynhild.

Egging and suttee: the rights, and rites, of women

Suttee – the word was borrowed into English from Sanskrit *sati* – is the custom of having a widow burn herself alive on her husband's funeral pyre. The British were horrified when they encountered it in India and banned it as soon as they had the power. But their ancestors, or some of their ancestors, had been doing the same, or worse, a thousand years before. The Indian rite depends on the custom of cremation, and the ancient North knew several burial customs, including burial, ship burial and barrow burial as well as cremation. Possibly the grisliest find ever made in England (though there is strong competition) was one in Sewerby, Yorkshire. There archaeologists found the grave of a young Anglian lady, laid out decently with her arms folded and her jewels round her neck. On top of her, though, was the skeleton of an older woman, not laid out decently at all, but still trying, in death, to push herself up on her elbows. She had been buried alive, and she couldn't push herself up because her back was broken. Her back had been broken by the heavy millstone thrown in on top of her as she sprawled in her mistress's grave. This was very likely a human sacrifice,[12] but not suttee, which, in theory at least, was voluntary, done by a wife, and a sign of devotion, whence its original Sanskrit meaning, 'a virtuous woman'.

Suttee does seem nevertheless to have existed among Scandinavians, for we have one very detailed account of just such a case, recorded by a travelling Arab in the 920s; in severely bowdlerized form it was taken into the movie *The 13th Warrior* (1999; see Chapter Eight). And it is a recurrent feature of the Volsung/Nibelung story, though the story still leaves undecided the question: what would make women volunteer to die with their husbands or their lovers? And did Gudrun do right to hold back? All three women remain enigmatic.

The first case is particularly oddly motivated, and it is that of Signy. 'The Saga of the Volsungs' says that her father, King Volsung, had ten sons, the eldest being Sigmund, and one daughter, Signy. Signy is married to

King Siggeir of Gautland, who takes offence when Sigmund will not give him the sword planted by Odin in the tree Barnstock, which only Sigmund could draw. Siggeir invites Volsung and his sons to visit his home, plotting (just like Atli with Gunnar and Hogni) to kill them there. When Volsung arrives, Signy warns her father to flee, but he refuses, saying – and this entire scene will be repeated in all essentials later on in the Nibelung story:

> [I] made the vow that I would flee neither fire nor iron from fear, and so I have done until now. Why should I not fulfill that vow in my old age? Maidens will not taunt my sons during games by saying that they feared their deaths, for each man must at one time die. No man may escape dying that once . . .[13]

This contains three characteristic elements. The (implied) argument that since death is inevitable, there is no point in trying shamefully to put it off echoes stanza 16 of the Eddic poem *Hávamál*, 'The Words of the High One' (that is, Odin):

> The coward thinks he can live for ever
> If he avoids battle.
> But old age gives no man mercy,
> Though spears spare him.

There is a logical error here – living forever is not the same as not dying right now – but Volsung has other arguments. One is just that he is old, with, it is implied, not many years to lose. But, finally, one should note that he thinks that even his younger sons have a powerful motive: they do not want to be taunted, and in particular not by women. Old Norse even has a special verb for women's taunting, which is *eggja*, 'to egg on' but also 'to whet, to sharpen, to put an edge on'. It is what so many Norse and Icelandic heroines do as they send their sons, husbands and brothers out, often reluctantly but never refusing, to kill and be killed.

Signy's father sends her back to her husband; Volsung is killed and his ten sons are captured. Signy then asks her husband, as a favour, not to have them killed quickly but to put them in stocks so that she can gloat over them. Siggeir thinks this is rather odd, but agrees. As they sit in the stocks, a grim old she-wolf visits nine nights in a row and eats nine of the sons up, leaving only Sigmund. Signy then sends a man to put honey on Sigmund's face and in his mouth. When the wolf comes, she licks the honey and tries to lick it out of Sigmund's mouth. But he catches her tongue and tears it out so that it is the wolf (Siggeir's witch-mother) who bleeds to death. (It is thought this scene may be depicted on the very-weathered hogback stone now in St Peter's Church at Heysham in Lancashire.) Sigmund breaks the stocks and escapes. Signy lives on for years with Siggeir and bears his sons. But she remains set on vengeance.

The story implies that Sigmund, hiding in the woods, cannot take vengeance without some assistance, and each time one of her sons by Siggeir reaches a useful age (ten), Signy sends him to Sigmund to be tested. The test is that Sigmund goes out, telling the boy to make bread from a sack of flour. But there is an adder, a poisonous snake, concealed in the flour, and the boy dares not touch it. When Sigmund reports this to Signy, she tells him each time to kill the boy, since he is useless. Signy then – note that she is the driving force in all this – determines desperate measures. She changes her shape, with the aid of a sorceress, goes to Sigmund's hideout, and lies with him. She thus conceives a child who is a Volsung on both sides of his lineage and will have the true hard heart of his ancestors. The saga does not mention it, but it seems there must be a price to be paid, for the child of incest is called Sinfjotli, which means 'spotty' or perhaps 'piebald': he has a birthmark.

Sinfjotli is a true hero. When his mother, as a test, sews his shirt sleeves to his skin and then rips them away, he does not flinch or cry out. Confronted with the sack of flour and the adder, he merely kneads the snake into the flour and bakes them together. He cannot drink poison like his father, but he is immune to a snakebite. Sigmund, who does not know he is the boy's father, thinks that Sinfjotli is rather odd, for he keeps insisting on taking vengeance on the person they both think is his father, Siggeir, but he accepts his assistance just the same. In the end, after other adventures, they burn Siggeir in his hall.

As the flames rise, though, Sigmund asks Signy to come out of the burning hall, to live honourably and happily. But she replies by confessing her incest:

> Sinfjotli is our son. Because of this he has so much zeal; he is the child of both a son and a daughter of King Volsung. In everything I have worked toward the killing of King Siggeir. I have worked so hard to bring about vengeance that I am by no means fit to live. Willingly I shall now die with King Siggeir, although I married him reluctantly.[14]

She walks back into the flames and dies.

This does look very like suttee, voluntary self-cremation with a deceased husband: she married Siggeir reluctantly, but she dies with him 'willingly'. The amazing thing is that there is no love in it. Nor does Signy seem to feel remorse at her repeated infanticides. Could it be self-disgust over her incest ('I am by no means fit to live')? Or is it just a point of honour? Her father fled 'neither fire nor iron', and she does not intend to do so either. As often in Norse literature, the gesture is dramatically obvious, but the motive remains obscure.

One might note that in the famous *Njáls saga*, Njal's wife, Bergthora, who is offered the chance to escape with the other women and children when their enemies come to burn Njal and his sons in his house – taking revenge for murders instigated by Bergthora – nevertheless refuses. In words rather like Signy's, she says, 'I was young when I was given to Njal, and promised him that we would both share the same fate.'[15] The two old people go back to bed. Their little grandson Thord also refuses to leave, reminding his grandmother that she promised they would always be together. No one tries to argue with him, for children have their honour as well. The three lie down with an oxhide over them and die of suffocation in their burning homestead. Njal and Bergthora's son Skarphedin – no one even thinks of offering *him* mercy – says, once more making a joke out of death, 'Father's going to bed early, as you'd expect, he's an old man.'[16]

The whole scene may be fiction, but Njal and his family were real people, the site of their homestead remains well known, and events like the burning certainly happened.[17] Once again, the account was thought by Icelanders to be true in its essentials, the sort of thing that could or should be said and done. Several times, scenes from the *fornaldarsögur*, the 'sagas of old times', like 'The Saga of the Volsungs', are rewritten in the homelier sagas of Icelanders, set now in farmyards, not kings' courts; but the spirit, expressed in plain or joking understatements, remains the same.

The price of a valkyrie's virginity

Signy's incestuous son Sinfjotli is poisoned by his stepmother. He knows the drink is poisoned but drinks it anyway, following the very bad advice of his father to *Láttu grön sía, sonr*, which Jesse Byock memorably translates as 'Filter it through your moustache, son.'[18] Sigmund, like other favourites of Odin, is betrayed by the one-eyed god, who breaks the sword he left for Sigmund with his spear Gungnir. The shards pass to Sigmund's infant son Sigurd.

'The Saga of the Volsungs' then switches, with something of a crash of gears, to 'the otter's ransom' – the treasure taken from the dwarf Andvari by Odin and Loki to pay the weregild they owe for accidentally killing a giant's son, shape-shifted into an otter. The treasure is taken from the giant by another son, Fafnir, who refuses to share it with his brother Regin, then shape-shifts into a dragon and lies down on his gold on the Gnita-heath. His hoard includes the ring Andvaranaut, which Andvari begged to retain when all else had been taken, knowing that if he retained it, he could win back all he had lost. A curse now follows it. The treasure and the Volsungs intersect when Sigurd reforges the broken sword and is led by Regin to kill his brother Fafnir. Then, warned by the nuthatches that Regin means to kill him – roasting and tasting the heart of Fafnir has given him the power to understand bird-speech – he kills Regin too and becomes sole possessor of the treasure and the ring.

No ancient author seems quite sure what happens next, though there is universal agreement – picked up by Wagner, though he is no more convincing in the big scene than anyone else – that a ring, or The Ring, or maybe two rings, must have been somehow central. The pivotal scene, in all versions, is the 'quarrel of the queens'.

Everyone agrees on some things. First, there was a woman of super-natural powers called Brynhild. The Norse versions (Snorri's *Edda* and 'The Saga of the Volsungs') see her furthermore as a valkyrie. The Old Norse word *val-kyrja*, and the Old English one *wæl-cyrga*, both mean the same thing: 'chooser of the slain, those dead on the battlefield'. They are a per-sonification of the fact that some warriors die while others live, and many deaths appear random. They act as harvesters for Odin, continually recruit-ing for his army in Valhalla. Brynhild, however, again in the Norse versions, has disobeyed Odin's order and given victory to the wrong man, and has accordingly been cast into an enchanted sleep within a circle of fire, from which she can only be released by a fearless hero who will ride the flame. The German versions have de-paganized this until she is just a woman of enormous strength who will marry no one who cannot overpower her.

Fearless or Herculean, this has to be Sigurd. The second matter gen-erally agreed, though, is that one way or another Sigurd wins Brynhild on behalf of Gunnar, king of the Burgundians. Gunnar wants the famous beauty protected by fire or by her own strength, but dare not or cannot win her himself. In return for Gunnar's sister Gudrun, Sigurd agrees to do it. He changes shape with Gunnar and then either rides the fire or wins the contests of strength; in the *Nibelungenlied* these are the long jump, the javelin and putting the shot. Either way, Sigurd woos and wins Brynhild, changes shape again and passes her on to Gunnar.

Brynhild has been won by treachery, then. Sigurd gets Gudrun in return, and all is well, until – again, universal agreement – the fact that it was Sigurd and not Gunnar who really won Brynhild is blurted out by

Gudrun to Brynhild, during the famous 'quarrel of the queens'. The strange thing here is that although the scene is vital and was admired so much that other saga authors reworked it in more everyday terms (just like Signy and Bergthora), still, no ancient author managed to make sense of it. (Although it should be remembered that eight vital pages from the oldest version, the Eddic 'Great Lay of Sigurd', have been lost at exactly this point.)

The other four each tell it in a different way, and one can see that they all have trouble with the motif of the ring (or Ring, or rings), which nevertheless none of them will leave out. There is, moreover, the vital but embarrassing question of quite what is meant by Sigurd 'wooing and winning' Brynhild, as tactfully phrased above.

Everyone agrees once again that the whole thing starts with a contest over precedence. In the Old Norse versions, this is marked in what one has to call a rather primitive way. In both Snorri's *Prose Edda* and 'The Saga of the Volsungs', the two women Gudrun and Brynhild are washing their hair in a river and argue over who has the right to wash her hair further upstream. Brynhild says she does, because she has the more valiant husband, Gunnar. Gudrun says no, it's her husband, Sigurd: he killed Fafnir the dragon. Brynhild then says – this is Snorri's *Prose Edda* version, and the traditional 'one step too far':

> 'It was a greater achievement for Gunnar to have ridden the flickering flame when Sigurd did not dare.'
>
> Then Gudrun laughed and said: 'Do you reckon it was Gunnar that rode the flickering flame [which guarded the sleeping Brynhild]? I reckon that the one that went to bed with you was the one that gave me this gold ring, and that gold ring that you are wearing and that you received as morning gift, that is known as Andvari's gift, and I reckon it was not Gunnar that won it on Gnita-heath.'
>
> Then Brynhild was silent and went home.[19]

There is something seriously wrong with this. In the first place, it has *two* rings. Gudrun is wearing a ring which Sigurd gave her, and which Brynhild gave to the man she thought was Gunnar, so she ought to be able to recognize it. One has to wonder why Sigurd was so tactless as to pass on a love token to his wife with the risk that the giver will recognize it.

But the revelation of the other ring is even more destructive, because Gudrun knows that Brynhild received her ring, from Sigurd, as a 'morning gift', which was traditionally given to the bride on the morning after the wedding night. *If*, that is, she proved to be a virgin, and in exchange for her virginity. This suggests that Sigurd did not hand Brynhild over to her husband untouched, and has furthermore (bad idea!) boasted of the fact to his wife. Most serious of all, the big shock is the recognition of the famous ring, the fatal ring Andvaranaut, known to belong to Sigurd ever since he won it from the dragon. This is what seems to silence Brynhild. But she has had it on her finger all the time! Has she not noticed? If she never recognized it before, then why should she be so shocked when recognizing it now?

We do not know exactly what version of the story the author of the *Nibelungenlied* was starting from – one big difference is that he knows the Gudrun figure as Kriemhild – but clearly he found much of this far too vulgar and embarrassing to be repeated. For one thing, in his world, queens do not wash their hair in the river and argue over precedence about who gets to stand upstream. Accordingly, in his poem Kriemhild and Brunhild argue over who has the right to enter church first, and they see it as a matter of social class, not whose husband is the bravest. Brunhild says she is the wife of a king, and is therefore a queen, while Kriemhild, though the sister of a king, is only married to a liegeman. Wives take rank from their husbands, not their brothers. So Brunhild should go first. Kriemhild then puts the fat in the fire by answering that while she may be the wife of a liege-man, Brunhild is the cast-off mistress of a liegeman, that is, her husband Siegfried. (Once again, the implication is that Siegfried has boasted of his sexual conquest to his wife, who seems to have been impressed by it.) For good measure, Kriemhild calls Brunhild a *kebse*, a slut or tart: she had sex with someone not her husband, and it was Siegfried who took her virginity.

Brunhild then starts to cry, in a very un-valkyrie-like way, and Kriemhild enters the minster before her. But on the way out of the church they start again. Brunhild asks for proof of the allegation that she has had sex with Siegfried. The dialogue continues:

> Kriemhild: 'I prove it with this gold ring on my finger, which my sweetheart brought me when he first slept with you.'
>
> Brunhild: 'This noble ring was stolen and has long been maliciously withheld from me! But now I have got to the bottom of it and I know who took it from me.'
>
> Kriemhild: 'You shall not make me the thief who stole it! . . . As proof that I am not lying, see this girdle which I have round me – you shared my Siegfried's bed!'[20]

This version also generates problems. The first is that the ring on Kriemhild's finger is not the famous ring Andvaranaut (of which the *Nibelungenlied* knows nothing), but just an anonymous ring. Also, it's not clear how Siegfried got it. Logically, Brunhild ought to have given it to him as a token, because then she would know that it must have been passed on by the man she slept with, whoever that was. But Kriemhild never says that's what happened, and Brunhild says the ring was stolen, in which case it could have been stolen by anyone.

The weakness of the ring motif as used here is shown up by the fact that Kriemhild here has to introduce a second token, the girdle – very often a symbol of sexual conquest, as a ring is a token of love or a sign of commitment. One other deeply embedded confusion in the *Nibelungenlied* story is that the author makes it quite clear that Brunhild's prodigious strength is tied up with her virginity: she has to lose her virginity before a normal man can cope with her. On the wedding night Gunther gets nowhere and winds up hanging on a peg. Siegfried takes over the next night and overpowers Brunhild, before handing her over to Gunnar, taking the ring and girdle before he does so. But did he take her virginity as well? And if not, why does he take the ring and the girdle? The courtly poet of the *Nibelungenlied* at this point gets embarrassed and says he doesn't know.[21]

Two rings, one of them Andvaranaut, worn without realizing it by Brynhild, who got it as 'morning gift'. One ring, not Andvaranaut, worn by Kriemhild (Gudrun), not given but taken as a sign of conquest. 'The Saga of the Volsungs' has another explanation, which is more logical, but at the price of creating enormous problems elsewhere in the story. In the saga, the two women are again bathing in the Rhine, there is a row about who goes out further, and Brynhild – this time it is she who says the one word too many – taunts Gudrun by saying her husband Sigurd was once a thrall. Gudrun says she is a fool to say that:

'It is not fitting for you to insult him, because he was your first man [*frumverr*]. He killed Fafnir and rode the wavering flames when you thought it was King Gunnar. He lay with you and took from your hand the ring Andvaranaut, which you can now see here for yourself.'

Brynhild saw the ring, recognized it, and became as pale as death.[22]

Now in some ways this is a good scene. This time there is only one ring, and it is Andvaranaut, and Gudrun has it on her finger. That's why Brynhild has not seen it before. Furthermore, Brynhild recognizes it right away: she knows that she owned it, she knows who took it – the man she thought was Gunnar. If Sigurd's wife now owns it, then the man who took it must have been Sigurd. It is that sudden realization that makes her go 'pale as death'.

But there is still a serious objection to it. If Sigurd has *taken* the ring Andvaranaut from Brynhild, he must have *given* it to her beforehand, because the ring is known to have come from the hoard of the dragon Fafnir, whom Sigurd killed. So when did he do that? And if he gave it to her as a morning gift, as Snorri says and as implied in the saga by the word *frumverr*, that means he must have taken her virginity *before* he wooed her for Gunnar (unless he took her virginity *while* wooing her for Gunnar, gave her the ring then, and took it back again, presumably the next morning, which is ridiculous).

This version forces on the saga writer a kind of plot doubling. Sigurd has to win Brynhild twice: once for himself, once on behalf of Gunnar. In between, he is given a potion of forgetfulness, so he does not remember his earlier vows. It is odd that Brynhild never reminds him.

The fourth version, *Þiðreks saga*, or 'The Saga of Thidrek', is refreshingly straightforward. In this, Brynhild asks why Grimhild (Kriemhild/Gudrun) is sitting in her, Brynhild's, high seat in her hall. Grimhild says it is because both seat and hall are rightfully hers. Taunts are exchanged, until Grimhild asks Brynhild, 'Who took your virginity, and who was your first man [*frumverr*]?' Brynhild says it was Gunnar. Grimhild says that it wasn't: it was Sigurd. Brynhild says, 'I was never Sigurd's woman and he was never my man.' To which Grimhild replies:

> 'I refute that by this gold ring, which he took from you when he had taken your virginity. He took this same ring from your hand and gave it to me.'
>
> And now when Brynhild sees this ring, she recognizes that she had owned it . . . And Brynhild thinks this matters so much that her body is now as red as newly shed blood, and she is silent and says not a word, stands up and goes away out of the hall.[23]

(Note that, like Volund, women too can have their feelings betrayed by autonomic nervous reaction, in this case flushing.)

This is actually the most sensible of the four versions we have. As in 'The Saga of the Volsungs' there is only one ring, and Grimhild/Gudrun has got it. The weak point is that, as in the *Nibelungenlied*, this ring is not The Ring, 'the Nibelung's ring', the ring we know as Andvaranaut. There is then no problem as to how Brynhild got the ring in the first place; but though the ring does its job in this scene, it does not connect the scene with the dwarf Andvari's curse, the dragon Fafnir's curse, the curse that will fall on Brynhild, Grimhild, Sigurd and Sigurd's murderers.

Unlike the *Nibelungenlied*, which refuses to comment, and unlike both Snorri's *Edda* and 'The Saga of the Volsungs', which declare that Sigurd kept his sword Gram between himself and Brynhild after he won Brynhild for Gunnar, *Þiðreks saga* makes no bones about declaring that Sigurd had sex with Brynhild at the time that he won her for Gunnar; in fact, this author says that Gunnar told him to do so, to take away her magic strength. But he was supposed to keep quiet about it, not take her ring, and of course, not tell his wife! *Þiðreks saga* is the clearest of the four ancient versions, but also the coarsest in sentiment.

Whatever the mechanics of it, in all versions Brynhild knows she has been deceived by her husband and Sigurd/Siegfried acting in collusion, and someone has to pay. Why pick Sigurd? As with Signy, Brynhild's motives are never clarified, but one can think of several. Killing Sigurd will injure Gudrun terribly as well. In 'The Saga of the Volsungs', when she realizes Sigurd is dead, Gudrun lets out a great wail of lamentation, and Brynhild hears it and laughs. The Eddic 'Short Lay of Sigurd' says:

> Brynhild laughed then,   the daughter of Budli,
> that one time   with all her heart,
> when she could hear   from her bed
> the daughter of Giuki   weeping bitterly.[24]

But then, with vengeance satisfactorily accomplished on both the man who betrayed her *and* the woman who taunted her, why does Brynhild commit suicide?

There is a kind of symbolism in the detailed instructions she gives for her own funeral pyre. Only 'The Saga of the Volsungs' gives the full story here. Snorri is laconic – 'Brynhild stabbed herself with a sword and she was burned with Sigurd' – and in the two German versions (counting *Þiðreks saga* as a translation from German) she just disappears from the story.

'The Saga of the Volsungs' tells a different tale. There, once Sigurd is dead, Brynhild curses her husband, Gunnar, distributes her treasure and stabs herself. Then she gives her instructions: make a pyre for her and Sigurd. Set between them a drawn sword, as when they lay together (she means the second time, when Sigurd took Gunnar's form). Build a pavilion over them, and it must be 'reddened with the blood of men'. Four of her men are to die and be burned with Sigurd; thirteen attendants are to go with her. There is a hint, in 'The Short Lay of Sigurd', that these deaths are supposed to be voluntary: in stanzas 49–50 of that poem she offers treasures to those who will take them, but:

All were silent,   considered what was best,
all together   offered answer:
'Enough have died,   we mean to live,
let the hall-maids   win honour.'

The 'hall-maids', then, have presumably volunteered already. Brynhild replies with scorn:

'I do not want   someone reluctant,
nor someone   who needs persuasion,
to lose life   for our sake.'

In the saga she also says, 'The door will not close on his heels if I follow him.'[25] A similar speech in the poem implies that she must follow hard on Sigurd's heels into the land of the dead, or be left out. (After all, as a lapsed valkyrie, Brynhild must know how people make the passage.)

As for her motive, surely this is simply suttee, the act of the virtuous woman. She regards Sigurd as her real husband, her *frumverr* or 'first man'; she means to go with him. Of course, she also had him murdered, but that does not affect her real feelings or her sense of what's right.

There is a parallel in the Icelandic *Laxdæla saga*, 'The Saga of the People of Laxardal', where at the very end of Gudrun Osvifsdottir's life – the name Gudrun has remained common in Scandinavia to this day – her son asks her whom she loved most. She replies with a list of her four husbands, and comments on each. Her son repeats the question, but all she will say is, 'Though I treated him worst, I loved him best.'[26] She means Kjartan Olafsson, whom she never married and whom she arranged to have murdered by her husband Bolli, seemingly because Kjartan was happy with another wife.

In Norse belief, it seems, killing someone doesn't mean you don't love them. And in any case, wives have a duty to their husbands. Signy did not love King Siggeir, but she turned back to burn with him just the same.

The griefs of Gudrun

This leaves Gudrun, Sigurd's widow. As said above, just under half of the extant Eddic poems, seventeen out of about 35, deal with the Volsungs and the Nibelungs, and of that seventeen, just under half again – seven or eight, depending how one sees them – involve Gudrun. The poems present two images of her. One is the grieving woman, the woman whose woes have been the greatest in all the world: in the 'First Lay of Gudrun' there is a kind of competition, as women gather round Gudrun after the murder of her husband Sigurd and tell their sorrows, in an attempt to get her to weep and, as we say, 'let it all out'. In the 'Second Lay' she tells her sorrows to King Theodoric, famous in Germanic legend as the most tormented of exiles (quite wrongly – he was a most successful king), so there is again an element of competition. There is a 'Third Lay', too, but the most powerful account of her sorrows is in the poem called 'The Whetting of Gudrun'. This, however, also includes the other image of Gudrun, as the woman set on vengeance, whose revenges invariably make things worse for herself and even create the sorrows she laments.

Gudrun's later story, in Norse tradition, goes like this. After the murder of Sigurd by Gudrun's brothers Gunnar and Hogni, they marry her off to Atli (Attila the Hun), by whom she has two sons. The story then develops as told in 'The Lay of Atli', and as summarized in Chapter One above: murderous plot, wolf-hair warning, dare accepted, deaths of Hogni and of Gunnar in the snakepit.

The story goes on to say that once her brothers are dead, Gudrun kills her own sons by Atli to revenge her brothers' deaths (like Signy), feeds them to Atli at a feast and then kills her husband and burns the hall down (like Signy again). But unlike Signy, she does not choose to join her husband in death. She escapes and is married a third time, to a King Jonak, by whom she has two more sons.

She also has one surviving daughter by Sigurd, Svanhild the beautiful. Svanhild is married to the mighty king of the Goths, Iormunrekk, but is accused of infidelity and trampled under horses' hooves. Gudrun then, disastrously, sends her sons by Jonak to avenge their half-sister's death. She and they know that this is a suicide mission, and in the Eddic *Hamðismál*, 'The Lay of Hamdir',[27] one of her sons answers his mother sardonically: when she lists her sorrows, as usual adding the taunts that he and his brother are a poor imitation of their ferocious uncles and that she is the only real Niflung left, Hamdir replies that her brothers showed their quality by murdering her husband; that her own murder of her sons by Atli hurt her as well as Atli; and her present attempt to wipe out another generation of sons will only give her something else to wail about. He concludes ironically:

> 'Every man should be   the death of another
> with sore-biting sword,   *without harming himself*.'[28]

His brother Sorli cuts off the conversation by saying, 'I have no wish to bandy words with mother; you both want to have the last word', but has the last word himself:

'What are you asking for now,   Gudrun, that will not
    make you weep?
You wept for your brothers   and your young sons,
close kinsmen,   sent into strife.
You will weep, Gudrun,   for both of us too,
we are doomed here on our horses,   will die far away.'[29]

The brothers half succeed in their revenge, cutting off Iormunrekk's arms and legs, but they fail to cut off his head, allowing him to give the fatal advice to his men to stone them to death, since swords will not bite on them. They die fighting, with a hint of regret from Hamdir, immediately repressed by his better-advised brother Sorli.

With that, apart from one very dubious exception (see Chapter Four), the line of the Volsungs and Nibelungs comes to an end. There is a hint in 'The Whetting of Gudrun' that she too commits suicide and burns herself on a funeral pyre. After being responsible, directly or indirectly, for the deaths of two husbands, two or three brothers, four or five sons, and other collateral damage, like to her stepson Erp, she might be thought to have good reason for suicide. But can she be seen as another case of the 'virtuous woman', like Signy, like Brynhild?

German writers trying to deal with the peculiar female ethic contained in the story certainly did not think so. What they found particularly incomprehensible was the idea that after her brothers had murdered her husband, Gudrun would still side with her brothers against her second husband, warning them about his plot and avenging them once they were dead. Surely she would have been on the other side? Blood may be thicker than water (whatever that means), but isn't love more important than kinship?

Gudrun, or Kriemhild as she is in the *Nibelungenlied*, accordingly becomes demonized. *She* is the instigator of the plot to kill her brothers, not Atli, *she* draws Theodoric into the final combat, *she* kills her brothers with her own hands and in the end is killed by Hildibrand, Theodoric's master-at-arms, indignant at her murder of prisoners.

Is this in line with the Norse heroine ethic? In one way it seems to be: Kriemhild is set on vengeance, just like Signy and Brynhild. But Signy directed her vengeance against her husband, though she chose to die with him, and Brynhild likewise revenged herself on the man she regarded as her real husband, Sigurd, again choosing to die with him. The Norse Gudrun has no quarrel with her first husband, Sigurd, does not die with him, and finds it impossible to take revenge within the family on the brothers who killed him. Perhaps one should conclude that in Norse eyes

Gudrun is only half a 'virtuous woman': she refuses the option of suttee, takes no revenge for her first husband's death and turns her anger against her second husband and the children she has had with him. In this, and the revenge she takes for Svanhild, she does admittedly show the same cruel hard-heartedness as Signy.

Each woman's story has its own dynamic, its own hard decisions and bitter prices. There is no overall rule, for each person, man or woman, or even child, must make his or her own decisions about honour. That is what made these legendary stories interesting.

Historical facts, psychological attitudes

Are these people just legend? Gunnar and his family are known to have existed, but we have no corroboration of the Volsungs' existence. Other characters drawn into the story come from quite different dates. Gundaharius and his family were wiped out in 437, and Atli, or Attila, died in 453, which is not completely incompatible. Iormunrekk, however, comes into the story after Atli's death, but his historical original, Ermanaric, died perhaps eighty years before; and Theodoric the Great, presented as a visitor at Attila's court, was not born until the year after Attila died. There has clearly been a good deal of 'cutting and pasting' in the early legends, helped by the understandable confusion of stories passed by word of mouth.

One may still sometimes see a trace of how all this could have come about. Though the *Lex Burgundionum* has nothing to say about any female *Gunda-runo, there is every likelihood that a Burgundian princess might have been carried off as a slave trophy by the Huns. Sixteen years later, Attila the Hun died after getting drunk at his own wedding, suffering a nosebleed and choking on his own blood. His wife, however, is named as 'Ildico', almost certainly the Germanic female name Hild with a Germanic dimunitive, as in the Dutch Winn-eke or English mann-equin. As Professor Ursula Dronke points out, it must have been a great temptation for Attila's Hunnish followers to put two and two together and get five: 'I cannot believe the great Khan died so ignominiously. The woman must have killed him. Was she not a German?'[30]

The thought that they had been revenged – perhaps by one of their very own princesses – might have cheered up the surviving Burgundians, who had taken further revenge on the Huns at the Battle of the Catalaunian Plains in 451. As for Ermanaric, the earliest account of his death says that he committed suicide in despair and fear of the invading Huns. But another version rapidly circulated which is identical with the Norse story, though much earlier, and which includes Sunilda, or Svanhild, her brothers

Ammius and Sorlius (Norse Hamdir and Sorli), the trampling by horses, and the king's non-fatal mutilation.[31] This too must have been 'bolted on' to Gudrun's story, as the fall of the Burgundians was 'bolted on' to that of the Volsungs. One may say that events tended to be remembered, but when it came to motivation, everyone was free to invent their own.

And that is the final question: what motivated not only the characters in the stories but the people who created the stories and the much larger number who knew them, admired them, embellished them, passed them on? To the modern mind it is amazing, almost incomprehensible, how so many thousands of men, over generations, took appalling risks in small boats and continuous hand-to-hand and face-to-face confrontations with edged weapons, for what do not seem to us to have been very great financial returns. Viking armies were often defeated, even exterminated, but there never seemed to be any difficulty in recruiting another one. And the women appear, from the Eddas and the sagas and from history, to have been just as committed to the hero(in)ic ethic as the menfolk, sometimes even more so, as this chapter has shown. The context for Bergthora in *Njáls saga* is very different from the cases of Signy and Brynhild, but all three wives do the same thing in the end, with varying motives and varying reasons for pride and guilt.

The one consistent feature is fearlessness, or the appearance of it. The culture rated this as the highest virtue, superior to what we think of as morality. It rated the shame of being taunted by the maidens (as King Volsung says), or by one's mother (like the sons of Gudrun), or by one's mistress (like the hang-back attendants of Brynhild) as the worst disgrace. Stories like those of the Volsungs and the Nibelungs – which clearly began to circulate very close to the historical events of the fourth and fifth centuries – energized the Second Viking Age, which reaches full force in the next chapter.

FOUR

Ragnar and the Ragnarssons: Snakebite and Success

With Ragnar *Loðbrók*, or Lodbrog, or 'Hairy-breeches' (renderings of the name vary), we begin to emerge from the legendary past, which may sometimes have had a historical base, to a historical era with some contemporary records, though these may often have been contaminated by legend: not quite from dark to light, but heading that way.

In this process, Ragnar is a pivotal figure. His ancestry, as declared in *Ragnars saga*, goes back to Sigurd Fafnir's Bane, and has clearly been invented to attach him to the Volsungs – in one manuscript, 'Ragnar's Saga' follows on directly from 'The Saga of the Volsungs'. By contrast, his sons, or men who were repeatedly identified as his sons, are not only historical figures but extremely important ones for the whole history of Britain and Ireland. (It is argued in Chapter Six that England and Scotland would not be as they are without them.)

The jury is still out as to whether Ragnar himself was a historical figure, and probably, poised as he is 'between history and myth',[1] no decision is possible. Nevertheless, a rational account of him could be reached once one strips out the evidently fictional elements – like his death in King Ella's snakepit, surely modelled on the much earlier legend of Gunnar's death in King Atli's snakepit. Moreover, even that fictional element, as expressed in the poems associated with him, gives a penetrating insight into the 'Viking mindset'. And finally, returning to his sons: archaeology has, not for the first time, literally 'unearthed' a grisly discovery that may well bear out early accounts of one of them, Ivar the Boneless.

The 'Death Song of Ragnar Lodbrog': where the comic books get their ideas

To start with the poems: ever since the legends and poetry of the old North started to be rediscovered in the seventeenth century, Ragnar has been the archetypal Viking, and the archetypal scene has been Ragnar singing his death song in the snakepit. The character Ragnar in the Kirk Douglas movie *The Vikings*, father of the movie's main hero Einar, is based on Lodbrog; so is the character Ragnar in the TV series *Vikings*.

Further clarifying the situation as regards the poems, the most complete one is 'Ragnar's Death Song', or 'The Death Song of Ragnar Lodbrog', which is now also known (for no very good reason) as *Krákumál*, 'The Song of the Crow'. This title was given it by Guðbrandur Vigfússon and Frederick York Powell in their groundbreaking 1883 edition of *Corpus Poeticum Boreale*, 'Complete Poetry of the North', and the name has clung on ever since. Vigfússon and Powell also printed a string of verses extracted from different parts of 'Ragnar's Saga', many of them spoken by Kraka, one of Ragnar's wives, but gave these no title.[2] I call them the 'Kraka Dialogues'. They contain the remark quoted in Chapter One about the 'piggies'.

The reception of the 'Death Song' is a classic case of 'riches to rags'. A hundred and fifty years ago, when Thomas Hughes – author of *Tom Brown's Schooldays* – was writing his intensely patriotic *Life of Alfred the Great* (1869), he imagined Alfred before the Battle of Ashdown as 'a youth who carried in his bosom the Psalms of David', while from the opposing camp of the Vikings, 'We may fancy . . . the song of Regner Lodbrog beguiling the night-watches'. The song seems to have beguiled Hughes as well – a great exponent of 'Muscular Christianity' with more than a sneaking feeling of respect for the undeniably muscular Vikings – for he goes on to quote the whole of stanza 22. The 'song of Regner' is set up by Hughes as a kind of ideological statement, almost as a pagan Bible opposed to the one that Alfred carries. Even before that, Sharon Turner (1768–1847), the first historian of the Anglo-Saxons, wrote that what set him working on the whole enterprise was 'The Quida, or death-song, of Regner Lodbrog'. Ragnar, of course, was definitely not an Anglo-Saxon, but this seems not to have worried Turner.[3]

That early admiration of the 'Death Song' is definitely *not* the opinion of modern scholars. In 1883 Vigfússon and Powell were unimpressed by it. The first 21 of its 29 stanzas were demoted to a smaller typeface, with a running translation that was frankly sketchy, though they relented after stanza 22, commenting, 'Henceforward the poem is of a nobler type, and we translate more fully.'[4] They made it clear, though, that they preferred the *other* set of verses associated with the death of Ragnar, which I have opted to call collectively the 'Kraka Dialogues'.

Vigfússon and Powell's negative opinion then became and has remained standard among scholars. Tolkien's friend and collaborator E. V. Gordon was especially severe, spending the best part of three pages of the lead-in to his *Introduction to Old Norse* complaining about the poem and the effect it had had on 'romantic taste'.[5] Gordon had a point, which was that the title *Krákumál* was not the only mistake the 'Death Song' had had forced on it.

What had happened was that when in the early seventeenth century people started rediscovering the Viking heritage, like the Codex Regius, a priest in north Iceland called Magnús Ólafsson discovered a manuscript of the 'Death Song'. He sent a transcript and a translation into Danish, with his own commentary, to the famous antiquarian Ole Worm. Passed on repeatedly, for many years this was the source of all knowledge and all translations of the poem. But while Magnús was a native Icelander, he was not skilled in the specialized diction of Old Norse verse and made several serious errors. In stanza 25, Ragnar says (looking forward to his afterlife in the house of Odin), 'we will soon drink beer *ór bjúgviðum hausa*', that is, literally 'from the bowed, or bent, branches of skulls'. The 'bent branches' that grow from (ox) skulls are of course drinking horns, so Ragnar is just saying, 'we will drink beer out of horns.' But Magnús saw only the word 'skulls' and assumed it meant that Ragnar was looking forward to drinking out of the skulls of his enemies – a motif that has never since quite gone away. In the René Goscinny and Albert Uderzo comic book *Astérix et les Normands* (1966), for instance, the Normans, or Norsemen, never say 'no' to *un petit crâne*, a little skull. (To be fair, there is indeed an old story about a Lombard king jokingly asking his wife to drink out of the skull of his enemy, her father; but even the other barbarians seem to have regarded that as 'not funny', and his angry bride promptly murdered him.)

Furthermore, in stanza 13 Ragnar, gloating over his many past battles, says of a stiff fight 'at the bay of the Hethnings', that 'when we were split-ting the helmets of the Goths [Gauts? Geats?], that was not (*vasat*) like laying a bright bride next to you in bed': in other words, it was tough work, not easy work. But Magnús did not recognize that the old suffix -*at* meant a negative and assumed that Ragnar was saying that splitting helmets *was* just like laying a bride, and so launched on the world the notion that, to Vikings, having sex and killing people had much the same sensation. He repeated the mistake in stanza 18, which really says 'at the field of Vika it was *not* like having women bring the wine', and in stanza 20: 'when we killed King Orn it was *not* like having a warm bath prepared by a maiden, it was *not* like kissing a young widow in one's own high-seat'.[6]

Magnús, however, got it wrong every time. The 'Death Song' is only saying, in its way, what is expressed in the *Bjarkamál* or 'Lay of Bjarki', namely that being woken to battle is *not* the same as being woken to 'wine and the whispers of women', and everyone has agreed that the sentiment in the 'Lay of Bjarki' is (meant to be) truly noble. Ragnar seems to think that while wine waitresses, sex and hot baths are fun, killing people is what you boast about. And he definitely does *not* think they are the same thing. Modern scholars nevertheless still turn away from the whole poem with a certain horror, as having set up far too many ultra-macho clichés. A fairly recent and authoritative comment on it remarks that there is no extensive modern study of it, and 'it definitely needs a new evaluation'[7] – which up until now it has not received.

The 'Death Song of Ragnar Lodbrog', looked at again

It may be simpler to start off by going back to the old evaluations. What Thomas Hughes clearly liked was the poem's ideology, while what also appealed to the 'romantic taste' deplored by E. V. Gordon was the faint hints of pathos – for after all, the very frame of the poem is that Ragnar is dying alone, and slowly, by snakebite, defeated, and surrounded by his enemies – all facts mentioned by him and immediately firmly repressed. Ragnar's credo, one might say, accepted for generations as the Viking creed, is the question 'do you want to live for ever, or live well and die gloriously?' He asks, and I give the notably direct original wording along with a literal translation:

Hví sé drengr at feigri	Why should a man be feyer [nearer death]
at hann í odda éli	though he in the shower of spear-points
öndurðr látinn verði?	be placed in the forefront?

One might think there is an obvious answer to this question, which is that if you are fighting in the forefront you are clearly 'nearer death' than if you are hanging back. But perhaps Ragnar is relying on the thought expressed in the Eddic poem *Hávamál*, 'The Words of the High One', quoted earlier, to the effect that even if one *does* keep out of the way of spears, one cannot keep out of the way of old age: death, one way or another, is certain. Ragnar goes on to state the heroic creed more positively:

Hitt telk iafnt, at gangi	I count that good to go
at samtogi sverða	to the drawing of swords
sveinn í móti einum . . .	man against man . . .

He looks back on his life with some surprise at what has happened to him:

Eigi hugðak Ellu	I never thought that (King) Ella
at aldrlagi mínu,	would be the death of me,
þás blóðvali bræddak . . .	when I was feeding the
	blood-hawks . . .

But the emotion is surprise, not regret:

Hitt lægir mik, jafnan	It always makes me laugh
at Baldrs föður bekki	that the benches of Balder's father
	(Odin)
búna veitk at sumblum . . .	I know are prepared for feasting . . .

As the snakebites start to take effect, Ragnar thinks that his sons would be there with him if they knew

hvé ófáir ormar	how no-few serpents
eitrfullir mik slíta	full of venom bite me

But again, the hint of self-pity vanishes, under the assurance of revenge:

móðernis fekk mínom	I gave my sons a mother
magom, svat hjörtu dugðu . . .	such that their hearts are strong . . .
sonum mínum man svella	my sons will swell (with anger)
sínn föður ráðinn verða . . .	for their father to be avenged . . .

The last lines of each of the last two stanzas then combine assurance with rejection, resignation with the last much-quoted words of paradoxical triumph:

oss munu æsir bióða,	The gods will invite me in,
esat sýtandi dauði . . .	in death there is no sighing . . .
lífs eru liðnar stundr,	The hours of life have passed,
læjandi skalk deyja.	laughing shall I die.[8]

Note, finally, the way in which a negative ('no sighing') is set against and capped by a much stronger positive ('laughing').

The characteristics of the northern death song, seen as a genre, have in fact been noted by Professor Joseph Harris of Harvard.[9] He counts as many as fifteen Old Norse examples, though that includes some marginal cases like the death song of Starkad, found only (like most of *Bjarkamál*) in Saxo's verbose Latin rendering. He also lists some eight or nine motifs found repeatedly, but the most striking one is this: the very last words of a death song were (should be? Or were expected to be?) about as emotionally flat as could be managed. Several are quoted in what follows, but a good one is Thorir Jokul's, as he was led to execution in 1238: *Eitt sinn skal hver deyja* 'Everyone must die one day'.[10] They are the correlative of the poker face that the hero is expected to display in moments of stress or disaster. Both the flat words and the poker face surely exist to express a cultural imperative – one that our more sentimental modern world is (on the whole, and with exceptions) ill-suited to appreciate.

No expressions of grief, then, or religious hope, or loving memory. However, just as with the breaches of the poker face rule, which show what is simmering underneath, hints of (some) emotions may be allowed just to leak out. Humour is allowed, though it must be ironic. Hjalmar, in 'The Saga of King Heidrek the Wise', remarks that he has many times fed the eagles on the bodies of those he has killed; now the eagle will come for him, 'he shall make his meal / on my blood now' (this time, the joke's on me).[11] Eirik Ragnarsson takes this a step further in the 'Kraka Dialogues'. If the ravens take his eyeballs, he remarks, that will be a poor return for the many he has given them. (There's just no gratitude in the world. Not in the heroic world, anyway.) The last words of Arrow-Odd say simply, give my regards to friends and family ('loved ones' would be the sentimental modern phrase), 'I won't be there' – which is about as factually unemotional as one can get. Yet the most downbeat ending of all may well come from Egil Skallagrimsson. It is discussed at the end of Chapter Five, too sad and specific to summarize here.

On one occasion it is as if even the very thought of going any further into unmanly emotion has to be extinguished. When Hamdir says in 'The Lay of Hamdir' what a pity it is that he and his brother Sorli killed their half-brother Erp instead of recruiting him – '[Iormunrekk's] head would be off now, if Erp had lived', so (it is implied) he wouldn't have been able to tell his men how to kill us – Sorli cuts him off short. He says, 'No man lives one evening beyond the decree of the Norns' (no regrets, we've done well).[12] Bar an eleven-word epitaph, those are the last words of the poem *Hamðismál* and of the whole Codex Regius. Repressed emotion, with just a hint showing: that's what gives words power.

Romantic poets liked the poems, and the situations, but they could never get their heads round the idea, the less said the better. The French poet Leconte de Lisle thus gave a stirring version of 'Hjalmar's Death Song' from 'The Saga of King Heidrek', but he had to change the ending. In his rendering it came out as (a switch on the Valhalla idea) *Je vais m'asseoir parmi les dieux, dans le soleil*, or 'I go to sit among the gods, in the sun.'[13] By contrast, the flat ending certainly existed in Old English and has not quite disappeared from modern English. Beowulf's last words are a strong contender for the '"That's It" Prize for Heroic Plainness'. Dying of dragon-bite, like Ragnar of snakebite, he says that fate has swept away all his kinfolk: *ic him æfter sceal*, 'I must after them.'[14] Not a word wasted. Even the implied word 'follow' has been deleted. Meanwhile, the very last words of Tolkien's *The Lord of the Rings* are, famously, '"Well, I'm back", [Sam] said.' One major author in the same field declared it 'the most heartbreaking line in all of modern fantasy'.[15] But that is the skill of the skald: to say much with little.

How, then, do Ragnar's 'famous last words' score against so much serious competition? Perfect for brevity, one must say: four words, counting *skal ek* as two. No one manages fewer – unless one counts Hogni from 'The Lay of Atli', who just laughs without saying anything. Very high for defiance. If one were to think that 'laughing' should lose points for being cheerful, one should remember that this is *malicious* laughter, always acceptable in Viking circles. And overall, considering the 'Death Song' as a whole, one ought to give it the credit it no longer usually gets for emotional variety, the turbulence swirling beneath what seems the plain surface. Ragnar's credo – both 'death song' and 'life song' or biography – expresses at once recklessness; rueful surprise, which never gets as far as regret, still less remorse; confidence that his pagan gods will treat him with honour; even more confidence, based, like Hjalti's words in the 'Lay of Bjarki', on birth pride, that his sons will avenge him; and, finally, a cheerful acceptance of fate. Those who live by the sword shall die by the sword, says the Bible. One feels Ragnar might reply, 'yes, and your point is?' Even dying by snakebite, while not the best of fates, is all in the game. Like losing your eyeballs to the ravens.

The secret of the poem's appeal, then, which scholars have preferred to turn away from and indeed deny, is that its emotions are more complex than one might think, especially – and here one can agree with Vigfússon and Powell – when it turns away from the list of unknown battles with the repetitive refrain 'We hewed with the sword' and the conventional motifs of reddened swords, cloven shields, falling corpses and food for the eagles, and gets closer to the imagined situation, the old warrior psyching himself up for death (as Beowulf so obviously does). To this one might add that the whole poem confirms a thought expressed in Chapter One: that just as the really unexpected and distinctive feature of the Norse religion was the idea of Ragnarok, where gods and heroes would march out to fight the giants and the monsters – knowing they would lose, but not considering the certain knowledge of defeat any reason to change sides – so Ragnar did not consider that his defeat and death by torment made him in any sense a loser. What Tolkien famously called 'the creed of unyielding will',[16] which says that the only defeat is giving in, is present in the 'Death Song', in the whole situation behind it, in the culture and the belief system of its composer and its original audiences.

It was surely thoughts like these that struck home to the scholars, and then the poets, of the seventeenth century and after, even piercing their armour of classical education and social prejudice. 'The Death Song of Ragnar' was one of the most popular early successes of the Gothic Revival. It was passed on from Ole Worm to Thomas Bartholinus the Younger – it was a major support for his theory about the Valhalla cult – and then to a string of translators of whom the most influential was Thomas Percy, who included the poem in his *Five Pieces of Runic Poetry* (1763). By 1814 a Ragnar-fancier could choose from two complete translations into Latin and as many as fifteen complete or partial translations into English.

One further ingredient in the new and exciting literary flavour that Gothic or 'Runic' poetry brought to the eighteenth- and nineteenth-century world was, moreover, a certain careless lack of decorum, a defiance of the 'correctness' that critics since Pope and Dryden had been trying to impose on poetry. If Dr Johnson could scarce 'check my risibility' (keep from laughing) at Shakespeare's use of common, vulgar words, like 'blanket' in a deeply tragic scene and speech in *Macbeth*, how much more of a shock was it to have a hero called Hairy-breeches? Even trousers were not really mentionable in polite society, let alone breeches, let alone (the horrid northern word) breeks![17] And then Ragnar talked about drinking beer in the halls of the gods: surely gentle-heroes should drink nectar or ambrosia, or at worst wine? And Ragnar boasted such a lot, and even boasted about laughing as he died. That was not decorous or gentlemanly behaviour, either, for as that eighteenth-century arbiter of manners Lord Chesterfield had put it, 'there is nothing so illiberal, and so ill-bred, as audible laughter'.

Translators accordingly liked the ideas and the scenario, but cut strange capers in avoiding vulgar wording. Ragnar's last line, 'laughing shall I die', virtually identical in Old Norse and modern English, came out as 'With Joy I seek that happier Shore' (William Bagshaw Stevens, 1775), 'With a smile I shall expire' (Richard Polwhele, 1790) and 'The smiles of death compose my placid visage' (James Johnstone, 1782). Placid? Who, Ragnar Hairy-breeches? Fortunately for Johnstone, the old hero and his sons did not hear that word.[18]

The poem was all very rude, very barbaric, very boastful and not gentlemanly at all – a feeling that has not quite gone away among the modern scholarly community. Still, no one then or now could deny its claim to 'heroic virtue', to use the eighteenth-century phrase. The Norse variety of heroic virtue was unexpected also in its incipient democracy: Norse poems might be complicated, even fantastically complicated, in their use of a special language for poetry. But Norse jarls, like Anglo-Saxon thanes, still *talked* the same way as karls and churls. Upper-class euphemisms and the social stratification of language had not yet been invented or imported. This may have given an extra thrill of daring naughtiness to the learned readers of the past – even if it still upsets too many of the *delicati* among the learned readers of the present.

Ragnar: the legend

Smash-hit of the eighteenth and nineteenth centuries the 'Death Song' may have been, but Ragnar does not owe his fame just to that one poem. When the Danish officials went on the search that led to Magnús Ólafsson unearthing that first manuscript, they were looking for support for their national chronicle, Saxo Grammaticus's *Gesta Danorum*, mentioned above, in Book IX of which Ragnar is already a prominent figure.

Saxo's is only the earliest of many surviving mentions – in his survey of the whole saga, Professor Rory McTurk counts eighteen separate pre-modern sources,[19] and that is for the legend, not counting possible references to the man – but of these the most important are Saxo, writing in Latin, and therefore never completely forgotten, and 'Ragnar's Saga', together with the *Þáttr af Ragnars sonum* (or 'Tale of Ragnar's Sons').[20] Both of these were written in Old Norse (strictly speaking, Old Icelandic), much later than Saxo, perhaps about 1400. Despite the difference in date, the Old Norse saga and the Latin chronicle are in close agreement. Saxo must have known a version of the story quite close to that of the saga, even if his interpretations are wobbly.

What is common to both Saxo and the saga owes a great deal to folk tale. In both, Ragnar's nickname is already attached to him, and they both give the same explanation for it. There was a Swedish or Gautish jarl called Herraud, or Heroth, who had a beautiful daughter called Thora. He gave her a little snake – Saxo, maximizing as usual, says two snakes – which she fed on beef, but the saga prefers the stranger notion that she put it in her chest, to lie on her gold. It is notorious that worms, or dragons, love to lie on gold, and when they do, the gold makes the dragons bigger and fiercer. In the end, Thora's pet dragon becomes gigantic in size and threatening in behaviour, and the jarl offers his daughter, and her gold, to anyone who will kill it. Ragnar, son of the Danish king Sigurd Ring, hears about this and determines to be a dragon slayer. To protect himself from the dragon venom, he has specially shaggy breeches made, and a shaggy fur cape, which he then boils in pitch. He also rolls in sand, so that the sand sticks to the pitch (Saxo's version is that he soaks the clothing in water and lets it freeze into ice). Either way, his clothes ward off the dragon-bite, he kills the beast or beasts, wins Thora and also gets his name, Hairy-breeches. Thora, however, fades out of the story, leaving two sons behind.

Ragnar's next major exploit is to win a second bride, and this exploit is told only in 'Ragnar's Saga', not in Saxo. It smacks even more of fairy tale than the dragon story, but, as said at the start of this chapter, it also leads back to earlier heroic legend and will lead forward to documented history. In fact, it acts as a kind of hinge. Just as Sigurd linked the legend of the prehistoric Volsungs to the genuinely historical Burgundian kings (the Nibelungs), so Ragnar acts as a pivot between legend and history, ancestors and descendants.

What happened with 'Ragnar's Saga', though, is that its unknown author spotted a gap in legend and decided to 'write into the gap'. In Chapter Three it was pointed out that the story of Sigurd and Brynhild and the ring Andvaranaut is full of unanswered questions, notably: who took Brynhild's virginity? What was meant by Sigurd 'wooing and winning' her for Gunnar? And where did she get the fatal ring that exposed Sigurd's deception, if deception it was? The author of 'The Saga of the Volsungs' dealt with this – followed by most modern narrators, including Wagner, William Morris and Tolkien – by saying that Sigurd 'wooed' Brynhild twice: once on his own behalf, when he entered the fiery ring set there by Odin, and once years later, after he had been given a potion of oblivion, on behalf of Gunnar. Most authors (including all the modern ones) prefer to believe that Sigurd acted like a gentleman both times, setting the sword Gram between him and Brynhild and delivering Brynhild to Gunnar untouched. The author of 'The Saga of the Volsungs', however, decided that this was not the case. Sigurd may not have betrayed Gunnar on the second occasion, but he *did* lie with Brynhild on the first, when he woke her from her enchanted sleep, and this coupling gave Brynhild a child, a daughter called Aslaug.

She, declared the author of 'Ragnar's Saga', was the second wife of Ragnar, once Thora faded out of the story. What happened was that after the death of her parents, Sigurd and Brynhild, Aslaug fled, to be fostered by a peasant couple. But since they were as low-class ugly as she was upper-class beautiful – here we are in Cinderella territory, and even closer to the Grimms' version of that tale, 'Allerleirauh, Rough-All-Ways', referring to Cinders's shaggy disguise – she dirties her face and wears rough clothes to stay hidden. She also changes her name and calls herself *Kráka*, Crow.

The disguise doesn't work. She is seen by Ragnar's men and is reported to him; he tests her intelligence by a complex riddle-game, and she becomes his wife. Under the name of Kraka, and later (for no obvious reason) the name of Randalin, she utters a number of verses in the saga, the ones I call the 'Kraka Dialogues'. And she bears Ragnar sons.

Ragnar: the man and his sons

It is the sons who are important. This is where we move away from legend (with a historical base) into history (contaminated by legend) – and incidentally, where Bernard Cornwell's *The Last Kingdom*, both book (2004) and television series, takes off. Putting it very briefly, men later identified as the Ragnarssons – and we are sure the men existed, though we cannot prove they were Ragnarssons – led the *mycel here* or 'great army' of the Vikings that in the years after 866 conquered much of England, killed the rival kings of Northumbria at York, ended the royal dynasty of East Anglia and made the king of Mercia a refugee in Rome. Only Alfred the Great of Wessex held out, and for another hundred years his descendants and the descendants of Ivar Ragnarsson (if Ragnarsson he was) disputed the rule of Britain and Ireland, with effects on English and Scottish politics lasting to this day.[21]

Before reaching that point, a lot of legendary accretion has to be deleted, starting with most of Ragnar's sons. If one puts together all the accounts in all sources, there were a dozen of these, by several different wives or partners. The number is quickly whittled down. Three are mentioned only by Saxo, who readily invented extra characters. Four more die young: Thora's two sons Eirik and Agnar, and two sons of Aslaug, Rognvald and Hvitserk. These four are mentioned in the 'Kraka Dialogues', where Eirik is given his own death song (the one that ends with ravens and eyeballs). Aslaug also says that Rognvald was the first of her sons to go to Odin, while Hvitserk was cremated on a pyre of dead men's skulls.

Taking out these seven uncorroborated or fanciful individuals, five are left. Sigurd *Ormr-í-auga*, Snake-eye, sounds promising but has no significant role in either the stories told by Saxo or the sagas: he may have been invented, with his nickname, to cement the connection back to Sigurd the dragon slayer. Bjorn *Jarnsíða*, or Ironside, starts to take us from legend into history, for he was an active leader of Vikings in France in the 850s, mentioned in two different contemporary accounts and remembered still as Bier *Costae Ferreae*, or Bier Ironside, by two more French chroniclers two centuries later. The contemporary accounts, however, do not describe him as a Ragnarsson or associate him with the others. He may just have been sucked into the legend, in the same way as originally independent stories were attracted into the Arthurian orbit.

That leaves just three. There is no doubt that they existed, for they appear again and again in Irish and English accounts, some of them contemporary with the events described. But, as with Bjorn, the contemporary accounts do not identify them as 'sons of Ragnar'. Scandinavian accounts, all of them written down much later, are quite sure that's who they were, but by that time a legend may have developed. It must nevertheless have developed earlier than either Saxo or the sagas, for about 1070 Adam of Bremen, writing a *History of the Archbishops of Hamburg*, identified one 'Inguar' (Ivar) as *filius Lodparchi*, 'son of Lodbrog'.[22] Even Adam, however, wrote two centuries after the momentous events associated with the three brothers – and there is little doubt that they *were* brothers – Ivar, Halvdan and Ubbi.

All one can say for sure is that these three brothers really existed, and at some early period, rightly or wrongly, began to be identified as sons of Ragnar Lodbrog.[23] (There is nothing to say they weren't.) As for Ragnar himself, for all the fairy-tale elements included in his legend, there certainly was a prominent Viking with a similar name active at about the right time.

Having expressed the doubts and uncertainties, one can turn to the story as the Vikings' descendants remembered it. Ivar, regularly nicknamed *inn beinlausi*, the Boneless, is agreed by all of them to be the leading Ragnarsson. Saxo adds an Ubbi, who does not appear in 'Ragnar's Saga'; and the *Anglo-Saxon Chronicle* adds the third of this trio, Halvdan, or, in Anglo-Saxon, Healfdene. It is this last item which takes us right out of legend and folktale into documented history (just like Hygelac/*Hugilaikaz), for the *Chronicle* was composed well within living memory of the events described, by someone who was extremely well-informed. In it, Healfdene appears several times between 871 and 878, while from 865 the *Chronicle* is completely preoccupied with the activities of the *mycel here*, the great army of Vikings, led in many other accounts (though the *Chronicle* does not name him) by Ivar.

A vital link comes in the *Chronicle* entry for 878 – a crisis year for both Vikings and Anglo-Saxons – which records that a Viking leader was defeated and killed with 840 of his men by the local levies in Devonshire. It was obviously a heartening victory for the men of Wessex, whose king, Alfred, was at that time hiding out in the marshes of Somerset and trying to rally supporters (and in later legend, 'burning the cakes'). Yet the chronicler does not know the Viking leader's name. What he does say with certainty is that he was 'the brother of Ivar (*Inwær*) and of Halvdan (*Healfdene*)'.[24] One manuscript of the *Chronicle* adds, furthermore, that the levies also captured the Vikings' 'Raven' banner,[25] while the later *Annals of St Neots* (*c*. 1120–*c*. 1140) states that the leader was called Ubbi and that the banner was woven by the three sisters of Ivar and Ubbi. If the raven on it flapped its wings, the Ragnarssons would conquer; if it hung limp, they would lose.[26] We don't have to believe in magic banners to accept the general agreement that there were three brothers, Ivar, Halvdan and Ubbi, later identified as Ragnarssons, and that these men dominated the military scene in the British Isles as a whole for close to twenty years.

Ivar's career is the critical one. It should be noted that the way his name is written in later Norse – *Ívarr*, with a long initial Í, pronounced Ee – could be a later development from the earlier *Ingvarr*, with a short initial I, in which case the Old English and Latin renderings of his names as *Inwær*, *Inguar* and *Hinguar* would be reasonable enough. So would the Old Irish *Ímair* (also variously spelled). If Irish records are taken into account, Ivar's career becomes fuller and more directed; indeed, one might say, geopolitically calculated.

One strong reason for identifying the Irish Norseman Ímair with the Inwær/Hinguar known to the Anglo-Saxons, as first pointed out by Alfred Smyth,[27] is that the records complement each other chronologically. Ímair is active in Ireland in 857–63 and then disappears from Irish records until 870, when he is found attacking and taking the great stronghold of the Strathclyde Britons, Dumbarton Rock. But between those years, 'In(g)uar' is found in Anglo-Saxon records, attacking and destroying the kingdoms of East Anglia, Northumbria and Mercia, to the last of which he returned in the early 870s, having won an unsurpassed string of major victories.

King Alfred's resistance over the next 25 years in Wessex is the main hero narrative of early English history – he is the only English king regularly labelled as 'the Great'. But the main surprise in the story ought to be the collapse of three of the four main Anglo-Saxon kingdoms, their kings killed or driven out, their long-established royal dynasties never to be heard from again. Yet the kingdoms must have been able to call on manpower and resources many times greater than that of their enemies. The facts demand more of an explanation than has regularly been given – and one is available. The trouble is that (as I explain below), like so much to do with Vikings, it is thoroughly unwelcome to the modern academic world.

Finally, it is the reality of Ivar, Ubbi and Halvdan that makes one think that their alleged father, Ragnar, may have been a real person as well. Ivar's well-documented career begins in Ireland in the year 857. That suggests he would have been born in the 830s, and thus Ragnar perhaps (allowing for early maturity in a dangerous age) in the 810s. This in turn would suggest an active career any time from the 830s to – remembering that Viking chiefs did not usually live long – the 850s or 860s.

This fits well with some mentions. In her recent study of the whole development of the legend, Elizabeth Ashman Rowe lists four 'contemporary and near-contemporary Frankish records' that mention a Viking leader called Reginheri, Ragenarius, Ragnerus or Ragneri, of which the fullest and most interesting is the *Translatio sancti Germani*.[28] These between them state that Reginherus, or Ragnar, attacked Paris in 845 and was paid 7,000 lb of silver to go away – probably troy or Roman pounds, only 12 oz (340 g) each in modern weight, but still a big pay-off: close to ninety manloads. The saints of Francia took revenge (according to their hagiographers) by afflicting the Vikings with dysentery, from which Reginherus is said to have died, but only once he got home – a conveniently undisprovable claim, one has to note. For what it is worth, and remembering Ragnar's boasts of many battles, none of them readily identifiable, the raid was remembered for the ruthlessness of its leader. He broke Frankish nerve by hanging 111 captive warriors in full view of their comrades the other side of the Seine, without any attempt at rescue being made. Professor Gwyn Jones remarks in his *History of the Vikings* that it is 'unnecessary to equate [this man] with his hairy-breeked namesake',[29] but the date fits. Rowe, by contrast, accepts that Reginherus may well have been the original of Ragnar, not yet known as 'Lodbrog'.[30] Noting the accounts that say that he was struck down by disease, once specified as dysentery, she adds the speculation that the unfortunate effects of dysentery – unstoppably loose bowels – may have been the cause of his nickname.[31] This is a theory one has to reject! If Ragnar had been famous for fouling his trousers, one can be sure that his loyal comrades, filled with Bad Sense of Humour, would not have called him anything as polite as *loðbrók*, or 'hairy-breeches'. They would have come out with something much ruder, perhaps *dritbrók*, which I forbear to translate.

Where, however, does this leave the story of Ragnar's capture by King Ella of York and his defiant death in the snakepit? King Ella himself was certainly a historical character, but not a very important one. The *Anglo-Saxon Chronicle* reports that in the year 866 – that is, the year after the *mycel here* of the Vikings is reported as landing in England – the Northumbrians replaced their king Osberht with Ella. The two kings put aside their differences for long enough to fight the Viking great army at York, but lost badly, both kings being killed.[32] Ella cannot have been in power long enough to execute Ragnar, given that it must have taken the Ragnarssons some time to organize a revenge attack, if revenge attack it was. It has been suggested, very plausibly, that the whole story of Ella's killing of Ragnar was invented, and hung on the handy peg of a known king, precisely to give a motivation for the attack on England by the great army, now said to be led by Ragnarssons.[33] By contrast, the *Annales Ryenses*, a late medieval chronicle mostly based on Saxo but with some added data, reports Ragnar's death in Ireland in 854, and that may be what really happened (of which more later).[34]

The grunting of the piglets

Summing up the interaction between history and legend just outlined: the real-world attack on York by the *mycel here* was reimagined as a revenge attack by their Ragnarsson leaders. The need for something to revenge created the unlikely story of Ragnar's death in the snakepit, which was modelled on the old hero-tale of King Gunnar. The whole situation inspired both the 'Death Song' and 'Kraka Dialogues', as well as the saga in which they are set, though this had other folk-tale sources too. These must have been known earlier than the date of the surviving saga, for Saxo in 1200 knew much of the story, including the snakepit and even the lines quoted already about the piglets grunting.

Ragnar's death in the snakepit, then, looks like fiction, or propaganda, but is one absolutely vital part of his legend. It shows how a hero should face death, defiant, with no regrets, showing self-mastery by amusement. But there are two other crucial parts of the legend, both found in more than one source.

One is the scene where Ragnar's sons are told of his death. This shows how heroes should take bad news. Impassively, of course: Vikings are not supposed to show their feelings, least of all pain, fear, dismay. But there would be no virtue in this if they didn't *have* any feelings. So the ideal response, as said already with reference to Volund and to death songs in general, is one in which the hero maintains a poker face and (if he says anything at all) says only something flat, joking, undeniable. But this lack of response should at the same time be betrayed by signs that are automatic, that cannot be controlled: Thor's knuckles whitening, Volund grinding his teeth. In a stanza from a lost poem, quoted in 'The Saga of the Volsungs' (Chapter 31), when Sigurd is finally rejected by Brynhild, he says nothing (naturally), but his breast swells with rage and grief so much that the links of his mail-shirt burst. The key belief is that the feeling is greater the more tightly it is controlled and the smaller the signs of inner struggle.

This, anyway, is the basis for the scene of the Ragnarssons being told of their father's death, recounted in essentially the same form in Saxo and in 'Ragnar's Saga'. In the saga it is King Ella's messengers who bring the news to four Ragnarssons, listed by the saga as Ivar, Sigurd, Hvitserk and Bjorn. When they actually make the announcement, Hvitserk and Sigurd, who are playing chess, stop their game, and Bjorn stops sharpening his spear. Ivar shows no sign of emotion, but just asks for the full story. When it gets to the point where they report the 'piglets would grunt' wording, Bjorn clenches his hand around the spear shaft so hard that it leaves an imprint on the wood. When the messengers get to the end, Hvitserk moves a chess piece, as if to show he is concentrating on his game – but he squeezes the piece so tightly that blood bursts out from under his fingernails. Sigurd, meanwhile, is cutting his nails with a knife, but he cuts on until the knife reaches the bone, without flinching. As for Ivar, his autonomic nervous system makes him first turn red in the face, then blue and finally pale. But he forbids Hvitserk's suggestion that the messengers should be killed. That is not the way to take revenge.

So what is? The answer is what has caused the most upset among modern historians and commentators. It is a major reason for their dislike of the whole romantic or 'comic book' image of the Vikings. (Which doesn't mean it can't be true.) In Chapter 39 of his *History of the Archbishops of Hamburg*, Adam of Bremen not only mentions Inguar, 'son of Lodparchus', but lists a number of 'tyrants' who embarked on 'piratical excursions' and then declares Inguar 'the cruellest of all, *crudelissimus omnium*, who killed Christians everywhere by torture'.[35] Ivar in fact stands accused of at least three ritual killings of defeated kings, by methods that would be described as 'cruel and inhuman' in any era, including his own.

The most notorious case is the killing of King Ella in revenge for Ragnar's death in the snakepit. The 'Tale of Ragnar's Sons' (*Þáttr af Ragnars sonum*) says that Ivar and his brothers, remembering how their father was tortured, 'now had an eagle cut on Ella's back and then had all his ribs shorn from his backbone with a sword, so that his lungs were pulled out'.[36] Scholars nowadays very much prefer to think that this whole procedure, 'cutting the blood-eagle', is a romantic fiction that never happened, but there are several references to it elsewhere. Chapter 30 of Snorri's 'Saga of Harald Fairhair' says that Jarl Einar of Orkney did exactly the same thing to an enemy, and the 'Saga of the Jarls of Orkney' describes the same incident much the same way.[37] (One might have been copying from the other, though there's no other sign of that.)

Stanza 26 of the Eddic poem *Reginsmál* ('The Lay of Regin'), from the Codex Regius, has Regin declare, 'Now the bloody eagle has been cut with bitter sword on the back of the killer of Sigmund'. Saxo too, writing earlier than the sagas, though maybe not the poem, has heard something like it, though his version is as usual both vaguer and more verbose: 'they ordered his back to be carved with the figure of an eagle, exultant because at his overthrow they were imprinting the cruellest of birds on their most ferocious enemy'.[38] But what Saxo and 'The Lay of Regin' describe is just a cutting, not a virtual disembowelling or turning inside out. The idea of the saga writers seems to be that the whole corpse, ribs splayed and lungs pulled out, would actually look like a spread-winged eagle, but whether they were right or not is not known: no one is likely to make the experiment.

It is possible that there was some ancient misunderstanding, for the 'Tale of Ragnar's Sons' quotes a few lines from a poem called *Knútsdrapa*, by Sighvat Thordarson, which makes many references to legendary history and was written in or near the year 1038.[39] Skaldic poetry like *Knútsdrapa* is notoriously hard to follow, but its four lines go like this:

> *Ok Ellu bak,*
> *at, let, hinns sat,*
> *Ívarr, ara,*
> *Jorvik skorit*

And in a more natural word order: *Ok Ivarr, hinn's sat Jorvik, let Ellu bak ara skorit.* Which means no more than (as with Saxo and *Reginsmál*) 'And Ivar, who resided at York, had Ella's back cut with an eagle', or possibly (the suggestion of Rory McTurk) 'by a sword'.[40] This could have been over-interpreted into the grisly surgery described by the 'Tale of Ragnar's Sons', the 'Saga of Harald Fairhair' and the 'Saga of the Jarls of Orkney' – in which case someone must have invented the bit about ribs and lungs. Sometimes there *is* smoke without fire.[41]

Furthermore, although the story about the killing of Ella obviously spread widely early on, the entry in the *Anglo-Saxon Chronicle* for 866, which was written well within living memory of the event, gives no hint that Ella did not just die in battle. The whole 'blood-eagle' business would be an easy story to invent as revenge for the death of Ragnar, and the death of Ragnar looks like an invention itself.

Just the same, Saxo deserves credit at least for asking what was the symbolic point of the eagle, even if his answer is unconvincing. Remembering the raven banner which the Devonshire levy captured from Ubbi Ragnarsson, and the many Viking coins that bear raven and eagle designs, the answer is more likely that warriors saw themselves as friends to the eagle and the raven by providing them with dead bodies to eat. A runic inscription from Gripsholm in Sweden commemorating the dead declares, 'In the east they fed the eagle', *drengiliga*, 'like warriors'.[42] An unrelated saga notes that the ritual killing of captured enemy leaders was intended as a sacrifice to Odin, to bring victory.[43]

Or – and this is the unwelcome thought hinted at above – there may have been another motive, not necessarily ruling out the sacrifice idea. The case of the East Anglian king Edmund, King and Martyr is well authenticated. He was killed in 869, as the great army returned from its attack on York, presumably because he proved less cooperative then than he had been three years earlier, when the army landed in East Anglia. (The date of his death is traditionally 20 November.) 'Hinguar' (Ivar) and Ubbi are said to have been those responsible, and not only is there a detailed account in Abbo of Fleury's *Passio sancti Eadmundi*, but Abbo gives the source of his information, repeated in the Old English version by Ælfric, writing in the Dorset monastery of Cerne. Abbo says that he got his story from St Dunstan, and St Dunstan heard it as told to King Athelstan by the man who had been Edmund's sword-bearer. At that time, Dunstan was a young man and the sword-bearer a very old one.[44] The dates are perfectly plausible. If the sword-bearer was a teenager in 869, he could have told the story as many as sixty years later, when Dunstan himself would have been a teenager and Athelstan would have been on the throne for five years. Of course, the story could have been hyped by the sword-bearer or by Dunstan, or (and most likely) by Abbo, operating within the conventions of the saint's life and with his own ecclesiastical axe to grind.

Nevertheless, the story as Abbo and Ælfric tell it is that all the blame lies on Hinguar. He offered Edmund the option of becoming his under-king. Edmund was advised by his bishop to take the offer, but refused, unless Hinguar would accept baptism. When confronted by the Vikings, he threw down his weapons, wishing to emulate Christ in the Garden of Gethsemane. He was then taken and tied to a stake 'as if put to the torture of the rack', while his ribs 'were laid bare as if by many gashes' and then shot with javelins until they looked like the bristles of a hedgehog. Finally, his head was cut off and thrown into the brambles, where it was guarded by a grey wolf until the head was able to call out to those who came searching for it. We are well into fairy tale here, but there is no doubt at least that Edmund was killed, though the *Anglo-Saxon Chronicle* reports that he was killed, like Ella, in battle, not as a martyr for Christianity.[45]

So far it has been possible to 'debunk' the repeated images of Ivar as a torturer who offered up rival kings as sacrifices to Odin for victory. Maybe there was no blood-eagle, and the deaths of Ella and Edmund were just business as usual for early medieval kings. Nevertheless, the Irish records, generally neglected by English-language historians, once again tell similar stories. Thus the *Cogadh Gaedhel re Gallaibh*, 'The War of the Irish with the Norse' – like Saxo, a late and admittedly fanciful text – lists a string of Irish kings killed by 'Amlaibh', or Olaf, associated with Ivar in the capture of Dumbarton, including 'Maelguala, son of Dungaile, king of Caisel … his back was broken by [on, or over?] a stone'.[46] The last detail is corroborated by a mention of pagan practice in *Eyrbyggja saga*, 'The Saga of the People of Eyri', where the Christian author mentions the establishment of a new assembly ring and adds 'in that ring stands Thor's stone, on which those men who were to be sacrificed were broken, and one sees still the blood-stain on the stone.'[47] Scholars prefer not to believe either the Irish writer or the Icelander, but these two, at least, cannot have been working in cahoots.

There is a really uneasy thought here for tender-hearted moderns, which is that maybe Ivar and his brothers were following a deliberate policy. *And it worked.* A Swedish professor, Anders Winroth, eager to clear his ancestors of their terrible reputation and to get rid of blood-eagles once and for all, retranslates the critical lines of the *Knútsdrapa* even further so they say only that 'Ivar, he who resided at York, caused the eagle to cut Ella's back,' that is, he fed the eagles on him.[48] (Which is fair enough, if you accept that all those native speakers of Old Norse got their grammar wrong and couldn't understand their own language. Bjarni Einarsson, a native speaker of Icelandic and so the nearest thing in the modern world to a native speaker of Old Norse, finds this implausible.)[49] But Winroth goes on to say that only his preferred version 'makes literary and historical sense'. Now, in the first place, there is no such thing as one exclusive 'literary sense'. Anything that appeals to readers makes a *kind* of literary sense, and blood-eagles have certainly done that: the 'comic book' version of Vikings couldn't do without them, and it turns up in the *Vikings* TV series as well (series 4, episode 18). But it is the 'historical sense' that is both obvious and unwelcome.

One has to think what the leaders of the *mycel here*, the great army, were aiming at. Surely they never intended to replace the native populations of Ireland and England with their own men? No, what they wanted was first to collect as much loot as possible, and then to displace the native upper classes: taking over the lands of the kings and nobles and especially of the Church, giving a healthy cut to their own followers but keeping as much of the former rent-gathering and tax-collecting system in place as they could. In large areas of England that seems to have been exactly what happened.

This was a procedure made much easier if there were no rival claimants still around. One fact not noticed much by historians is that Edmund, King and Martyr had a brother, Edwold, who might have been expected to make some attempt at recovering the throne. What he did, however, was to go almost as far away from East Anglia as he could get in England, to become a hermit at Stockwood in Dorset.[50] He became the patron saint of Cerne, a few miles off; it is strange that Ælfric, who wrote many lives of English saints, including St Edmund's, while he himself was at Cerne in the late tenth century, says not a word about Edwold. He may have regarded Edwold as a traitor to the English cause. Anyway, there was no comeback by the old and well-established East Anglian dynasty, from brothers, sons, cousins or collaterals. In pre-Viking eras dead kings were never short of unlikely would-be successors. But with people like the Ragnarssons around, it was easy to have second thoughts about claiming a throne.

Even more surprising than the East Anglian collapse is the folding of the large and powerful kingdom of Mercia. Their king, Burhred, simply gave up and retired to Rome in 873, after the Viking great army took Repton, presumably taking the crown jewels and royal treasury with him. The *Anglo-Saxon Chronicle* reports that the great army 'conquered all that land', but it clearly didn't.[51] Much of South Mercia remained firmly English and increasingly firmly allied with King Alfred's Wessex resistance policy. Burhred, one feels, had just had enough, like Edwold. Being a king made you a certain target, and (if the Ivar legends are correct) not just for merciful beheading.

If, as has been suggested, the mysterious alderman Ethelred, who controlled South Mercia in Alfred's lifetime, was in fact the son of Burhred as well as the nephew and son-in-law of Alfred, and so the rightful king of Mercia, it is striking that he never seems to have called himself King of Mercia – though his Welsh enemies, at least, thought that is exactly what he was.[52] Post-Ivar, Anglo-Saxon royals seem to have been reluctant to accept kingship. It must have been a scary business for Alfred, hiding out in the Somerset marshes in the late 870s with his wife and family. He knew there would be no negotiation for any of them if caught.

The tide turned in 878 when Ubbi, last of the three real-life brothers, was killed by the Devon militia, as said above; Halvdan had been killed in a sea battle off the Irish coast the year before. Most of his men had already decided they had campaigned enough and were satisfied with their new roles as landowners in Yorkshire.[53] And Ivar, after a warlike career of almost twenty years of unbroken success, had already died 'of sickness in England' and there, according to the 'Tale of Ragnar's Sons', was 'laid in a mound (*heygðr*)'.[54]

Where was the mound? And why was he called *inn beinlausi*, the Boneless? It is possible we have an answer to at least the first question, and it casts a light on events at least as lurid as the much-doubted blood-eagle.

Archaeology at Repton: boar's tusk and jackdaw's wing

For more than fifty years now, professional scholarship has concentrated on 'the Viking achievement'[55] and deplored the popular and romantic concentration on berserkers and blood-eagles. Not for the first time in this volume, however – see the comments on Lejre and the Skjoldungs in Chapter Two – archaeology has failed to stay in line with scholarly wishes. One of the most remarkable studies of modern times has left everyone wondering, and wondering whether there is, after all, a connection between what was discovered and none other than Ivar Ragnarsson.

In a sense, the discovery was made more than three centuries ago, only to be ignored until it was almost too late. It took place in the vicarage garden by St Wystan's Church in Repton, Derbyshire. In 1686 a labourer called Thomas Walker was digging there when he came upon an old stone wall supporting a mound. To his surprise, part of the roof fell in, and he found himself looking at a large underground chamber. In his own words, taken down from his dictation forty years later, in the chamber he found 'a stone Coffin, and with Difficulty removing the Cover, saw a skeleton of a Human Body Nine Feet long, and round it lay One Hundred Humane Skeletons, with their Feet pointing to the Stone Coffin'.[56] Walker took the skull from the giant in the coffin and gave it to the local schoolmaster, after which it disappeared. In the three hundred years after 1686, the site, still known locally, was repeatedly entered, everything of possible value removed and the arrangement of the skeletons thoroughly disturbed. Only in the 1980s was a proper professional study made. Its conclusions are various, but – as often with archaeology – difficult to interpret.

First, the body in the coffin was the only one buried intact, and it was a man of considerable size, though not nine feet tall. Second, Walker underestimated the number of other bodies. There were at least 264, about fifty of them women. Third, the male bodies were men of fighting age, fifteen to 45, and 'massively robust': the excavators comment that it was like uncovering a cemetery of the Brigade of Guards, men picked for their size.[57] On the other hand, the bodies do not seem to have been battle casualties, since few of them bore signs of wounds. Most of them were identifiable as Scandinavians by the isotopes in their teeth, and radiocarbon dating places them in the Ragnarsson era, the later ninth century. On the other hand once again, some of them were older and may have been bones dug up from the Mercian royal cemetery while someone was making the D-shaped fortress that incorporated the walls of the church.

Further, though most of the skeletons in the chamber did not show signs of combat trauma, not far away there was a grave that very definitely did. It held a man who was certainly a Viking, which we know because he had a Thor's hammer round his neck as a pendant. He had been stabbed through the eye and had then suffered a terrible slash across the tops of his legs that had gone so deep he must have been emasculated. He had also been disembowelled. He was buried with his hammer, a scabbarded sword, the wing of a jackdaw – as a substitute for an Odinic raven? – and a boar's tusk between his thighs (perhaps to replace his severed penis?). A young man was buried beside him, and not far away another Scandinavian, from Sweden, was buried with a gold ring and a few coins from the mid-870s. Two further discoveries were three children and a teenager buried just outside the mound that held the coffin and the skeletons; 'one cannot help but fear', writes Professor Robin Fleming, 'that their last hours were terrifying.'[58] Finally, not quite 5 km (3 mi) away was a site with almost sixty burial mounds. But the men in them had been cremated, which at that time was not the Christian custom, and horses, sheep and dogs were burned with them, presumably – like the children? – as sacrifices.

What all this means will obviously never be clear. Nevertheless, Repton is where the *mycel here* finally crushed Mercian resistance and sent King Burhred into exile, in the winter of 873. The D-shaped fortress, which took in the church but cut its trenches without regard for the old and venerable royal cemetery, must have been the work of invaders, making themselves secure in hostile territory. The invaders were Scandinavians, the coins buried with the dead Swede support the 873 date, and the burials and cremations are not Christian. How did so many strong men of fighting age die, if not in battle? The scourge of all pre-modern armies, especially encamped in cramped quarters, without medics and with zero sanitation, was always diseases like dysentery, typhus and cholera. One may remember that Ivar himself 'died of sickness and was laid in mound', according to Irish records in 873.[59]

The thought has accordingly occurred that what Thomas Walker stumbled on may have been the tomb of Ivar Ragnarsson himself. Certainly the man in the stone coffin was a Viking, he died at the right date at a place where Ivar is known to have been, and he was a man buried with every mark of (pagan) respect, including, it would seem, human sacrifice. The real puzzle is why stack all the other bones around him? Burying warriors with their victims, and great ones with their servants to be their slaves in the hereafter, is a familiar custom, and that might apply, though not very worthily, to the bones of long-dead Mercian royals. But most of the skeletons seem to have been companions of the man in the coffin, not his enemies. Was it a gesture of fellowship?

Something we can well guess at is the effect all this had on the local population, abandoned by their king and his guards, though seemingly not without a bit of a fight (the Viking with the boar's tusk). No doubt the locals were subject to random killings, robberies, rapes, abductions. They had to observe the desecration of a holy site, if they weren't conscripted to do the digging themselves. They could not have avoided the stink of the burnings. They must have been terrorized. And the Vikings, though not terrorized, must also have been on their guard, in hostile territory many miles from their escape route, the sea, and very much outnumbered by the Anglo-Saxons – who, if their leaders had only got their act together, could have made life very difficult for foragers, detachments, stragglers and sentries.

The unwelcome conclusion is that in the behaviour of Ivar, his brothers and his father (if the Reginherus of Frankish sources was his father) – mass hangings, the raven banner, targeting of royals, public rituals making horrible examples of captured kings – there was a strong element of psychological warfare. Making a public and memorable display of royal executions may or may not have been advertised as a form of sacrifice to Odin, but it could very well have been what the twentieth-century learned, to its sorrow, to call *Schrecklichkeit*, deliberate terror tactics. And once again, *it worked*. To return to Professor Smyth's comment about there being a 'psychopathic element' in Viking culture: to us, maybe, but perhaps there was a method in the madness.

As for the question of why Ivar was called *inn beinlausi*, the Boneless: it seems no one knew, even in ancient times. The author of 'Ragnar's Saga' says it was because Ragnar insisted on consummating his marriage to Kraka/ Aslaug on their wedding night, even though she was menstruating: she tells him in two lines of the 'Kraka Dialogues', 'you will do long-lasting injury to my son / you are too eager to beget one who will have no bones'.[60] So when Ivar is born, he has gristle instead of bone, though he still grows to be immensely tall. He has to be carried everywhere, but acts as the counsellor and planner for his brothers. The Repton excavators give this idea a very cautious mention, while it has also been suggested (and here compare the much more plausible case of Egil Skallagrimsson in Chapter Five) that Ivar may have suffered from *osteogenesis imperfecta*, brittle bone disease.[61] It seems unlikely just the same that Viking armies would carry anyone around who could not look after himself, no matter how wise his counsel.

Another idea is that Ivar may have been sexually impotent. This runs into two problems: one is that if a leading Viking was sexually impotent, it would probably be unwise to mention it to him, let alone use it as his nickname. The other is that Irish records give Ímair/Ivar two sons, Sigfrid and Sigtrygg, while the 'Grandsons of Ivar' dominated the early tenth century from their double strongholds of York and Dublin. His great-grandson squared off against King Alfred's grandson Athelstan at the Battle of Brunanburh in 937, and though defeated he came back with interest only three years later. Olaf Sigtryggson *Cuaran* was another 'Ivaring', or member of the *Uí Ímair* clan, the 'O'Ivars' – prominent in Irish politics until the 980s.[62] So Ivar's genes are probably still at large. Both the 'gristle' theory and the 'impotence' theory look like people guessing from a known nickname, as was the case with *Hugleikr*, mentioned earlier.

Perhaps the best suggestion was made by Nora Chadwick, who pointed out that *beinlauss* could mean not 'boneless' but 'legless'.[63] To us, dragons are creatures like crocodiles, with legs as well as wings. But in Norse they were *ormar*, 'worms' or snakes, and the Ragnar legend has worms as the pets of Thora and the explanation for 'Loðbrók', and in the nickname of Sigurd, *ormr-í-auga*, Snake-eye. So Ivar might have been called Ivar 'No-legs', meaning were-worm: not an insulting title and one highly suitable for a dragon-king. Not quite 'Mother of Dragons', as in *Game of Thrones*, but similarly respectful.

Adam of Bremen called Ivar 'the cruellest of all tyrants'. Abbo of Fleury called him 'the most unconquered'. Florence of Worcester called him 'the most pagan'.[64] *Crudelissimus, invictissimus, paganissimus.* To his contemporaries Ivar was the man who took Northumbrian York and Irish Dublin, Mercian Repton and British Dumbarton. If his father Ragnar Hairy-breeches came to represent Viking defiance in defeat, Ivar the Boneless showed the Viking capacity for success. He and his allies argu-ably shaped the whole later history of England and Scotland. Professor Smyth declares that it is Ivar, rather than the many other contenders such as 'King Arthur', Alfred the Great, or Athelstan *sigrsæll*, 'the Victorious', who deserves to be called 'the greatest war-leader that the British Isles had seen before the coming of the Normans'.[65] Whether psychopath or perfectly sane.

FIVE

Egil the Ugly and King Blood-axe:
Poetry and the Psychopath

There are some forty 'sagas of Icelanders', and close on fifty *þættir*, or short stories about Icelanders, but of them all only one gives a full and plausible picture of a Viking hero – that is, one who makes his reputation and does his most famous deeds outside Iceland, in Scandinavia itself and in the raiding grounds of the British Isles. Most Icelandic heroes are essentially homebodies. Their sagas may contain some dreamed-up adventures abroad, in which they show up the Norwegians and compensate for the Icelandic colonists' 'cultural cringe'. But they then come home to become involved in the main events of their lives as described in their sagas, which is fighting with their relatives and neighbours.

The exception to the rule is *Egils saga Skallagrímssonar*, 'The Saga of Egil Skallagrimsson', or 'Egil's Saga' for short. This brings its hero, with some of his friends and enemies, into the relatively well-recorded milieu of Anglo-Saxon England during the Viking wars of the mid-tenth century. But even more important than the saga's relative historical verifiability is the fact that Egil shows the dark as well as the admirable side of the Viking ethic better and in more detail than any other. He was mean, in every sense of the word: so mean even the other Vikings noticed.

This did not prevent him from being also the greatest named poet, or skald, of the Viking world. Viking poetry was not a matter of daffodils and nightingales and soulful private epiphanies.

But what made him so mean?

Descent from trolls . . .?

'Egil's Saga' describes him physically like this:

> He sat upright, but with his head bowed low. Egil had very distinctive features, with a wide forehead, bushy brows, and a nose that was not long but extremely broad. His beard grew over a long,

wide part of his face, and his chin and entire jaw were exceptionally thick. With his thick neck and broad shoulders, he stood out from other men. When he was angry, his face grew harsh and fierce. He was well built and taller than other men, with thick wolf-grey hair, although he had gone bald at an early age.[1]

The description comes from a moment just after Egil has (according to the saga) won a vital battle for the English king Athelstan, at the cost of his brother Thorolf, who is not only Egil's brother but also something like his minder: the sensible one who can keep his dangerously unpredictable brother under partial control. As he sits at the victory feast, Egil puts his sword across his knees and starts half-drawing it, then slamming it back in its sheath. He says nothing amid the merriment, and – very unusually for him – refuses drink, while he 'just raised and lowered his eyebrows in turn'. The significance of the last gesture is not at all clear, but it *is* clear that he is in a temper over something and liable to lash out. King Athelstan sensibly, if silently, draws his sword, puts a large gold ring on it, walks over and extends it to Egil, who likewise takes it on the point of his sword. He clasps it on his arm, puts down his sword and helmet, takes a drink, stops playing with his eyebrows, and composes an extempore poem.

Athelstan later hands over two chests of silver as payment for Thorolf – there will be trouble over these later – and says some kind words, further mollifying Egil. Sagas very rarely explain what people are thinking, or explain what we are to think about their actions, but it looks as if Egil has been feeling underappreciated, thinking that he has won someone else's battle at too high a family cost. But is it Athelstan's recognition or his money that cheers him up? The saga also notes that Egil (again very much unlike his normal behaviour) has buried his brother with clothes and weapons and a gold ring on each arm. Was he sulking about losing his brother, or losing the gold rings? And did he bury them under pressure from social convention, or as a gesture of love and respect, which he then regrets?

Of course, the saga is just a story, written three hundred years after the events in it, and much of it (as I shall show) should be considered as a historical novel, not a history.[2] Nevertheless, it does offer a consistent and highly individualized picture: Egil, it tells us, was (1) fierce, (2) poetically talented, (3) greedy for money, and (4) bitter ugly. 'Fierce' is common enough for saga heroes, though there are exceptions. There are other sagas about skalds, too, though an unusual amount of poetry said to be composed by Egil has been preserved, and the claims for its authenticity are likely to be true.

Greed for money is more unusual. While the point of raiding is, obviously, to make a good haul, as the sagas often say, what is really respected in most sagas about Icelanders is generosity, readiness to help out – if not with outright gifts of money then with hay or food or assistance in paying compensations. Rich people are good people, because they can afford to be.

But Egil is not like that, and his notorious stinginess is a family trait. Very late in life, his father, *Skalla-Grímr* – meaning 'bald Grim' – suddenly asks his son what happened to the silver King Athelstan gave him. Grim obviously thinks he should have a share of it as payment for the death of his other son. Egil replies evasively, saying he will let his father have money any time he needs it, but 'I know you have kept a chest or two aside, full of silver.'[3] After Egil has ridden off on a visit, Grim brings out a large chest and a cauldron and rides off with them. He comes back without them – he is thought to have buried them in a bog – and dies sitting on the edge of his bed.

This is an extreme case of 'spending the kids' inheritance', as the only fun Grim gets out of it seems to be the knowledge that no one else will get the money, in particular his chiseller of a son. Egil in extreme old age does much the same thing. His first plan, the saga says, was to take Athelstan's silver to the *Lögberg*, or 'Law Rock' at the Althing, or national assembly, and then throw it into the crowd for the pleasure of seeing the assembly fight for it. When this is vetoed by his son-in-law, also called Grim, who has been looking after him for years, Egil waits until he and his daughter are out of the way and then rides off with the famous two chests, and two slaves to do the digging.

Neither the money nor the slaves come back, and Egil admits freely that he killed the slaves so no one would know where the money was. (People in Iceland are still looking for it in the Mosfell ravine, where old coins have occasionally washed up.) Grim buries his father-in-law, like Thorolf, with his clothes and weapons, but unlike Thorolf, without gold rings. If you spend the kids' inheritance you must expect a minimal funeral.

Nor does the matter end there, and it was not only the author of *Egils saga* who knew about the stinginess of the Myramenn family (the Miremen, the Fen-people). In reading Icelandic sagas it is a good rule always to try to figure out who is responsible for the main event or disaster, and it is never easy. Most sagas describe what modern air-crash investigators would call an 'error chain', with several opportunities to break the chain, none of them taken.[4] In *Laxdæla saga*, 'The Saga of the People of Laxardal', the central event is the killing of Kjartan by his cousin Bolli. What causes it? Certainly, the fact that Bolli told lies to Gudrun Osvifsdottir and persuaded her to marry him when her preferred lover Kjartan was out of the country. Gudrun may then have sent Bolli off to kill his cousin out of mere anger and jealousy – though it certainly crosses Bolli's mind that she might have expected Kjartan to win the fight, which would have left Gudrun, not for the first time, a widow and free to make new arrangements, possibly involving Kjartan. But then why was Bolli so anxious to cut out his cousin, with whom he was on very good terms, by stealing his intended?

The trouble there started two generations back, when their grandfather Hoskuld bought an expensive Irish slave girl from a Russian. The really galling things about this were, first, that she turned out to be a princess, the daughter – though this looks very like the usual Icelandic brag about noble origins – of someone plausibly identified as King Muirchertach *na gCochall gCroicenn*, Muirchertach 'of the Leather Coats' (d. 941);[5] and second, that her illegitimate but unexpectedly well-born son Olaf the Peacock, father of Kjartan, turns out to be smarter, richer and more favoured than his legitimate half-brother Thorleik, father of Bolli. He is furthermore held to have inherited much more than he should have done, including the intangible but vital family 'luck'. So there is a grudge there from way back, a feeling on the part of everyone in Bolli's family of having been demoted unjustly to number two.

However, an even more immediate reason involves the Myramenn and their avarice. In the 'Laxdalers' Saga', Olaf the Peacock, the concubine's son, marries Egil's daughter Thorgerd: in view of her family pride a very good way of showing he has arrived. A Norwegian called Geirmund then asks for their daughter Thurid, and Olaf, who can see the future, turns him down. Geirmund then bribes Thorgerd to talk her husband round, which she does. The marriage is a disaster. Geirmund, predictably, runs out on Thurid, and Thurid decides to arrange her own childcare and alimony settlement by dumping their baby on Geirmund and stealing his precious sword with the razor edge and the walrus-ivory handle, 'Legbiter'. Geirmund tries to buy it back, but Thurid refuses out of spite, and Geirmund puts a curse on it.

This is the sword that Bolli uses to kill Thurid's brother Kjartan. While the killing is therefore partly Bolli's fault and partly Gudrun's, and Hoskuld's fault from way back, as well as Thurid's for giving the precious sword to the wrong man, one contributor to the whole chain is certainly Thorgerd, with her ignoble and short-sighted sacrifice of family prospects for money. That's just like her father and grandfather, some would say, and so is the savage way in which she drives her remaining sons on for vengeance for their brother.

And then there is the ugliness. The saga explanation is clear. Like the greed for money, it's in the family. Egil's great-great-grandfather is Ulf the

Fearless, of whom nothing else is known. His son Bjalfi, however – about whom even less is known, since he does not have so much as a nickname – married a wife called Hallbera, and *she* is the sister of Hallbjorn Half-troll, the father of Ketil *Hængr* (Salmon or Trout?), himself the progenitor of another famous family, the *Hrafnistumenn*, the men of Hrafnista. There are four sagas and a *páttr* about him and his descendants.[6] All are in effect fairy tales, about fighting legendary monsters, giants and trolls.

Hrafnista, however, is a real place, an island off the coast of northern Norway, in Hålogaland; its modern name is Nærøy, from the earlier *Njarðar-ey, the 'island of [the god] Njorth'. It has to be remembered that Norway is an extraordinarily long-drawn-out country, more than a thousand miles (1,600 km) south to north, and Hrafnista is very close to the Arctic Circle and the limit of possible Norse habitation. Or should that be possible *human* habitation? In 'Ketil's Saga', it is clear that while the Hrafnistumen are the furthest people to the north, there are other creatures beyond them; and it's also fairly clear, though never at any point admitted, that Ketil's father, Hallbjorn Half-troll, has some kind of arrangement with them. When Ketil, like all saga heroes, starts showing signs of restlessness, his father tells him very carefully which fjords he can go into and which he cannot.

Ketil, of course, again like all saga heroes, takes no notice and goes into one of the forbidden fjords. There he finds smoke-houses and blubber pits, and in them not just walrus meat and polar bear meat, but human meat too. He lies in wait for the mighty, intelligent, man-eating hunter, who is of course a troll, and kills him. After this, Ketil too starts making his own arrangements with the trolls, including marrying one of them and reinforcing the troll bloodline, which he himself has from his father.

What all this means is not clear. Some suggest that by 'trolls' the Norse meant to indicate the Sami hunters who do indeed live to the north of Hålogaland. But the Sami are quite familiar in sagas and in non-fictional works – an important part of Norwegian kings' income came from the Sami tribute of furs and hides and other high-value items like walrus ivory, and no one calls them trolls. Nor does Sami ancestry square with the reputation for unusual size and strength of part-troll families like Egil's.

Maybe the whole idea is a projection of the natural fears of people living in the unusually hostile landscape and climate of sub-Arctic Norway, something well understood also by their Icelandic descendants. But in any case we can see that the author of 'Egil's Saga' meant to indicate that the troll blood inherited from what must have been Hallbera's troll mother runs true, but not consistently, in the Myramen. Egil's grandfather is called Ulf, like his great-great-grandfather, but where the latter's nickname was 'the Fearless', the former is called *Kveld*-Ulf, 'Evening Wolf'. What this means is that it is not a good idea to visit him when it's getting dark. He is thought to be a shape-shifter, a were-thing of some kind – visitors don't hang around to investigate further.

The next two generations both show the same pattern. In each there are two brothers, and while one is the typical saga hero, handsome, gifted, cheerful, generous and so on – what in the wrestling world used to be called a 'blue-eyes' – the other is dark, ugly, bald and (overwhelmingly) mean. Both the 'nice guy' brothers, that is to say, Egil's brother and his father's brother, are called Thorolf. Egil himself takes after his father, Skallagrim, in looks and temperament. Some of the Hrafnistumen emigrated to Iceland as well, and Egil carries the sword Dragvandil, which came to him from Grim Hairy-cheek, son of Ketil Hæng (himself presumably a quarter troll) and his full-blood troll wife Hrafnhild. Egil is the way he is because he's part-troll.

. . . or genetic disease?

That is the old and fantastic explanation for Egil's looks and behaviour, but there is now another one, put forward in the eminently sober and respectable pages of *Scientific American* by Professor Jesse Byock of the University of California, Los Angeles.[7] Places in Iceland mentioned in Icelandic sagas usually remain well known, and Egil's farm at Borg and his funeral mound close by are no exception. Egil, however, is no longer in the mound where he was first buried. He died a pagan, but his daughter converted to Christianity and, the saga says, had his remains moved to the church at Mosfell.

When that church was pulled down to make way for a new one many years later, they found an unusually large skeleton under the altar, which they took to be Egil's. The priest, Skapti Thoroddson, picked up the skull and was amazed by its size, even more by its weight, and furthermore by the fact that it was ridged all over 'like a scallop-shell'.[8] Skapti accordingly put it upon a wall and, in the true spirit of scientific inquiry (as practised by Norsemen), hit it with the back of his axe as hard as he could. The skull did not break or dent, but just turned white at the point of the blow. If that is what his skull was like many years after death, the saga author concludes, it is no wonder that Egil did not have to fear the blows of little men while he was alive.

Professor Byock draws another conclusion, based partly on the strange detail of the scallop-shell-like skull ridges. He thinks that Egil Skalla-grimsson in reality suffered from Paget's disease, a genetic defect that results in the build-up of bone, especially skull and facial bone. Some sufferers also show exactly the kind of skull ridges noted by Skapti Thoroddson. Even the detail of the skull whitening when struck makes sense, for 'when subjected to a blow, the soft, pumicelike outer material of the enlarged Pagetic skull gives way to a white, hardened, highly resilient core.'[9] Paget's sufferers take on a lion-like appearance. The weight of the head also makes the head droop; note the description of Egil at King Athelstan's feast, where he is sitting 'upright', but his head is 'bent down'.

Professor Byock also regards as authentic the short poems in which Egil, in extreme old age, describes his symptoms. Some of these – cold feet, blindness, impotence – are too normal in old age to be diagnostic, but Egil also complains about the way his head sways on a neck that cannot support it. Finally, Paget's disease is hereditary. In 1982 a study of Western European sufferers found it was most common in the British Isles, but that survey excluded Scandinavian countries on the assumption that their small populations would not include enough cases to matter. Further checking by Professor Byock, however, found ten cases being treated at the Icelandic National Hospital in Reykjavik, with more at the City Hospital not far away. There is every possibility, then, that a medieval Icelander could have carried the gene for Paget's disease, and it fits what we are told in the saga about Egil, including symptoms that no medieval author is likely to have known enough about to invent: something that further reinforces notions of the saga's reliability, at least on some things.

Family disputes, making enemies

Where sagas are less historically reliable is when they start to show signs of artistic patterning. In the case of 'Egil's Saga' the pattern is especially clear. The political background of the saga is dominated by the attempts of successive kings to impose their authority on the entire enormous extent, but scattered population, of Norway and the Norwegian colonies in the Atlantic islands, including Iceland, the Faroes and the Orkney and Shetland islands.

According to saga tradition, most particularly in *Heimskringla* – the sequence of sixteen kings' sagas written by Snorri Sturluson, probably in the 1220s, and covering the period from prehistoric antiquity to the death of King Magnus Erlingsson in 1184[10] – the first man to try to do this was King Harald Fairhair. In legend he was taunted by a prospective bride who said she would not waste her maidenhood on a petty king who could not make himself master of a proper realm. Harald accordingly swore he would not cut or comb his hair until he had brought all of Norway under his rule, and he succeeded in doing this by a series of campaigns against the many other petty kings of his time.[11]

This exercise in centralization, or nation-building, was naturally resented by many, since it involved paying taxes and surrendering the freehold rights that the farmers regarded as natural and hereditary. The Icelanders themselves insisted that a major motive for the settlement of Iceland was the refusal of their noble and libertarian ancestors to submit to tyrannical rule, which led to the founding of the Icelandic republic – an extremely aberrant state by medieval European standards, with no king, army, navy, taxes or central authority other than the very tenuous authority imposed by the annual *thing* (or parliament). The matter was still a vital one in the time when the sagas were written, three or more centuries after the time of Harald Fairhair, when Icelanders were still trying to maintain their independence. Indeed it caused the death of Snorri Sturluson, the author of *Heimskringla* and possibly of *Egils saga* as well, for – as well as the usual family squabbles over money and inheritances – he was thought to be a secret agent of the Norwegian kings plotting to suppress the republic, or possibly a double agent, taking the money but not doing the job. His ignominious death in his own cellar in 1241 has already been noted. The kings got their way in 1261, when Iceland came under Norwegian rule, not regaining independence (by this time from Nazi-occupied Denmark, not Norway) until 1944.

Egils saga centres on the notion of collaboration with or resistance to the rule of Harald Fairhair, followed by his son King Eirik Blood-axe, so-called for his determined elimination of many of his half-brothers. The central clash is between Egil and Eirik, and the most critical and dramatic scene is the moment when Egil, shipwrecked on the English coast, comes into the power of the bitterly hostile Eirik, by then (according to the saga) exiled from Norway to become king in York. The only way Egil can save his head is by composing the poem *Höfuðlausn* in Eirik's praise, in a set time and under supernatural difficulties: *Höfuðlausn* means 'head-loosing' or 'head ransom'.

But the saga works by a kind of ratcheting up. From the very beginning, when Harald starts his campaigns, there are two opinions in the family of Kveldulf, still at this point firmly based in north Norway. The Thorolfs, the well-adjusted, upwardly mobile, nice-guy side of the family (the ones where human genes have overpowered troll ones), think that the right strategy is to cooperate with the new regime and go into royal service. This is what Thorolf senior does, while his father Kveldulf and his brother Skallagrim hang back, make excuses and sit on the fence, without managing to fool King Harald at all. But things go wrong. Despite loyal service, Thorolf senior is slandered to the king, accused of keeping back the king's share of the valuable Sami tribute, and there is a sequence of provocations and retaliations. In the end, it comes to open warfare. King Harald in person gives Thorolf his death wound, and Thorolf – who has made a determined attempt to reach Harald and killed the standard-bearer at his side – dies with the remark 'Now I took three steps too few,' meaning three steps short of reaching and killing the king (a classic last words throwaway line).[12] Although the king shows signs of respect for Thorolf (guilt or remorse are not emotions very well developed in saga characters), Thorolf's family decides to emigrate en masse. They carry out revenge strikes first, assisted in this by their dangerous half-human Hrafnistumen relations.

Then it all happens again. Thorolf junior, out in Iceland, decides that *his* future lies in the wider scope of Norwegian politics, so makes friends with King Harald's most favoured son, Eirik, and Eirik's wife, Gunnhild, and seems launched on a profitable career in royal service – until things go wrong, this time caused by Thorolf's uncontrollable brother Egil.

All this raises the question of factual reliability. Egil's hereditary ugliness has been given a realistic explanation. But the similarity in the stories of the two Thorolfs looks too neat to be true, and indeed the two Thorolfs look as if they are there to show up in more relief the nature of their family and their hero relative. The issues that cause the trouble with the kings in successive generations also look like a narrative doubling. As one might have guessed with Egil's family, they deal with inheritances disputed between half-brothers and half-sisters and questions of legitimacy, and are presented with the curious moral neutrality and liking for legalistic complication of the whole Viking ethos: Egil (just like a modern lawyer, one must admit) will take either side of an argument to suit his own advantage. And, as happens fairly often in sagas, he will offer to settle matters in single combat if the law doesn't work out right. To which the equally common saga response is for the enemy to make it clear that it won't be *single* combat – fair fight? Whose crazy idea is that? – and Egil and his supporters are well outnumbered. Also, Egil's enemy Onund has King Eirik Blood-axe behind him.

At the end of it all, Egil, driven from the law court, ambushes Onund and kills him and his brother, as well as Eirik's foster-son. He then does something unforgivably mean-spirited. As Egil sails away in flight, Rognvald, King Eirik's ten-year-old son, steers bravely to intercept him. Egil just cuts the boy down: child murder without even Volund's excuse of prior torture and mutilation. He then leaves Norway rapidly, raising as he goes a *niðstöng*, a 'mocking pole', with a horse's head on it and runes carved on the shaft, pronouncing a curse on the *landvættir*, the spirits who guard the land, until they shall drive Eirik and Gunnhild out of Norway. Which they do.

But before considering the involvement of Egil and Eirik with Anglo-Saxon politics, which is where they come into the light of verifiable history, it is worth asking what is or are the point(s) of the long and confusing family negotiations that take up so much of 'Egil's Saga'. From the point of view of Icelanders of almost any age, they show a noble resistance to the tyranny of kings, made clearer by the repeated demonstrations, through the Thorolfs, that even the most loyal service to such people will get you nowhere. Along with this there seems to be a kind of argument that says that the original settlers of Iceland had no choice but to emigrate, because they were being continually cheated of their property rights.

Perhaps the saga author was trying to show how error chains work. Or perhaps he was really a kind of early Thomas Hardy who wanted to show that 'character is fate' and that while all kinds of accidents happen, the real driving force is the intransigence of the 'half-troll' character. There is a vicious streak throughout that side of the family. Skallagrim nearly kills his own twelve-year-old son, Egil, in what seems to be a kind of ice hockey, and does kill another player and a woman who intervenes – they should have known not to go on playing after sunset, when the troll side of the family comes out. By our standards, Egil and his sons overreact to almost everything. Egil bites out a man's windpipe in a duel. His son Thorstein gets into the typical Icelandic row over fodder – a vital matter in a marginal subsistence economy dependent on milk and meat – and the person confronting him says contemptuously that he is not afraid of his threats. To prove it, he sits down to tie his shoelace. The Norse did have a concept of fair play, and in similar scenes in other sagas duellists take no advantage of the other man taking a break. But Thorstein simply beheads the sitting man with his axe. When Egil is magnanimously given the right to arbitrate, he imposes an evidently unjust and ungenerous arbitration. 'Egil's Saga' is not a feel-good story. It backs up the argument that Viking society had a 'psychopathic' element in it. Or in their view, troll genetics.

Ethnic conflicts in the British Isles

What bearing does this have on the real historical events mentioned in the saga, and how far can this saga's account of anything be trusted? As said above, much of the time the saga should be taken as a historical novel, but once Egil and Eirik become involved with English politics, cross-bearings can be taken on it from relatively reliable and sometimes contemporary English and Irish sources. To make any sense of them, though, one has to set them within what must have been even at the time an immensely confused and confusing set of religious, political and most of all ethnic conflicts within the British Isles and Ireland.

The exceptionally tangled situation in Ireland and Scotland is considered further in the next chapter, but the situation in tenth-century England was in essence a clash between two rival dynasties. Back in the ninth century (as described in Chapter Four), Ivar and his brothers, and their associates and later successors, had eliminated the royal dynasties of Northumbria, Mercia and East Anglia, but had been beaten off by King Alfred in Wessex. Meanwhile, as argued by Professor Alfred Smyth, and largely confirmed by later research, the 'descendants of Ivar' had established a kind of dual kingdom in York and Dublin. The pattern in this unusually cohesive family was for the senior family member to control York, with a junior relative in Dublin, the latter taking over when there was a vacancy in York and the next in line moving up to Dublin.

Meanwhile, in between the 'sons of Ivar' in York and the 'sons of Alfred' in Winchester lay Danish Mercia, with its Five Boroughs, controlled by separate groups of Viking descendants: Derby, Nottingham, Leicester, Stamford and Lincoln. Even more critically disputed was English Mercia, the modern counties running in an arc from Cheshire and Staffordshire down to Middlesex and London and containing much of the manpower, and the best agricultural land, of all England. The front line between Danish and English Mercia ran along Watling Street, approximately Chester–Stafford–Northampton–London, with Essex as a defiantly English projection into often Scandinavian-controlled East Anglia.

The real situation in the tenth century was, accordingly, delicate, if in a way symmetrical. There was Wessex in the south, under a succession of strong kings – and the strong not-queen Æthelflæd, Alfred's daughter, 'Lady of the Mercians' – building one fort after another in a kind of pawn push to annex English and threaten Danish Mercia. In the north were the descendants of Ivar, drawing support from Ireland while trying to extend their control to Danish Mercia and block the Wessex advance. The whole situation was further complicated by the long-standing hostility between Danish and Norwegian Vikings, while the Celtic kingdoms of Wales and Scotland were waiting all the time for their opportunity.

This tangled situation is the one into which first Egil and then Eirik Blood-axe forced themselves. And here the sagas of both Egil and Eirik find some confirmation (as also some contradiction) in contemporary sources.

Egil and Eirik in Hiberno-British politics

Egil's first visit to England, according to the saga, comes before relations with King Eirik in Norway have broken down completely, though after a fight over drinks Egil's brother Thorolf remarks, with the usual understatement, 'I think that what you have done will make it inadvisable for us to go to Norway this autumn.'[13] Both brothers head south.

The saga then contains a mixture of information and misinformation. It declares that Alfred the Great was 'the first king of his kinsmen to be sole ruler [of England]', which is not true at all. Having got Alfred wrong, though, the saga author is perfectly correct in saying that Alfred's son was Edward and that Edward's son was Athelstan the Victorious. The saga is also pretty much correct in saying that when Athelstan succeeded to the throne, 'some of the noblemen who had lost their realms to his family started to make war upon him' and that these were 'British [i.e. from Wales], Scots and Irish'.[14] Athelstan's father and grandfather had defeated the Danes, first as raiding armies and then as the controllers of the Five Boroughs, but they cannot be said to have gained power over them, nor much over the Welsh princes, over whom they exercised at best an uneasy protectorate. As for Scotland and Ireland, Wessex and Mercia had no border with the one and no sea power to reach the other. But it is true that Athelstan faced a coalition of enemies with a coalition of his own.

His coalition was Wessex and English Mercia, while the *Anglo-Saxon Chronicle* is very clear about that of his enemies. In a long and exultant poem inserted into the entry for 937 it identifies them as 'the men of the Scots', 'the ship-fleets', 'those who sought out the land with Anlaf . . . lord of the Northmen' and 'Constontinus, the old warrior'. Beaten by the sons of Edward, the poem said, Constontinus left his son dead on the battlefield, and the Northmen fled in their boats, 'bloody survivors of darts, disgraced in spirit . . . over deep water, to seek out Dublin'. They left the corpses to the eagle, the raven and the wolf. The poem ends triumphantly and with a sense of long history:

> Never yet in this island was there a greater slaughter, of people
> felled by the sword's edges, before this, as books tell us, old author-
> ities, since Angles and Saxons came here from the east . . . warriors
> eager for fame, proud war-smiths sought out Britain over the broad
> sea, overcame the Welsh, seized the country.[15]

The poem's 'Constontinus' was Constantine II, King of Strathclyde – his Roman name is a reminder of the Welsh/British/Cumbric claim to be the inheritors of Rome and the only valid owners of Britain. Anlaf, 'lord of the Northmen' must be Olaf Gudfridsson, great-grandson of Ivar the Boneless, and the *Chronicle* is quite right in saying that he fled back to Dublin. The story does not end there, for both sides continued to slug it out, but Brunanburh was certainly a big score for the Anglo-Saxons, if not the decisive victory they claimed.

But who won the victory? The Anglo-Saxon poet says it was the men of Wessex and Mercia, but 'Egil's Saga' says it was Egil, acting as a mercenary. (Vikings, whether Danes, Norwegians or Icelanders, would after all fight for or against anybody if the pay was right.) According to the saga, Egil and Thorolf came to King Athelstan with three hundred men, were well received, and marched with him to the battle of Vinheith, which all have agreed must be another name for Brunanburh. Their main enemy, according to the saga, was one Olaf the Red (Old Norse Olaf, Old English Anlaf), who was descended from Ragnar Hairy-breeches (if you believe the saga genealogies, this is correct for Olaf Gudfridsson, Ragnar's great-great-grandson). The saga also thinks that Welsh chieftains were on his side, and they may have been. A Welsh poem survives from about this time, the *Armes Prydein Vawr*, which prophesies the day when all the enemies of the English will get together, Welsh and Scots and Irish and Vikings, and drive the hated 'Saxons' back to where they came from. ('In your dreams, boyo,' as any English rugby player or supporter will remark.)

'Egil's Saga' then gives a detailed but probably completely invented account of the battle, designed to show that the victory was all down to Egil and Thorolf and their Norwegians.[16] Olaf sends two earls to make a preliminary night attack, and the English commander takes to flight, but the day (or rather the night) is saved by Egil and Thorolf, who defeat the earls. Thorolf indeed runs berserk and ceases to protect himself, slinging his shield and striking out two-handed with his heavy lance, until he kills one earl's standard-bearer, runs the earl through, lifts him in the air and plants his butt-spike in the ground to make a grisly trophy. In the morning, Athelstan puts Egil at the front of the main army but puts Thorolf in the second line, on the grounds that no one can be sure where the Scots are likely to turn up. Thorolf is indeed ambushed and killed, and when Egil sees his standard retreating he knows Thorolf cannot be with it, for he would never retreat. He calls his men together – taking them out of the front line opposing Olaf's main force?, surely not – and charges over to avenge his brother. The saga says that 'King Olaf was killed there' (actually, he got away to Dublin, as mentioned) and that 'King Athelstan won a great victory there', though for Egil this was at very great cost. A scene follows of Thorolf's burial, Egil's disturbing behaviour at the feast and

Athelstan's placation of him. Despite tempting job offers from Athelstan, Egil returns to Norway, where he immediately gets involved with Onund and the disputed inheritance and offends Eirik and Gunnhild irretrievably by the killing of their son Rognvald.

The surprising thing asserted by the saga is that Eirik, king of Norway, then got involved in Anglo-Saxon politics. One must surely wonder whether this is true and how it could have come about. According to 'Egil's Saga', the reason, for Eirik, is obvious. According to *Heimskringla* – and bear in mind that both *Heimskringla* and 'Egil's Saga' could well be by the same man, Snorri Sturluson – Eirik was the favourite son of Harald Fairhair and chosen to rule the entire recently united kingdom after his father's death in old age. But *Heimskringla* names seven wives of Harald and remarks that when he married Eirik's mother he 'let go' eleven others. Eirik, accordingly, had any number of half-brothers, all determined to dispute unified rule, and though he killed several of them – hence his nickname, Blood-axe – he was eventually forced out by the popular Hakon the Good. Eirik then sailed to the Orkneys, traditional refuge of defeated contenders, and by the mid-940s was looking for a new power base.

According to the D manuscript of the *Anglo-Saxon Chronicle*, which is well informed about northern affairs, he had found it by 948, when King Eadred, successor to Athelstan and Edmund, raided across all of Northumbria 'because they had taken Eric [Yryc] for their king'.[17] But why would the Northumbrians do that? It seems so out of line, given the long dominance of York by the descendants of Ivar, that it has been argued that the 'Yryc' of the *Chronicle* cannot have been the same man as the Eirik of the sagas.[18] A slightly later entry in a different manuscript of the *Chronicle*, however, calls the Northumbrian Eric 'son of Harald', which is right for Blood-axe.

Perhaps the explanation is this. By the late 940s, the Wessex dynasty descended from Alfred, and the York-Dublin dynasty descended from Ivar, had clashed three times, in 937, 940 and 942, with the score so far 2–1 to the English. At that point a deal was made, with the two senior York-Dublin kings accepting baptism. But as soon as they could, the pagans reneged on their conversion, and as soon as they were strong enough the Wessex kings chased their rivals out. The odd thing is that according to the sagas the Northumbrians, led by their evidently English Archbishop of York, Wulfstan, instead of either thankfully accepting English Christian rule from Wessex-Mercia, or else keeping up their old loyalty to the Ivar dynasty, issued an invitation to the royal but homeless – and pagan, and Norwegian – Eirik Blood-axe instead. One might think that they meant to maintain their independence and keep a precarious balance by bringing in a puppet king with no connections to either side; one who, moreover, had good warlike credentials but no personal power base and who would accordingly do pretty much as he was told by the Northumbrian power brokers.

A further whirl of expulsions and returns nevertheless took place, the final act in it being the death of Eirik. *Heimskringla* says that he was killed in an enormous battle along with five other kings, while 'Egil's Saga' says that he was killed 'on a Viking raid' (Ch. 68). The most plausible account, however, comes from a later English chronicler, Roger of Wendover, who says that he was killed 'in a lonely place called Stainmore'.[19] This makes good geographical sense. Even now there are few clear routes across the Pennines north of York, and for practical purposes one has a choice of the A684 through Leyburn and Hawes to Kendal, the main A66 from Scotch Corner to Penrith, or the old Roman road the Stanegate (now superseded by the modern A69) which ran behind Hadrian's Wall from Newcastle to Carlisle. Stainmore is at the highest point of the A66, a good place for an ambush. Roger of Wendover also reports that the killing was carried out by Maccus, one of the York-Dublin family, but organized by Oswulf, the English high-reeve of Bamburgh. If Oswulf's loyalties were ethnic rather than separatist, he may have wanted to clear one Scandinavian contender out of the way for the eventual permanent English takeover of York.

Eirik was remembered, however, in the fine heroic poem allegedly commissioned by his widow Gunnhild, *Eiríksmál*.[20] The poem opens with Odin in Valhalla asking, 'what is the noise?' His attendant Bragi says the bench boards creak as if Balder were coming back from the dead – not a wise thing to say to Odin, whose failure to bring his son back from Hel proves the less-than-omnipotence of the Norse gods. Nonsense, says Odin, the noise must be the coming of the great Eirik. He sends the two greatest of his Einherjar, the warriors who wait with him in Valhalla, to greet the new hero; they are Sigmund and Sinfjotli. Sigmund asks, competitively, why the fuss about this new guy Eirik? Odin tells him Eirik has borne bloody sword in many lands. Bragi asks why Odin has then taken victory from him, and Odin replies with a famously enigmatic remark: 'Because it cannot be known for certain when the grey wolf will attack the seat of the gods.'[21] What cannot be known for certain, even by Odin, is the date of Ragnarok, when the grey wolf Fenrir will come. Odin wants his team of warriors in Valhalla to be as strong as possible when the moment comes. And for that, they have to be dead. So he harvests them with his valkyries, characteristically betraying his best and bravest worshippers, notably Sigurd's father, Sigmund, whose sword he broke on the battlefield with his own spear, Gungnir.

Sigmund then welcomes Eirik and asks who he has brought with him from the battlefield. Five kings, says Eirik, and I am the sixth. It is these lines that perhaps gave rise to the *Heimskringla* story of an enormous battle, but in fact the five kings seem to have been Eirik's sons and supporters.

All the above at least accounts for what Eirik was doing in York and gives us possible dates for his final clash there with Egil Skallagrimsson, some time between 947, when he fled Norway, and 954, when he was killed. Their encounter is well described in the saga and authenticated by two things: the saga's account of Egil's shipwreck on the English coast, and the long poem *Höfuðlausn*.

One use of poetry: ransoming your head

According to the saga once more, Egil, back home in Iceland and by now hopelessly at odds with Eirik after killing his son, became moody and decided to visit King Athelstan again (though in reality Athelstan had died several years before). He sailed down the eastern coast of Scotland and northern England, having carefully avoided the Orkneys as the jarl there was known to be in alliance with Eirik, but then ran into a storm as it was growing dark. He and his crew noticed nothing until there were breakers both on the seaward side and in front of them. There was no choice other than to make for the land. They did this and sailed in to wreck the ship at the mouth of the Humber.

The odd detail here is the breakers 'ahead of them', meaning to the south, and 'on their seaward side', that is, to the east, with the English coast to the west.[22] It sounds as if they had sailed into an enclosed north-facing bay, which is not easy to imagine by the mouth of the Humber, as a glance at any ordinary map will show – though a proper navigational chart would tell a different tale. Is this story, then, just made up to motivate a shipwreck, and a wholly imaginary confrontation at York with King Eirik, while excusing the hero from any accusation of poor seamanship?

Surprisingly, and rather as with Paget's disease, there is a modern and rational explanation, put by Alan Binns, the great authority on Viking (and modern) ships and sailing.[23] Binns – who incidentally acted as adviser for the Kirk Douglas *Vikings* movie and had a cameo in it – says that there is indeed just one place on the northeast coast that fits the data exactly, and that is the long peninsula of Spurn Head. This stretches down across the mouth of the Humber, but has to seaward off its southern tip a curving shoal, known for centuries as the Binks. Binns points out that in some circumstances the shoal does indeed raise breakers, that there can be a strong tidal set into the angle between it and Spurn Head itself, and that a Viking ship coming down from the north, with its relatively poor ability to sail to windward, could well be lured in too close to the flat coastline and find itself unable to escape. Even the detail that Egil's men managed to save most of their cargo is feasible, since there is a small gap between Spurn Head and the Binks, with a relatively sheltered beach where goods would not have to be carried through the surf. Particularly important is the fact that the relationship between shoal and mainland, while constantly changing, is cyclic and predictable. The given circumstances of the wreck fit the mid-tenth-century period of Egil's voyage, but *not* the early thirteenth-century period of the saga's composition, when the Binks were much less dangerous.

Binns admits that the whole story could of course have been pure invention, but concludes that 'it is odd that [the saga account] fits the conditions which must have obtained at that time and place in the mid-tenth century so well, and would not have fitted any other place on the coast or any other time'.[24] The saga story, then, could be literally true, in which case a particular detail of a tenth-century shipwreck was known to a thirteenth-century author – passed on, presumably, by word of mouth and presumably within the family (for Snorri Sturluson could trace his own descent back to Egil through his mother, Gudny).

The saga goes on to say that Egil found out once he was ashore that Eirik was now king in York, not far away, and Gunnhild with him, mother of the boy he killed. He thought it undignified to try to hide or escape – partly because he knew everyone would recognize his trollish features immediately – but pinned his hopes on his friend and wife's cousin Arinbjorn, known to be in York and in favour with the king. Arinbjorn decides on a mixture of flattery, quibbling, legalistic argument and a touch of threat. He meets Egil and goes to Eirik with all his men, fully armed. Once Egil has been recognized – Eirik sees him over the heads of all the others – Egil embraces the king's feet and makes a short appeal to him in verse. Both Eirik and Gunnhild say that's no good, he must be killed at once. Arinbjorn, quibbling, says he can't be killed right now because 'killing at night is murder'[25] (the normal rule is, only if the killing isn't declared). He succeeds in getting a decision put off and takes Egil home, telling him it would be a good idea to appear next morning with a twenty-stanza poem in praise of the king. Egil says, naturally enough, that he can't think of anything good to say about Eirik, but he is told to get on with it. Then Gunnhild takes a hand.

Gunnhild 'Kingsmother' is the saga authors' favourite wicked queen. It was she, in 'Njal's Saga', who blighted the marriage of her lover Hrut Herjolfsson for wanting to leave her and for denying that he had an intended in Iceland. She cursed him, not with impotence but with the opposite: when his wife Unn Mordsdottir divorced him, the reason she gave was that 'When he comes close to me his penis is so large that he can't have any satisfaction from me.'[26] According to *Heimskringla*, furthermore, Gunnhild was a witch-woman from Finnmark who learned sorcery from the Finns. 'Egil's Saga' says only that Egil cannot concentrate on the long poem he has to have ready before morning because of a swallow that chatters constantly outside his window. Arinbjorn realizes that it is some kind of shape-changer and keeps guard until dawn so that Egil can finish his poem: all readers have concluded that Gunnhild was the swallow.

In the morning, Egil and Arinbjorn report again to King Eirik, and Arinbjorn makes it clear that if Egil is to be killed, he will have to be killed too, and though he does not make a direct threat, he still has all his men, armed, inside and outside the hall. Egil breaks the tension – for even an implied threat is liable to be taken as a challenge – by starting to recite his poem: twenty stanzas, 72 lines long.

As has been said already, Viking poetry is very different from modern poetry. In it, no marks are awarded for delicate sentiment or piercing insight. What is valued is concision, obscure allusion, grammatical complication and above all technical virtuosity: every syllable has to be exactly right according to complex rules. Snorri Sturluson included in his *Prose Edda* both a long section, *Skáldskaparmál*, or 'The Art of Skaldic Poetry', and a 'List of Metres' (*Hattatal*) with rules and examples of more than eighty different types.[27] The simplest of these is the *fornyrðislag*, or 'old-word metre', of the *Bjarkamál*, quoted in Chapter Two. The rest get progressively more complicated.

Egil's *Head Ransom* is in a variety of *rúnhenda*. Just to show how that works, here are lines 17 to 22, in the original (to show the rhyming and alliteration), in close line-by-line translation, and finally (third column) in a version that makes clear sense. Note that 'spear-field' means shield, while 'seal's field' means sea.

Vasa villr staðar	Wasn't wrongly placed	The play of spears
vefr darraðar	the weaving of spears	was there in front of
fyr grams glöðum	before the king's glad	the king's glad shield-wall,
geirvangs röðum,	spear-field's ranks,	
þar's í blóði	where in blood	where the waves
í brimils móði	in wrath the seal's	broke in blood,
völlr of þrumði	field broke,	roared beneath his banners.[28]
und véum glumði.	roared under banners.	

Hné folk á fit	The host sank on shore	The host sank on shore
við fleina hnit.	beneath the shock of darts.	beneath the shock of spears.
Orðstír of gat	Glory got	From this Eirik won
Eiríkr at þat.	Eirik from that.	glory.

There is no doubt about the technical virtuosity of this – one rhyme, half-rhyme or syllable in the wrong place and Egil would have been a goner – and although Eirik never stops glaring at Egil, he concedes that the poem is 'well delivered'[29] and grants Egil his head – this time. He is not to think this means any sort of reconciliation.

However, even admirers of skaldic poetry are bound to ask the question: but does it mean anything at all? Egil's whole 72 lines in effect say no more than the *Eiríksmál* did in one and a half, namely that Eirik had borne a bloody sword in many lands. The lines above appear to describe a battle on a coastline, but no one knows where it might be. In fact the whole poem – quite different from the *Krákumál* or 'Death Song of Ragnar' – contains virtually no place or personal names. The Old English praise poem on the *Battle of Brunanburh* has far more factual detail. One could argue that this proves Egil's whole poem a later fake. Alternatively, one could say that the poem just backs up what Egil himself says in the saga, that when it comes to praising Eirik he has nothing prepared: 'you killed a lot of your brothers but the kid Hakon was too much for you' doesn't seem quite the thing, in the circumstances.

Opinions about the poem, then, differ. But it is certainly very skilful. Professor John Hines says it remains 'seriously undervalued by both literary critics and cultural historians'.[30] It plays cunningly on the setting, as both Eirik and Egil are importing something – battle and poetry, respectively – to the English shores, and it also keeps up an extended conceit, and a highly flattering one, that links king and poet together as artists in their respective fields. This could all be the work of an imaginative recreator, but the poem is set in a historical context that we know to have been real and which didn't last long. The person who wrote 'Egil's Saga' (probably Snorri Sturluson) did get important facts, like the dates of King Athelstan, wrong, but that invalidates the saga, not the poem. The whole scenario is, moreover, mentioned very briefly in another poem alleged to be by Egil, his *Arinbjarnarkviða* or 'Lay of Arinbjorn', where Egil says that for the mead of Odin (that is, poetry) he got back *hattar staup*, the 'knob of the hat' (his head). As with the 'scallop-shell' skull and the shipwreck details, there is no obvious reason for someone to fake the whole complex poem.

There may even be a wry joke in the very title, *Höfuð-lausn*, 'head ransom', but more literally 'head-loosing'. *Háls-lausn*, 'neck-loosing', is the final payment a slave makes to buy himself freedom, presumably marking the moment when they take off his iron collar. Egil would then be making an ironic comparison between himself buying life with a poem, and a thrall buying freedom with mere cash. The one action is aristocratic, inspired, upper class, the other mundane, commercial, vulgar. But both the warrior and the thrall are operating under the same kind of compulsion, and the warrior might as well admit it. Hjalti made the same kind of ironic comparison in *Bjarkamál*.

Meanwhile, looking at it from Eirik's side, the poem and the story about it show the Viking idea of a point of honour in Eirik's sparing of his enemy: characteristically qualified, hard-edged, unsentimental, and not including anything seriously foolish like forgiveness.

Another use of poetry: dealing with death

The relationship between prose and poetry in Old Norse literature is a complicated one. Some of the *fornaldarsögur*, the sagas of old times or legendary sagas, incorporate or are based on older poems, sometimes much older poems.[31] Some sagas, further, look like long explanations of pre-existing poems, such as Snorri's *Ynglinga saga,* or 'Saga of the Ynglings', which looks very like an extended write-up of information derived from the old poem *Ynglingatal*, 'The List or Tally of the Ynglings'. On the other hand, there's nothing to say that poems could not have been constructed later on to fit in to existing sagas – and if 'Head-loosing' is a fake, and if Snorri was the author of 'Egil's Saga', there could not be a better person than Snorri to fake it. Still, and in general, in pre-literate societies poetry is likely to be older than prose. It is easier to remember, and if it is written according to strict metrical rules – as is definitely the case with Old Norse poetry – then mistakes and misrememberings show up immediately and are likely to be corrected.

All this just raises the question, with reference to 'Egil's Saga': which came first, the poems or the story? The saga contains just over fifty poems attributed to Egil himself, and eight further stanzas either by his troll-line relatives Kveldulf and Skallagrim, or else said to him, usually as a veiled warning. Most of the poems are single stanzas, but three of them are longer: 'Head-loosing' is 72 lines, and 'The Lay of Arinbjorn' and the *Sonatorrek*, 'Loss of My Sons', are a hundred lines each.[32]

So, were the poems composed to fit the saga? Or did the author know the poems and try to fit a saga round them? To take just one example each way, it seems unlikely that the woman who warns Egil of a trap in the farm of Armod actually did so in verse: someone made that up to fit the story. But the scrap of verse in which Egil complains about his son spoiling his good silk cloak seems to have no narrative point: it's there because someone remembered it. Poems fill out 'Egil's Saga', all the way from the ones Egil is said to have composed at the age of three, for which he was rewarded with three snail shells and a duck egg, to the ones he composes in old age about his infirmities, which Professor Byock regards as genuine and personal enough to be diagnostic. Most of them relate to his adventures, some of them very closely, like 'Head-loosing' itself or the stanzas composed in praise of Athelstan, with their flattering anti-Celtic refrain 'Even the highland deer's paths / belong to mighty Athelstan now'.[33]

But after Egil makes his getaway from York and returns to Norway, and then to Iceland, the saga seems to lose shape and become episodic. The first half of the saga works by 'ratcheting up', as Kveldulf's family fall in and out with one king after another, all leading up to the irrevocable breach with Eirik and Gunnhild and Egil's lucky escape. But after that there is not much of a pattern. Egil fights duels, fails to make his peace with King Hakon the Good, does a bit of raiding, and shows his skill as a runemaster by healing a girl suffering from a misspelled or wrongly carved charm. Then he goes home to Iceland. Several of these incidents look as if they have been extemporized from scraps of poetry that just happen to have been remembered. The major events of Egil's life are now poems.

Of these the greatest is *Sonatorrek*, often called 'Loss of My Sons' but perhaps better called the 'Difficult Avenging of Sons'.[34] This is prompted by the death of one son in particular, Bodvar, to whom Egil was much attached, though he had lost another son earlier, Gunnar. Bodvar was 'exceptionally promising and handsome, big and strong like Egil and Thorolf at his age;[35] in fact (remembering that Egil had never been called 'handsome') a perfect example of the good side of the family, lost ever since the death of Thorolf junior. But Bodvar drowned in Borgarfjord, and his body washed ashore at Einarsnes. Egil goes to fetch him, opens the burial mound of his father, Skallagrim, and puts his son in it next to his grandfather. Then he goes and lies down on his bed and bolts the door.

It is a common scene in sagas – as mentioned twice already – for heroes to say nothing of their emotions but to betray them by some uncontrollable physical symptom. In this case, although Egil says nothing, and no one dares to speak to him, the saga says that he was wearing a laced tunic and laced leggings, and that he swelled so much – with grief? with anger? with bottled-up emotion? – that all the laces tore. This may be an imitation of Sigurd's response to Brynhild's rejection, mentioned earlier, but, as often in sagas of Icelanders, scaled down socially, from heroic mail-shirt to domestic laced tunic. Egil then refuses food and drink, and they realize he is intent on starving to death.

At this point his wife sends for his clever if avaricious daughter Thorgerd, wife of Olaf the Peacock, mentioned at the start of this chapter. She declares loudly on arrival that she too means not to eat or drink until she goes 'to join Freyja', which is to say until she dies, and asks her father to let her in as she means to tread the same path as him: 'I do not want to live after my father and my brother are dead.' Egil lets her in, and she lies down on the other bed. After a while he asks her what she is chewing, and she says it is seaweed, to make her die sooner. She offers him some. Then she calls for water. Egil comments that seaweed makes you thirsty, so Thorgerd offers him a drink. He takes it, but what is in the horn is not water but milk. He only realizes what he's done after he has drunk it. 'We've been tricked,' says Thorgerd as her father angrily bites a piece out of the horn, 'Our plan has failed.' She quickly changes the subject to the idea of composing an elegy for Bodvar, which she says she will then carve in runes on wood; they can commit suicide later. After all, she says, they can't trust her brother Thorstein to compose an elegy, and it would not do for Bodvar to die unsung.

As in the scene with Athelstan after the death of Thorolf, Egil responds to this appeal to his pride, composes the poem and manages to, as we would say, 'externalize' his grief. The poem is strongly traditional, with hints in it of the mythical poems of the *Poetic Edda*, but also too appropriate to the circumstances, too personal, to be (one would imagine) a later invention. Egil says that his grief is greater because his son never reached his prime; because he has buried too many of his kin already; because there is no one on whom to take revenge and (a classic Egil touch) no chance of compensation. The guilty parties are Ægir and Ran, the Norse god and goddess of the sea.

But what about Odin? Odin took Bodvar (line 43), Bodvar is with Odin now – though, note, he did not die in battle. *Eiríksmál* builds on the belief that Odin takes the best in order to reinforce his army of Einherjar, which is why even his favourites cannot trust him: what he gives one day he will take away the next. Christians also say, 'The Lord giveth and the Lord taketh away', adding resignedly, 'blessed be the name of the Lord', but Egil takes a more independent attitude to his god. In the last four stanzas of *Sonatorrek* Egil turns from what has been both a lament and an *ævisöngr*, or 'life song', to something more like a death song, though an individual one. Odin was good to him for a while, says Egil, and he was loyal to Odin, but he trusted Odin too much, because the god took away Bodvar. Now he no longer worships Odin. He concedes that Odin gave him his two great gifts, which remain a consolation: poetic skill and (typically Egil, one might say) the ability to make enemies.

Most surprisingly, Joseph Harris has pointed out, Egil sees himself as a kind of Odin analogue who has lost his son as Odin lost Balder, and lost him in such a way that he can find no satisfaction in revenge. But Egil's recasting of Odinic myth is a kind of 'minority report' questioning the 'official mythology'.[36] It hints at the idea of old men – King Aun, King Harald Wartooth, Starkad the Old – sacrificing their sons and relatives for long life or victory. Did one-eyed Odin create an analogue of himself in the blind god Hod, to kill his son Balder? Has Egil lost two sons, Bodvar and before him Gunnar, as payment for the two gifts Odin sent him? *Sonatorrek*, one could say – and the individuality of the thoughts make its authenticity seem all the more likely – is a poem racked by what we call survivor guilt.

There is another Odinic thought in the poem as well, Professor Harris argues. If Odin takes those who die sword in hand, then Gunnar and Bodvar will never be received in Odin's Valhalla of the heroes, for Bodvar drowned and Gunnar died of disease. Unless, that is, their father in the poem has designated them as sacrifices to Odin – sacrifices, he says, he made unwillingly? As for Egil himself, he knows he at least will never go to Valhalla, but instead to Hel, at once death, the goddess of Death, and her gloomy underworld, for in the end Egil will die in his bed, the 'straw death' shunned by many as ignoble. There is no one to designate him as a sacrifice or to pay a price for him. But even that fate does not daunt him, any more than the snakes daunted Ragnar. The last lines of *Sonatorrek*, flat and plain, as is right for the end of a death song, run:

Skalk þó glaðr	Still I shall gladly
með góðan vilja	with a good will
ok óhryggr	and not grieving
heljar bíða.	wait for death.[37]

The flat ending should not disguise the poem's complexity of emotion – sadness, guilt, resignation, defiance – any more than Ragnar's ending disguises his blend of stoicism and recognition. The stronger the feelings, the less you must show them.

The saga ends with further anecdotes on unconnected topics: Egil's poetry – he took pleasure in conversing with young men about the art of poetry; his long elegy for Arinbjorn; his son's extremely unsporting killing of a rival herdsman; and Egil's final hiding of his treasure and murder of the two slaves who helped him. The poetry, the avariciousness and the ruthless cruelty all remain connected right to the end of the saga, as they do in the sad, hard-hearted ending of *Sonatorrek*.

Although Egil's children would become Christians – Iceland accepted conversion in the year 1000 by decision of the Althing – and although 'Egil's Saga' was written by a man whose family must have been Christian for generations, the picture of Egil is of a man still formed by pagan beliefs – 'deeply immersed in Odinic myth',[38] as Professor Harris says – even though in the end he turned his back on his god. In its correct Old Norse form the god's name is *Óðinn*, in Old English *Wóden*, and the Old Norse *óðr* and Old English *wód* are both commonly translated as 'mad'. But Egil is not a madman. Could he be called a psychopath'?

A standard modern definition of the latter term is 'a person who is mentally ill, who does not care about other people, and who is usually dangerous or violent'.[39] Egil is certainly the latter. Not only does he kill armed opponents, in war or duel, he kills a ten-year-old child (Eirik's son Rognvald) and he murders his own slaves. Yet he clearly cares about *some* other people, like his brother Thorolf, his son Bodvar and his relative Arinbjorn. Is he, then, a sociopath? A modern definition here is, 'someone who behaves in a dangerous or violent way towards other people and does not feel guilty about such behavior'.[40] That fits Egil again, but by his lights he has done nothing to feel guilty about: his violent actions are either retaliations against threats or disputed legal decisions, or what he sees as insults, or else – like the slave murders – they are done to defend his property. None of this would be excusable in the modern world, but then, in the modern world – as said earlier with reference to Volund – we have police forces and a system of non-personal law enforcement.

Perhaps the best modern term for Egil is 'amoral familist'. He has feelings of responsibility and affection, but they apply within the family only. Even that, though, is not quite accurate, for Egil also has something like a code of honour, in which not responding to threats or insults is the wrong way to behave. At least one can say that, by the standards of his society, which had its own 'coherent cultural system' (to borrow a phrase from Professor Hines),[41] Egil is not 'mentally ill'. There is just one thing about him which the saga author seems to regard as part of his personality and not admirable. It is his stinginess, the greed for money – and that, as his daughter Thorgerd shows in 'The Laxdalers' Saga' and as his son Thorstein shows in the scuffle over hay, may be genetic. It goes with the troll blood.

Going back to the words *wód* and *óðr*, a better translation for them might be 'inspired'. They testify to a belief in some superhuman and inexplicable force that allows men and women to see the future – the Latin word *vates*, 'prophet', is from the same root – and to call down curses, as Egil does on Eirik and Gunnhild. It is the same force that puts immortal poetry into mortal heads and makes warriors and berserkers impervious to fear, pain or wound. Like the god Odin, it cannot be trusted. It will always let you down in the end.[42]

None of this thought complex about madness and inspiration is much appreciated, still less believed in, in modern society, and even people like Egil viewed parts of it with ironic suspicion. But they were part of the culture. Much of the remainder of the Viking story deals with the clash between Christians and pagans, and it was the attractions and advantages of the old culture, so hard for us nowadays to feel, that the missionaries had to find ways to overcome – and which we now have to find ways to understand.

PART II

Moving to the Bigger Picture

The five preceding chapters have been able to centre both on outstanding personalities – Volund, Gunnar and Gudrun, Hygelac and Hrolf, Signy and Brynhild, Ragnar and Ivar, Egil and Eirik – and on outstanding poems from the Codex Regius, from *Egils saga* and from other sources as well.

The next three chapters are not so fortunate. Chapter Six has an outstanding poem, Chapter Seven the enigmatic personality of Hastein, and Chapter Eight has both a death song and a death. But the death is of someone nameless, like most Vikings and their victims, and the death song fades back into prehistory.

These gaps are compensated by a new variety of sources, stemming from the Vikings' other main cruising grounds outside Britain and Scandinavia: first Ireland and the Celtic fringes of north and west Britain; then the empire of the Franks, or Francia, which included the Low Countries and much of Germany as well as France; and then the great rivers of Eastern Europe, which led to the civilized empires of Byzantium and the Muslim world. No account of the Vikings is complete which does not take them into consideration.

Yet our sources for events in these areas, though often extensive, include little in the way of biography. Indeed, reading them makes one aware of what remarkable achievements the sagas were, even late and unreliable ones like 'The Saga of King Hrolf'. Dudo of Saint-Quentin's Latin *Historia Normannorum* or 'History of the Normans', was written far closer in time to the events he describes than 'The Saga of King Hrolf', or Snorri Sturluson's sagas of Egil and of the Norwegian kings, but his account of 'Ganger-Hrolf', founder of Normandy in both legend and real life, a man who lived four hundred years later than his namesake, has almost nothing credible to offer. Dudo, brought up on saints' lives and anxious to show his rhetorical mastery, operated on the principle 'more is better'. His hero 'Rollo' – Dudo's version of *Hrólfr* has become enshrined in the TV series *Vikings* – wins every battle; is opposed only by cowardly and treacherous enemies; has no vices at all, since everything he does is fully justified; and shows not a spark of individuality. One has to concede that the legendary *Göngu-Hrólfs saga* or 'Saga of Ganger-Hrolf' is no better. It seems that the Scandinavian world preserved little memory of the settlements in Normandy.

The accounts surviving of Viking activity in Eastern Europe are often much more valuable, for there the 'Rus', as they were called, came under the sharp-eyed, if often disgusted, observation of men from the civilized world of Islam, in the Near East and in Spain. But these observers saw the Vikings only en masse, commenting on their culture – often remarkably, and sometimes first-hand – but not on the individual personalities of men they did not recognize and whose names they did not know. Finally, as Donnchadh Ó Corráin remarks, 'the Irish monastic scholars provide the most detailed and dispassionate account of the Viking wars'[1] (though one might dispute his term 'dispassionate'), but again, individuals are hard to pick out. Especially early on – before the two sides began to intermarry – Irish chroniclers probably had neither opportunity nor inclination to learn the names of the enemies they fought, whose language (unlike the Anglo-Saxons) they could not understand.

Yet in spite of all the reservations above, these three main areas, Ireland and the Celtic world, Francia and Normandy, and the Scandinavian 'Wild East', all have their major place in the Viking world and in any account of the Viking ethos. They bring up sharply some vital questions about history and about psychology. What determines the fate of battles? Why do they so often not go according to past form? What qualities did a successful Viking leader need, and what tactics worked against them? An overpowering question: what made Vikings 'go Viking'? Was it just lust for adventure? And if not, what were the likely returns for an average rank-and-filer, and for a successful leader?

Answers to all these questions are necessarily speculative, and historians do not like speculation. Avoiding it, however, puts one in the position of the man in an old music-hall joke. The sketch opens with a man crawling around on stage under a light. A second actor comes on and asks the first what he's doing. He says, 'I'm looking for the sixpence I dropped.' The second actor gets down on his knees to help, and after crawling around for a while, he asks, 'Where exactly did you drop it?' The first man points back to the darkest section of the stage, yards away. 'Then why the dickens are you looking for it here?' 'Because that's where the light is.'

To put it less allegorically, if you only ask questions to which answers are known already, you don't learn much. Or, putting it yet another way, where certainty is impossible, probability will have to do.

The questions underlying the three chapters that follow are ones to which we do not already have answers; and the chapters are devoted to the three geographical areas listed above.

SIX

Weaving the Web of War:
The Road to Clontarf

Ireland and the Celtic northwest of Britain may well have been the place where the Vikings began to practise their raider skills. It was remarked in Chapter Two how strange it is that the first recorded attack on Britain should be the arrival of Norwegians from Hordaland at Portland, in the very centre of the English south coast. Portland is a good 950 km (600 mi.) from the southwestern tip of Norway, most of it open sea, a crossing as long as the one to Iceland – which Scandinavians did not discover until the 870s, three generations after the affair at Portland.

By contrast, the Shetland Islands lie on the same latitude as Bergen – Viking navigators could easily check for latitude – and are no more than 320 km (200 mi.) away. From them the Orkney Islands are less than 160 km (100 mi.), and from the Orkneys one can steer round the north coast of Scotland, through the Hebrides (the *Suðreyjar*, or Southern Islands, to the Norse) and down to Ireland. From there, Wales and the long peninsula of southwestern England can be kept in sight all the way. Archaeologists have found traces of Scandinavian settlement in the Orkneys dating to as early as 800. There is no clue as to what happened to the original inhabitants of Orkney or Shetland: both groups of islands were Norse-speaking through most of recorded history, English taking over only in the eighteenth century. Presumably the pre-Viking populations were just wiped out, or assimilated, to use the preferred modern term, like the *papar*, the Irish monks who astonishingly found their way to Iceland even before the Scandinavians, but who, again, left no trace behind them.

The Irish situation: Viking training ground

One may well think, then, that the new era of sea-borne assaults from Scandinavia began with Norwegians, specifically, preying on the small, scattered, poorly armed populations of the northern and western islands of Britain, followed by further probing and reconnaissance of the richer lands to the south. The shrine of St Cuthbert on Lindisfarne was as well known to the Celtic world as to the Anglo-Saxon one. The raiders of 793 could have heard about it from Scottish sources. That raid was followed two years later by the sack of St Columba's Iona, off the western coast of Scotland, which was attacked twice more in 802 and 806, after which the monks moved to what they regarded as a safer place, Kells in Ireland, in 807.

In this they were probably mistaken, for Ireland itself had already been attacked – beginning in 795, according to the *Annals of Ulster* – and the attacks were about to become seasonal. If one can believe the account of the *Cogadh Gaedhel re Gallaibh*, 'War of the Gaedhil [Irish] with the Gaill [Foreigners]' – which is often difficult, as we will see – then in the forty years or so after 812, when 'the foreigners first began the devastation of Erinn', at least sixteen fleets of the Gaill arrived on Irish shores, 'great sea-cast floods' of them, 'so that there was not a point [of Erinn] without a fleet'.[1] They were fiercely resisted, according to the patriotic chronicler, writing three centuries after 812: he counts many defeats for the Gaill, the foreigners, and if one adds up all the Norse casualties claimed during those years (though most of the battles do not have a casualty list attached) they come to more than four thousand.

Things were only going to get worse for Ireland, though, for before too long the news had spread, and powerful competition appeared for the first set of invaders. This occurred round about 850, two generations or so after the first Viking attacks. A new leader called Thorir appeared, said to be the deputy of the king of *Laithlind*. He was quickly disposed of, but then the 'king of the foreigners' (perhaps of *Laithlind*) despatched a fresh army, whom the Irish called the *Dubgaill*, the 'dark foreigners', also known as 'new foreigners', in opposition to the *Finngaill*, the 'fair' or 'old foreigners'.[2] These have traditionally been identified as, respectively, Danes and Norwegians, but this is probably an anachronism. In the early ninth century neither Denmark nor Norway existed as entities, and loyalties were more local and more personal. It would help if one could be sure where *Laithlind* was. Could it have been Scotland, or the by this time Norse-settled Scottish islands? But that is where the Old Foreigners must have made their bases, while the king of *Laithlind*'s army were New Foreigners.

More significant is the fact that the New Foreigners are said to have been led by one *Ímair* (Old Norse *Ívarr*), and he looks very like the *Inwær* of Anglo-Saxon accounts, whom later Scandinavian sources insist, rightly or wrongly, was Ivar Ragnarsson. His descendants, the *Úi Ímair* or O'Ivar dynasty, are prominent in the history of Ireland for the next 150 years and more.

The main reason for identifying Irish *Ímair* with the *Inwær* of the *Anglo-Saxon Chronicle*, as Professor Alfred Smyth pointed out, is that they are chronologically complementary.[3] *Ímair* is logged in Irish sources from 851 to 863 but then reappears in 870. Those intervening years were the years of the 'great army' in England and the overthrow of Northumbria, Mercia and East Anglia, with the events at York and Repton, discussed earlier. Similarly, the Healfdene whom the *Anglo-Saxon Chronicle* identifies as Inwær's brother, and who was said to have left England in 875 to continue raiding after the settlement of his men in Northumbria, looks like the *Albann* killed in battle against the *Finngaill* or Old Foreigners at Strangford Lough in 877.[4]

Be that as it may, *Finngaill* and *Dubgaill* began a bitter contest in which both sides allied themselves with Irish factions, notably the over-kings of the feuding Northern and Southern Úi Néill clans. This was probably more of a 'turf war' than a national contest, and Dark Foreigners, it has been suggested, is just a term for 'Ivar's associates', the men under his leadership.[5] Quite what that group was composed of, no one can say. Apart from *Albann*/Halvdan, none of the many other 'Ragnarssons' mentioned earlier show up in Irish records, which is not surprising, as most of them were imaginary. On the other hand, Irish chronicles repeatedly mention one *Amlaíb* (Olaf, earlier *Anlafr*), said to be the son of the king of *Laithlind*, in regular alliance with Ivar, and said also to be his brother – though this may be no more than an inference from their long alliance. The great feat of Ivar and Olaf in alliance, as far as the Irish were concerned, was their long and successful siege of Dumbarton Rock in Scotland, the stronghold of the Britons of Strathclyde, from which they returned to Ireland with two hundred ships and a great plunder of slaves, English and British and Picts. This had immense consequences (discussed later).

Nevertheless it was the *Úi Ímair* who caught the eye of the Irish chroniclers, which is to say Ivar's sons and grandsons and later descendants. 'The War of the Gaidhil with the Gaill' declares that 'they alone sustained half the troubles and oppressions of all Erinn.'[6] The twelfth-century writer sums up the situation of the ninth century by saying that:

> numerous fleets of Danes and pirates . . . demolished [Erinn's] beautiful ornamented temples, for neither veneration, nor honour, nor mercy for [lands of sanctuary], nor protection for church, or for sanctuary, for God or for man, was felt by this furious, ferocious, pagan, ruthless, wrathful people. In short, until the sand of the sea, or the grass of the field, or the stars of heaven are counted, it will not be easy to recount, or to enumerate, or to relate what the

Gaedhil all, without distinction, suffered from them: whether men or women, boys or girls, laics or clerics, freemen or serfs, old or young – indignity, outrage, injury, and oppression. In a word ...[7]

But the account goes on for many words!

Even that excerpt, however, shows some of the difficulties of using the many Irish documents, sometimes 'detailed' indeed, but not so often 'dispassionate', as Donnchadh Ó Corráin claims. What one would like is some of the hard-headed analysis given by some of the writers of the *Anglo-Saxon Chronicle*, like the writer of the entry for 897, who after a long account of a five-year campaign remarked that the raiders had not 'utterly crushed' (*eallunga gebrocod*) the English people.[8] He added dispassionately that the worst thing was the heavy death rate among the king's thanes, names and titles given. There may be reasons why this kind of analysis was not possible in Ireland, including the greater linguistic barrier between Old Irish and Old Norse as compared with Old English and Old Norse.

Also, one cannot help thinking, the situation itself was intolerably confused. In their attacks on the Anglo-Saxon kingdoms, the Vikings were opposed by remarkably centralized states: Mercia, Northumbria, East Anglia, Wessex. Although these could accordingly field relatively large armies, if those armies were defeated and the royal dynasties either eliminated or driven into exile, then Viking rulers could hope to install themselves and their followers as replacements for the native kings and nobles now dispossessed. Anglo-Saxon England had a harder shell, one might say, but a kernel inside it. By contrast, the plethora of petty kings and statelets in Ireland – as many as 150 of them – all of them perfectly accustomed to fighting each other, might have been easy to deal with one at a time but could never be dealt with, even diplomatically, all at once. The existence of half a dozen provincial overkings, notably the chiefs of the mutually hostile Northern and Southern Uí Néill, did not make matters any easier.

To this confusion was added the very bitter animosity of rival gangs of Vikings, whoever they were; the confusing loyalties of jarls of the Orkneys, the Hebrides, and the Isle of Man; and, as time went by, the existence of communities of *Gall-Goídil*, 'foreign Gaels', (as the Irish called them, or in Old Norse, with mangled pronunciation, *Gaddgeðlar*): people of mixed Norse and Celtic descent. These gave their name to the Scottish province of Galloway, and the Gallowegians long retained a reputation for exceptional ferocity and barbarism. One of the authors of the Irish *Three Fragments*, or *Fragmentary Annals of Ireland*, describes them as 'a people who had renounced their baptism' (for the Irish at this period had been

Christian for centuries) and adds that bad as the Norsemen were, their children by Irish or Scottish wives 'were worse by far, in whatever part of Ireland they used to be'.[9] In any case, many of them were not in Ireland but in the raiding centres of the Scottish islands, the Isle of Man between Britain and Ireland, or Galloway, within sight of the Irish coast but inaccessible to any king without a fleet.

One might sum up, not entirely out of line with the *Cogadh* above, by saying that in the ninth and tenth centuries the Irish fought the Vikings; one set of Vikings fought another set of Vikings; Viking leaders from both factions used the Irish to fight the other Irish; Irish kings conversely used Vikings to fight other Vikings; everyone fought for his own hand; and round the whole dogfight lurked the mixed-race and mixed-religion (but mostly apostate) Hiberno-Norse, whom everybody hated, either for being traitors to God (the Irish view) or for being bastards both literally and metaphorically (the prevailing Norse view). In sagas set in Iceland, far from the scene of conflict, a stock character is the surly Hebridean, or Hiberno-Norseman, with a chip on both shoulders, never accepted into the Icelandic community and rarely tolerated for long.[10]

The anarchic situation seems indeed to have reached a peak of ferocity. The most disgusting passage of all accounts of Viking behaviour must surely come from the *Three Fragments* once more. This describes how King Mael Sechlainn of Tara, who had just murdered Cinaeth, son of the king of Cianachta, having him 'drowned in a dirty streamlet' (a traditional but ignominious form of execution), sent emissaries to a group of Vikings. This eleventh-century text identifies them as 'Danair', Danes, who had just defeated a group of the 'Lochlannach', who were possibly Norwegians:

> When [the Irish emissaries] arrived [at the Viking camp] the Danes were cooking, and the supports of the cooking-pots were heaps of the bodies of the Norwegians, and even the spits on which the meat was [roasting] rested their ends on the bodies of Norwegians, and the fire was burning the bodies, so that the meat and fat that they had eaten the night before was bursting out of their bellies. The messengers of Máel Sechlainn were looking at them thus, and they were reproaching the Danes for it. That is what the Danes said: 'They would like to have us like that'.[11]

It is not easy to say what makes this scene so uniquely repulsive. The indifference to death? The juxtaposition of cooking and cremation? The men eating while corpses actually regurgitate food? The non-activation of what ought to have been a natural thought, namely, 'these men were eating yesterday as I'm eating now, so maybe the food I'm putting in my mouth now will come out . . .'.

But this is a thought that does not need to be pursued. Of course, it could be part of the Irish atrocity narrative, but the *Three Fragments* were written earlier than the *Cogadh*, are based in part on earlier accounts and are taken to be more reliable. And the indifferent, shoulder-shrugging response of the Danes is much more characteristic of Scandinavian understatement than of Irish hyperbole.

A Viking queen in Dublin?

The different phases of Viking activity in England are perceptively noted by the authors of the *Anglo-Saxon Chronicle*. At first they are just raiders who arrive in the summer, any time after 789 (a Kentish charter of 792 shows precautions already being taken for coastal defence). Then, an ominous sign, they start to seize island bases so they can stay over the winter, as they did in 850–51, on either the Isle of Thanet or the Isle of Sheppey, both off the Kentish coastline again. Then they arrive as organized armies with the intention of taking over whole kingdoms, as the 'great army' did from 865. Ten years later – a final stage – the raiders have turned into settlers with no intention of going home: that year Halvdan's men 'divided up the land of Northumbria; and they were ploughing and providing for themselves'. This was such a major change that one copyist of the *Chronicle* couldn't understand it. He saw the word *ergende*, 'ploughing' – from the verb *erian*, related to our word 'arable' – but assumed it was a mistake and 'corrected' to *hergende*, 'raiding', which is what you expect Vikings to do.[12] But ploughland was the prize now, not cash and slaves.

The *Chronicle* notes that the same thing happened that year with 'Rollo' and his men in Normandy. This progression from raid to settlement did not, however, take place in Ireland, or did so only to a limited extent. There the 'foreigners' could be negotiated with, certainly allied with, but never assimilated. It is significant that there must have been some communication in England between invaders and defenders, for the *Chronicle* occasionally notes what the Vikings themselves said or thought, and the chronicler for 893 knew not just what happened but sometimes why: the Danes did not take an opportunity to get away following their defeat in 893 because their king was too badly wounded to be moved. That snippet of information must have come from the other side.

By contrast, it was almost forty years before an Irish chronicler managed to identify a named individual among their enemies, one 'Turgeis' (probably a rendering of Thorgest). He arrived in 839 with what is said to be 'a royal fleet' and 'assumed the sovereignty of the foreigners of Erinn', keeping it for at least a few years. Among the many abbeys plundered was the abbey of Armagh, and special offence was given because 'the place where Ota, the wife of Turgeis, used to give her audience was upon the altar of Clauin Mic Nois' (Clonmacnoise being some 175 km/108 mi. from Armagh).[13] Later chroniclers add that she did so naked. This is probably just further scandalizing, but the implication is that she was practising the kind of shamanic magic that the Icelanders called *seiðr*.

It was in Turgeis's time that further assaults were launched, first on southern France and then on both Christian and Islamic Spain, in 844. A glance at the map shows that one could reach France in easy stages from southern Ireland, with landfalls at Cornwall and Cape Finisterre, after which one could again coast as far on- or offshore as required. As might have been expected, the Andalusians under Abd ar-Rahman II proved a tough proposition, but the following year Abd ar-Rahman thought it worthwhile to send an embassy to the king of the heathens.

We do not know who this was. (Indeed, it is only fair to say that there is doubt about the whole story.)[14] Nevertheless, an account of the embassy survives, in Arabic,[15] but unfortunately the ambassador, al-Ghazal, 'the gazelle', so-called because of his good looks, spends most of the text boastfully describing his flirtation with the queen of the heathens and omits almost everything we would now take an interest in. The land he reaches from Spain is described as 'the first of the lands of the Vikings . . . one of their islands . . . three days' sail, that is three hundred miles from the mainland . . . around the island are many other islands, all populated by Vikings'.[16] This could indicate Ireland, Britain and the islands from Shetland to Man, which would have been a great deal easier to reach than, for instance, the Danish archipelago. (Surely even al-Ghazal would have noticed the long run-up through the English Channel and along what are now the French, Dutch, German and Danish coasts as far as the Skaw, or Skagen.) Al-Ghazal also declares that the Vikings had mostly become Christian – which at this time they certainly had not – and had given up their practices of fire-worship (never a Viking custom) and incest (subject to definition). Was the king of the 'Madjus', the fire worshippers, Turgeis/Thorgest? Or some other candidate? al-Ghazal once again does not say – though characteristically, what he does say is that he competed with the Vikings at everything, from scholarship (?) to martial arts, and won all contests.

The important thing, for him, however, was his relationship with the queen, whose name is given as Nud (Aud? Ota? It's not identifiable). She was, al-Ghazal alleges, quite besotted with him, stunned by his rather elementary flattery, sending him presents, insisting on seeing him every day. What seems to have been especially titillating to the Arab ambassador, not used to female freedoms, was her forward and independent behaviour. When he was warned about the risks of his behaviour by other members of the embassy, he tried to cool matters off and eventually told Nud why he was doing so. But she replied that he need not worry:

> We do not have such things in our religion, nor do we have jeal-ousy. Our women are with our men only of their own choice. A woman stays with her husband as long as it pleases her to do so, and leaves him if it no longer pleases her.[17]

There may be some faint truth in this, for by Mediterranean standards Viking women had considerable civil rights, including divorce. But the account of the embassy goes on, much less plausibly, 'It was the custom of the Vikings before the religion of Rome reached them that no woman refused any man.' By now we are deep in Male Fantasy Land, as may have been the case all along. Just the same, 'When al-Ghazal heard her say this, he was reassured, and returned to his previous familiarity.'

Little, then, can be learned from this account about the real situation in Viking Ireland in the time of Turgeis. In any case, Turgeis was drowned at almost exactly this time, 845, by the Irish, in Lough Owel. Nevertheless, news of what was happening in Ireland, and at least some report that there was profit to be made there, must have spread in the Scandinavian homelands, for the next major development was, as said above, the arrival of a very large fleet of the *Dubgaill* or Dark Foreigners, and with it the appearance of Ivar.

Professor Smyth has even made out a case for saying that this fleet of 851 was led by none other than Ragnar Lodbrog himself and that Ragnar was actually killed in Ireland – the story of his execution by King Ella at York being a later invention.[18] Whether this is true or not – it is based on an interpretation of an unreliable addition to Saxo Grammaticus, him-self deeply unreliable[19] – the newcomers clearly looked like upsetting the whole balance of power in what the *Finngaill* or Old Foreigners had come to regard as their territory (including the northern and western isles of Scotland, by now heavily Norse-settled). It is not surprising then that a few years later a counterbalancing fleet arrived, led by '*Amlaibh*, [son of] the king of Lochlainn',[20] perhaps from Norway. He and Ivar dominated the politics of the European Far West for twenty years. Can he be identified?

The man in the Gokstad ship

There are far too many Olafs in Scandinavian history for anything to be certain, but Olaf, 'King of Dublin', to whom all the Vikings of Ireland submitted in 853, is often linked with Olaf the White, who appears repeatedly, with full genealogy, in later Icelandic sagas. He was of special interest to Icelanders because his wife, Aud the Deep-minded, daughter of Ketil Flatnose of the Hebrides, was one of the earliest settlers in Iceland, and important Icelandic families claimed descent from her and Olaf's son, Thorstein the Red.

Professor Smyth has, however, argued that in the Icelandic sources, written more than three hundred years after the events, this major Norwegian expedition of 853, led by one Olaf or another, has been confused with a later expedition. Smyth's view is that Olaf the White was the same man as Olaf, Elf of Geirstad (*Ólafr Geirstaða-álfr*), another petty Norwegian king (of whom fantastic tales were later told). He goes on to put forward an argument that has since been quite definitely disproved but is nevertheless too enticing to leave out,[21] and which, furthermore, makes a point about reality in the Viking Age.

What Smyth suggested was that Olaf the White, aka Olaf Elf of Geirstad, might also have been the man buried in one of the two most famous Norwegian ship burials, the Gokstad ship – Gokstad being only a few kilometres northeast of *Geirstaðir*. The ship is tree-ring dated to around the year 890, which fits with Olaf's withdrawal from Ireland, while still in his prime, in 871, and the man buried in it was tall, strong and very high-status, as shown by his burial goods, ship included – all of which fits with what the Icelanders say of King Olaf the White (though it is hardly diagnostic, given that Viking leaders tended to be physically formidable). Smyth also believed (and this is where his theory broke down) that the buried chieftain was an old man who suffered from chronic arthritis. This fits a poem about Olaf Elf of Geirstad, preserved, as so often, by Snorri Sturluson in 'The Saga of the Ynglings' (Ch. 49), which says that he died of *fótverkr*, leg pain.[22]

Unfortunately, many people, almost up to the time of writing, have been misled by the results of the first Gokstad autopsy from the nineteenth century. A scientific reappraisal from the University of Oslo in 2007 changed these completely.[23] The dead man was not an old fellow crippled by arthritis but a man in his forties, almost 183 cm (6 ft) tall and extremely muscular – indeed unusually so, for he had a tumour on his pituitary gland that would have affected his production of growth hormone and made him perhaps as formidable as Egil Skallagrimsson with his Paget's disease. As the Eddic poem *Hávamál* comments, though, in Viking times, however tough you were there was always someone just as tough: stanza 64 declares, 'he finds who mixes with the brave ones / that no one is singly the boldest'. The dead man of Gokstad, physical anomaly though he was, had died not from disease but from slash, stab and club wounds, inflicted by two or three attackers. If a jackdaw could substitute for an Odinic raven, as suggested earlier for the dead man with multiple battle wounds at Repton, one wonders what the peacock buried in the Gokstad ship was supposed to represent, along with the twelve horses, six hounds, 64 shields and much else.

The Gokstad burial was a chieftain, no doubt, maybe one of the many petty kings of Norway, but he cannot have been Olaf Elf of Geirstad, for he did not die of gout or pain from arthritis. He also seems to have died too young to have been Olaf the White. As for Olaf, 'King of Dublin', he is reported as having been killed in Scotland in 874. Death in battle was a standard fate for royal Olafs.

Irish Vikings and the creation of Scotland

Smyth's argument that this later forgotten or misremembered Irish Olaf was critical for the whole history of the British Isles is not affected, however, by rejection of the Gokstad identification or uncertainty about the Olaf the White identification. What seems to have happened is that after an initial heavy defeat of the Old Foreigners by the incoming New Foreigners, Olaf's arrival with his fleet in 853 restored the balance between the two groups.[24] Olaf the probable Norwegian and Ivar the possible Dane then sensibly made common cause, in 858 defeating the coalition of Mael Sechnaill, by this time High King of Ireland, and Ceitil Find (probably Ketil Flatnose), leader of the Hebridean faction of *Gaddgeðlar*; Olaf was married to Ketil's daughter Aud the Deep-minded of Icelandic fame, but it is typical that the (temporary) marriage did not prevent war between husband and father-in-law.

After 858, Olaf and Ivar operated successfully and cooperatively, but it looks as if pickings in Ireland were growing thin. There was no chance, either, of the Vikings completely replacing the native population, as they did in Orkney and Shetland, or dominating them, as they did in the Hebrides, or turning from raiders to settlers, as they did in England. It seems that Olaf and Ivar had given up on making a profit in Ireland – Ivar's search in 863 for hidden treasure in the ancient tombs along the Boyne looks like a move of desperation – and had taken their by this time battle-hardened troops off to, respectively, Scotland and England.

The success of Ivar and his brothers in England was covered in Chapter Four. What was perhaps even more fateful for the British Isles was Olaf's success in Scotland. Scotland in the ninth century was already multi-ethnic and multi-linguistic. It had English-speaking Angles in the southeast and the modern border counties; Britons speaking a language related to Welsh in the southwest, with their capital at Dumbarton, 'Rock of the Britons'; Gaelic-speaking incomers from Ireland in the north and west, these latter especially exposed to Viking pressure; and increasing numbers of Norse speakers competing with or replacing the Gaels of the islands and the Britons of Galloway. The largest bloc, however, was the mysterious Picts, occupying the north and centre of the country, who also spoke a language related to Welsh but perhaps had another of their own, related to nothing on earth and surviving only in names and inscrutable inscriptions.

Briefly, what happened in the late ninth century was that Kenneth MacAlpin (Cináed mac Ailpín, traditional founder of the Scottish kingdom and king of Dál Riada) married his daughter to Olaf and allowed Olaf to hollow out resistance among the Picts by raiding them repeatedly. This opened the way for the Scots of Dál Riada in the northwest to establish their own control over what was the greater part of the country. Their takeover was much assisted by Olaf and Ivar's combined siege and conquest of Dumbarton in 871 (which broke the power of the Britons), while the Anglian settlers of the southeast and border country had already found themselves on their own following the collapse of the Northumbrian kingdom under the earlier attack of Ivar and his brothers.[25]

Smyth concludes, 'It was against this background of rapidly changing events and movements of people that the kingdom of Scotland was born.'[26] To which one could add that something similar happened in England, too. In both countries, Viking assault destroyed established states and seemed to be creating a condition of anarchy. But in both cases the long-term result was that the one survivor of the previously established states – respectively the Scottish Dál Riada and English Wessex – profited from the elimination of what had been equal or superior competitors to create a hegemony and eventually unify what became the medieval and modern realms of England and Scotland. When one looks at it like that, the most significant event of the ninth century, certainly for British and maybe for European history, was the alliance of Olaf and Ivar.

Ireland, meanwhile, remained divided, in a welter of splits and alliances. Nevertheless, from about the 870s, when Olaf returned to Norway and Ivar died, perhaps at Repton, a general pattern emerged. There was not much to be gained by the Vikings any more through raiding for accumulations of money and church treasuries: they had either gone or become much better defended. There was no prospect of land settlement except in limited areas under the control of the Viking ports, like Waterford, Wexford, Limerick and especially Dublin. Where there was still money to be made, it came from slaves, for whom there was steady demand from silver-rich Islam. So what grew up for several generations was 'A delicate balance ... between the Norse leaders and the Irish kings of the interior, whereby Dublin survived, for the most part, unmolested, and the Norse for their part desisted from serious attempts at conquest'.[27] Meanwhile, the sons, grandsons, great- and great-great-grandsons of Ivar, all the way from Sigtrygg I to Olaf Kvaran (d. 981) and Sigtrygg IV 'Silkbeard' (d. 1042), concentrated their energies – successful except for a temporary exile from Dublin from 902–16, and fluctuating fortunes in York – on maintaining their power along the east–west axis of York and Dublin, two increasingly important trading centres. It was only their final fadeout that allowed Britain and Ireland to settle into something like their later political shapes.

The road to Clontarf: valkyries and the web of war

As we have seen, the long Viking interaction with Ireland and Scotland had massive consequences. Nevertheless, it remained unproductive as regards sagas, biographies or famous endings. For all their importance, there are no stories about the deaths of either Ivar or his associate Olaf. Yet the Irish Viking experience produced one striking ending, at the Battle of Clontarf, fought on Good Friday, 23 April 1014; and one of the great poems of the Viking age, *Darraðarljóð*, 'The Song of the Pennants'; which furthermore gives us some insight into what was the central Viking experience: hard-fought hand-to-hand battle.

If the Battle of Stamford Bridge in 1066 put an end to Viking ambitions in England, Clontarf had done the same thing some fifty years earlier for Ireland. In it Brian Boru, High King of Ireland, faced an army composed as usual of several elements: the Danes of Dublin led by Sigtrygg Silkbeard, great-grandson of Ivar; the Norwegian-descended forces of Sigurd, jarl of Orkney; a hastily recruited band of Vikings led by a renegade deacon called Brodir from the Isle of Man; and the forces of the Irish king of Leinster (for to every Irish High King there was at least one rival, challenger or dissident). The battle ended in complete victory for Brian, who nevertheless died on the field, together with his son and grandson. After it, while the *Óstmenn* or 'Easterners' remained a presence in Ireland up to the time of the Norman invasion a century and a half later, they had only commercial, not military, power.

The main Norse account of the battle, and the poem *Darraðarljóð* attached to it – possibly wrongly – come to us only by strange chance. Both form a kind of coda to the greatest of the sagas of the Icelanders, *Njáls saga*. Njal himself has an Irish name (Níall), but almost all of the action of this saga takes place back home in Iceland. Some of the participants make rather perfunctory voyages abroad, seemingly something of a rite of passage for a proper hero, but the real core of the story concerns not battles for loot and treasure and slaves, but disputes over precedence – asking someone to move down one on a bench is enough to trigger multiple killings – or over divorce settlements, or over hay, one of the dominant motifs of real Icelandic sagas. Icelanders had to feed their cattle indoors over winter, and if spring came late or they miscalculated how many cattle they could keep after the autumn slaughter, farmers could lose all their stock and be wiped out – so asking someone for hay in early spring and being turned down was more than enough to create hard words, reprisals and, in the end, the burning of Njal in his farmstead at Bergthorsknoll, with his wife and sons.

The only warrior to escape the burning, however, is presented as a professional Viking, a friend of the Njalssons, Kari Solmundarson. He rescues two of the Njalssons from attack by other Vikings somewhere in the north of Scotland and escorts them to Jarl Sigurd of Orkney, after which they help Sigurd in battle on the mainland of Scotland and go raiding on their own account down as far as the Isle of Man. Kari goes to Iceland with the Njalssons and marries their sister Helga. He gets away from the burning, hidden by smoke, but his little son dies in the fire after refusing to leave his grandparents.

Kari then embarks on a one-man vendetta against the Burners. At Jarl Sigurd's court in Orkney – where King Sigtrygg of Dublin happens to be paying a visit – he hears one of the Burners telling a lying and shameful story about how Skarphedin Njalsson wept from pain and fear when he was trapped. Kari bursts in and slashes the head off the liar before the whole company. The head bounces on the table before the king and the jarls present. Even by Viking standards this is a breach of etiquette, but people speak up for Kari, and the saga notes prosaically that 'they cleaned off the tables and carried out the dead body.'[28] The business end of the meeting, though, is Sigtrygg of Dublin's request for help against the Irish from Sigurd of Orkney. Sigurd agrees, on condition that he gets to become king of Ireland and to marry Sigtrygg's mother, Kormloth or Gormflaith, an Irish lady, famous beauty and queen of the former Irish High King Niall *Glundubh*, 'black knee'. (One can see how interrelated the Norse and Irish were by this time.) Sigtrygg, however, treacherously makes a similar promise to Brodir, the Viking ex-deacon from the Isle of Man.

Kari then continues his one-man vendetta, but the other participants of the meeting in Orkney sail to battle against Brian. The short account of the battle given in Chapter 157 of *Njáls saga* is fairly close to the much longer account given in the *Cogadh Gaedhel re Gallaibh*. The two forces squared off against each other. Or, to put it the way the *Cogadh* does:

> Then the fearful, murderous, hard-hearted, terrific, vehement, impetuous battalion of the Danmarkians; and the fine, intelligent, acute, fierce, valorous, mighty, royal, gifted, renowned, champions of the Dal Cais [Brian's tribe] . . . met in one place; and there was fought between them a battle, furious, bloody, repulsive, crimson, gory, boisterous, manly, rough, fierce, unmerciful, hostile, on both sides; and they began to hew, and cleave, and stab, and cut . . .[29]

In fact there were, as usual, Scandinavians and Irish on both sides, and even the observers were mixed. Brian's daughter was watching and so to speak cheering on her father's troops, but she was watching with her husband, King Sigtrygg, who eventually became so annoyed that he struck her. Nevertheless, Brian's Irish got the upper hand, though his son Murchadh and his grandson Toirdhelbach were killed.

At the end, though, Brian – who was 88 years old and moreover did not wish to wield weapons on Good Friday – was left almost alone as the fighting moved away from him. Brodir the Viking apostate, who had previously backed out of the battle, eventually noticed the old man praying and was told who he was. He went over and cut him down – after which there are two versions of what happened (see below). Both versions, however, agree that it was a disastrous defeat for the forces of Viking Dublin and the *Inis Gaill*, the islands of the foreigners; while Brian 'was he that released the men of Erinn, and its women, from the bondage and iniquity of the foreigners'.[30]

Such an event might be expected to be marked by portents, as Hastings was by Halley's Comet. *Njáls saga* lists several. At Svinafell in Iceland, blood fell on the priest's Good Friday stole. Another Icelandic priest saw such a vision that he was too shaken to sing Mass. Back in Orkney, there was a man called Harek who had been left behind by Jarl Sigurd but had received a promise from the jarl that he would be the first to learn what happened. In Orkney after the battle he thought he saw the jarl – who had died at Clontarf 'pierced through by a spear'[31] – and went to meet him. But Harek and the jarl rode behind a hill, and neither was ever seen again.

The Song of the Pennants

The most terrible vision, however, came in Caithness, according to the saga, seen by a man called Dorrud. *Darraðar* is the genitive form of the name *Dörruð*, so *Darraðarljóð* could mean 'song of Dorrud'. That name is found nowhere else, though, and it seems that the saga author, who knew the title of the poem, invented the name in order to explain it. General opinion now is that the name means 'Song of the Pennants', or perhaps 'Song of the Spears'. Egil used the word in his poem *Höfuðlausn*, and John Hines has argued that it is there deliberately and imaginatively 'polysemous'.[32]

The poem became much more famous in English after it was translated by Thomas Gray, in 1761 (published 1768), as 'The Fatal Sisters: An Ode'. If *Krákumál* was the favourite Viking image-setter of the nineteenth century, *Darraðarljóð* was the favourite of the century before. Modern scholars, once again, tend to avert their eyes. It has too many of what they regard as Viking clichés in it – though no one disputes its genuineness.

Its most prominent cliché is valkyries. They have certainly become part of the modern Viking 'imaginary', though the most prominent image-maker for them was Richard Wagner, in his opera *Die Walküre*. The operatic connection, with the music for the 'Ride of the Valkyries', has produced a general image of stout ladies in armour, liable to burst into song. The real image is more threatening.

What Dorrud saw was twelve female riders, who dismounted and went into a woman's room. He went up and looked through the window, and saw

> women inside and that they had set up a loom. Men's heads were used for weights (*kljána*), men's intestines for the weft and warp (*viftu ok garn*), a sword for the sword beater (*skeið*), and an arrow for the pin beater (*hræll*).[33]

What they are weaving is, as Thomas Gray put it, 'the crimson web of war' and the fate of those fighting in the battle. It is clear that the twelve women are valkyries – though there were other types of ominous females in Viking folklore, like the 'goddesses' or *dísir* who killed Thidrandi, in another saga, for converting to Christianity.[34] But the women seen by Dorrud *must* be valkyries, for the Old Norse word *val-kyrjar* means 'those who choose the slain', and that is exactly what these women are doing. Both they and their weaving can be seen as developments of natural and widespread observations, or questions, about reality.

First, there is an element of luck in all warfare; as noted in Ecclesiastes, 'The race is not always to the swift, nor the battle to the strong' (9:11).

Great heroes can be killed by puny creatures like Vogg, who avenged King Hrolf on King Hjorvard (see Chapter Two), or just by bad luck. But what makes bad luck? One theory, applied to King Sigmund in 'The Saga of the Volsungs' and then to King Eirik in *Eiríksmál*, is that this is all the doing of Odin, notoriously eager to recruit great champions for his army in Valhalla. The greater the champion you are, the higher the likelihood that Odin will arrange for you to meet death in battle, if necessary appearing himself, as he did to Sigmund, breaking the sword he himself had given Sigmund using his own spear, Gungnir. (Regin would reforge the shards of it for Sigurd into the sword Gram, in the 'broken sword' motif.) It is only an extension of this theory to say that Odin delegates this role to his daughters, the 'choosers of the slain'.

In addition, the idea of the spinners who spin men's and women's lives goes back into prehistory. It is another natural development: no one knows how long a life will be. All lives, short or long, are in the end cut off, like threads. So who does the cutting, and who spins the threads? In ancient Greek, the answer was the *Moirai*, or 'apportioners', three of them, one to spin the thread of life, one to determine its length and one, Atropos, 'the blind fury with th' abhorrèd shears / [who] slits the thin-spun life'.[35] In Norse something like the same role is ascribed to the Norns, three of whom act as the apportioners of fate, their names meaning (roughly) Past (*Urðr*), Present (*Verðandi*) and Future (*Skuld*).

Darraðarljóð takes these ideas a considerable stage further, for in it the valkyries are not just spinning but weaving, a much more complex operation. To follow the image one needs to have some idea of the whole process of loom weaving.[36] This was once of course a very familiar sight in every Norse household, where housewives span their own yarn and wove their own cloth. In essence, single threads need to be woven together. The threads are set up on a vertical frame. These threads (the warp) must be under tension, so each thread needs a weight (loom weights are often found among the remains when weavers' sheds have been burned down). Alternate vertical threads then have to be separated by a bar at the top, the shed-rod, and a movable one lower down, the heddle-rod, so that a horizontal thread (the weft) can be passed through: for instance, odd-numbered vertical threads separated for a passage right to left, after which the process is repeated with even-numbered threads, this time the horizontal thread moving left to right. The horizontal threads are attached to a shuttle, which a skilled weaver flicks from side to side and back again, with proverbial speed: in the Bible Job says, 'my days are swifter than a weaver's shuttle' (7:6). (From this right-to-left and back again movement we have retained the idea of shuttle-runs and shuttle-buses, while the word itself is related to 'shoot'.)

Every now and then, finally, the weaver packs the weft firmly, using a sword-shaped implement called a beater.

All of this, as said above, must have been far more familiar in ancient times, when every farmstead had a loom – there is one set up in the main hall of the Viking Ship Museum at Roskilde in Denmark – and both *Njáls saga* and *Darraðarljóð* use specialized vocabulary that has given translators trouble, such as *skaftir* (heddle-rods?) or *hræll* (given as 'shuttle' above, but some say 'pin-beater'). The whole activity nevertheless creates an image of speed, repetitive but flickering motion. What, though, makes the weaving of the valkyries such a powerful image of battle?

The first thing that is vital to understand is that a battle between two sides is not like a modern game between two sides, though people often compare them. In most modern games there is one focus for attention: the ball. In a battle, everything is going on at once, and any of it may be decisive. Even in a small-scale Viking Age battle one can be sure thousands of missiles would be thrown or shot, many thousands of blows struck. The aggregate would become clear – winning or losing – but what actually decided the result? No one could really tell. Certainly, as said above, when it came to any individual's fate, luck had to play a large part. Luck measured out by the valkyries, or Odin, or other supernatural creatures who might be stalking the battlefield.

As Neil Price puts it in his outstanding account of both 'the Viking Way' and 'the invisible battlefield':

> None of this [supernatural intervention] can be seen by the ordinary Viking, of course, but what else could explain that lucky spear-cast, that man's amazing survival after such a blow, the incredible accuracy of that arrow? Why else would such a dexterous warrior trip like that, and how could such an imbecile manage to bring down that veteran of many battles? Where did this awful downpour come from, when the sky was clear an hour ago?[37]

No wonder Vikings carried lucky charms and were sometimes buried with them (like the amulet, jackdaw wing and boar's tusk of the horribly mutilated casualty at Repton). But unpredictability is hard to accept, as is the idea that everything is random chance, and that is where the valkyries weaving the web of war come in.

Weaving demonstrates the creation of something fixed and solid from separate strands, by fast and flickering motion: uncertain present becoming unalterable past, one might say. Also, in some cases, the creation of a pattern. And that is exactly what the valkyries do, with human lives, to determine the course of a battle. And that is precisely what they are doing as they chant the 88-line poem.

In the first three ten-line stanzas they describe what they are doing. They set up the weighted warp threads, which are the lives of men. They cross the warp (*vefr*) of men, that is, the threads of life, with a red weft (*rauðum vefti*), death in battle. They beat and pack the woven threads with a *skeið* or 'sword-beater'. To quote Gray again (with an echo of the witches in *Macbeth*):

> Shafts for shuttles, dipt in gore,
> Shoot the trembling cords along.
> Sword, that once a monarch bore,
> Keep the tissue close and strong.

The original actually says nothing about 'once a monarch bore' – Gray is trying to raise the tone – but makes it clear that what the valkyries are doing is simultaneously packing the fabric with their sword-like 'beaters' and controlling the play of swords on the battlefield; in Russell Poole's translation, 'With our swords we must strike / this fabric of victory'. All the valkyries' tools and materials are death-related: the threads are entrails, the loom weights are severed heads, the heddle-rods are spears, the shuttles are arrows, and the whole web is packed tight with swords.

Then three eight-line stanzas each begin, 'Let us wind, wind, the web of the pennants'. Poole points out that winding up a large web as the weaving progressed, with all its loom weights attached – like the strip of a sail in the Roskilde demonstration – was heavy work, involving the use of levers set into the head rod, and sometimes done cooperatively, so that the poem is a kind of work song, of a realistic kind. But looking at it magically, what the valkyries are doing is determining what is happening on a battlefield far away: 'we will go forward', they sing, 'where our friends are trading weapons'. We can see the shields that guarded the king, but 'let us not let his life leave him. Only valkyries can choose the dead'.

In three further eight-line stanzas they sing the result of the battle: 'Lands will now be ruled by those who once inhabited only headlands ... the men of Ireland will suffer a grief which will never grow old ... the sky will be stained with blood as the battle wardens sing their song'. Finally the weavers congratulate themselves:

> we sang well many songs of victory for the young king. Let the one who listens learn the song of the spear-women and teach it to many. Now let us ride our horses hard, bare-backed, with drawn swords, away from here.[38]

The poem moves from the perfect tense, in describing what has been set up, to the present tense, to tell what is currently happening, to the future, detailing what the valkyries will do, and then it is over, the web is woven (*vefr ofinn*). As Poole says, it's a 'running commentary' in which the valkyries both act out and decide what happens to the combatants on the battlefield. Even the stages of the battle are represented, from the exchange of thrown spears, the *skothríð* or 'storm of shot', to the close-quarter work with sword and shield. As Professor Price points out, the names of valkyries are aspects of the battle experience: Paralysis, Mist or Confusion, Din, Sword-time, Spear-shower, Shield-gnawer.[39] 'The Song of the Pennants' is acting out a battle, and its weaving image is surprisingly realistic.

What caught the eighteenth-century fancy, however – and has on the whole disgusted the more tender sensibilities of the twentieth- and twenty-first centuries – is the delight in, to put it no more frankly than the poem does, blood and guts. But one has to say again that the image is a complex one – just as 'Ragnar's Death Song', that other dethroned favourite, is more complex emotionally than scholars have allowed – and, moreover, an image that tries to say something about the nature of reality. Events are not in our control. Our intentions clash with other people's. Outcomes are uncertain. All of which is absolutely true of human conflict.

One doubt, though, about 'The Song of the Pennants' is that the battle described does not sound much like Clontarf, though it does have rather close echoes of Norse experience in Ireland. The Irish will know lasting grief? Not Clontarf. The battle will see new lands acquired by people who once ruled only headlands? Very apt for Norsemen operating from island bases in the Hebrides, but not at Clontarf. And victory for a young king? Again, not Clontarf, for the victor Brian Boru was 88. It looks as if this was a poem composed on another occasion: Nora Chadwick pointed to a victory won almost a hundred years before, in 919, over the Irish king Níall *Glundubh*, 'black knee'.[40] The victor then was also a King Sigtrygg, and both battles were fought near Dublin, so the two events could easily have been confused. Or, the poem might have been picked up by the author of *Njáls saga* and just grafted on to his main narrative as too good to waste. Poems can last a long time. Many centuries later, Walter Scott reported that the song was still known in Orkney. When an antiquarian clergyman started to read Gray's version to the inhabitants of Ronaldsay, they stopped him, saying they knew it already and that they had even sung it to him before, in their own Norse dialect (which he hadn't understood). They called it 'The Magicians', or 'The Enchantresses'.[41]

'The Song of the Pennants' was not the last act for the saga author, who also gives his own account of the death of Brian Boru, which differs from the Irish account of the *Cogadh Gaedhel re Gallaibh*. Both stories agree that Brian was left unguarded as his men pursued the fleeing Vikings and was then seen by one Brodir (Norse version) or Brodar (Irish version). The Irish account says that 'Earl Brodar' at first walked past the old man, until one of his companions recognized him. Brian and Brodar then struck at each other, Brian severing both Brodar's legs and Brodar splitting Brian's skull.[42] In the Norse version there is no counter-stroke from Brian (who was after all 88 years of age and, as we have already heard, did not wish to wield weapons on Good Friday). Brodir cuts him down. The blow simultaneously beheads the king and cuts the arm off a boy who threw up an arm to protect him: the king's blood spills on to the stump and heals it immediately.[43]

The saga account then goes on to say, more plausibly, that when the king's men hear Brodir boasting that he has felled the king, they turn back and take Brodir alive, smothering his men's weapons with tree branches. The captors are Kerthjalfad, the king's foster-son, and a Viking mercenary on Brian's side – not the only one – called Ulf of Hreda. Ulf cuts Brodir's belly open, 'and unwound his intestines from his stomach by leading him round and round an oak tree; and Brodir did not die until they had all been pulled out of him'.[44] Brodir, the Christian apostate from the Isle of Man, had the misfortune of being one of the *Gaddgeðlar* of mixed race and uncertain religion whom nobody liked. Killing not only a king, but a very old man, may have been regarded as deserving special punishment.

The smart answer of Thorstein Sidu-Hallsson

According to *Njáls saga*, Kerthjalfad, by contrast, does grant his life to an Icelander who had been fighting against him, one Thorstein Sidu-Hallsson. When the battle has been decided and the losers are running for their lives with Kerthjalfad after them, there is one man who does not run, and that is Thorstein. When Kerthjalfad catches up with him, Thorstein is casually tying his shoelace. The Irish prince asks why he isn't running. 'Because I can't reach home tonight,' says Thorstein, 'my home's out in Iceland.'[45] As wise-crack answers go – they are something of an artform in Icelandic sagas – this is not a terribly good one, though good enough to be repeated in Thorstein's own saga as well as *Njáls saga*. One should ask what are the inner mechanics of this demonstration of self-possession by Thorstein, and of generosity by Kerthjalfad.

Unpacking the dynamics of a fictional conversation may seem a pointless or impossible task, but it can show how people thought or were expected to think; and there is now a powerful tool available, generally called 'pragmatic linguistics', most readily defined as the art of hearing what people don't say. Most of us are quite good at it, but it is strongly dependent on cultural assumptions.

In this case, one begins by asking what would be the likeliest reason for not running from a lost battle. The short answer is that you would demonstrate that – remembering Hjalti's *Bjarkamál* stanzas – you are one of the *ættum góðir men*, the 'men of good birth', *þeir es ekki flygja*, 'those who do not flee'. Very likely we are meant to understand that that is Thorstein's secret motivation. Running for your life is undignified behaviour.

On the other hand, not fleeing is a signal that you are not afraid. And even today – in the rougher parts of town – wearing a tattoo reading 'No Fear' is likely to be taken ill by those whose self-image requires that they *should* be feared. It is a challenge. And challenges, like dares, have to be taken up.

Tying a shoelace can therefore be seen as a provocative act – or alternatively, as a compliment. Putting yourself at someone's mercy may show that you trust them to act honourably and not take advantage. This is what happens in the short but excellent Icelandic short story 'The Tale of Thorstein Staff-struck'.[46] There the great champion Bjarni of Hof is forced by public opinion to take revenge on a poor farmer called Thorstein, though secretly he thinks that his own men have been in the wrong all along. The two fight for a long time and then agree to take a break. Bjarni puts his sword down, and Thorstein picks it up and comments on it. Bjarni is at his mercy, then, but Thorstein merely hands the sword back. They fight on, and then Bjarni says, 'My shoelace is loose.' Thorstein tells him to tie it up, and this time not only takes no advantage but even lends his opponent a shield to replace his broken one, and a sword with its edge undulled. Still they fight on, but eventually Bjarni concedes the competition in fairness – if that's the word for it; sportsmanship, maybe? The Viking word is *drengskapr*, see Chapter Nine – and they come to a deal, which involves taking their anger out on those who have pushed the pair of them into fighting.

This is a happy ending, between two honourable men. It will be remembered, though, that yet another Thorstein – son of Egil – does not act the same way. In a dispute over grazing, a man called Thrand says to him, 'Now you'll find out whether I'm scared of your threats, Thorstein' and sits down to tie his shoe.[47] Now that is not a compliment but a provocation, in fact a gesture of contempt, a challenge, a dare. Thrand said he wasn't scared of Thorstein Egilsson and now he is proving it, and that's offensive. As one might expect from one of the notoriously mean and touchy *Myramenn*, Thorstein instantly beheads him.

Kerthjalfad could, then, take Thorstein Sidu-Hallsson's behaviour as a display of contempt, and at that moment it was unlikely to be taken as a gesture of trust. So he asks his question, and the wrong answer here would surely be fatal. Thorstein's answer, 'Because I can't reach home tonight,' shifts the situation on to a different plane. It implies that the other losers are not fleeing for their lives but are running just because they are anxious to get home. So Thorstein not joining them does not mean that he scorns to flee (and so is superior morally to the others), or that he is not afraid of Kerthjalfad (because running isn't about saving your life, just about getting home) – merely that he is in a different situation from the others. Fleeing and not fleeing are just options dictated by circumstance – in this case, Thorstein's home being unreachable.

Note that Thorstein is not surrendering. He does not throw down his weapons, kneel and beg for mercy. That would be undignified too. But he stakes no claim to superiority, offers no challenge, no threat. It is as if he is offering Kerthjalfad a draw. By doing so he puts Kerthjalfad in a slightly difficult position. He could say, 'Well, *you* won't see Iceland again', and strike Thorstein down, but there is no credit in killing someone defenceless. What Thorstein has done is put himself in a neutral position: not quite submissive, not at all threatening or challenging. Kerthjalfad can spare him without losing face.[48]

In a way, that is what happened with the Vikings in Ireland as a whole. After Clontarf they did not man their ships and sail away, turning their backs on the island in flight. But they abandoned any claim to sovereignty or domination. They ceased to be a threat. They lived on for generations as a commercial community, the *Óstmenn* of Dublin and the other ports. Sigtrygg, great-great-grandson of Ivar, lived on until 1042, but after that the Ivar dynasty is unrecorded.

Nevertheless, as far as we can tell, there was very little assimilation. There was high-class intermarriage between Irish and Viking families; there must have been a good deal of concubinage to produce the *Gaddgeðlar*; and DNA evidence from modern Iceland indicates a considerable Celtic strand in the population, almost entirely inherited through the female line.[49] But the communities didn't mingle on even terms. There was too high a level of linguistic difference and of cultural intolerance. The Viking experience in Ireland, then, ended in failure.

Things would be different elsewhere.

SEVEN

Two Big Winners:
The Road to Normandy

I n the long term and real world, the most successful Viking of all time
must be *Göngu-Hrólfr*, whom the Victorians called Ganger-Hrolf,
which means not Hrolf 'Gang-leader', applicable though that is, but
Hrolf 'the Walker'. He was the founder of the Duchy of Normandy, ceded
to him by Charles the Simple of France about the year 911. To quote
Orkneyinga saga ('The Saga of the Jarls of Orkney'), he was the son of Jarl
Rognvald of Norway and his wife Ragnhild,

> and it was their son Hrolf who conquered Normandy. This Hrolf
> was so big that no horse could carry him, which is why he was
> given the name *Göngu-Hrólfr*. The earls of Rouen and the kings
> of England are descended from him.[1]

He was the great-great-grandfather of William the Conqueror (and so
an ancestor of the present Queen of the United Kingdom, Elizabeth II).
The name the Franks gave him, Rollo, has gained new if mistaken fame
from the TV series *Vikings*.

Nor was his influence only on genealogy and celebrity, for the duchy
he founded spawned a whole series of Norman conquerors, who in the
centuries after 1066 came to rule Sicily, Cyprus, much of modern Greece,
the kingdom of Outremer in what is now Israel and Lebanon, and eventually even the Canary Islands. Historians have been reluctant to see any
carry-over from the Vikings in this, noting that the Normans were rapidly
assimilated into French ways, becoming Christians, speaking Norman-
French, and most of all abandoning the old Viking axe-and-ship raiding
pattern in favour of the new Frankish weapon-system. This combined
mounted lancers and foot archers, including crossbows, and not only did
it win at Hastings, it also, fifteen years later at the Battle of Dyrrhachium
in what is now Albania, won the replay.[2] There the Byzantine emperor's
famed Varangian Guard (by now largely dispossessed Anglo-Saxon or

Anglo-Danish axemen) once again dealt with charges from lancers fairly easily, but made the mistake of following up too enthusiastically and were cut off, forced to keep close order by the threat of mounted charges, and then shot by archers in a kind of scissors-paper-stone contest.

Nevertheless, there is rather surprising evidence – so surprising that it has generally gone unnoticed – to suggest that Viking legends remained known even in southern Europe for longer than the consensus view would have it. It comes from Santa María la Real, Sangüesa, in northern Spain. A whole century after Hastings, masons employed to sculpt the front of the church opted for some reason to decorate it with scenes from the legend of Sigurd and the Nibelungs as told in the poems of the Codex Regius. One can still see quite clearly Sigurd stabbing the dragon Fafnir from below; Sigurd roasting the dragon's heart that enabled him to hear the warnings of the birds; the birds themselves sitting behind him; and, facing all this, badly worn but recognizable, Sigurd's daughter Svanhild being trampled to death by the horses of King Iormunrekk. Why the masons thought this was appropriate, what the local bishop made of it all, and what in the world the inhabitants of Sangüesa thought about these strange figures for the next eight centuries – none of this has ever been explained. And when the scenes were belatedly recognized, in 1959, the recognition was immediately forgotten, until the rediscovery was made by Andrew Breeze of Pamplona University in 1991.[3] Professor Breeze accepts Cynthia Milton's suggestion of 1959 that the Sigurd legends may have been the idea of a Norwegian knight of the Knights Hospitaller of St John, who were in charge of the defence of Sangüesa from 1131 to 1351. This could be so, but Norman knights were much more common in southern Europe in the twelfth century than Norwegian ones. Breeze, and Milton before him, furthermore lists a number of neglected late-period Sigurd scenes from England, the Isle of Man and even Freising, near Munich; there may be more, still unrecognized.

We see, alas, what we expect to see, and ignore what doesn't fit. But it is certain at least that Norse mythology and heroic legend remained alive in Scandinavia (not just Iceland), and perhaps in Normandy, longer than the official unification and Christianization narrative would claim. A piece of runic graffiti found in the permafrost of Bergen waterfront shows that as late as 1185, up in the north, someone was wishing a friend well in the names of Thor and Odin ('Thor receive you! Odin own you!') – and it is not the only one.[4] There is dispute about what Raoul de Tesson meant by shouting *Tur aie!* at the Battle of Val-ès-Dunes in Normandy (1047), as reported in the *Roman de Rou* or 'Romance of Rollo', by the Jersey poet Wace.[5] Probably he was just identifying himself as Lord of Thury, not calling on Thor for help. But *Tur aie!* is very similar to the normal Norman war cry *Dex aie!* (God help!) which Wace quotes immediately afterwards. Maybe Wace (or a scribe) took it to mean 'Thor help!'

Whatever happened later, it is certainly true that Ganger-Hrolf, unlike most of the Viking heroes in this book, not only died in his bed but is now commemorated by a tomb in the cathedral of Rouen, under a splendid effigy with the Latin inscription 'Rollo lies in his temple, father and first Duke of the Normandy, which he devastated and founded. Worn out by toil, he died aged more than eighty, in the year 933.'

No famous last stand or heroic defiance of death for him, then – and so, accordingly, no real saga. There is a 'Saga of Göngu-Hrolf', but it is totally fictitious and deals for the most part with romantic adventures in Russia. The translators of *Orkneyinga saga* note severely, at the foot of the quotation above, that Rognvald's son 'should not be confused with his namesake, the hero of *Göngu-Hrolfs saga*', which they also translated.[6] A century and a half later someone wrote this biographical saga, as the author indeed declares, just for people's entertainment, on a historical basis of nothing but a name. It is somehow appropriate that investigation has also revealed that the bones under the marble tomb cannot be those of Hrolf/Rollo.[7]

Despite his tomb and his frequent appearance in Frankish annals, then, almost nothing is known for sure about the real-life Ganger-Hrolf. Nevertheless his career is instructive, first for the history of the Carolingian kingdom of Francia, much more extensive even than modern France; but also, more relevantly for this work, for what it suggests about two vital Viking issues: profitability and integration. To understand these, one has both to speculate (as said above, not a method popular with historians) and to take in evidence from sources underused by historians: linguistic history, and the information concealed in place names.

Hastein makes a killing

Ganger-Hrolf, it should be said, has a competitor for the title of Most Successful Viking, if not in the very longest long term. This was a man of whose name we cannot even be sure. He figures prominently in, first, the *Historia Normannorum* or 'History of the Normans', completed shortly before 1020 by Dudo of Saint-Quentin, a cleric writing for Hrolf's great-grandson Duke Richard II – Dudo served as his chancellor; and following that, in the *Gesta Normannorum Ducum* or 'Deeds of the Dukes of the Normans', written by a monk called William of Jumièges some fifty years later, with several further supplements by different authors.[8]

The name of Hrolf's predecessor and competitor for the Most Successful title is rendered in Dudo's Latin as 'Alstignus', while William prefers 'Hastingus'. He also appears in the *Anglo-Saxon Chronicle* as 'Hæsten', and his real name may well have been *Hásteinn*, though a number of other suggestions have been made. (For convenience, Hastein is here adopted throughout.) Whatever his name, his career and exploits are recorded widely, notably by a whole sequence of Arabic writers (who did not know his name at all), for he led a long and extraordinarily adventurous raid into Moorish Spain, from where he went on to southern France, and (perhaps only in legend) on to Italy with the ambition of sacking Rome. The raid ended badly – or at least with heavy casualties, though it may still have made a substantial profit for the survivors – and Hastein went on to contest with Hrolf for power in Francia and, more than thirty years later, to give Alfred the Great of Wessex a great deal of trouble, perhaps in the end and remarkably, getting the better even of him.

His career, as reconstructed, goes like this. According to William of Jumièges, the Danes, suffering from overpopulation because of the habit among the men of taking many wives, had a law by which all sons had to be expelled except for the recognized heir. Among those expelled was one 'Bier Costae Ferrae', or Bjorn Ironside, met already in Chapter Four as one of the less well authenticated sons of Ragnar Lodbrok. Like Adam of Bremen, and at about the same time, William uses the name or nickname 'Lotrocus', though he knows nothing of any of the better-recorded Ragnarssons. He declares that King Lotrocus expelled his son Bjorn, and that Bjorn went into exile with his *pedagogus* Hastein. 'Pedagogue' is an odd word to use in this context, for it normally means the guide or teacher of a schoolboy, in Roman times usually a slave, and one cannot see what kind of relationship this would correspond to in the Viking world. Be that as it may, the exiled younger sons set sail, not forgetting to mark departure by human sacrifice, 'pouring out human blood to their god Thor'.[9]

According to William, the pair then arrived, in 851, at the city of Noyon in the Vermandois. This seems to be a mistake for 859.[10] If one ignores William's error for the moment, it seems that in 859, and probably remembering the successful raid on Paris by Ragnar a few years earlier (7,000 pounds of silver as well as unknown amounts of loot taken before the ransom was paid), Bjorn made another attack on Paris. It is quite likely that the repeat raid gave rise to the belief that this second leader was the son of the first. Before resistance could be organized, Bjorn had taken the abbey of St Denis and had had to be paid off with astonishing amounts of gold and silver. The Franks under Charles the Bald then did manage to gather a force large enough to pursue Bjorn and besiege him in his camp at Oissel, on the Seine 13 km (8 mi.) south of Rouen, but were then drawn off by the ongoing civil war between Charlemagne's descendants. Charles took the easy if short-sighted course of hiring another Viking war band under a man called Weland (*Vǫlundr*) to finish Bjorn off for him, but Bjorn simply paid Weland a cut of his profits to let him withdraw. One imagines that Weland had already received a payment in advance from Charles – how were these deals arranged when neither side could trust the other? – so everyone did well, except, of course, the looted Frankish churches and unfortunate Frankish taxpayers. (Many years later, in the entry for 1011, the *Anglo-Saxon Chronicle* would lament that the worst thing a king could do was dither: 'All these misfortunes befell us through lack of decision, in that they were not offered a pay-off in time; only after they had done great evil, *then* a truce and peace was made with them.'[11])

By 859, however, still following the account of William of Jumièges, Bjorn and Hastein really had joined up and arrived at Noyon, on the river Oise, a tributary of the Seine. William, probably drawing on local memories in his own home, says they killed the bishop of Noyon, burned down William's own monastery of Jumièges, sailed on to Rouen, made a base, which included slave quarters, on an island near Nantes, and burned down Angers, Tours and Orléans as well as half a dozen other cities. They kept this up, he thinks, for about thirty years.

William's chronology and his whole itinerary of devastation must be even more badly out here, for in fact the next and most famous exploit of the Bjorn–Hastein partnership is much better dated and must have started very soon after the attack on Noyon. According to Dudo this time, but followed by William, it was Hastein who decided that the pair should set their sights higher and attack the most famous city of all, not Paris or Rouen or Tours but Rome, aiming, says William, at 'the imperial crown' – an unlikely ambition, one must say, for the most ambitious of Vikings, since it had no money attached to it, only prestige. Both Dudo and William then tell a circumstantial story of how the Vikings, having got themselves all the way across the Bay of Biscay, round Portugal and through the Strait of Gibraltar, headed on without incident to Italy. There they found themselves at the city of Luna (modern Luni), near the Gulf of La Spezia. Thinking this was Rome, but finding its walls unscalable, the Vikings pretended that their lord wished to be baptized before death and then to be buried in the monastery. Of course, the coffin was a Trojan horse, full of weapons as well as containing Hastein, and at the right moment the mourners seized the weapons and took the city. Finding out too late that he had conquered a minor city, not Rome, Hastein ordered a massacre before sailing back to Francia.[12]

Almost all of this must be nonsense – the fake coffin trick is widely reported, ascribed for instance much later to Harald *Harðráði* and turning up yet again in the TV series *Vikings* (series 3, episode 10); and sailing from northern France through the Strait of Gibraltar and on to Italy without incident cannot be true. But in fact something like it did take place and is recorded, with dates and details, by much more reliable contemporary sources in Arabic.

As reported in the previous chapter, by the 850s the Vikings were not unknown to the Moorish world of Spain, for in the year 844–5 (AH 230) an attack, probably made from Viking bases in Ireland, is recorded by one Ibn al-Khutia (his name means 'son of the Gothic woman', a reminder of the earlier Gothic conquest of Spain).[13] His account is corroborated by Christian Spanish chronicles, which report marauders in Asturia, northern Spain, in the summer of 844. Later that year they came down with many ships (one report says eighty, another 54) and sailed boldly up the Guadalquivir to Seville. According to al-Khutia, and the much later writer Ibn Adhari, the 'Madjus' (pagans, fire-worshippers) took Seville and held it for some weeks, burning down the great mosque, until the emir Abd ar-Rahman II gathered his forces. The invaders fell back, using their many captives as a bargaining point, but were eventually defeated, many ships being burned. The emir, it is said, sent two hundred heads to Tangiers as tokens of his victory. The differing accounts nevertheless suggest that the Vikings had a long run of success, with merely local forces being afraid to challenge them, and a number, maybe a large number, got away with who knows how much in loot.

The Muslim world was alarmed enough to send an embassy (described in Chapter Six) to the 'king of the Madjus' – the account of which, as said above, contains little useful information and a large amount of male fantasy. But flirtatious ambassadors aside, reports on the Seville raid back in the Viking world may have pointed to opportunities as much as risks. One thing was absolutely certain: the Muslims had even more gold and silver, *a great deal* more gold and silver, than even the richest of Frankish or English churches and monasteries. Risks, in any case, were part of the day's work.

In 859 (AH 245), then, the Vikings tried again, and this extended raid, or expedition, which lasted until 861, must be the one of which Dudo and William give their very truncated version. Ibn Adhari is this time the main reporter, and though he lived even later than Dudo and William he is thought to have been copying from authors of the tenth century, maybe within living memory of what happened.

According to him, the Madjus arrived in 62 ships. They were seen coming, for the Muslims by this time had guard ships out, and when they got to the mouth of the Guadalquivir, aiming for Seville again, they found strong forces waiting for them. So they went on to Algeciras by the Strait of Gibraltar, which they took, once more burning down the mosque, before crossing over into Africa. They took many prisoners there, offering some for ransom, and sailed on to hit the Balearics – Mallorca, Menorca and Formentera – all of them probably relatively undefended. Then they went on into France and sailed up the Rhône, at which point reports come in from Frankish chronicles. They plundered Nîmes and Arles, as usual from an island base in the Camargue. It was at this point – if there is any truth in Dudo's and William's reports at all, which by this stage begin to look at least plausible – that they went on to Italy with the ambition of attacking Rome (or anywhere else that looked a likely prospect).

So far so good, one might say, but getting the loot back was often a problem. The returning ships were intercepted by the fleet of Emir Muhammad of Cordoba, and at least a few were lost, and many more are said to have foundered in a storm in the Bay of Biscay. Before that, however, they had had another large payday on the return voyage, reaching Pamplona in northwest Spain, where they captured and then ransomed its Christian governor, Garcia, for – it is said – 90,000 gold dinars, or nearly half a ton of gold. Quite how much this would come to in terms of the usual Viking currency, pounds of silver, is hard to say. The ratio was probably much less than the current 75:1, but even at 12:1 or 15:1 Hastein and Bjorn's payoff for the governor alone would come out to half as much again as what Ragnar got for Paris. If the ships carrying the money got back safely – and Hastein and Bjorn did get back, and one can bet that the big money never went very far from their safe-keeping – then the survivors must have thought they had had a very profitable trip indeed.

To Vikings looking back, the 860s and 870s must have been remembered as a happy time for them, and conversely a very unhappy one for the inhabitants of Ireland and Britain and northwest Europe generally. In 865 the Ragnarssons launched their invasion of England, which led to the takeover of three Anglo-Saxon kingdoms, reaching a high point in 876, when their successors very nearly eliminated Alfred as king of the last hold-out, Wessex. France must also have been alive with opportunist war bands, though Hastein, no doubt loaded with loot from his Mediterranean expedition, and even more with prestige, switched his attention from the Seine to the Loire. There, following the well-tried Viking practice, he set up an island base at Noirmoutier. In 866, in alliance with the Bretons, he killed Count Robert the Strong in battle at Brissarthe. In 872 he not only captured Angers, on the Loire, but instead of razing it to the ground as usual he settled in as its new master – a dangerous escalation, parallel to the Viking takeover of York and the subsequent sharing out of land in Northumbria for permanent settlement at almost the same time. Though he was dislodged by for once effective counter-action, Hastein merely retreated to Noirmoutier to remain a lasting menace.[14]

Resistance was, however, stiffening. Alfred beat a Viking army at Edington in 879 and forced a treaty on their king, Guthrum. In 885 another large-scale attack on Paris met serious if unofficial resistance, led by Count Odo, whose father had been killed by Vikings twenty years earlier. The resisters were promptly let down by their king, Charles the Fat, but Odo came again and won another victory, at Montfaucon, in 888, this time against Hastein. Hastein, predictably undismayed, was back again threatening Paris in 889, but France was no longer a place for easy pickings, and Hastein began to look across the Channel.

Hrolf and Hastein: competition among the predators

At about this time, however, Hrolf – or Rollo, as the Norman chroniclers chose to call him – must have appeared on the scene. If he died in his eighties in 933, as his tomb asserts, then he would have been in his prime as a warrior by about 880. Since he was the ancestor of Dudo of Saint-Quentin's patron Duke Richard II, Hrolf was bound to get a good write-up in 'The History of the Normans', but Dudo's chronology is non-existent, and the story of his interaction with Hastein (Alstignus) is hard, though not impossible, to resolve.

One clue is that according to Dudo, Hrolf, having been expelled from Denmark by his father, in the usual unlikely story, then heads not for Francia but for England, led by a dream. There he makes a deal with an English king called Athelstan. Even in Dudo's shaky chronology this can hardly be the famous King Athelstan, Alfred's grandson and Egil Skallagrimsson's employer, who reigned from 924 to 939 and died in his forties even later than Hrolf did as an octogenarian: the two men were a good two generations apart. However, part of the deal between Athelstan's grandfather Alfred and the Viking king Guthrum was that the latter should accept baptism and take a baptismal name – which was Athelstan. Guthrum/Athelstan then established himself as King of East Anglia, ruling an English population under Danish control and attracting increasing numbers of Danish permanent settlers. East Anglia then, like Northumbria and Danish Mercia, remained liable to assist Viking armies while officially at peace with Wessex and English Mercia.

A deal with the East Anglians in the 880s, then, looks quite a likely alliance for a newcomer on the raiding scene, though an ominous one for the future. The idea is contradicted by Dudo, who declares that Hrolf's attack on Walcheren, at the mouth of the Scheldt (datable to 870), was rescued by English supplies and reinforcements, for which Hrolf was suitably grateful; and also by Dudo's assertion, with one of his very rare dates, that following Walcheren Hrolf made yet another attack, in 876 on Jumièges and the by then ruined city of Rouen, which would eventually be his capital.[15]

In the early 870s it is unlikely that any pro-Viking ruler in England would have had resources to spare or any interest in helping out a competitor. In the 880s, by contrast, they might have had restless subjects to employ safely and profitably overseas. But as Dudo's editor bluntly comments, 'enough can be deduced from the surviving contemporary sources to demonstrate that [Dudo's] history is all wrong, throughout the work.'[16] The best that can be hoped for is a general picture, based presumably and at best on oral recollections by old men in the 1010s, of what grandfather had told them about events more than a hundred years before. (And it should not be forgotten that no Viking is likely to have had any idea of the Anno Domini system of recording dates: after a few years had elapsed, all estimates could be well off.)

Nevertheless, one interesting hint for the future was Anglo-Danish involvement across the Channel. Another was relationships between poachers and gamekeepers, Viking incomers on the make against Vikings with their own established interests to guard – in this case, Hrolf versus Hastein. And here Dudo, followed by William, does for once have an interesting story to tell.

According to both, Hrolf called a council of war at Rouen, where his men told him, 'as if having foreknowledge of future events . . . "This land is fertile . . . but it is devoid of warriors and knights. Let us subject it to our power, and claim it as our own".'[17] Dudo, of course, writing 150 years later, *did* have knowledge of future events and was writing a retrospective account of the foundation of Normandy, an 'origin myth', with this as a crucial moment. And in fact the moment when Vikings decided to stop being raiders and start being colonists really *was* a crucial moment. Though when it was, no one can now tell, nor can one know what affected the decision.

Dudo then goes on to say, however, that Ragnold, the Frankish leader, called Hastein to him and said, 'You, who are sprung from that same nation: give us your advice on this affair.' One may well ask why Hastein was being asked to advise the Franks, and William of Jumièges, supplementing the story, explains that Hastein had been granted the town of Chartres, so that he now had a stake in seeing off raiders.[18] Hastein accordingly agreed to act as an ambassador to the new invaders, and he and Hrolf's men then had a conversation, perhaps calling out across the river, as Byrhtnoth and the Viking spokesman do in the Old English poem *The Battle of Maldon*, fought a century later. The conversation, with my comments appended, goes like this:

Hastein says that as 'representative of the king's authority', he commands them to say 'who you are, and where you come from, and what you want?' [Tactless, for Vikings are unlikely to respect any king's authority, and respond badly to commands.]

They reply: 'We are Danes, and we have sailed from Dacia. We come to conquer Francia.' [Plain-speaking with a vengeance.]

Hastein: 'By what title does your chief hold office?' [Someone like Hastein would not need to ask such a question: this is the question of someone used to an organized state with a clear chain of command.]

The natural reply is: 'By none, because we are equal in power.' [Not true in fact, but a Viking asset was very likely their 'flat' social structure. Killing their leaders was not as demoralizing to them as it was to other armies.]

Hastein then asks what has brought them. Is it by any chance the fame of a certain Hastein, i.e. himself? [Is he fishing for compliments?]

'We have. Now that one was marked out by a good omen, and he made a good beginning, but he was fated to die a bad death in the end.' [Perhaps they recognized him and were applying some psychological pressure.]

Finally, the vital question: 'Are you willing to bow your necks to Charles, king of France . . . and accept many grants of land from him?' [A demand plus a sweetener.]

Predictably, 'We will never bow the neck to any man . . . That grant of land will suit us best which we win for ourselves, with weapons and the sweat of battle.' And the Danes tell the ambassadors to be off, and quick about it.[19]

Hastein then goes back to report that he thought it too risky to offer battle. But saying this, however sensible, always laid someone open to the charge of cowardice, or in this case treachery, and a Frank called Roland says contemptuously, 'Why are you all taking this man's advice? The wolf will never be caught by the wolf, nor the fox by the fox.' Stung by these words, Hastein says: 'From now onwards there will be no word against battle spoken by me.'[20]

Roland, the brave Frank, then leads an attack on the Danish earthwork and charges through its gateway, apparently left unblocked. But of course it is a trap, and he is killed. The others, Ragnold and Hastein among them, look at his dead followers and, according to Dudo, 'turned their backs and escaped in flight'. The curious thing is that Dudo modifies the sentence just quoted with the word *hilares*:[21] they fled 'laughing'. What at? The gullibility of poor Roland? Relief at their own safety? Or, possibly, satisfaction by Hastein – marked out by William as *per omnia fraudulentissim[us]*, 'most deceitful in every way'[22] – at seeing someone taken in by what may have been his own collusion, a trick to get rid of a danger man. Later copyists changed the word to *celeres*: they fled 'rapidly'.

Dudo has no more to say about Hastein and from then on follows the career of Hrolf/Rollo, which he portrays as a sequence of triumphant battles in England supporting the mysterious Athelstan, and in France using crafty if unlikely devices like making a fort out of animal carcases with the flayed hides hanging down, a sight that completely daunts attackers. Dudo concedes that Hrolf was actually defeated at Chartres – though this seems to have been many years later – William further explaining to his patrons, Hrolf's descendants, that Hrolf retreated from his unsuccessful siege of the town 'as a wise man, not a timid coward'.[23] (The worst feature of Latin chronicles is that there are never any shades of grey: heroes are always heroic, villains always villainous. That's why it's such a relief to read a saga.) By that time, however, as far as William was concerned, Hastein was out of the story. He was tricked into abandoning his grant of Chartres by a warning that King Charles was out to get him and, 'Terrified by these words', sold out to Count Theobald of Arles. He collected all his possessions (this at least sounds realistic), but then, William says vaguely, *peregre profectus disparuit* – he 'wandered off and disappeared'.[24]

He did not. Hastein does not sound the sort to have been 'terrified', and he quite certainly did not disappear, whatever William may have thought. But the Dudo/William 'origin myth' continues to the big scene in which Hrolf 'put[s] his hands between the hands of the [Frankish] king, which neither his father, nor his grandfather, nor his great-grandfather had done for any man'.[25] In exchange for this he is granted 'as an allod and property' (we might say freehold) all Normandy between the river Epte and the sea, as well as the king's daughter as his wife. Further conditions are that he undergo baptism and – the important one – that Hrolf will now defend the mouth of the Seine, and so close off one of the main Viking approach routes. The grant was extended eastwards in 924 and 933, first to the land round Caen and Bayeux and then to the peninsula of Cotentin and Avranches.

In a famous scene, the assembled bishops say that for a grant like that, the new duke ought to kiss the king's foot, but Hrolf flatly refuses: 'I will never bow my knees at the knees of any man, and no man's foot will I kiss.' (This is very like the 'wildlings' in *Game of Thrones*, who despise 'kneelers'; or the Victorian poem 'The Private of the Buffs', commemorating Private Moyes, who when captured during the Opium Wars refused to kow-tow to a Chinese mandarin and was executed for it.) Dudo adds comedy, for Hrolf orders one of his men to kiss the king's foot as his proxy, but the Viking, stubborn as his leader, hoists the foot in the air instead of grovelling 'and laid the king flat on his back'.[26] Victorian rankers, Viking rankers: both groups obedient only up to a very limited point, and not subservient at all.

Hastein's last exploit: the Vikings meet new tactics

The accounts in Frankish and Arabic annals say little or nothing about Viking tactics, and historians have been content to say that Viking success was largely caused by their shipborne mobility and ability to achieve surprise. This assertion deserves at least a little scrutiny. One obvious thought is that Viking longships, sweeping their way along the relatively narrow rivers of northwest Europe, must have been vulnerable to random sniping from the banks. Any huntsman with a bow could loose off a few arrows and be far away by the time a ship pulled to the bank and landed avengers. The same tactic repeated at every bend in the river would cause a steady drain of casualties – wounded men can be more of a nuisance to the survivors than dead ones. Did Vikings use mounted detachments along the riverbanks as a screen? Or did they have a policy, like some armies in recent history, of taking such terrible reprisals against areas where partisans or *francs-tireurs* operated that the locals made sure it didn't happen?

Viking armies also had to feed themselves, which involved foraging on land. Foraging is not best done by large groups or by men on foot. It needs horsemen, spread out to cover as much ground as possible, and one would think also a supply of carts. All these requirements create further vulnerability, which could have been exploited by determined leadership. No doubt tactics and counter-tactics of this sort were part of the mental equipment of any successful Viking leader. But the Frankish annals in particular, written by monks concerned above all with the fate of their own communities, usually the final stage of a Viking raid, have nothing to say about such matters.

This is one of the main differences between them and the *Anglo-Saxon Chronicle*. The latter is a composite work written over several centuries, in several places and by many compilers, but it is generally thought to have been begun as a project in the 890s, the last decade of King Alfred's reign, in his kingdom of Wessex and (many believe) at his personal instigation. Its account of 'Alfred's Last Wars' was certainly written by a cleric, or clerics, but not by monks: by that time, after a century of Viking attacks, there were no proper monasteries left in England. It is markedly realistic and unusually well informed. One strange fact is that the Alfredian chronicler sometimes seems to know not only what happened but what was supposed to happen but didn't; he was writing at the West Saxon headquarters, one might say. From his account and those of his successors, one gets at least some idea of the moves and countermoves of attackers and defenders. On the other hand, he can be detected, here and there, covering up for his king. To quote the Duke of Wellington on Napoleon, Hastein 'humbugged' Alfred.

By the early 890s Alfred had clearly worked out a strategy for defeating Vikings. He had spent most of his early life fighting the 'great army' of the Ragnarssons and their successors, unsuccessfully to start with, and in 876 almost disastrously. In that year he was nearly caught napping after the Christmas festivities by a sudden winter raid aimed at him personally. He had to hide out in the marshes of what are now the Somerset Levels, and though the 'burned the cakes' story is a later legend, he must have been tempted to do what the King of Mercia, his brother-in-law, had done: take the crown jewels and flee to Rome. If he had been caught there is no doubt the Vikings would have killed him and his wife and children, including his son Edward, himself in due course to become a hammer of the Vikings and father of the great King Athelstan. Perhaps the killing would have been done with one of the Ragnarssons' atrocity demonstrations. Remarkably, Alfred held on, managing to rally the levies of the neighbouring counties from his hideout, beating the Vikings badly at Edington, and imposing a treaty on King Guthrum/Athelstan, which the latter, for once, stuck to. But Alfred had every reason for spending the next decade seeing that this critical situation never happened again.

The centre of his strategy was fortresses, typically earthworks with a stockade. A document called the Burghal Hidage survives from this time and stipulates how these were to be manned.[27] The rate was four men to every 5 m (16 ft 6 in) of wall, each hide of land (normally 48.5 ha/120 ac) supplying one man for the defences. The largest burh, then, Winchester, needed 2,400 men (as did Warwick, which must have been added to the list later, in the reign of Alfred's son Edward), guarding a perimeter of something over 2.75 km (1 ¾ mi.) and drawn from an area of some 1,165 sq. km (288,000 ha, or 450 sq. mi). A distance of 2.75 km is about right for the old boundaries of the town. The modern county of Hampshire, of which Winchester is and was the county town, is 1,400 sq. mi. in area, about 7,000 hides, but it contained four other smaller burhs, so the figures for garrisons are fairly consistent. Arrangements must have been made for call-up, and certainly were for rotation, though neither always worked. Such forts, one should note, would act not just as refuges for the local population, but more importantly as bases from which to attack Viking vulnerabilities – like their foraging parties, and the ships from which they forayed, which would now have to have strong guards permanently in place. Their garrisons could be local levies, not fit to make fast marches or stand in a battle line but good enough to defend a wall. And Alfred had other ideas as well. Hastein and his competitors tested them from 892 onwards.

What the *Anglo-Saxon Chronicle* says in its entry of 892 is that the 'great army' (the one once commanded by the Ragnarssons, whose later movements in Francia the Anglo-Saxons had been carefully monitoring) 'were provided with ships' at Boulogne (by whom? The Franks, anxious to get rid of them?) and came over 'horses and all'.[28] One imagines they cannot have fitted horses for every man into undecked longships, but even a few would equip raiding parties to go and round up more on landing. They arrived on the Lympne river in Kent, a short crossing from Boulogne, and rowed inland 6.5 km (4 mi.). There was supposed to be a fort there – presumably the one listed in the Burghal Hidage as *Eorpeburnan*, though the site has not been identified – but in any case, the chronicler reports, it wasn't finished, and the garrison consisted only of a few men of 'churl' rank – meaning no thanes, none of the military aristocracy. (The chronicler, one notes, is already making excuses: the Vikings had help from the Franks, they had horses on arrival, the Kentish ealdorman had not done what he was supposed to do . . . and there are more to come.) This army, which had 250 ships and perhaps as many as 7,000 men, promptly made a base at Appledore.

At the same time, and maybe in cahoots, Hastein (Hæsten in the *Chronicle*), crossed with eighty ships to the mouth of the Thames and made a base at Milton Regis, some 32 km (20 mi.) away. A different chronicler then takes over from the year following (894, correctly 893), and he continues to write, very informatively, but still with a deducible perspective. He says that what Alfred did was not what one would expect – to pick one army and attack it – but to first collect his forces from the shire levies, after which:

> [he] went so that he camped between the two raiding-armies, at a convenient distance from the fortress in the wood [Appledore]

and the fortress on the water [Milton Royal], so that he could get at either if they wanted to seek any open country.[29]

Alfred had in fact invented the doctrine of the 'fleet (or army) in being'. He did not have to fight the Vikings as long as fear of his army prevented them from leaving their bases – which meant, of course, they were not making any profits. Meanwhile they still had to forage, and what ensued sounds like violent 'patrol activity'. Quoting the 893 annal again:

> Then afterwards [the Vikings] went through the forest [the Weald of central Kent] in gangs and mounted groups, on whichever edge was without an army [Alfred's army]; and almost every day [the Vikings] were sought by other groups, both from [Alfred's] army and also from the strongholds [the fortified boroughs], either by day or by night.[30]

In other words, Viking detachments could evade Alfred's main army of the levy in its base somewhere on the higher ground of the Kent Downs, then heavily wooded, but were continually harassed both by detachments from the main army and from the burh garrisons. Here the Anglo-Saxons must have had the advantage of knowing the paths and tracks, especially if, as the chronicler says, they were scouting and patrolling at night in dense forest. In a way, the continual dogfights were forerunners of the actions fought in the skies over Kent in the Battle of Britain almost 1,050 years later.

The plan worked well, especially since 'The king had separated his army into two, so that there was always half at home and half out, *except for* [a significant exception] those men who had to hold the fortresses [the borough garrisons]'. The chronicler claims, rather clumsily, that the great army was only on the loose twice, once before it made its base, and so before Alfred had got his forces together, and once when it finally tried to break out. At that point the story becomes confused, not so much from what the chronicler says as from what he (surely deliberately) chose to leave out – until overcome by indignation.

Reading his lines as well as reading between them, what happened was that the great army of Appledore decided to break out, with what booty they had managed to accumulate. They headed north to Essex, on the other side of the Thames estuary, 'to meet the ships' (what ships? There had been no mention of ships in Essex beforehand). The Wessex levy, however, intercepted the Vikings, as it was supposed to, beat them at Farnham some 80 km (50 mi.) to the west and recovered the plunder they had taken. But by this time – the chronicler does not say this directly, the information coming from a good and more neutral source a hundred years later – Alfred was no longer there, having handed over command to his son Edward, later King Edward the Elder. The levy thought they had the Vikings penned, but they somehow got across the Thames where there was no ford (presumably swimming or on rafts) and then made a base on an island in the river Colne. They really were penned there, the chronicler says, well informed as ever, because their (unknown) king was wounded and they did not want to move him.

But at that point the rotation policy failed. The English levy

> besieged them there for as long as they had food; but they had completed their call-up, and used up their food, and [added indignantly by the pro-Alfred chronicler] the king [whose absence had not previously been noted] was on his way there [to relieve them] with the division which was campaigning with him.[31]

And then other things happened. The Northumbrians and East Angles (presumably this means, the Danish settlers in Northumbria and East Anglia, but there could be some doubt about this, on which more below) sent two fleets to attack the West Country, and Alfred had to turn his army round and march west to deal with them, though he did send a small detachment to London.

The real question that ought to have struck historians of the period is what happened to Hastein while all this was going on? The chronicler was crystal clear at the start of this account: two armies, at Appledore and Milton Regis, King Alfred blockading them both. Then suddenly attention focuses on the Appledore army and nothing is said about Hastein's smaller force. We would never be able to solve the question if indignation on behalf of his king had not swept over the chronicler again. For a few lines he follows the track of the detachment sent to London:

> They went on until they came to London town, and then, with the inhabitants of the town and the help which came to them from the west, went east to Benfleet [in Essex north of the Thames]. Hæsten had come there with his raiding-army, which earlier settled at Milton; and also the great raiding-army had come there, which earlier settled at Appledore on the mouth of the Lympne. Hæsten had made that fortification at Benfleet earlier, and was then off on a raid, and the great raiding-army was in occupation. Then they [the English] went up and put that raiding-army to flight, broke down the fortification, and seized all that was inside

it, both money and women and also children, and brought all into London town; and all the ships they either broke up or burned or brought to London town or to Rochester.[32]

So, Hastein had moved across the Thames to Benfleet in Essex. His were the ships that the Appledore army was making for. He was out raiding, unchallenged by any Wessex army (though Essex was by this time part of Alfred's domain, which London was not). But at Benfleet the scraped-together Anglo-Saxon forces won what must have been a smashing victory, perhaps against a much-reduced garrison, taking plunder and hostages and the ships as well.[33] But they failed to nail Hastein – though they did capture his wife and sons.

At this point indignation overcomes the chronicler, who continues:

> And they brought Hæsten's wife and two sons to the king; and he gave them back to him [why ever would he do that?], because one of them was his godson, and the other Ealdorman Ethelred's. They had received them before Hæsten came to Benfleet, and [Hæsten] had granted [the king] hostages and oaths, and the king had also granted him much money, and did also when he returned the boy [boys, surely?] and the woman. But immediately they came to Benfleet and the fortification was made, [Hæsten] raided [Alfred's] kingdom – that very quarter which his son's godfather Ethelred, had to hold; and again a second time, he was engaged in raiding in that same kingdom at the time when his fortification was broken down.[34]

In other words, while Alfred was covering both armies at once, he must have made a deal with the smaller one led by Hastein: accept baptism, give hostages, and we'll let you pass unchallenged, with a substantial 'sweetener' as well. For years the official Wessex policy had been *not* to follow the Frankish practice of paying Vikings to go away – it just encouraged them to come back again. But on this occasion the king did it, however the 'sweetener' was disguised. Alfred must have hoped that doing a deal with Hastein would work as (moderately) well as the deal with Guthrum had fourteen years before. But it failed. Hastein took the sweetener, profited from the truce to cross the Thames and get away from Alfred's threateningly aggressive army, made his new base at Benfleet, and then went back on all the assurances he must have given: a real failure for Anglo-Saxon diplomacy. The chronicler very nearly goes as far as criticizing his king for what he surely saw as an act of misplaced chivalry.

After that, Hastein really did 'wander off and disappear', as far as our records go. The combined remainder of the two Viking armies broke out again and was chased across England by the ealdormen of three counties plus 'king's thanes' collected from the burh garrisons. When the pursuers caught up, the Vikings were besieged on the Severn until they had eaten all their horses and were close to starving. Even then they broke out, and though the chronicler claims very heavy casualties among the Vikings, he also admits to the same among the Anglo-Saxons. A second break-out got as far as Chester, and here the pursuers used scorched-earth tactics:

> [they] besieged that fortification some two days, and took all the cattle that was outside there, and killed the men they could ride down outside the fort [the foraging parties]; and burned up all the corn, and with their horses ate up all the neighbourhood.[35]

The Anglo-Saxons, then, had worked out Viking vulnerabilities. They were hard to beat, and even harder to finish off, but essentially they were not interested in pitched battles, which they fought only if they had to. Stop them spreading out, stop them foraging and plundering, or make it unacceptably dangerous, and some of them would realize this was not a paying proposition. The trouble was, it all required a high level of organization and coordination, which sometimes broke down. And Alfred's diplomatic strategy did not work. In the whole panorama of Viking history, it rarely did. Vikings were very clear about their own self-interest.

One does wonder what happened to Hastein. Did he get away, with some proportion of the loot he had accumulated, to die a 'straw death' in retirement in Denmark, or perhaps in the Danish colonies in England? He had been a menace to Christianity, and to Islam, for more than thirty years and been quite ready to fight his countrymen, like Hrolf, in addition. His 'humbugging' of Alfred shows he was still earning his title as *fraudulentissimus*.

He was the Vikings' Viking. But he was getting out of date.

The third phase of Vikingdom

Loot, slaves, land: those were the three main sources of profit for Vikings, and in a very rough way they represent the main phases of their activity. The phases are in a way recognized by the *Vikings* TV series, but what the scriptwriters have done is foreshorten Viking history. The series opens with the raid on Lindisfarne in 793; soon Ragnar is raiding Paris, which occurred in 851; not long afterwards, Rollo, who died in 933, is noting (series 2, episode 3) that 'rich soil' is the true wealth; by series 4 he has become a defender of Francia, as he was from about 911; and in the next episode he is getting his hair cut and taking French lessons. The blood-eagle scene, however – which if it happened at all was a good fifty years earlier – is still in TV Rollo's future, as is the takeover of East Anglia, also in reality some fifty years earlier. In our modern Viking imaginary, then – just like our modern Wild West imaginary – dates aren't very important. Yet the TV series *does* indicate changes of policy by the Vikings, or changes of target, even if it speeds them all up.

Going back to the idea of three phases, loot from abbeys and cathedrals, cities and trading centres was the earliest and most convenient kind of profit, but it had the disadvantage of not being sustainable. Once a church treasury, with its accumulation of gold and silver over many years, had been looted, its plate melted down or cut up into shares, it would take many years for any accumulation to build again.

Slaves were much more renewable (a development which the TV series on the whole ignores), and in Ireland this seems to have become the main reason for attacking church festivals and gatherings. Slaves could be very profitable indeed (as will be demonstrated later), but they had drawbacks too. They had to be guarded and transported. Worse, buyers had to be found for them – buyers with cash. What one might call the domestic market in Scandinavia cannot have amounted to very much: Icelandic sagas often mention Celtic thralls, but the island's whole population can only have been in the tens of thousands, and a slave's labour might not be worth what it cost to feed him (though concubines were a different matter). Selling Christian slaves in Christian countries, Franks to Anglo-Saxons, or vice versa, or for that matter Franks to Franks, needed a well-policed market and was always likely to arouse opposition from the Church. The Islamic world had an inexhaustible demand for male and female slaves, but the problem was getting them there (see Chapter Eight).

So there remained land, the basic source of wealth in the European economy at all times up to very nearly the present. But this must have presented its problems, too. As previously noted, a large part of the Ragnarssons' army decided they had done enough, and the *Anglo-Saxon Chronicle* entry for 877 (really 876) records flatly, 'Halfdan [Ragnarsson] shared out the land of Northumbria, and they were ploughing and provid-ing for themselves.'[36] But the question that needs to be asked (but rarely is, for it can only be answered speculatively) is: who had previously owned the land they were ploughing?

Dispossessing individual small farmers would be easy enough initially – obviously a small Yorkshire village, with maybe a dozen or twenty able-bodied men in it, could offer little resistance to a Viking army, or even a well-armed ship's crew. But permanently dispossessing 'peasant proprietors', as they are called in academic language, would be a risky business. Peasant proprietors are deeply attached to their land – naturally enough, since it is their sole livelihood. Even if the previous owner of a farmstead was killed, there would be relatives, neighbours, runaways hiding out in the woods likely to retaliate. An ex-Viking living on his own in a farmstead could not expect to sleep easy – and living on his own, ploughing his own land as a *bóndi* or independent farmer, must have been the ambition of many Vikings.

But after all the battles, there must have been many casualties among the Anglo-Saxon 'thegnage', the military aristocracy. Replacing *them* would be an easier business. A successful Viking might take over the land of a dead Anglo-Saxon thegn, perhaps retain the 'home farm', and then tell the 'churl' tenants of the former thegn that they were now his tenants, sharecroppers as they perhaps always had been. A wise Viking might even ensure that they got better terms from him than from their previous lord.

An even safer target would be Church land, worked by tenants of a monastery or a cathedral. The monks were no longer there, nor the bishops – lists of Northumbrian bishops cease for a century or more. Their previous tenants might readily accept a mere change of masters, especially when they realized church tithes were no longer payable. Another factor is that dead thegns must have left many widows, as happened after the Norman Conquest of 1066, and daughters with no means of support. Military conquests are carried out by men, who in most cases do not have wives with them (apart from top men like Hastein). A natural solution is to marry into the relics of the native aristocracy.

As it happens, we have one suggestive clue to the situation, which is the sundial above the porch at St Gregory's Minster in Kirkdale, North Yorkshire, probably the most heavily Scandinavianized area in Britain. The inscription of this reads as follows, as near as possible word-for-word:

> Orm, son of Gamal, bought this church when it was all broken-down [*tobrocen*] and fallen-down [*tofallen*] and had it raised new from the ground in honour of Christ and St Gregory, in the days of King Edward and Earl Tosti. And this is the day's sun-mark [*solmerca*] at every line. And Haward made me and Brand the priest.[37]

The bit about the *solmerca* (regularly misread as *tide*, 'time', rather than *tane*, 'line') means that you can tell the time from the rays carved on the stone. The inscription is in rather non-standard Old English (though *sólmerki* is Old Norse), and the names of the king and the earl indicate a date around 1050. By that time, Northumbria was once again under the rule of the Anglo-Saxon King Edward the Confessor and had also once again become Christian. All the names on the inscription are, however, apart from Edward, Norse names: *Ormr, Gamall, Hávarðr, Brandr*. Earl Tosti himself – brother of King Harold Godwinsson, who lost at Hastings, and the man who joined the 'last Viking', King Harald of Norway, to fight his own brother at Stamford Bridge the same year – was one of a completely multiracial family. His father Godwin was an Anglo-Saxon; his mother Gyda was Danish; three of his brothers had Anglo-Saxon names, Gyrth, Leofwine and Wulfnoth; while his brothers' names Harold and Sweyn are Anglicizations of the Norse *Haraldr* and *Sveinn*. Tosti itself is short for Thorstein. By 1050 it must have been hard to tell ethnic English and ethnic Danes apart.

More significant, however, are some questions not usually asked. Orm Gamalsson was clearly a Christian, proud of rebuilding the church. But how had it come to be 'broken-down and fallen-down'? Also, he says he bought it, but who sold it to him? It must have ceased to be Church property. The tenth and eleventh centuries are usually seen as the story of how the Anglo-Saxon kings of Wessex, Alfred's descendants, established their authority over the Danish-settled areas, the Danelaw, and re-established Christianity: a story of national unification. But behind that, not so welcome to patriotic historians, are indications that not only was much of England still controlled by Viking descendants, but there was also (as in Ireland) widespread English apostasy, made profitable by takeover of Church property.

Viking aftermath

In brief, Halvdan Ragnarsson's followers melted over the years into the countryside, with results still evident in the English language and on the map of England. To take the latter first, if one looks at any area of Yorkshire or Lincolnshire, and to a lesser extent other counties, one can see a strange mixture in place names.[38] At the foot of Langstrothdale in West Yorkshire is a village now called Kettlewell, which once meant 'stream in a narrow valley'. In Domesday Book, however, its name is Chetelewelle. One difference between Old English (OE) and Old Norse (ON; closely related languages) is that Anglo-Saxons said *ch-* and *sh-* where Norsemen said *k-* and *sk-*. So even now Northern English uses 'kirk' (ON *kyrkja*) where Standard English says 'church' (OE *chiriche*). Not far from Kettlewell is

Skipton, once Shipton. Other doublets still in the language include 'shirt' and 'skirt', once the same thing, and – two very clear split-the-difference forms – 'screech' and 'shriek'.

Meanwhile, the next village up the valley from Kettlewell/Chettlewell is Starbotton, 'valley where stakes were obtained', combing the ON *botn*, 'innermost part of a valley', and a first element which could, in OE or ON respectively, be *stæfer* or *stavr*, two words for 'stake' spelled differently but pronounced the same way. A bit further up the valley, Hubberholme is pure OE: the *ham*, or home, of a lady with the distinctively OE name of Hunburg. Three kilometres away, though, lies Yockenthwaite, which combines the ON *þveitr*, 'a meadow' or maybe 'an enclosure' that belonged to 'Yocken'. But Yocken as pronounced by English or Norse speakers is Old Irish *Eoghan*. Yocken must have been a Hiberno-Norseman, a descendant perhaps of the *Gaddgeðlar*, one of those who filtered into northwest England from Ireland.

It makes one wonder what language they were speaking in Langstrothdale in the unrecorded years of the ninth to eleventh centuries. 'Langstrothdale' itself is OE, but would be much the same in ON. An answer increasingly favoured – after some patriotic resistance – is that the inhabitants of the Danelaw evolved a mixed language (or 'creole', though the term isn't accurate).[39] And, more surprisingly and rather out of line with the approved version of national history, that *this*, not King Alfred's West Saxon, is the main ancestor of modern English. As one can see from what we might call 'the arm-and-leg' problem.

Many words in modern English are borrowings from Norman French, which became Law French, and histories of the language regularly provide lists of the new concepts introduced by the post-1066 invaders, of which the most significant may well be 'castle' (French *château*, Norman French *chastel*) or 'prison'. New things, even if unwelcome, need new words. But many words in modern English, words that descend from ON, are not new concepts at all. 'Arm' is just the OE *earm*, but 'leg' is ON *leggr*. Obviously, Anglo-Saxons did not need a new word for 'leg' – they had one of their own, *sceanc*, pronounced 'shank', a word that has survived with different or specialized meaning. So why drop it and use a foreign word? The same question applies to a number of pairings (the modern word derived from OE always given first):

earth and sky (ON *sk*ý; OE used *heofon*, modern 'heaven')
live and die (ON *deyja*; OE used *steorfan*, 'starve')
ham and eggs (ON *egg*; OE said *ægru*, later 'eyren')
right and wrong (ON *rangr*; OE more simply *unriht*, 'unright')

The critical pair, though, has to be 'wife' and 'husband'. *Wíf* is OE (ON being *kona*), but *húsbóndi* is ON (replacing OE *ceorl*, modern 'churl'). Children growing up in mixed-language families must have picked whatever seemed best. Old Norse infiltration extended even to exceptionally common words like 'she' and 'they', perhaps because the Old English words for personal pronouns were so similar to each other (*he*, *heo*, *hie* for 'he' and 'she', and the last one did duty for 'her' and 'they' at once) that non-native speakers readily confused them.

In England, then, Viking settlers were, to put it briefly, absorbed, as a result of many social and linguistic accommodations and compromises, of which one can give only an overview here. The fact was, the two societies were not all that different – a situation very unlike what happened in Ireland, where Viking settlement remained confined to major towns and ports and where the *Östmenn*, 'Men from the East', stayed a separate group. And different also from what happened in Russia, where the Vikings eventually disappeared into the Slavic majority, leaving little linguistic trace behind them.

As for the Normandy of Hrolf/Rollo, its similarity to the English Danelaw is even closer than one might have thought, with suggestive implications not entirely welcome to national myth.

The followers of Rollo

The situation in Normandy has been especially closely studied by M. Jean Renaud, who has written a biography of Normandy's founder, *Rollon, chef Viking* (2006), and also a general survey, *Les Vikings et la Normandie* (1989). This includes a chapter on Norse words found in modern Norman dialect, some fifty of which have passed into standard French. Renaud has also made a very detailed study of place names, *Vikings et noms de lieux de Normandie: Dictionnaire des toponymes d'origine scandinave en Normandie* (2009). The results of the latter in many ways duplicate what one finds in the English Danelaw. ON words for features of the landscape figure frequently as place name elements. Examples from modern Normandy include:

-bec, from ON *bekkr*, 'stream' (e.g. Caudebec, 'cold stream';
    cf. Caldbeck in Cumbria)
-dalle, from ON *dalr*, 'valley' (e.g. Dieppedalle; cf. Deepdale
    in Lancashire and North Yorkshire)
-gard, from ON *garðr*, 'yard, enclosure' (e.g. Auppegard;
    cf. Appelgarth, North Yorkshire)

-gate, from ON *gata*, 'path' (e.g. Holgate, Houlgate; cf. Holgate,
   West Yorkshire)

-homme, -hou, from ON *hólmr*, 'island, dry land in marsh'
   (e.g. Le Hommet; cf. Hulme, Cheshire)

-tuit, from ON *þveitr*, 'clearing' (e.g. Grintuit, *'Grim's Thwaite',
   no exact Danelaw parallel but cf. Grimsthorpe
   in Lincolnshire and Yockenthwaite in Yorkshire)

The above are only a selection from more than sixty Scandinavian elements describing natural features, most of them appearing several or many times in Renaud's study. To these one can add the evidence for Scandinavian origins of modern Norman names, of which Renaud lists many more. These are not always listed separately, so an accurate count is difficult, but they include La Hastinguerie, from *Hásteinn*; Havardière, from *Hávarðr*; La Quetterie, from *Ketill*; Le Mesnil-Opac, from *Óspakr*; Les Néels, from *Njáll* (derived from Irish Níall); Romesnil, from *Hrólfr*; Turgisière, from *Þorgisl*; La Tostinière, from *Tosti < Þorsteinn*; and anything from thirty to a hundred more.

Scandinavian personal names in the English Danelaw are even more frequent, going all the way alphabetically from Asenby in North Yorkshire, from *Eysteinn*, to Ugglebarnby in the same county, which is an ON nickname: *Ugla-Barði* or 'Owl-Barthi' (why did they call him that?). Several hundred ON names can be picked from the surviving place names of the Danelaw, and those several hundred must imply a much larger number of settlers, for after all not everyone gets a place named after them.

The same ought to hold good for Normandy, where there is, however, a problem both with the Scandinavian words for natural features and with those for people: neither can always be told from what would have been their near-equivalent Anglo-Saxon forms. To be at all sure about their source one needs early records (like Domesday Book) that have not been affected by the processes of change to which place names are especially subject. The Thor- names, of which Renaud finds twenty examples, are distinctive, for Anglo-Saxons had stopped using Thor- as a name element before the Viking era. But does for instance L'Aumonderie derive from ON *Ásmundr* or OE *Osmund*? The same goes for L'Ozourie – *Ásulfr/Oswulf* – and many others, to some of which there might also be a native Frankish equivalent. One cannot always tell from the worn-down modern forms.

Still, there is a strong suspicion here, amounting very close to certainty, that many of the settlers in Normandy did not come directly from Denmark or Norway, but from England. They may, of course, have been pure Danish or Norwegian by blood, making them second-generation emigrants. But one starts to wonder where a late-era Viking like Ganger-Hrolf recruited his armies. Dudo of Saint-Quentin and William of Jumièges have the idea that Hrolf got substantial assistance from England. And by his time there had been Scandinavian settlers in England for a generation or more. Did he too recruit the English equivalent of the *Gaddgeðlar*, men of mixed Anglo-Danish stock who like Hiberno-Norsemen (remembering *Eoghan* or 'Yocken' from Langstrothdale) had abjured their Christianity, thrown in with the winners and decided to take their identity from their Scandinavian fathers rather than their Anglo-Saxon mothers? What reality lies behind L'Étantot, the *topt* or homestead of Athelstan? Or Dénestonville, the (Latin word) *villa* of Dunstan? Or indeed Englesque-ville, 'the English farm', which looks like a hybrid of OE *englisc*, with a final -sh, and ON *enskr*? As an aside, the only runic inscription found in Normandy is written not in the Viking version of the runic alphabet, but the Anglo-Saxon one.[40]

One may remember further the complaint in the *Anglo-Saxon Chronicle* about fleets appearing from 'the Northumbrians and the East Angles' to attack Wessex and support Viking armies.[41] Historians have been quick to explain that this must mean the *Danish settlers* in those territories, not the conquered natives. But the Anglo-Saxon kingdoms had usually existed in a state of war with each other. It might not have been hard to fill the ships with English or half-English recruits. It was very much part of King Alfred's policy, and his descendants', to give their wars an ethnic dimension and to present themselves as natural protectors of all *Angelcynn*, 'the English race', or even, later on, as protectors of Anglo-Danes against Norwegians coming in from Ireland.[42] One might suspect, though, that if one could interrogate some bearded ruffian from a tenth-century Viking fleet, give him some powerful inducement to tell the truth and then ask him his name, he might shuffle awkwardly and confess, 'well, it's Ragnar now, of course, but I was baptized as Edward. You won't tell anyone, will you?'

In twentieth-century conditions, when all Europeans, including the British, were sensitive to any accusations of being collaborators or 'quis-lings', this was not a welcome thought. But national boundaries then were not as we draw them now; nor were national loyalties. Northwest Europe, in short, was a melting pot. And it was Vikings who supplied the heat.

While most of the heroes in this book are men who died gallantly, defiantly, expressing the Viking ethos of unbreakable will in the face of death or torture, many Vikings must have preferred to look at different role models: men who took gold and silver by daring and deceit, and kept their winnings, like Hastein. Men who seized land and kept it as a lasting inheritance for their descendants, like Hrolf. Winners, sometimes in the very long term. Not only they but their followers were men who left their mark both on the landscapes of England and France, and on the languages we speak to this day.

EIGHT

Furs and Slaves, Wealth and Death: The Road to Miklagard

In Western eyes, the Viking image has remained one of raiders from the sea. The Viking Age began (or so the conventional story has it) with sudden hit-and-run irruptions like the one on Lindisfarne in 793 that so panicked Alcuin. It developed with Vikings seizing bases from which to mount more continuous attacks, on islands from Shetland in the far north of Britain to the Isle of Sheppey in the southeast, as well as other sites anywhere along Europe's Atlantic coasts. Another development was the creation of harbour bases controlling or trying to control a larger hinterland, predominantly Dublin. In the end, raiding would turn to conquest and settlement, in Scotland, northern England and Normandy, and then to full-scale national takeover of England under King Knut.

Nevertheless, the connection with sea raiding never entirely went away. The final phase of the British Viking wars was inaugurated with the defeat of the alderman Byrhtnoth in 991 at Maldon, in the estuary of the River Blackwater, a battle whose course was partly determined by the tides. The writer of the *Anglo-Saxon Chronicle* entry for 1006 notes that it had been the English boast that if the Vikings ever got to *Cwichelmes Hlæw*, then they would never get home again – the point being that *Cwichelmes Hlæw*, now Cuckhamsley Hill in Berkshire, is about as far from the sea as you can get in England. The Vikings took the dare, which they must have heard about (but how?), reached Cuckhamsley Hill unchallenged, and then marched on, carrying their plunder to the sea. The chronicler adds bitterly that 'the people of Winchester could see [them], proud and unperturbed, when they went by their gates.'[1] The English still thought of the Vikings as sea raiders, and it was a sign of national demoralization when they came to be more.

The response of modern Western historians has, naturally, been to take this image as the default one and to build it up with a particular interest in the Scandinavian (not really 'Viking') expansion across the northern seas and on to Iceland, Greenland and the northern coasts of America.

The surviving native tradition has a bias in the same direction, for most of what has been preserved comes from Iceland, and the Icelanders naturally took special interest in the histories of Norway and of the British Isles, from where most of their ancestors came.[2]

Wild East, not Wild West

But all through the Viking Age, things were happening elsewhere that were arguably as dramatic, as daring and even, globally speaking, more important – not in Western Europe and the Atlantic regions but in what to the Vikings was the 'Wild East'. To saga writers this was the home of giants and dragons and creatures of folk tale, and in reality the home also of civilizations far more advanced than anything the impoverished west could muster, and possessing the lure of fantastic wealth. It is our misfortune that the expeditions across the Baltic and deep into the Eurasian land mass, stretching as far as the Black Sea and the Caspian, Constantinople and (indirectly) Baghdad, long remained a venture for Swedes and in particular for the inhabitants of Gotland, an island off the Swedish coast.

These people came late to Christianity and its vital accompaniment, literacy, and much of their story remains untold. Except – and this is a big exception – for the fact that the people they came into contact with – Greeks, Arabs, Persians – were perfectly literate and have left considerable accounts of their side of the story, which still get less space than they might in Viking histories. 'I have never seen bodies more perfect than theirs,' commented the Arab traveller Ibn Fadlan some time in the early 930s, of a group he met out on the steppe, 'They were like [i.e. as tall as] palm trees'. He added, less obligingly, 'They are the filthiest of God's creatures.'[3] A hundred years later, his countryman Miskawayh was complimentary again, though again with a developing undertone of disgust and incomprehension: 'They are a formidable nation, the men huge and very courageous. They do not recognize defeat; no one turns back until he has killed or been killed.' Writing earlier than Ibn Fadlan, Ibn Rusta from Isfahan agreed: 'They have great stamina and endurance. They never quit the battlefield without having slaughtered their enemy. They take the women and enslave them. They are remarkable for their size, their physique, and their bravery.' When a son is born to one of them, says Ibn Rusta, the father throws down a sword and tells the baby, 'I leave you no inheritance. All you possess is what you can gain with this sword.' Marwazi from Merv, writing in the early twelfth century, agreed about their valour and courage, but reflected that it was fortunate that they had never taken to horses: 'If they had horses and were riders, they would be a great scourge to mankind.' They were weird, though, thought Miskawayh. Even their boys were suicidal.[4]

The men they were talking about they described as the 'Rus', a word whose etymology is uncertain. Could it mean men from Roslagen, a district in Sweden? If these were the first Scandinavians to arrive, their name might have been adopted for all successors, just as the Islamic world later used 'Frank' to mean any Western European. Or could 'Rus' derive from the verb *róa* and mean 'the rowers, the oarsmen'? Though the word has come down to us as 'Russians', it's clear that the Rus were at least initially Scandinavians, though the Scandinavian elite eventually merged with the native populations of Eastern Europe, mostly Slavs. Their names, when preserved, and some scraps of language written down by people who knew no Norse, are Scandinavian: Askold and Dir for Hoskuld and Dyri; Oleg and Olga for Helgi and Helga; Vladimir for Valdimar and Igor for Ingvar (the name that would become Ivar in the west), as well as many others. The largely lost epic of the Rus, however, was very different from that of the western Vikings, even if they came from adjacent homelands. It was a river story, not a tale of the sea.

The 'Wild East' that was exploited by the Swedes and Gotlanders from (as far as we know) the early 800s looks like nothing so much as the conquest of North America by the British and French getting on for a thousand years later. In both cases, invaders arriving initially by sea found themselves confronting a vast land mass, far bigger than anything they knew in their own countries. In both cases, much of it was covered in forest, about which they knew nothing – *Myrkviðr inn ókunni*, say the old Eddic poems, 'the unknown Mirkwood'. Behind the forest there were vast tracts of steppe, or prairie, which were too far beyond their resources to even think about controlling. The whole area was inhabited by bewildering numbers of mostly hostile tribes, which neither first-millennium Swedes nor second-millennium French and British could so much as keep track of: Abenaki, Penobscot, Wampanoag, Mohegans and Hurons and Ojibwe and Iroquois in North America, and a thousand years before, Drevlians and Yotvingians, Esti and Polovcians and Pechenegs, Prussians and Latvians. Both sets of incomers, moreover, protected themselves by forts or stockades; the Norse term for the world of the eastern rivers was *Garða-ríki*, the 'country of the Garths', a garth being an enclosure – it's the same word as the English 'yard' – expanded to mean a township. What became Novgorod was to them *Holmgarðr*, 'island city', and of course the greatest city of all, Byzantium, was *Miklagarðr*, 'big city'.

Some things in the two situations were different, however. The power differential between natives and incomers was not the same. The Rus, or

Scandinavians, had no guns. Nor were the people they faced still living in the Stone Age: they had iron weapons like the Rus, and though like Native Americans they were hunter-gatherers as well as agriculturalists, agriculture was probably a larger part of their lives than hunting and gathering – which meant larger populations. Also, while in both cases part of the motive for penetration of the land mass was access to much richer civilizations on the other side of it, in the case of the Rus those civilizations were really there and (with difficulty) accessible. The lure of the Orient that drew Columbus was by contrast a major error, not securely exposed for centuries.

Nevertheless, the first probes of the Rus into the Eurasian land mass must have been much more like something out of Fenimore Cooper than, say, the modern *Vikings* TV series. It was an affair of forests and fur trappers, canoes rather than longships, and most of all, rivers.

Geography, prehistory, poetic fossils

The critical area for the Rus penetration of the Eurasian land mass was the region of the Valdai Hills in northwest-central Russia, now midway between Moscow and St Petersburg. Rivers run from here in different directions.[5] Two drain north and west into the Baltic Sea, on the coast facing Sweden: the Daugava, also called the Western Dvina, which runs for more than 1,000 km (600 mi.) from the Valdai Hills to the sea at Riga, now capital of Latvia; and the Lovat and the Volkhov, which flow first from the Valdai again into Lake Ilmen and then on to Lake Ladoga, to reach the Baltic a little further north than the Daugava. Three much larger rivers run the other way, to the south. The Don flows for almost 2,000 km (1,200 mi) from southeast of Moscow into the Sea of Azov, an arm of the Black Sea almost cut off by the Crimean peninsula. The Dnieper runs even further, for 2,200 km (almost 1,400 mi.), to reach the Black Sea itself west of the mouth of the Don. And an even larger river, the Volga, the longest and largest in Europe, flows for almost 3,700 km (2,300 mi.), first to the east and then bending away to the south, to reach the Caspian Sea close to Astrakhan. These rivers have remained vital to the whole self-image of Eastern Europe, especially Russia, right into the present, with great cities founded on all of them – sometimes by the Rus, such as Kiev on the Dnieper or Novgorod close to Lake Ilmen, though this was not the case with Volgograd, formerly Stalingrad, on the Volga.

For the Rus, though, the important fact is that the headwaters of these rivers all cluster relatively close together. In the eighteenth and nineteenth centuries, canals were made to connect them up, linking for instance the

Dnieper with the Daugava. There are also tributaries and smaller rivers, such as the Pripet and the Niemen (another that runs into the Baltic). Dark Age Scandinavians did not have the resources to make canals. But they were well able to organize trans-shipment and indeed portages. They could row upriver from the Baltic along the Daugava or the Niemen, or up the Volkhov to Lake Ilmen and the Lovat, and then row downriver along the Don, the Dnieper, even the Volga, from where they could sail across the Black Sea to Byzantium, or across the Caspian to the Islamic Caliphate, the heartlands of classical and Mesopotamian civilization. The rewards for this must have verged on the fantastic (of which more below), as, of course, were the risks. But Vikings, whether westerners or easterners, seem to have heard the word 'reward' much better than the word 'risk'.

But how did they know that any of this was even possible? It is a sign of the 'periodization' of much historical inquiry that the question does not seem often (or ever) to have been asked, but it is quite possible that the Swedes and Gotlanders knew a good deal more about the Eurasian land mass than historians have been prepared to consider. They had old connections dating back half a millennium to the fall of the Roman Empire.

No people get more of the blame for that fall than the Goths. They called themselves *Gut-þiuda*, the Goth-people, but the etymology of their name is doubtful. Were they in some way connected with Gotland, the Swedish island? Or with the inhabitants of what are now the Swedish provinces of Östergötland and Västergötland, with their capital at what in English is called Gothenburg? It seems at least plausible, and the Goths' own native traditions insisted that they emigrated out onto the steppes of Russia from the north. One thing we are quite sure of is that the Goths spoke a Germanic language, now classified as East Germanic, unlike the Scandinavian languages, which are North Germanic, and English, Dutch and German (and so on), which are West Germanic. The further back one goes in time, however, the more all these language groups resembled each other. In the fifth century, the time of the fall of the Roman Empire, and even in the sixth, the time of King Hrolf and King Hygelac, Goths and Anglo-Saxons and Swedes could all probably understand each other. We know, for instance, that North Germanic became markedly different from the others only in the immediately pre-Viking period.[6]

This explains some peculiar facts, brought to light, as it happens, by Christopher Tolkien, the son of the author of *The Lord of the Rings*. What he noticed was that even in very late Icelandic legend there is still a trace of awareness of the Goths and their old stamping grounds in the Carpathian Mountains, home of Count Dracula and the source of several great rivers, including the Vistula.

That trace occurs in the saga known variously as *Heiðreks saga*, 'Saga of King Heidrek the Wise' (Christopher Tolkien's title) or *Hervarar saga*, 'Saga of Hervor'. It is a compilation that includes among much else the poems 'Riddles of Gestumblindi' (of great interest to Tolkien Senior); the 'Waking of Angantyr' (one of the first Norse poems to find an appreciative modern audience, describing Hervor calling her dead father from his barrow to give her the sword Tyrfing); and the 'Battle of the Goths and Huns', of which Christopher Tolkien made a further extended study elsewhere.[7] The vital detail, however, occurs in a mere scrap of poetry. Angantyr – a different Angantyr from Hervor's dead father – seeking revenge for his own father Heidrek's killing, comes upon the murderers fishing in a river by a forest and overhears one of them, who has just beheaded a fish using the sword Tyrfing, say: 'The pike has paid, by the pools of Grafa, / For the death of Heidrek under the fells of Harvad [*und Harvaða fjöllum*].' Angantyr kills the murderers and recovers his father's sword. The important point here, though, is that, to quote Christopher Tolkien's comment: 'The view is not challenged, I think, that *Harvaða-* is the same name in origin as "Carpathians".' He adds in a footnote: 'The stem *karpat-* was regularly transformed into *χarfaþ-* by the operation of the Germanic Consonant Shift (Grimm's Law).' He concludes 'These four lines are a fragment of a lost poem ... that preserved names at least going back to poetry sung in the halls of Germanic peoples in central or south-eastern Europe.'

The saga also contains other non-Scandinavian place names, notably *Danparstaðir*, which 'seems certainly to contain the Gothic name of the Russian river Dnieper, which is called *Danaper* by the sixth-century Gothic historian Jordanes' and which was the accepted boundary between East- and West-Goths. By such survivals, Tolkien argues:

> one is probably being taken back a thousand years even beyond *Heiðreks saga* to the burial-place of Gothic kings in south-eastern Europe and the high stone in their chief place, on which the king stepped to have homage done to him in the sight of all the people.[8]

If, however, such linguistic fossils and scraps of poetry could survive a thousand years, being translated by the regular development of language change from Gothic to Norse, what other information might also have survived? Not for anything like as long as a thousand years, nor to far-off Iceland, but as a living tradition among the Goths' relations in Sweden? We know that a relict population of Goths, still speaking Gothic, survived in the Crimea into the sixteenth century. (Some late period inscriptions, still in classical Gothic, were discovered only in 2015.)[9] So Norsemen from

Gotland or Gothenburg, rowing down the Don, might well have bumped into their Gothic-speaking distant cousins at the end of their journey, perhaps surprising neither of them. It seems very likely, then, that information about the exploits and whereabouts of the Goths and related East Germanic peoples in the early centuries of the first millennium remained known in Sweden all the way through to the Viking era. Especially useful would have been awareness of the layout and extent of the major rivers and the river network that linked them.

Byzantium: raiding and trading

At some point, then, and we do not know when, men from eastern Scandinavia began probing up the rivers from the Baltic coast, and then down the rivers that led to the south, perhaps especially the Dnieper. As said above, their experience must have been like that of the Franco-British 'woodsrunners' and *coureurs des bois* venturing cautiously into America, up the Hudson, St Lawrence and Delaware rivers and eventually along the Missouri and Mississippi. The immediate pay-off in both cases may have been the same: furs – beaver from the rivers of America, fox and marten and squirrel from the forests of Eurasia. But once again there were some differentiating factors, notably the kinds of people the pioneers had to deal with. We have some valuable if inevitably patchy and suspect accounts of the process, though all of them from the other side, from Greek, Slavic or Islamic sources. And there are once again some suggestive linguistic clues.

We know that Swedes had come downriver to Byzantium by the 830s, for a group of them had to be repatriated via France in 836 on the orders of the Byzantine emperor Theophilos, their river route home being blocked by hostile tribes.[10] A hundred years later they were much more firmly established. Very close to 950 the Byzantine emperor Constantine VII Porphyrogenitus ('born in the purple') wrote a guide to foreign policy for his son Romanus, *De administrando imperio*, or 'On the Governance of the Empire'. Section 9 of this deals with the Rus.[11]

These people, the emperor wrote, come down the Dnieper from Novgorod and other cities, assembling at Kiev. They come in what he calls *monoxyla*, 'single keels', which are essentially disposable boats, possibly dugout canoes. The Rus buy the hulls in spring from their Slav tributaries, finish them and fit them out with masts, sails and rudders for the summer voyage. Size and weight have to be kept down, because a major obstacle on the Dnieper is a series of rapids or barrages. Constantine lists seven of these, giving their names in (garbled) Norse and Slavonic. Some of them can be passed, carefully, by edging along the riverbank, but others have to be bypassed on land, by dragging the boats (presumably on rollers) or physically carrying them. The other main danger comes from the Pechenegs, steppe nomads who lay ambushes, especially at the narrows below the seventh barrage. The Rus go down in convoy, ready to fight, all putting in together if a *monoxylon* gets stranded. They take a break at St Gregory's Island, which the Pechenegs apparently cannot reach, and eventually arrive at 'the district of Mesembria [probably modern Nesebar, on the Black Sea coast of Bulgaria], and there at last their voyage, fraught with such travail and terror, such difficulty and danger, is at an end'.[12]

The names of the Dnieper barrages have attracted a good deal of modern attention, for some of them are decipherable even in their garbled form (such as 'Essoupi', *ei sofa*, do not sleep, or 'Leanti', *hlæjandi*, laughing [water]). There is some archaeological corroboration of Constantine's account. Five tenth-century Scandinavian swords were found in 1928 in the riverbed at the seventh barrage, which Constantine notes as an ambush site.[13] In 1905 a runestone was discovered by the Dnieper estuary, set up by one Grani in memory of his comrade Karl.[14] But the most valuable parts of *De administrando* are mostly hints. The only trade goods mentioned by the emperor are slaves – especially valuable, maybe, because they did not have to be portaged but could do some of the portaging – but clearly there were other materials loaded on the boats, and they must have been high-value items, to compensate for the 'difficulty and danger'. It is significant that in the winter the Rus leave Kiev and make the 'rounds' of 'the Vervians and Dragovichians and Krivichians and Severians and the rest of the Slavs who are tributaries of the Russians'.[15] It seems that the Rus had carried over the Norwegian practice – of which we have a very detailed account, see Chapter Nine – of levying tribute, basically protection money, from hunter-gatherer populations – Sami in the case of the Norwegians, Slavs in the case of the Rus – payable, in the case of the Sami but probably the Slavs as well, in skins and furs, feathers (for beds), wax and honey. An interesting point, though Constantine places no stress on it, is that the Rus show strong cohesion. They come in convoy, they back each other up, no boat is left stranded. Like d'Artagnan and the Three Musketeers, it's 'All for one, and one for all'. To betray one's *félagi* (fellow, partner in a deal involving goods, *fé*) was *níðingsverk*, a contemptible deed, as one Swedish runestone from Söderby angrily proclaims.[16]

Some of these claims find a little support linguistically. The major account of the coming of the Rus is the *Primary Chronicle*, written in the early twelfth century, and here the author steadily uses the term 'Varangians' as well as Rus. It survived as the designation of the Byzantine Emperor's famous Varangian Guard. This clearly derives from the Old Swedish *vær-gengi* and means 'someone in an agreement', just like *fé-lagi*. This suggests that, like medieval Hanseatic merchants or nineteenth-century whalermen, the members of a Rus trade convoy bound themselves to act cooperatively and share the proceeds at agreed rates. The word 'Varangian' survives in Russian as *varyag*, 'trader, pedlar', which suggests that this is how the Varangians were at first or sometimes seen.

Another suggestive term is Serkland, a name used in several sagas and on several runestones, though it is not clear what it means or to which area it refers. The Gripsholm runestone thus declares, in three lines of alliterative verse, that Harald and Ingvar:

furu trikila fiari at kuli	[They] fared like bold men far for gold
ok a:ustarla arni kafu	and in the east gave [food] to the eagle,
tuu sunar:la at sirk:lan:ti:	died in the south in Sirkland[17]

It is a famous, almost emblematic statement of the Viking urge (the British Museum exhibition 'Vikings: Life and Legend', 2014, quoted it prominently, but silently cut out the word **trikila** (*drengiligr*), 'like bold men' – not the preferred image in scholarly circles). But what was meant by 'Sirkland'? Could that be Sarkland, the place where people wear 'sarks' (shirts), that is, robes, not trousers? Or could it be 'the land of silk', from Latin *sericum*?

Or could it be 'Forty-land'? The Russian word for the number forty is *sorok*, but the word is 'completely anomalous in the Russian numerals system'. Andrew Jameson claims that it 'almost certainly denotes the number of small furry animal skins demanded as tribute by the Vikings as they travelled along the Russian river system on their way to and from the Black Sea', perhaps from each household from which they took protection money.[18] The *Primary Chronicle* notes (just after its description of saunas) that the Khazars imposed a tribute of a white squirrel skin on each hearth of their tributaries, while Oleg the Varangian charged 'a black marten-skin apiece'.[19]

Rarity furs clearly had special value. One Arabic commentator says that a black fox-skin went in Baghdad for 100 dinars,[20] though the amount is hardly credible: a dinar was a gold coin, heavier than a silver dirham, and worth maybe twenty times as much. Would it have sold for 2,000 dirhams? Dirhams were heavier than pennies, so maybe 3,000 silver pennies, 5.5 kg (12 lb) or more in weight? For one skin? Even a fraction of that would have made the fur trade the Dark Age equivalent of the trade in cocaine today. We know, however, that many thousands of dirhams did indeed fetch up in Gotland.

These are speculations, but the *Russian Primary Chronicle* does give a coherent account and time frame for the arrival and consolidation of the Rus.[21] According to this twelfth-century writer (using earlier written sources and writing in Old Church Slavonic), the story began with three brothers called Rurik, Sineus and Truvor (i.e. *Hrœrekr, Signjötr* and *Þorvarðr*). There seems to have been a prehistory, as suggested above, for according to the chronicler the native inhabitants first drove out the 'Varangians', but then, finding themselves incapable of self-rule, in the early 860s invited the three brothers to come in from overseas. Rurik established himself at Novgorod, near Lake Ilmen, and soon took over his brothers' cities also – in the process founding a dynasty, the 'Rurikids', which held rule in Ukraine and Russia until 1598.

Meanwhile, two other men, Askold and Dir (*Höskuldr, Dýri*), took over Kiev and from it launched the first of several unsuccessful attacks on what the *Primary Chronicle* calls 'Tsargrad', Constantinople. Before he died, Rurik bequeathed the care of his infant son Igor to a relative called Oleg, and Oleg eliminated Askold and Dir. (Vikings honoured deals among themselves, but without a deal, it was every man for himself.) It was forty years before Oleg ventured to launch a second attack on 'the Greeks', and was bought off, though the amounts given are again impossible to believe – 5.5 kg (12 lb) of silver per oar bench, forty men to a ship and two thousand ships would make several hundred tons of silver – however one calculates it, an awful lot to portage and more than anyone ever got from Danegeld in the west.[22]

Oleg died – mysteriously, as will be explained later – and Igor took over. In 941, according to the *Primary Chronicle*, he made a third attack on the Greeks, which was routed by 'Greek fire' (petroleum pumped out under pressure and ignited).[23] He tried again a few years later but was persuaded to withdraw by his understandably cautious retinue, and was killed soon after by the 'Derevlians' (cf. Russian *derevo*, 'tree', so 'forest-dwellers'). His wife Olga, daughter of his guardian Oleg, avenged him several times over, and he was succeeded by their son Svyatoslav.

Despite his Slavic name, Svyatoslav was Norse on both sides of his ancestry (as far as we know) and continued to behave in Viking style. He was Prince of Kiev in the time of Constantine VII Porphyrogenitus, who mentions him, and he too led an expedition against the empire in 971, rallying his men when they seemed on the point of defeat, first by the Bulgars and then by the Greeks. Leo the Deacon saw him when he came to make his deal with the emperor and was unimpressed, first because he wore the same clothes as his companions and second because he took his turn at the oars along with others – all this deeply contemptible to the hierarchy-conscious Byzantines, but very much in the egalitarian spirit of Viking armies.[24] The *Primary Chronicle* notes his austerity and hardiness more admiringly, saying that on campaign he used neither tents nor wagons nor kettles but instead slept on a horse blanket and ate what we would call jerky, strips of dried or roasted meat. Svyatoslav was bought off like his predecessors but was ambushed at the cataracts on the Dnieper by the Pechenegs, who plated his skull with gold and made a drinking cup out of it. (Vikings did not drink from skulls, though this has become part of their image, but they knew people who did.)[25]

After Svyatoslav, the *Primary Chronicle* reports a welter of civil strife, first between the sons of Svyatoslav – Vladimir I came out the winner – and then between the sons of Vladimir, Yaroslav coming out the winner. Yaroslav married a Swedish princess, Ingigerd Olafsdottir, and appears as King Jarisleif in several sagas set in the eleventh century, including *Heimskringla*. By the time of his grandson Vladimir II Monomakh (d. 1125), however, the rulers of Kiev had become speakers of a Slavic language. The Viking Age was over in west and east, and the rivers of Don and Dnieper were becoming part of Greek and then Russian Orthodox Christianity.

The caliphate of Baghdad: just raiding

The Dnieper was, however, not the only route taken by Varangians, nor were the riches of Byzantium the only attractive target. There was also the longer route down the Volga, which led to the Caspian Sea, on or near the shores of which lay the rich cities of what are now Azerbaijan and Iran. Attacks on this were particularly well recorded by a number of writers in the highly literate world of the Islamic Caliphate.

The first attack seems to have been some time around the 870s and is mentioned by Ibn Isfandiyar, a native of Merv in Turkmenistan on the old Silk Road, though he was writing more than three hundred years later. He also records a second attack in 910, though this was a small and perhaps exploratory affair of only sixteen ships.[26] It must have been successful enough to trigger a much larger repeat only two years later, however, and this one is described by al-Mas'udi, who was almost a contemporary (writing *c.* 943) and is known to have visited the Caspian area in person.[27] The same raid is described in greater detail, but without taking the story to its disastrous finish, by Miskawayh, writing a century later.[28]

The geography of both accounts is suspect-to-impossible, at least to start with. Al-Mas'udi says that the Rus fleet came down the Don, not the Volga, and asked permission from the king of the Khazars to cross his territory in return for a half-share of the loot, permission being readily granted. But how could they move their ships (five hundred of them, according to al-Mas'udi) from the Don to the Volga? By portage? Miskawayh is even vaguer: he clearly has no idea where the Rus came from or how they arrived on the Caspian. As far as the Muslim world was concerned, these attacks effectively came from nowhere.

Al-Mas'udi and Miskawayh between them are clear and convincing, however, on what occurred once the Rus did arrive within the Muslim known world. Miskawayh has already been quoted on the size and courage of the raiders. He adds that they go armed and armoured, with spear and shield, sword and dagger, also habitually carrying tools, axe, saw and hammer. He says that they first attacked the city of Barda, in Azerbaijan, and were met by the governor of the area with about six thousand men, mostly local volunteers. These were taken aback by the Rus, whom they expected to behave 'like Greeks or Armenians', and were speedily routed by their fierce onslaught. The Rus seem then to have tried to make a deal with the city inhabitants, promising them some sort of immunity as long as they stayed out of the fighting. The town mob, however, continued to throw stones at them and shout *Allahu akbar!* and so were told to evacuate the city; when they did not, 'the Rus put them to the sword' – though Miskawayh then contradicts himself by saying that they took more than ten thousand families to ransom, charging the very moderate rate of 20 dirhams per man. Still the Barda-ites dithered, and the Rus 'slew them to the last man' – though once again Miskawayh admits that some escaped or paid up (the price now having risen to everything the victim possessed). Females and young boys were kept as slaves. Repeated attacks got nowhere, but eventually the Rus, suffering from what sounds like dysentery, the scourge of medieval armies – Miskawayh says they gorged on fruit, to which they were not accustomed – found themselves besieged. Many of them died, and the rest made a successful breakout back to their ships.

Miskawayh adds that when one of the invaders died, he was buried with his weapons, and also his wife or his slave – though it is unlikely the Rus had brought any actual wives with them. Many of the buried swords were dug up and valued for their quality. He ends by saying that the Muslims were deeply impressed by their enemies' prowess and refusal to surrender. Several people told him the story of five Rus who were trapped in a garden, one of them a mere beardless youth, a chieftain's son. Though much outnumbered, they refused to surrender and killed many times their own number. In the end the boy climbed a tree and killed himself, or, as Miskawayh puts it, 'stabbed himself in vital organs until he fell dead'. Al-Mas'udi then continues the story, saying that the Rus easily defeated an amateur naval force sent against them and continued raiding round the shores of the Caspian until they returned to the Volga. Here, however, the Muslim Khazars reneged on the agreement made with their king and attacked the by now depleted Rus, eventually killing many or most of them.

The Caspian seems to have been another case of 'a bridge too far': good pickings and feeble resistance, but hard to reach and even harder to return from, through hostile territory, when laden with attractive loot. It was possibly the Khazar attack on the fleet returning which led to al-Mas'udi's story of a prior agreement and the land crossing of the Khazar country. More plausible would be Khazars leaving the Rus alone on their passage through, down the Volga, knowing that it would be easier and more profitable to catch them on the way back.

One can only conclude by saying that the Rus do not seem to have done particularly well by raiding into the Caspian. More significantly, there is no sign that they managed to set up direct trade relationships with the Caliphate, even though that was the final market for many of their goods.

Dealings with Byzantium via the Black Sea went better for them. As regards raiding, although they suffered repeated heavy defeats from the better organized Byzantine forces, they also had the occasional profitable success, as noted above. The *Primary Chronicle* records, meanwhile, repeated and detailed treaties for trading, which must have carried on continually, except, perhaps, when a new Prince of Kiev decided he had to make a demonstration of his power and warlike skills. Trade with Byzantium must have profited both sides, for the Byzantines could 'sell on' to the Muslim world. It was profitable to the Rus as well, for their trade goods largely came free, extracted by force and extortion from the Slavic peoples in the basins of the Don and Dnieper. And furs were not the only, or perhaps even the most valuable, commodity first extorted and then traded.

Economics of the Rus

The magnetic attraction that powered the Viking Age was money and bullion. As the runic inscription quoted above declares so economically, 'they fared like bold men far for gold'. The attraction was even stronger in the east than in the west. After the collapse of the Roman Empire, much of Western Europe ceased to be a money economy for some centuries.[29] English kings, for instance, began to coin their silver pennies only during the time of King Offa (r. 757–96). But England, like the rest of northwest Europe, no longer had native sources for gold and silver, their mines long since exhausted.

One result was the end of the 'Golden Age' for Scandinavia. It has been suggested that the very motive for the disastrous raid of King Hygelac (Chapter Two) may have been the cessation of inflows of precious metal, cut off by the Merovingian kings of France.[30] But the Merovingians had no gold or silver mines either, and much of the now limited quantities of precious metal was increasingly dedicated to the glory of God in the form of church plate, reliquaries, altar furniture and so on. Churches and monasteries were accordingly major targets for Viking attack from the start. It has even been suggested – by Anders Winroth, always keen to stress the Viking positives – that Viking raids had a beneficial function in putting this wealth back into circulation and so into the economy.[31] (Not much consolation, of course, for those who had been robbed.)

The situation was different in the east, and the magnetic pull so much the stronger. Both the Byzantine and Islamic empires had far greater quantities of gold and silver, both already mined and still being produced from mines in Afghanistan, Egypt, Moorish Spain and other locations in Eurasia. For northerners, the two ways of getting it were raiding and trading, and while the former was no doubt more attractive, as already noted it was not notably successful. But what were they trading? And was 'trading' (always approved of by academic historians) not in fact a by-product of raiding (a much less welcome thought)?

Besides furs, the really valuable commodities traded, if one can call them that, must have been slaves and mercenaries: both capable of production, if again one can call it that, by the undeveloped economies of Northern Europe, and, putting it coarsely once again, with limited production costs. The Byzantine emperor Basil II constituted his famous Varangian Guard in 988, enabled to do so openly by the Christianization of Kiev under Vladimir I. But no doubt men of the Rus had also seen the advantages of a regular paymaster well before that. At a pay rate of 40 gold solidi a year, each one worth as much as a dinar, a Byzantine guardsman was making at least as much as a successful recipient of Danegeld in the west, and a great deal more reliably. Part of this was based on their solid reputation for martial efficiency, to which Greeks and Arabs alike paid tribute – the eleventh-century Persian writer Marwazi says that one of the Rus was equal to several warriors from anywhere else, though he notes that they had no cavalry tradition.[32] Failure to cope with cavalry was indeed a weakness, as would be shown at Hastings in 1066 and in the last stand of the Varangians at Dyrrhachium in 1081, but in stand-up fights, sea battles and guard duties the Varangians were worth their pay. Such mercenaries – if they survived, and if they were prudent enough to keep their cash – enjoyed immense prestige when they returned home, as Icelandic sagas often insist.

Nevertheless the real money, one fears, was probably in the slave trade. Professor Michael McCormick's exhaustive study of the *Origins of the European Economy* (2001) comes up with several unwelcome conclusions. The most far-ranging is that what revived the collapsed post-Roman economies of Western Europe was the slave trade, in particular the trading of slaves to the far richer Muslim world. Figures are hard to find and are inevitably patchy, but the markup was certainly very high. One price recorded by McCormick is 150 dinars, paid in Baghdad in the late 700s for a 'beautiful girl' – close on four years' pay for a Varangian, and even more than for a black fox-skin![33] But even less valuable slaves went for three or four times the European price if traded to the Muslim world, and the demand, says Professor McCormick again, was insatiable.[34]

Much of the Viking world was involved in this trade, but we know very little about how it was organized. As the word 'slave' suggests, a major source of supply must have been the Slavic tributaries of the Rus. But Vikings also took slaves from all across Western Europe. Then the question has to be: where did they sell them? The domestic market in Scandinavia would have been easily saturated. Slaves from the North had long been sold in Southern Europe – one may remember the story about Pope Gregory determining on the conversion of England as a result of seeing Anglo-Saxon boys on sale in a Roman market and regretting that such fair children should be heathens. But this market was at least slowed by the conversion itself, and by injunctions against selling Christians to foreigners. Heathen Vikings, of course, felt no such restrictions; to quote McCormick:

> In the north, it was easier for Vikings to capture Franks, Anglo-Saxons, and Irish, directly and for free, than to pay Franks or Frisians for them . . . In an extraordinary irony of history, the European [i.e. Frankish] Empire which had once profited by supplying slaves from its subjects and neighbours became itself a leading source of supply.[35]

But where to sell them? An evident market was Moorish Spain, readily accessible by sea from Ireland especially and with no inhibitions about buying Christian slaves. But many western captives must have made the long and roundabout route from Britain and Ireland across to the markets in Scandinavia, to be sold on to the Rus and taken down the great rivers to the real profit centres in what are now Greece and Turkey, and further on in the Muslim Caliphate.

One small but in several ways revealing vignette is given in *Laxdæla saga*, 'The Saga of the People of Laxardal'. One of the early heroes of the saga, Hoskuld Dala-Kolsson, goes to an assembly on the Brenn Isles, off the mouth of the river Gaut in southwest Sweden. There he meets a man said to be 'the wealthiest man the guild of merchants had ever known' and tells him he wants to buy a slave girl. The merchant offers him his choice of twelve – they are in his trading booth, but hidden behind a curtain – and Hoskuld picks out one who seems beautiful to him but is shabbily dressed. Her price is 3 marks of silver, which, as Hoskuld says, is 'three times the normal price'. Before he hands over the money, the merchant says that the slave girl has one defect, which is that she appears to be a deaf-mute, for he has never been able to get a word out of her. Hoskuld buys her never-theless, and sleeps with her that night. In the morning he gives her fine clothes to replace the shabby ones she got from the merchant.[36] The saga goes on to reveal that she is not mute at all, for after Hoskuld takes her back to Iceland and she has had a child by him, she is caught talking to her baby and admits that her name is Melkorka; she is in fact an Irish princess, daughter of King Myrkjartan (Muircheartach 'of the Leather Coats'?), captured at the age of fifteen.[37] It is noteworthy that Hoskuld's wife, the Icelandic Jorunn, is dominant enough to prevent Hoskuld from keeping Melkorka as a concubine, and he has to set her up in a separate establishment, after which she marries a local farmer. Her child, Olaf, also rapidly outdistances Jorunn's children in wealth and prestige, which leads to serious trouble later on in the saga, so the saga appears to be offering a kind of happy ending for Melkorka's story.

Nevertheless, the points in the story that seem likely enough are, first, that the wealthy slave merchant is called Gilli *inn Gerzki*, Gilli 'from Gardariki' or Gilli the Russian, and he is wearing a 'Russian hat', presum-ably one of top-quality fur (perhaps as a kind of advertisement for his wares). What would have happened to Melkorka if Hoskuld had not bought her in Sweden? Presumably she too would have gone on with Gilli to his homeland, and maybe on 'down the river' to Kiev or Byzantium, or even Baghdad. In which case her price would have shot up stratospherically, for (going by McCormick's figures) even Hoskuld's exceptional 3 marks of silver, about a pound and a half in weight, or 360 pennies, or perhaps 300 dirhams, would have looked average-to-low there, even for a male slave of no special quality (if she had survived the journey, of course, a factor the likes of Gilli no doubt figured in as a business expense). Further points one could note are that while there was indeed a 'domestic market' for slaves in Scandinavia, the well-established rights of Scandinavian women worked against the formation of harems; while at the same time there was a 'great circle' route for slavers from the far west of Europe to the far east. Slave traders who used it also had the reputation, at least in Iceland in later centuries, of being both fair dealers (with their customers) and enormously rich.

There is plenty of evidence, indeed literally tons of it, for the second half of that reputation at least. The island of Gotland has proved to be the best place in Europe for seekers after Viking treasure. Arab coins turn up even in England: three single finds, including a now lost dirham from Cordoba close to my home in Dorset – and five hoards, notably the Cuerdale Hoard, datable to after 905, which contained seven thousand coins as well as hacksilver (silver ornaments cut up, presumably to be divided by weight). But these are dwarfed by the Gotland hoards.[38] More than seven hundred have been found on the island and been archaeologically registered – no one knows how many have not been declared – which, given that the island had only about 1,500 medieval farmsteads, indicates that every other farming family, admittedly over some ten generations, not only buried a hoard but then *lost track of it* (whereas most carefully buried hoards are of course retrieved by their owners). The largest such hoard, from Spillings, weighed in at 67 kg (nearly 150 lb) of silver, or 335 marks (more than 100 Melkorkas, at home-market rates). Much of the coinage recovered is in the form of Arabic dirhams, more than 80,000 of them, with another 40,000 in Sweden, all of this completely dwarfing any British discoveries. Archaeologists suggest that the prevalence of Arabic coins indicates that these are the proceeds of trade (English coins are more likely the result of extorted tribute).

Once again, this fits the current academic preference for the 'peaceful Scandinavian trader' image, as against the 'bold men who fed the eagles' Viking image. But one has to ask again, what were the traders trading? What did Scandinavia have to sell? It was suggested above that fur was the cocaine of the Viking Age, but perhaps – black fox-skins apart – furs were more like marijuana: bulk trade, steady demand. It was slaves, and especially slave girls and boys to fill harems and provide the harems with eunuchs, that were more like cocaine.

A final economic point is that things could change. The exhaustion of silver mines in the Muslim world in the late tenth century, coupled with the disruption of the Khazar-Samanid alliance around 1000, led to a sharp decline in silver exports to the Viking world.[39] Just as the Merovingian grip on gold may have provoked the disastrous sixth-century raid of *Hugilaikaz (discussed in Chapter Two), so the late tenth-century drop in silver coming from the east may have contributed to the renewed quests for Danegeld silver in the west.

Many deaths . . .

The Swedish domination of the eastern Viking world has meant, regrettably, that very little account of it was passed into the Norwegian or Icelandic traditions of the western Viking world, with none of the bravura stories of last stands and heroic deaths such as have been recounted in earlier chapters. Such stories there may have been. Nora Chadwick noted, rather wistfully, that the *Primary Chronicle* brightens up and becomes more animated in some places, as if there the author had something to build on.[40] Oleg's son Svyatoslav, Prince of Kiev, at one point makes a rather characteristic speech of encouragement to his troops in a difficult situation: 'Let us not disgrace Rus', but rather sacrifice our lives, lest we be dishonoured. For if we flee, we shall be disgraced.' The princess Rogned, or *Ragnheiðr*, also comes out with a piece of female tactlessness, reminiscent of the princess who refused Harald Fairhair, when she refuses Prince Vladimir 1: 'I will not draw off the boots of a slave's son.'[41] But on the whole the reflections in sagas of the eastern experience are disappointing to fanciful, notably in *Yngvars saga*, 'The Saga of Yngvar the Far-Travelled', and *Eymunds þáttr*, 'The Story of Eymund Hringsson'.[42]

There is no doubt that these have *some* connection to Gardariki. King Jarisleif of *Eymunds þáttr* must be Yaroslav, son of Vladimir 1 and married to the Swedish princess Ingigerd, mentioned above and a major figure in the saga. But Eymund himself seems to be an invented character, and his saga 'a construct of conventional material'.[43] *Yngvars saga* looks even less well-based, a farrago of fantastic events: giants, dragons, demons, alluring but fatal females, a strange beast (an elephant?) that carries a tower on its back, and even, drawn from learned legend, cyclopes like Odysseus' victim. Picking reliable information out of this seems a lost cause. Yet, as the saga's translators note, the saga author is careful to give his source, a lost Latin work written around 1180 in Iceland by Odd Snorrason, and he names Odd's three oral informants, one of them a priest called Isleif who says he heard the tale at the royal court of Sweden.

The modern translators of *Yngvars saga* ask, accordingly:

> Were there still members of the Swedish royal family in the middle
> of the twelfth century who cherished the memory of a talented, tragic
> kinsman, who had penetrated deeper than any other Scandinavian
> before him into the mysterious territories of the east?[44]

One has to say 'probably not' to the last part of the question, given how deeply many Scandinavians had definitely penetrated into Eurasia; and the motive ascribed in the saga to Yngvar, a wish to find the course of the greatest of the 'three rivers flowing through Russia from the east', seems the wrong way round. What interested the Rus were the rivers that flowed *to* the east, and to the south, and they had no trouble finding the sources of the Don, Dnieper or Volga. It was where they *came out* that was interesting and at first unknown.

Nevertheless, there is no doubt that there was someone called Yngvar who led an expedition in the eleventh century far into the east and who, like the saga hero, never came back. More than twenty runic inscriptions, carved in stone, mostly from the same area in northern Sweden, mention men who went with Yngvar and did not return,[45] as on the Gripsholm stone already quoted. Others commemorate Sæbiörn and Gunnleif, Gunnvid and Thorbiörn, Baki and Skardi, Ulf and Beglir and a dozen more, all fathers or sons or brothers, steersmen and shipowners, several of them praised as being a **trek** or **trik snialan**, a *drengr*, a bold man, all of whom went **miþ ikuari**, 'with Yngvar', and died **o sirklanti**, 'in Serkland', in the east. It must have been a considerable disaster to cost the lives of so many men of the runestone-erecting class. But we do not know what Yngvar's target was, or what went wrong. There was an attack on the Caucasus in the 1030s, on Byzantium in 1043, and Scandinavians fought in a civil war in Georgia in the 1040s. Just as likely, though, there were no survivors and no word ever came back of the doomed expedition.

The word 'doomed' makes a link with another famous Kievan Rus death, that of Oleg, the true founder of the Rurikid dynasty, which may also have been remembered in garbled form in the west. Norse heroic legend had a predilection for stories of doomed heroes. At the end of 'The Lay of Hamdir', Sorli reminds his brother that 'No man lives one evening beyond the decree of the Norns'. Likewise the Eddic poem on the 'Battle of the Goths and Huns' ends with Angantyr saying sadly over the body of his half-brother Hlod, whom he has just killed, 'We are cursed, kinsman, / your killer am I! / It will never be forgotten. / The Norns' doom is evil'.[46]

In both cases, one should point out, human miscalculation has a lot to do with the disaster. Hamdir and Sorli arrogantly refuse the assistance of their half-brother Erp, whom they will not acknowledge as a brother, and their arrogance makes the difference between success and failure. Angantyr, by contrast, was ready to acknowledge and negotiate with his half-brother Hlod, until his adviser Gizur arrogantly and provocatively used the word *hornungr*, 'bastard'. But as a character in 'The Saga of Gisli' says, 'The words of fate will be spoken by someone.'[47] Humans make the mistakes, but something supernatural prompts them to do so (a theme well picked out by J.R.R. Tolkien in *The Silmarillion*).

Such is the case with Oleg, founder of the great Rurikid dynasty. According once again to the *Primary Chronicle*, Oleg asked his 'magicians', some time early in his reign, what would be the cause of his death, and they told him it would be his favourite horse.[48] Oleg accordingly gave orders that the horse should be fed and cared for but never brought into his presence. Years later, after his successful attack on Byzantium, he remembered the horse and asked his squire what had happened to it. He was told it had died, and he laughed at his magicians, saying, 'Soothsayers tell untruths, and their words are naught but falsehood. This horse is dead, but I am still alive.'To make sure, he goes to see where the horse's bones lie, dismounts and stamps triumphantly on the skull. A snake crawls out of it and bites him in the foot, from which he dies.

Strangely, the same story is told in another legendary saga that has connections with the world of the far east and far north, *Örvar-Odds saga*, 'The Saga of Arrow-Odd'.[49] This is the third and longest of the sequence of sagas dealing with the 'men of Hrafnista' (for which see Chapter Five). It details many adventures and battles, and like *Heiðreks saga*, discussed above, contains long poems which may be older than the saga and perhaps the basis for it. The whole saga, however, is framed by a story virtually identical to that told about Prince Oleg. Odd is told by a prophetess that he will live for three hundred years and will never settle down, but that nevertheless a horse called Faxi will be the death of him. Odd kills Faxi, buries him in a mound of sand and boulders, and goes off on his long adventures, which end with him becoming king of 'all Gardariki', married to a beautiful Russian princess called Silkisif (probably a garbled form of the Greek Elizabeth). He nevertheless decides to return home, where he looks sadly at the ruins where he used to play. He then – just like Oleg, for 'the words of fate will be spoken by someone'– tempts fate by saying, 'there's not much likelihood now of that prophecy coming true that the old witch prophesied about me long ago. But what's that lying there, isn't it a horse's skull?' It is, for Faxi's mound has been eroded by time. He prods it with his spear and an adder crawls out and bites him, from which he dies.[50]

It is at least a strange coincidence that a story told about a Russian prince of the tenth century should also be told about a Norwegian hero from a family with strong connections to Russia. Nora Chadwick suggested that there were early poems about Odd and that such a poem may have been the basis for the story in the *Primary Chronicle* about Oleg, which is possible, if unprovable.[51] As he lies dying of snakebite, like Ragnar, Odd nevertheless composes a poem of 71 stanzas, which is at once a death song and a 'life song', that records his exploits:

With sword we set on sons of men
and destroyed their wooden gods . . .
Then I was happy,
For less time than I expected . . .
. . . Here we must part;
bear to Silkisif and our sons
my greeting; I won't be coming.[52]

. . . and a murder

The last three words of Odd's poem, *kemk eigi par*, make for a good stern ending, at once triumphant, sad, without self-pity. Nevertheless, the final death scene in this chapter deserves to go to someone much more unfortunate, completely anonymous, her life and her name forgotten, her death preserved only by chance – a death that nonetheless has an echo, a disturbingly real-life one, of much more famous ones from northern legend. It is the death of a slave girl, recorded by another Arab who came in contact with the Rus and now very well known in outline from the opening scenes of the movie *The 13th Warrior* (1999).

In the year 921 a native of Baghdad called Ahmad Ibn Fadlan was sent by Caliph al-Muqtadir on an embassy to the Muslim king of the Bulgars, who had asked for the blessing of the Commander of the Faithful, and also for money to build a fortress against his Khazar trade rivals. Ibn Fadlan wrote a long account of his voyage, on which he encountered many peoples. But what has attracted the most attention is a passage in which he describes another party of visitors to the Bulgars, whom he called 'the Russiyah'.[53] They were traders and had camped by the river Atil (probably Itil, the capital of the Bulgars, on the Volga near modern Kazan). Ibn Fadlan's praise of these people's physique has already been quoted, as has his disgust at their lack of hygiene: Arabs were readily disgusted by people who did not wash ritually after urination, defecation or having sex, but the Rus in Ibn Fadlan's account were even worse when they *did* wash, for they all used the same bowl of water, spitting and blowing their noses in it as well as washing hands and hair and wiping their combs.

In among this mix of praise and blame Ibn Fadlan notes many things. All the Rus, he says, carry axe, sword and dagger all the time and are never parted from their weapons. Their swords are broadswords of the Frankish type, and each man is tattooed from his neck to his toes. The women wear brooches with knives dangling from them, and torques or neck rings of different metals indicating wealth and status, as well as necklets of ceramic beads bought for a dinar a bead. They all have booths in which they display the beautiful slave girls they have brought for sale, but they themselves have sex with the girls, in front of their companions. Ibn Fadlan observes disapprovingly – it's poor business practice – that they do not stop even if a customer turns up. They also sacrifice to idols, asking their gods to send them rich customers who will buy everything and not haggle over the price. They quarantine their sick and hang thieves. When a poor Rus dies, he is burned in a boat. Funeral rites of the rich, however, are more complex, and this is what Ibn Fadlan goes on to describe in detail, for a chieftain of the Rus died while he was there.

This, he says, is what happens among the Rus at a rich man's funeral. First, his wealth is divided into thirds. One-third goes to the man's family, but the other two-thirds go on funeral expenses: one-third for his burial clothes and one-third to buy alcohol for the day of the final cremation, for these people 'drink *nabidh* [beer?] unrestrainedly, night and day, so that sometimes one of them dies with his wine cup in his hand'. But it is the practice of human sacrifice that most attracts the Arab's attention (and since then, the attention of Western scholars). What happens, according to Ibn Fadlan, is that the man is put in a temporary grave while his grave clothes are prepared. His slave girls and boys are asked who will die with him, and on this occasion one of the girls says, 'I will.'

There is then no going back. While they wait for the clothes to be prepared the girl victim is escorted everywhere and 'spends each day drinking and singing, happily and joyfully'. Meanwhile a boat is landed and propped up on blocks, inside which is set up a kind of pavilion, containing a bed. The corpse is exhumed and then dressed in a rich manner and placed in the pavilion, propped up on cushions, with food, drink and his weapons. A dog, two horses and two cows are also sacrificed, their meat put in the boat. In the meantime an old woman has appeared, 'a witch, thick-bodied and sinister'. The Rus call her the Angel of Death.

The girl victim then visits each of the booths of the other Rus, and in each the owner has sex with her, saying: 'Tell your master I only did this for love of him.' A kind of wooden door frame is made, and the girl is raised up three times to look over it, after which she cuts off the head of a hen. Ibn Fadlan says that he asked an interpreter what the girl was saying when she looked over the frame and was told that the girl said she saw, successively, her parents, her relatives, and finally her master sitting in Paradise and calling her. She then gave away her bracelets and anklets, boarded the boat, and was given cups of *nabidh* to drink. Ibn Fadlan comments, 'I saw that the girl did not know what she was doing.' She tried to enter the pavilion on the boat, but got her head caught between the boat and pavilion. The old woman freed her and took her into the pavilion, while the watching Rus banged their shields so that none of the other slave girls present could hear any cries and be frightened for their own futures. Six men entered the pavilion and all had sex with the victim, after which the men strangled her with a cord while the Angel of Death stabbed her with a dagger. Then the chief mourner walked naked round the boat, backwards, with one hand over his anus. And then they burned boat, pavilion, master and victim, so that all were reduced to ashes within an hour. One of the Rus laughed at this and said to Ibn Fadlan that Arabs were fools, because they put their loved ones into the ground for worms, whereas 'we burn them in an instant, so that at once and without delay they enter Paradise.'[54]

The account has caused revulsion among modern commentators, who have been quick to try to shift the blame onto other people, preferably non-Europeans. It is argued that Ibn Fadlan's 'Russiyah' may not have been Scandinavians at all; or that they may have been subject to 'foreign influence' (nomads, Khazars, Pecheneg skull-drinkers, whatever); or they were in a state of 'ethnic/social fluidity', that is, somewhere along the line that turned Norsemen into Slavs; or that some of what he describes is hearsay.[55] It is true that there are some things Ibn Fadlan cannot have seen, like the final gang rape and murder inside the pavilion, and for some things he had to rely on an interpreter. Nevertheless, he says he was an eyewitness to events right up to the murder of the slave girl, and he writes like one – note the detail about the girl getting confused and getting her head stuck. Neil Price has, furthermore, noted how several of the details given in the account – the temporary grave, the burial clothes, the prodigious funeral drinking – also appear in Scandinavian archaeological record.[56]

Revulsion at the whole story is natural, but one ought to look harder at what causes it, and how far there is, unfortunately, corroboration for putting the blame on the Vikings. First and most obviously, the whole idea of human sacrifice, killing others 'to ease [your] own death', as Tolkien's Gandalf put it, is cruel, selfish, pointless. It is perhaps inevitable that the sacrifice should be borne by the weakest in society, women and people of low status like servants and slaves: though these two groups need not be the same. The *Flateyjarbók* version of 'The Saga of Olaf Tryggvason' reports that Queen Sigrid the Haughty left her husband King Eirik of Sweden because 'it was the law in Sweden that if a king died the queen should be laid in mound beside him', and she knew Eirik 'had not many years to live'.[57]

There is then the claim, or pretence, that the victim is a volunteer. Someone has to say, 'I will,' but we do not know what pressure was put on the potential victims to say the fatal words – which cannot be taken back. Queen Brynhild in the Eddic 'Short Lay of Sigurd' scornfully refuses anyone who does not want to die with her, but that sounds like a noble ideal (and in any case, at the end of the poem she claims that five serving girls and eight other servants will be burned with the lovers, as well as her own personal 'foster-man', given her by her father).[58] What would have happened on the banks of the Volga if every slave had said 'no'? One notes that the girl victim seems to have been kept not only under guard but also permanently drunk during the long ten days while people were fussing with the master's grave clothes. Finally, the element of gang rape looks like mere opportunism. 'Tell your master I only did this for love of him,' indeed! Few would believe that this was done only out of duty and affection, any more than was the last act of rape and murder, done out of sight and concealed by noise, as if even the mourners knew it should be kept secret.

But how much of this scene might be plausible, even for Vikings? First, there is evidence for human sacrifice among Scandinavians, both documentary (lots of this, regularly dismissed by historians as exaggerated) and archaeological. The grave at Ballateare in the Isle of Man, excavated in 1946, contained a warrior buried with his weapons in a coffin, but also the body of a young woman, her skull sliced through by sword or axe. Recent discoveries at Flakstad in Norway have also been interpreted as slave sacrifice, with child sacrifice at Trelleborg in Denmark,[59] and in a Viking context at Repton, as described in Chapter Four.

Second, the cremation, in a boat, is a curious custom that nevertheless looks entirely characteristic for Scandinavians, not steppe nomads. The beheading of the hen is, moreover, reminiscent of Saxo Grammaticus's story of Hadding, the witch who guided him to the wall around the Undying Lands, killed a cockerel and threw it over the wall. Next moment he heard it crow, before he himself had to turn back to the mortal world.[60] Is the girl being assured she will not have to turn back and will come back to life on the other side of the wall? The door frame over which the victim is lifted to see into Paradise suggests some similar belief. Finally, the mode of death, simultaneous strangling and stabbing, recurs in accounts of sacrifice to Norse gods, primarily Odin, such as the death of King Vikar (hanged and stabbed) in both Saxo and *Gautreks saga*.[61]

As for gang rape, though Norse accounts are praiseworthily fastidious to avoid mentioning it, there need not be much doubt that it happened. Round about the year 1000, Wulfstan, Archbishop of York, wrote a furious diatribe against his Anglo-Saxon countrymen, *Sermo Lupi ad Anglos*, whose sins, he claimed, were what had brought disaster on their country. One of the main accusations levelled against the Christian English is that too often, many of them club together and buy a woman as a joint purchase between them and practice foul sin with that one woman, one after another, each after the other like dogs with no care for filth, and then for a price they sell a creature of God – His own purchase that He bought at a great price – into the power of enemies.[62]

Buying a slave (who from?), gang raping her and then selling her, quite likely a Christian, on or back to the Vikings: this is behaviour, Wulfstan implies, that they have learned from the Viking enemies with whom he is preoccupied. If so, this would certainly be a good case of 'ethnic / social fluidity', but one where the blame cannot be passed off to steppe nomads. And there are other uncomfortable similarities for Northern Europeans in Ibn Fadlan's account, like the addiction to alcohol, the careless attitude towards customers and the spare-no-expense funerals. All round, it seems hard to shift responsibility for this sad and cruel event on to other ethnic groups.

The best part of the 'Viking way of death' is the refusal to grieve for oneself or to give in, even when undergoing death alone, defeated, by torture. The insistence of Gunnar or Ragnar that death cannot break the spirit, and that the spirit is what counts, is wholly admirable, as are – with more of a stretch of the imagination – the point-of-honour deaths of noble women like Signy and Brynhild. Even in those deaths, though, there's a mean streak, which comes out more obviously in Egil, his father Skalla-Grim, Bodvar's nose-biting companion Hjalti, and some of the characters to be seen in succeeding chapters. The costs were borne by people like the now nameless girl on the Volga. Where had she been traded from? The Rus-folk's Slavic tributaries? Ireland? Or England? She fell into the hands of *drengir*, bold men no doubt, as they often claimed to be. They were people traffickers just the same.

It is a strange irony that though she has no grave and no memorial, quite unlike Ganger-Hrolf, father of kings, with his marble tomb in Rouen, the fate of the nameless slave girl has by now, as a result of *The 13th Warrior*, probably reached more people than have ever known about Hrolf. Rightly so: the fate of her and those like her underlies the Gotland hoards, the birth of Russia, the basis of Viking wealth.

PART III

The Tale in the North

S ources for the seven chapters preceding have been extremely various. By contrast, the events of the next three chapters come in large part from an almost consecutive sequence of three kings' sagas from Snorri Sturluson's *Heimskringla*. Snorri takes his story as a whole all the way from prehistoric antiquity up to the death of King Magnus Erlingsson in 1184; and since he was writing probably in the 1220s, he could still have collected information about King Magnus at least from living informants, while by then written documents had also become familiar in the Northern world. But how did Snorri know about events that happened, in the case of the forthcoming three chapters, more than two hundred years before he wrote?

Snorri was a learned man, with books available to him. Three Latin accounts which he certainly drew on are mentioned in what follows. He used them as inspiration, however, not as sources of information. Historical writing had, furthermore, begun in Norway before his time, with works like the Latin *History of the Antiquity of the Norwegian Kings* by the monk Theodoricus, written about 1180; later 'synoptic' or survey-histories in both Latin and Old Norse; and early sagas, including the 'Saga of the Jomsvikings'.[1] Noting the existence of these, however, only pushes the question of sources further back. Where did these pre-Snorri authors get *their* information from? There is no escaping the conclusion that much of it (if it was not complete fiction) must have come from oral tradition, from stories passed on by word of mouth.

In Icelandic circumstances, this is readily explicable. Icelanders were then (and still are) interested in and proud of their ancestry. Some of them still claim to be able to trace their descent from saga heroes of a thousand years ago: Snorri himself was a descendant of Egil and the Myramenn.

It's clear that many families preserved the memory of ancestors who had fought at Hjorungavag or Svold or Stiklastadir. Moreover, the two originating works of Icelandic history are the *Íslendingabók*, 'Book of Icelanders', and the *Landnamabók*, 'Book of Settlements', both written a hundred years before Snorri, by Ari Thorgilsson and (possibly) Sæmund Sigfusson respectively, both named 'the Learned'.[2] The latter work lists more than 3,500 personal names and nearly 1,500 farmsteads, and the only way it can have been compiled is by asking people who first settled their areas and who claimed which strips of land – information that current owners would not readily forget. The greater part of the many kings' sagas by Snorri and others, including other individual sagas by named authors and several compilations made before and after Snorri, must have come from accounts and anecdotes, likewise preserved orally and stitched together, so to speak, by the saga authors. Gísli Sigurðsson, in his important book on *The Medieval Icelandic Saga and Oral Tradition* (2004), calls such bodies of locally known information 'immanent sagas' and has shown that they lie behind many sagas of Icelanders, with both great consistency and apparent contradictions (as one might expect of stories remembered by different factions in a local quarrel).

A further important and independent source of information – which, however, created problems of its own – was the corpus of skaldic verse, much of it contemporary with the events it celebrated, if biased and frequently inscrutable. No one was in a better position to know, remember and interpret this than Snorri, with his detailed knowledge of poets, poetry, poetic diction and poetic metre, as revealed in the last two sections of his *Prose Edda*. The first of the sixteen sagas making up *Heimskringla* ('The Saga of the Ynglings') derives almost entirely from the poem *Ynglingatal*, or 'List of the Ynglings', by Thjodolf of Hvin. It was not the only such poem. The *þula*, or mnemonic list, was a poetic genre across the Northern world – see for instance the Old English poem *Widsith*, quoted in Chapter Two – and as with many tribal peoples the job of a *þyle* (like Unferth in *Beowulf*) was to know them. Examples include *Haleygjatal*, 'List of the Men of Halogaland', and the poem *Kálfsvísa*, a list of the horses heroes rode to a famous prehistoric battle on the ice of Lake Vaner in Sweden, as well as *Dvergatal*, the 'List of Dwarfs' from which Tolkien drew his names for *The Hobbit*.[3]

One comes, then, to the issue of reliability. First, oral tradition is not good on dates. It must be remembered that for the whole of the Viking Age, and after, most people had no idea 'what date it was', having no fixed system of reckoning. Events might be dated with reference to other events – 'five years after the fall of King Olaf', for example – but putting a number on a year came in only with the Christian system. Second, one has of course to allow for conscious bias or unconscious misremembering on the part of oral informants. In my own case, to be personal, I remember accounts going back to 1914 (the shelling of Hartlepool by German battle-cruisers), told to me by relatives at first and second hand. On checking against written sources, they and other similar stories proved to have significant but explicable errors: my grandfather was not going to admit that the Germans got away, and mentally conflated their successful raid with a failed one three weeks later, where one of the battle-cruisers was indeed sunk. Without the documentary sources I would have believed my grandfather.

On the other hand, a great deal of history never made its way into any document. Such things are likely to be more first-hand than what is later written down. One has to add that in our fully literate society, where we are used to having documentation for everything, people are careless about passing on stories orally. This was not the case even in post-Christian Iceland. It's striking that as late as the 1390s the priests Jón Thórdarson and Magnús Thórhallsson, compiling *Flateyjarbók* for the rich farmer Jón Hákonarson, still found extensive material to add in to the kings' sagas, including material not known to (or more likely quietly ignored by) Snorri, such as the extended stories about Thorgerd Holgabrud and her role in the defeat of the Jomsvikings, detailed in the next chapter.[4]

Finally, and this is a familiar problem with all historical works, one has to allow for the intentions of the author. Snorri's two major themes are the unification of Norway, against fierce resistance, by a succession of hero-kings starting with Harald Fairhair, and – very much connected with that project – the Christianization of Norway, once more against fierce resistance, by much the same set of kings, this time acting as aggressive and unscrupulous missionaries. As noted at the start of Chapter Nine, there may have been another story, from the heathen side, later censored out of existence.

In the chapters that follow, then, while Snorri's *Heimskringla* accounts form the main thread, as much corroboration as possible is drawn from other accounts, while contradictions are also noted. The main source of uncertainty remains – and we should be grateful for it – Snorri's mesmeric ability to tell a tale. Many saga writers are good, one or two may be even better – see the examples in the final chapter about sagas of Icelanders – but Snorri eclipses them all in scale and ambition.

NINE

The Jarls and the Jomsvikings:
A Study in *Drengskapr*

ometimes, sagas get lost. We know there was once a *Skjöldunga
saga*, a saga about the Skjoldungs, the legendary pre-Viking kings
of Denmark, because the Icelander Arngrímur Jónsson made a
Latin summary of it in the sixteenth century;[1] but we do not know what
Arngrímur cut out, altered or perhaps misunderstood. We also know there
was once a saga about an Icelander called Gauk Trandilsson, a real person,
mentioned several times elsewhere, because the scribe of the compilation
Möðruvallabók listed the saga and left a space for it[2] – but something
went wrong and a copy was never made. Conversely, sometimes we have
two versions of the same event, from different angles. In *Vatnsdæla saga*,
'The Saga of the People of Vatnsdal', the family 'enforcer' for the men of
Vatnsdale is a thug called Jokul. The saga brags that he arranged to fight
a duel with one of the district's other hard men, Finnbogi, but Finnbogi
did not show up, and Jokul raised a *níðstöng*, a 'shame pole', to taunt his
rival. 'The Saga of Finnbogi the Mighty' admits the fact, but claims that
weather made the road to the duelling ground completely impassable and
says nothing about the *níðstöng*. One can see that there were probably two
stories circulating among different families or supporter groups in the area
within days of the event, or non-event, and one can only guess as to which
was nearer the truth.[3]

This chapter, accordingly, turns on one saga that we do have, *Jómsvíkinga saga*, 'The Saga of the Jomsvikings', and one we no longer have
but which is thought to have existed, *Hlaða-jarla saga*, or 'The Saga of
the Jarls of Hladir'. There is good reason why the latter should have been
deleted, or censored out of existence, for it very likely ran counter to the
main themes of the many kings' sagas recorded in Icelandic. These between
them give what one might call the official account of the unification of
Norway under a succession of hero-kings, several of them also committed
to a policy of forcible conversion to Christianity. But no doubt there were
people who had their own reasons for not going along with royal policy,

and who were well able to stand up for themselves, and these included the Hladir jarls.

To understand the Hladir jarls, one needs to understand the geography of Norway. As remarked already in Chapter Five, Norway is a very long country, with the modern capital, Oslo, closer to Rome than it is to North Cape: its very name comes from the *norðr vegr*, the 'north way' that runs up the long coast to the very tip of Europe. It was also remarked in the same chapter that Egil Skallagrimsson's far-northern relations, the 'men of Hrafnista', were generally regarded as being weird because they had cross-bred with trolls. As it happens we have a fairly long account of life in the far north, dictated to scribes at the court of King Alfred by a Norseman whom the Anglo-Saxons called Ohthere (his real name probably Ottar). Ottar claimed to live further north than any other Northmen, and much of what he said seemed weird to the Anglo-Saxons, though we can now see that it is perfectly realistic, or at least explicable: his herd of reindeer, his killing of sixty whales in two days with only five assistants, his voyage of exploration all the way round North Cape into what is now the White Sea.[4] Ottar also made it clear that, just like the Rus, most of his wealth came from tribute extorted from the people he calls 'Finns', the nomadic hunters of the Sami people. They paid him stipulated quantities of furs, feathers, 'whale bone' (maybe walrus ivory), bear-skin and otter-skin coats, and ropes made from seal and walrus hide. Ottar said nothing about paying a toll on this tribute to the king of Norway, and perhaps, in the 880s and 890s, no such toll existed. By Egil's time a generation and more later, it did, and the kings of Norway took it very seriously, for the tribute from the far north consisted of luxury goods and must have made a substantial proportion, not of Norway's gross domestic product, but certainly of its profitable exports. As noted, it was the accusation that Egil's uncle Thorolf was not paying King Harald his cut that led to Thorolf's death and the exile of the family.

Between the kings of Norway in Oslo, however, and the far northerners like Ottar and the Hrafnistumen, lay the jarls of Hladir, in their home territory round Trondheim. One can accordingly say, very summarily, that most of Norwegian history during the Viking era was dominated by the clash between the two most habitable and populated areas of Norway, the Eastland and its surrounding districts, centred on Oslo to the south, and the Trøndelag, far up the coastline to the north, with the intervening Atlantic districts of the Westland shifting their allegiance to and fro as circumstances dictated.

That history was further framed by four major battles. They were: (1) Hafrsfjord, near Stavanger, fought not far off the time when Ottar was talking to King Alfred. Its traditional date is 872, twenty years earlier than Ottar's report to Alfred, but it was probably in reality rather later. In it King Harald Fairhair, originally a king somewhere in the Eastland but by this time also controlling much of the Westland, defeated an attack from the north and by tradition became the first *einvaldskonungr*, or sole king of the whole of Norway. It was this battle that according to Icelandic tradition led to a mass exodus by those who would not accept the southern victor's rule and preferred to settle Iceland. (2) Hjorungavag, some 320 km (200 mi.) north and almost a century later, which was a triumph for the Tronds against an attempt to impose rule from the south backed by the King of Denmark. (3) Svold, in the year 1000 (though there are considerable doubts about where this battle was fought), another win for the Tronds, this time backed by both Danes and Swedes, against Eastland and Westland together. (4) Stiklastadir, fought in the Trøndelag in 1030, and leading to yet another defeat for the king from the south.

One can see even from this brief survey that the persistent attempts by the Westland and Eastland kings to take over the northern territories failed repeatedly, though the north is where most of the battles were fought. And while the many surviving royal sagas insistently make heroes of the southern kings – defeat, as this book consistently points out, is a requirement for a proper hero-story, not, as Hollywood would see it, a disqualification – the core of the opposition to them came from the jarls of the Tronds, with their base at Hladir on the southern side of the Trondheim fjord.

That is why we wish we had the lost 'Saga of the Jarls of Hladir'. It might redress the balance of the stories that survive and fill out the evidence of skaldic poems – for the jarls were well served at least by their skalds.[5] What we do have, however, is *Jómsvíkinga saga*,[6] which builds up to its account of the Battle of Hjorungavag, the sorcery-assisted victory of Jarl Hakon of Hladir and his son Jarl Eirik. There are two other extended accounts of the battle, one in 'The Saga of Olaf Tryggvason' as found in Snorri's *Heimskringla*, and one in the longer saga of the same name in the compilation *Flateyjarbók*: both are used here to fill out the *Jómsvíkinga* version.

The Saga of the Jomsvikings: the Baltic professionals

'The Saga of the Jomsvikings' is an anomaly among the many sagas that survive, even more so than 'Egil's Saga', discussed in Chapter Five. Some forty of the sagas surviving are sagas of Icelanders. 'The Saga of the Jomsvikings' is not one of those: it does mention Icelanders, notably Vigfus, son of Killer-Glum, but only peripherally. We also have a number of kings' sagas, as well as Snorri's *Heimskringla* sequence. Kings certainly figure in 'The Saga of the Jomsvikings', which moves in the world of royal politics, but it has no royal central personage. Another accepted category is sagas of old times, of which the most famous is 'The Saga of the Volsungs'. *Jómsvíkinga* resembles them in its resolutely heroic spirit and its often fantastic quality, but it is not about 'old times'; it's about relatively recent Viking history. It is accordingly often left out of collected editions and does not figure much in modern scholarly discussions. All one can say is that we wish we had some more like it.

The saga starts far away from Norway, in south Scandinavia, with particular interest in the islands and the southern shore of the Baltic. What it says is that (cutting out a good deal of build-up to the main events) a man called Palna-Toki, from the Danish island of Fyn, found himself caught up in the civil war between King Harald Bluetooth of Denmark and his son Svein Forkbeard, both of them very well-attested historical characters. Eventually Toki shot King Harald from ambush. This brought him no gratitude, however, from Svein, and Toki fled east across the Baltic to the land of the Wends. After a while, King Burisleif (or Burizlav) asked Toki to settle on the coast of his kingdom to protect it against raiders, and Toki took the opportunity to build a stronghold called Jomsborg, with a harbour big enough to take 360 longships.

The first element in Jomsborg, Jom-, may indeed come from a Finnish word and mean 'pool', which would make Jomsborg analogous to Dublin in the west (Dublin meaning 'black pool', from Old Irish *dubh linn*). The saga says there was a stone arch over the entrance to the harbour, with iron gates, and a tower over the arch with *valslǫngur*, 'battle slings' or catapults mounted. The stronghold was a base for Toki's picked men, who became known as the Jomsvikings, and he established laws they had to follow: only those aged between eighteen and fifty were allowed to join; no one was to flee or show fear; comrades were to be avenged and loot shared; women were not allowed to enter Jomsborg; no one could be away longer than three days; disputes were forbidden, and inherited feuds were to be settled by Toki.

How much of this is fact and how much fancy? The arch, gates, tower and catapults all look like wild exaggeration, and there is no evidence for the existence of anyone called Palna-Toki. On the other hand, there was a Duke Boleslav of Poland, there were Scandinavian settlements with garrisons on the southern Baltic, and Jomsborg, well attested from several sources, is generally identified with the Polish town of Wollin, which in the late tenth century had a trading settlement and a walled citadel, with clear signs of Scandinavian occupation.[7]

As for the laws of the Jomsvikings, they are in the first place quite sensible and indeed have similarities with early modern Articles of War or King's Regulations. We also have an early Danish code for a group of warriors, the *Lex Castrensis*, written in the twelfth century for King Valdemar I but claiming to be based on rules drawn up by Knut (Canute) the Great, son of Svein Forkbeard; and this lays down broadly similar regulations 'to restrain the boldness of the unruly ones'.[8] Rules were framed about sharing duties, avoiding provocation and settling disputes. Penalties included, for the first offence, losing seniority, and for three offences, going to the bottom seat and being pelted with bones. There was a ritual also for expelling incorrigibles, who could and should thereafter be attacked with impunity.

There is also the strange phenomenon of the 'trelleborgs'. The first of these (which was called Trelleborg) was discovered in the 1930s in Denmark, but since then six more have been found in Denmark and southern Sweden. All were circular fortifications, all had four gates at the points of the compass, with two roads dividing the circle into quadrants, and within each quadrant were four or more identical longhouses. They differ in size, the biggest of them, at Aggersborg in north Jutland, being 240 m (780 ft) across, but the uniformity of their layout suggests that they are all part of some centralized plan, and built at the same time, in the later years of the reign of Harald Bluetooth (d. *c.* 985) – Trelleborg itself has been dated by the tree rings in its wood to 981. Were they barracks? Or training grounds? The name Trelleborg could mean 'the slaves' fort', which again might mean that they were built by slave labour, or possibly that they were meant as giant barracoons or slave pens. But they do look like barracks for something like a national army:[9] the first trelleborg, with its sixteen longhouses, could have held upwards of six hundred men, while the biggest one, at Aggersborg, looks well placed for an army thinking of heading for Norway – or for England, as Danish armies did in the time of King Svein. So the idea of a disciplined community of warriors, whether in Denmark or on the shores of the southern Baltic, does not seem unlikely at all.

The saga goes on to introduce two new sets of characters, one pair from the Danish island of Sjælland – Sigvaldi and his brother Thorkel the Tall – and another pair from Bornholm, Bui the Broad and his brother Sigurd. After Palna-Toki's death, Sigvaldi takes over. A settlement is patched up between the Jomsvikings and King Svein, but bad blood remains, and is increased by a highly unlikely story involving King Svein being palmed off with an ugly sister while Sigvaldi gets the pretty one. It is this that makes Svein determined on revenge, and he uses the Jomsvikings' rashness and honour code against them.

What he does is host a banquet, get the Jomsvikings drunk, and then suggest it would be highly suitable to follow the old custom of *heitstreng-ing*, making boastful vows.[10] The participant (as described in other sagas) stands with one foot up on a stone, stump or bench and declares: *Nú stíg ek á stokk, nú strengi ek þessi heit*, 'Now I stand on the stock, now I make this vow' – such vows, of course, having to be fulfilled on penalty of universal disgrace. Sigvaldi, who cannot be totally drunk, suggests Svein should lead, and he does, with the vow that 'before three years are past I shall drive Ethelred, king of England, from his kingdom or kill him otherwise and so gain possession of his domain.'[11] The dates do not fit exactly, but Svein did in fact start his attacks on England in 1002, though it took him eleven years to drive Ethelred out and be crowned king of England. The saga allows us to infer that this had been his intention all the time.

The Jomsvikings, however, had to respond with something of similar scale – Svein tells Sigvaldi, 'let your vow be as far-reaching as mine' – but had nothing prepared. Sigvaldi then says the fatal words, trying to match Svein's, 'I swear . . . that before three years are past I shall ravage Norway with as many men as I can assemble and drive Earl Hákon out of the land or kill him; or else my lifeless body will remain in Norway.' (Earl Hakon was the current jarl of Hladir.) His brother Thorkel then says, rather care-fully, that he will follow Sigvaldi and not flee before he does. Bui, Sigurd, and Palna-Toki's young grandson Vagn say much the same thing, but Vagn adds his own coda: he will kill a man called Thorkel Leira and have sex with his daughter without the permission of her family. (*Leir* means 'clay', and *leira* is a mud flat, but it's hard to see how these might become a nickname: I leave this one untranslated.) In the morning Sigvaldi can't remember anything about his vow, but naturally there are people there to remind him and the others what they committed to. The only surprise is that they set off right away, with sixty ships of Jomsvikings and sixty more extorted from King Svein.

But what made Jarl Hakon of Hladir the target? Why would profes-sional raiders based on the southern shore of the Baltic sail or row more than 1,000 nautical miles (1,852 km) to Trondheim? It is certain that two sides, whoever they were, did clash at Hjorungavag. But to explain the geo-politics of it, one has to go back further in the legendary history of Norway.

The jarls of Hladir: holdouts in the north

The Icelanders' origin legend has already been mentioned, in Chapter Five. According to the Icelanders – as detailed in 'The Saga of Harald Fairhair' – emigration to Iceland was started by the proud reply of a maiden. Harald, hereditary king of the Westfold and adjoining districts, and king by conquest of several more, sent messengers to the daughter of a petty king of Hordaland, on the Atlantic coast, offering to make her his concubine. Gyda replied that she did not intend to waste her maidenhood on a man who was king of only a few districts. Spelling it out, she wanted a man like King Gorm of Denmark or King Eirik of Sweden, who would have solitary rule over all Norway. Only such a man could be called *þjóðkonungr* or *einvaldskonungr*, a people's king, a 'sole ruler', the king of something like a modern nation state.[12]

When her answer was reported to Harald, he did not take offence, but agreed that she was right, and made a *heitstrenging* of his own: he would not cut or comb his hair until he had brought all Norway under his rule or died in the attempt. He then started a process of conquest, district by district, brought to a climax at Hafrsfjord perhaps around AD 885, after which he won the lady. The story could easily be a Snorri invention, based on no more than the king's nickname, *Hárfagri* or 'Fairhair'. But Norwegian unification under Harald Fairhair, and the subsequent flight of those not prepared to be unified, is the basis of Icelandic historical tradition.

If it was Harald's aim to win Gyda and unify Norway, however, Harald seems to have thought little of either achievement. He had many wives besides Gyda, including Ragnhild, Svanhild and Ashild, all daughters of jarls or kings and all (unlike Gyda) bearing sons ready to squabble for power. As noted earlier, he is said to have 'let go' eleven less well-connected wives on marrying Ragnhild: a skaldic poem says he 'turned away the maidens of the Holmrygir, and the Hordar, and all those of Heidmork' (all the wives taken from subsidiary Norwegian kingdoms, in fact), when he married the Danish king's daughter.[13] But he did not disinherit all their children. Before he died he assigned some fourteen districts to almost as many sons, a natural recipe for trouble, with or without stepmother jealousy: Eirik Blood-axe, notorious for killing several of his half-brothers, was just one of his sons.

During all this turbulence down south, the jarls of Hladir seem to have done very well for themselves. The founder of the dynasty was called Grjotgarth, which in English would mean 'grit garth' or 'stone yard'. The name might suggest that the family home was in the rocky and infertile north; Eyvind the Plagiarist's skaldic poem *Háleygjatal* makes it clear that Jarl Hakon traced his descent back to the earliest rulers of Hålogaland, including a King Sæming, an immigrant from Sweden on the other side of the mountain range the Keel.[14] His name may be connected with Suomi, the Finnish name for Finns, the Sami people. They were, then, far-northerners by descent, like the Hrafnistumen. Grjotgarth's son Hakon nevertheless picked out the winner from the south early on, joining up with Harald and helping him to subdue the whole Trøndelag, with its many petty kings. Harald married Hakon's daughter Asa – though that was not much of a distinction, presumably – and Hakon stuck by him, losing two sons in Harald's wars of conquest and being killed himself while trying to impose his authority on the district of Sogn, south of Trondheim.

Subsequent murders and manoeuvrings need not be detailed here – except to note that Norway went back to being basically fragmented and ungovernable – but eventually Hakon Senior's grandson, Jarl Hakon, was confirmed by the Danish king Harald Bluetooth as ruler of all the provinces of Norway from Rogaland northwards, with all royal estates and revenues: though this must have been only an acceptance of the real position. Jarl Hakon was then, in effect, 'Half-king' of Norway.

Goodwill, however, was not transferred to Harald's son Svein Fork-beard. When the latter succeeded, insecurely, to his father's rule, the power of Jarl Hakon may well have looked like a provocation. The chances are, then, that the expedition against Hakon was not an attack by the Jomsvikings, assisted by some Danes, but an attack sent out by the Danish king, with the assistance of Baltic mercenaries, Scandinavians and 'Wends' (Poles or Lithuanians) all mixed together. And there was another bone of contention, though not one likely to have troubled King Svein very much. This was that Christianity had been making its way into Scandinavia. Harald Fairhair's successor, Hakon the Good, had tried to impose it in Norway, with little success, and Harald Bluetooth had tried in Denmark, with rather more. The great runestone raised at Jellinge by the latter Harald says:

> haraltr kunukR baþ kaurua kubl þausi aft kurm faþur sin auk aft þąurui muþur sina sa haraltr ias sąR uan tanmaurk ala auk nuruiak auk t(a)ni (* karþi *) kristna

> King Harald ordered this stone to be carved in memory of his father Gorm and his mother Thyri. This Harald is the one who conquered all Denmark and Norway also and made the Danes Christian.[15]

Harald had not conquered all Norway, and probably had not made all the Danes Christians either, but in any case Jarl Hakon, the 'half-king', went out of his way to challenge the latter boast. He submitted to baptism himself, but promptly sailed north and made a great sacrifice. When two ravens appeared – the birds of Odin – he took it as a sign that the old gods were with him. Earlier, says Snorri, Hakon had sailed along the Norwegian coast giving orders that 'over his whole realm ... people should maintain [heathen] temples and rituals, and this was done'.[16] His father, Sigurd, had been prepared to mediate and compromise. Hakon was not, or was willing to do so only under compulsion; and in his own country there was no one who could compel him.

The Danes and the Jomsvikings were sailing, then, to take on someone unusually well established. And Hakon had the support of his son Jarl Eirik, low-born, popular, quick to strike and in control of further territories granted him by the former Danish king Harald.

'The Saga of the Jomsvikings', as one might expect, sees matters from the point of view of the Jomsvikings; and since, whatever one thinks about the reality of the battle, there is no doubt that the side with the alleged Jomsvikings in it lost, there has to be some kind of excuse, or excuses. The first one given is that Jarl Hakon found out they were coming. In their first attack, the reeve or mayor of Tønsberg got away, though he lost his arm to a sword-stroke. When he got to Hakon, he was asked if there was any news, and replied, making a fetish of the usual Viking imperturb-ability, 'There is not much news yet, but it might develop into something important,' and then showed his stump.[17] Hakon sent out the war arrows to all his sons, and by the time the Jomsvikings rounded Lindesnes to row up the coast to Hladir, he had 360 ships, three times the Jomsvikings' numbers (which is, of course, excuse number two). Then the Jomsvikings were decoyed into Hjorungavag bay by a herdsman who told them the jarl was there with only one ship (excuse three). But in the end it came down to the usual head-on clash, ships locking prow to prow and the crews fighting hand to hand.

Sigvaldi squared off against Jarl Hakon. The young Vagn Akeson squared off against Jarl Eirik. Bui the Broad was opposed by a collection of nobles including Thorkel Leira. Once Bui started to get the upper hand, Eirik had to row over to straighten the home side's line, but when he did so the ships still facing Vagn started to give way, and Eirik went back, laying his famous warship *Ironbeard* – later to become even more famous at the Battle of Svold – alongside Vagn's ship. The Icelandic author gives two of the four Icelanders present credit for stemming the Jomsviking attack. When one of the Jomsvikings, Aslak *Hólmskalli* or 'Bald Patch', boards Eirik's ship and starts to hack his way along it, blows bouncing off his bald and helmetless head with no effect, Vigfus, son of Killer-Glum, picks up an anvil (just like Li'l Abner) and smashes Aslak's skull in with it. At the same time, Thorleif *Skúma* ('Cross-eye', perhaps) hits Vagn with the oaken club which he has just made for himself, and drives him back on to his own ship.

Still, the Jomsvikings are winning. Jarl Hakon goes ashore and uses his last resort. The impenitent heathen calls on his supernatural protector, his *fulltrúi*, the one in whom he has full faith: Thorgerd Holgabrud.

Thorgerðr Hölgabrúðr, the troll-goddess

Thorgerd Holgabrud is mentioned several times in the surviving literature of Old Norse, without ever quite coming into full focus. (Snorri in particular omits her entirely from his account of Hjorungavag, Chapter 41 of 'The Saga of Olaf Tryggvason'.) She is a supernatural figure. But is she a goddess? If so, she is certainly not one of the familiar Æsir pantheon. If anything, her connections are rather with the opposing Vanir pantheon. One sug-gestion – since the god Frey belongs to the Vanir – is that Thorgerd may be, or may once have been, identical with the giantess-maiden Gerd, with whom Frey fell in love and whom he gave up his magic sword to possess. The loss of it will be his downfall at Ragnarok.[18]

But she may not be exactly a goddess at all. Even her name is recorded differently, as *Hölga-brúðr* or *Hörga-brúðr*, and in each case the *-brúðr* element may be replaced by *-troll*. *Hölgabrúðr* would mean 'bride', or per-haps only 'friend', of Holgi, and he, according to Snorri's *Prose Edda* (Sk. 52), was the founder of Halogaland, named after him. *Hörga-brúðr* could mean 'friend of the altars'. As for calling her a troll, that could be just rudeness, but there is some support for it. In 'The Saga of Ketil Hæng' – Ketil was mentioned in Chapter Five as the son of Hallbjorn Half-troll and the ancestor of Egil Skallagrimsson – Ketil is out one night on his home island, far in north Halogaland, when he encounters a female troll, and they exchange a few words. They are not friendly words, because while Ketil is a quarter-troll himself and married to a full-blood troll, he is also a troll killer, but they do recognize each other: he calls her *fóstra*, 'foster-sister'. The female troll tells him she is on her way to a trolls' meet-ing, or *trölla þing*. There, she says, she will meet prominent troll leaders, including Thorgerd Horgatroll.[19]

Whether goddess, troll wife or giantess, Thorgerd was in any case closely connected with Jarl Hakon. Her cult was presumably a family one, brought down from the far north by Hakon's ancestors, so she should perhaps be ranked as a female *fylgja*, a family guardian spirit.[20] In the *Flateyjarbók* version of 'The Saga of Olaf Tryggvason' (Ch. 326) – but not in Snorri's better-known account in *Heimskringla* – Hakon is said to have a temple at Hladir that contains an image of her, eventually destroyed by the mission-ary King Olaf.[21] *Njáls saga* mentions another temple dedicated to her and owned jointly by Hakon and his friend Gudbrand of the Dales; and there was a third, built in her honour in Iceland by a settler from the Trondheim area, though she turned against him and killed him for a theft committed against her 'brother' Soti, a *draugr*, or animated corpse.[22] Whatever it entailed, the cult of Thorgerd seems to have been well established in and specific to the Trondheim area, though its earlier connections are with the far north, and even with the Finns or Sami who live (according to Ohthere/ Ottar) outside and beyond what he regards as normal human habitation.

This is the power that Jarl Hakon calls on, according to both 'The Saga of the Jomsvikings' and 'The Saga of Olaf Tryggvason' as found in *Flateyjarbók*, at the crisis point of the battle. Both sagas agree that he retired into a wood and called on his *fulltrúi*, but she did not respond, rejecting all offers of sacrifice, even of human sacrifice. In the end, Hakon offers her his seven-year-old son Erling, who is immediately killed by Hakon's thrall Skopti. Hakon then returns to the battle, saying that he has now invoked Thorgerd and her sister Irpa. As the fighting starts again, a storm blows up, with violent hail that blows into the faces of the Jomsvikings and beats back their spears and arrows. Then men with second sight start to see Thorgerd fighting against them. An arrow flies from each of her fingers, striking a man each time. The Jomsvikings carry on fighting, but Hakon calls on his protector again, and the storm comes back more violently than before, and now men see that there are two witch-women on the earl's ship shooting arrows at them.

At this point Sigvaldi says, 'We did not swear any vows to fight against witches,' and pulls his ship out of the line, calling on the others to flee. Bui has his lower jaw cut off by a blow from one of the Icelanders on Hakon's side, says (or presumably mutters) 'The Danish woman in Bornholm won't think it so pleasant to kiss me now,' picks up his gold chests and jumps overboard, calling on his men to follow. (Does he mean they should commit suicide rather than surrender or be taken?) Thorkel and Sigurd, who had each vowed only to follow as far as Sigvaldi led, then turn tail as well. Only young Vagn is left, and he and seventy surviving Jomsvikings are picked up off a skerry in the morning, unable to offer resistance, being close to death from wounds and exposure.[23]

What follows is one of the most famous scenes of death defiance in Old Norse literature, but one needs first to finish the story of Hakon and Thorgerd. According to Snorri's version of 'The Saga of Olaf Tryggvason' in *Heimskringla* (Chs 45–9), what happens is that after his decisive victory at Hjorungavag, Hakon begins to become unpopular with the Trondheim farmers because of his continual demands for women. His attempt to seize the wife of a farmer called Orm triggers a popular revolt, which coincides with the arrival of King Olaf, the new king of (southern) Norway, intent on his mission to stamp out heathenism. Hakon, caught without his troops, goes into hiding with a thrall called Kark. They visit the home of a favourite mistress called Thora, who hides them both in a pit beneath an underground pigsty, or *svínabœli*. King Olaf arrives, defeats and kills Hakon's son Erling (who has the same name as the sacrificed child), and leads the farmers to the home of Thora. There he proclaims a great reward for the man who kills Hakon. And Hakon and Kark, hiding in the pit close by, hear him say it.

Now, can a jarl trust a thrall? Nora Chadwick remarks that the scene in the pigsty, as told by Snorri in *Heimskringla*, is 'perhaps the most tremendous and terrible scene in Norse literature'.[24] (One might add that setting such a scene in a pigsty would be completely unthinkable in classical literature: what happened to heroic dignity?) Be that as it may, both men stay in the pit as night falls, and Kark dreams a dream of Olaf putting a gold necklace round his neck. Hakon tells him it could be a red necklace that he receives. Hakon does his best to stay awake, but eventually falls asleep, and Kark cuts his throat in the night. But can a thrall trust a king? When Kark takes the jarl's head to Olaf for the reward, Olaf has Kark beheaded as well, as Hakon had predicted.

The scene is dramatic enough in itself, but Chadwick has suggested it means more than appears on the surface. She argues that the human mistress Thora and the supernatural protector Thorgerd are one and the same, but told in two different traditions, 'one sober and realistic, the other fantastic'.[25] *Flateyjarbók* has combined them, while Snorri's *Heimskringla* opts for the rational version. In the crisis of the farmers' revolt and the arrival of the missionary king Olaf, Chadwick argues, Hakon does what he did before and relies on the help of his protector Thorgerd/Thora. But her magic powers are nullified by the *mana*, as we would call it, of the Christian king. And the *svínabœli* with a pit under it, though regularly translated 'pigsty', should be seen as a barrow, perhaps a hidden underground shrine connected with the boar cult of Frey.

In another account of a trolls' meeting, one speaker says that she had been dear to Jarl Hakon, and that she lived in Gaulardal, where Hakon met his end. If the speaker was Thora, Thora too was a troll, maybe identical with Thorgerd. Another troll speaker says she tried to kill King Olaf in his bed; as did Thora's sister, according to Snorri. Once again, as Chadwick says,[26] it looks as if we have two accounts of the same incidents, one set ascribed to human beings for human motives, the other to supernatural women trying to defend or avenge their worshipper.

It should be noted,[27] finally, that Thorgerd, or Gerd, the protector of the Hladir jarls, perhaps gave rise to the rather redundant wife of Ragnar

Hairy-breeches, Lathgertha (now Lagertha in the *Vikings* TV series), in Saxo's *Gesta Danorum*. *Hlað(a)-Gerðr*, or Gerd of Hladir, would be *Laðgerðr* in Danish. Saxo dragged characters in from anywhere and has a record of not understanding names.

Jarl Eirik intervenes

Going back to the captured Jomsvikings again, Norse tradition gave them little chance of mercy or of treatment according to the Geneva Convention. As recounted in their saga,[28] the job of executing them is given to Thorkel Leira, whom Vagn had gone out of his way to insult, and the victorious Norwegians come along to watch them die. With a guaranteed audience, the Jomsvikings do their best to play up to it. One man after another makes some impassive or stoical remark before being beheaded. One of them reminds those present that the laws of the Jomsvikings prohibit fearing death or speaking a word of fear. The ninth in line refuses to kneel and be beheaded, saying he will face the blow and not flinch. The tenth makes a coarse remark about the mysterious Thora and is immediately killed, at Jarl Hakon's order.

The luck of the men waiting to die changes when they appeal to the unpredictable Norse sense of honour, or perhaps – BSOH again – humour. The eleventh victim asks for someone to hold his hair back as he is beheaded so that it does not get bloodstained, and someone comes forward and twists it over his head. As the blow falls, the prankster jerks his head back sharply so that the sword cuts off the hands of the helper, and then jumps up, saying – in triumph, or in amusement? – 'Whose hands are in my hair?' Jarl Hakon says to kill everyone remaining without further fuss, as they are too hard to manage, but his son Eirik gives the joker, who is the son of Bui, his life.

The next person waiting to be beheaded turns out to be Vagn, who has got the tether rope twisted round his foot so that he cannot stand up. Thorkel Leira, the executioner, asks him what he thinks about dying, and he replies, 'It won't worry me ... provided I first fulfil the other part of my vow.' Eirik asks him what that is, and he repeats that he means to kill Thorkel Leira and have sex with his daughter. Thorkel, naturally, resents this and rushes at Vagn straight away, but another Jomsviking trips him. He falls over and drops the execution sword, which cuts the tether rope. Vagn picks it up and promptly kills Thorkel with it, saying, 'Now I've fulfilled half my boast.' Hakon again says to kill him immediately, but once again Eirik countermands the order and offers Vagn a place in his own retinue – which Vagn refuses to accept unless the other surviving Jomsvikings are also given their lives. This, after some further negotiation, is what is agreed.

'The Saga of the Jomsvikings' closes with some remarks about what happened to the main personages. Vagn fulfilled his boast by marrying Thorkel's daughter Ingibjorg – though that seems to be not quite what he had vowed to do, which implied dishonourable intentions towards her. Bui, who had jumped overboard with his treasure chests, was reputed to have turned into a 'worm' or dragon, so he could continue to guard his gold even in death – if indeed he had died, for in other stories dragons are said to be men who have buried themselves alive with their gold and so turned into dragons as a particular kind of deathlessness. Jarl Hakon of course died the grim and shameful death just described. And Sigvaldi, whose boast started the whole expedition and who then turned away in the face of Thorgerd Holgabrud's hailstorm, went home to his wife for a bath and a massage. His wife, though, noting his lack of wounds and unmarked skin, taunted him by saying that she should put wheat powder on him to keep his skin so white (which is what aristocratic women did: she is calling him a girl). That was not the end of him, and he took a prominent though once again dishonourable part in the killing of King Olaf Tryggvason, as described in the next chapter.

Sigvaldi's brother Thorkel the Tall went to England and distinguished himself there by changing sides in 1012, to fight for King Ethelred, famous as 'the Unready'. His motive, however, may have been praiseworthy. Knut's army, with which he was serving against Ethelred, had captured Ælfheah, Archbishop of Canterbury, later honoured as St Alphege. When the old man refused to cooperate in negotiations for his own ransom, the angry Vikings pelted him with bones, the punishment threatened for defaulters in the twelfth-century warriors' code mentioned above. One of them then finished him off with an axe.[29] Thorkel joined Ethelred almost immediately afterwards. The chronicler Thietmar of Merseburg, writing very soon after the murder, says that Thorkel tried to save the old Archbishop, offering everything he owned except his ship as ransom for him.[30] One would like to think that he thought this killing of an old and unarmed man, who had stood up bravely to threats and would not buy his life at others' expense, was *ódrengiligr*, beneath the dignity of a *drengr* or warrior, and changed sides in disgust. Or maybe he figured if the troops were getting out of hand, it was time to go . . .

Finally, though 'The Saga of the Jomsvikings' does not say so, Jarl Eirik, though dispossessed of his lands and his father's after his father's murder and the coming to power of Olaf Tryggvason, pursued an active career as a raider in the Baltic and eventually had his revenge at the Battle of Svold (see Chapter Ten). He then ruled Norway for twelve years (1000–1012), still without bothering to take the title of King, and was then, like his old enemy Thorkel, called to England by King Knut, his brother-in-law. By this time, the struggle between King Ethelred and successive invasions, mostly by Danes, had been going on for fifteen years, with neither side managing to get a decisive victory – indeed the stubbornness of the English resistance, despite notably incompetent leadership, is said to have killed King Svein Forkbeard in what sounds like a stroke. This left his son Knut trying to get the upper hand against Ethelred's son Edmund, nicknamed admiringly by his enemies *Jarnsíða*, 'Ironside', a struggle concluded only when Edmund died.

The decisive battle that led to a negotiated peace (and Knut's subsequent takeover) was fought in 1016, and the *Anglo-Saxon Chronicle* records a long list of English casualties, 'all the chief men in the English race'. The one who had made most impression on his Danish enemies, however, Edmund apart, was Ulfcytel *Snilling* (the Bold?) of East Anglia, a man with a Danish name, presumably a descendant of the Danes who had settled in the area 150 years before, now thoroughly naturalized. In his first battle against the invaders in 1004, the *Chronicle* records, there was once again English disorganization and failure, but it notes Ulfcytel's determination to fight nonetheless. All surviving manuscripts of the *Chronicle* agree that 'if [the East Anglians] had been up to full strength [the Danes] would never have got back to their ships, as they said themselves', and two manuscripts add that '[the Danes] themselves admitted that they had never met with harder handplay in England than Ulfcytel gave them.'[31]

Snorri's 'Saga of St Olaf' gives Jarl Eirik the credit for defeating and killing 'Ulfkel' *Snilling*, as the saga spells his name, in the battle eleven years later. The same saga declares that Knut asked for Eirik's help because of the latter's fame, Eirik 'having won victory in the two battles which were reputed to have been the fiercest in the Northern lands',[32] that is to say, Hjorungavag, against the Jomsvikings, and Svold, against Olaf Tryggvason. If Eirik also deserved the credit for defeating the most dangerous of the English leaders, Ulfkel/Ulfcytel, at the Battle of Ashingdon, then he could claim, so to speak, a hat-trick of decisive and hard-fought victories.

This feat ought to have made Jarl Eirik Hakonarson the most famous of all the warriors of the Viking North. But he was on the wrong side politically as one who resisted the unification of the modern state of Norway, which made him unpopular with later nationalist historians. And he was on the wrong side as regards religion, which made him unpopular with medieval Christian chroniclers. That is probably why we can only surmise the existence of the *Saga of the Jarls of Hladir', and we have no suitably striking death scene for him, as we have for so many of his competitors in the prestige stakes. The last of his battles, however, seems to have been what caused his death. He died in England, Snorri says, *of blóðlati*, 'from loss of blood'. One wonders whether this was a haemorrhage, as Finlay and Faulkes translate it,[33] or the effect of wounds.

Mass executions: what do we know?

Returning to the scene of the beheading of the Jomsvikings, one might ask, first, is it in any way realistic? It does look like a classic example – Bartholinus might have said *the* classic example – of 'contempt for death among the pagan Danes'. Later scholars are much more likely to say it is a classic case of literary posturing, full of famous last words, famous last gestures, just the kind of clichés that have animated the Viking 'horned helmet' or comic-book tradition ever since.

Obviously we will never know what was said by the Jomsvikings after Hjorungavag, if there were any Jomsvikings there. Strangely enough, however, we do now know something about mass beheadings. In recent years two Viking Age mass graves have been discovered, both in England. One was found in the grounds of St John's College, Oxford (just outside what used to be my office window, as it happens), and the other during the digging of a relief road for the sailing events of the 2012 Olympics, on the Dorset Ridgeway above Weymouth (just a few miles from where I now live, as it happens: history can be very close).

Archaeologists are fairly sure about the St John's site. It contained 35 bodies, all male except for two juveniles whose gender could not be identified. Most were in the 16–25 age range, 'All were robust and taller than average', and many showed evidence of previous combat wounds that had healed. Scandinavian origin was probable. Carbon dating placed the date of death somewhere between 893 and 978. The excavators concluded that this was probably a 'mixed group of professional soldiers, perhaps a raiding party with Scandinavian origins'.[34] They must have been cut off from support, or perhaps underestimated the strength of local defence forces – as with the much earlier raiders of Hjortspring and Nydam.

The Ridgeway site has proved in some ways both more problematic and, with reference to the Jomsviking scene, more suggestive. Early reports declared that what had been discovered on the Ridgeway was one pit containing 54 headless skeletons, and close by, a pile of 51 skulls. It was certainly an organized mass execution, as the excavators say, the 'single largest context of multiple decapitations ever found from this period'.[35] The numbers, however, are not so secure as first reported. The skeletons were higgledy-piggledy, having been thrown into the pit and then also disturbed by the road builders' mechanical digger. The number is now somewhere between 46 and 52, and there may be as many as five skulls missing – though the archaeologists found a ready explanation in the Old English word *heafod-stoccan*, 'head-stakes'. The site of the Ridgeway execution is extremely visible from both sides of the last ridge before the sea, and it is also by the intersection of two well-used old roads. It would be a natural place to put heads on stakes, as a warning.

The bodies were once again all male, all in the Jomsviking age range, 21 of them under 25, only two older than 45. They were definitely not local, analysis of the isotopes in their teeth revealing that they came from Northern Europe, including possibly the Baltic states, Russia and Belarus, and even from north of the Arctic Circle (a Hålogalander?). One had horizontal grooves cut into his front incisors, a fashion also known from Scandinavia. They were not especially robust, heights being average for Viking Age Denmark, about 173 cm (5 ft 8 in), but they had relatively marked 'upper body robusticity' – oarsmen, one might conclude, not marchers or horsemen. The archaeologists concluded that they were 'a group of athletic individuals who had been performing repetitive strenuous activities from a young age'.[36]

Unlike the St John's victims, however, there was little sign among them of previous combat wounds. Perhaps, the archaeologists suggested, they were 'relatively inexperienced warriors'.[37] One suggestion has been that these were victims of the massacre of Danes in England ordered in 1002 by King Ethelred, but there were several other recorded incidents which would fit the carbon dating, such as the ravaging of Portland a few miles away in 982, and attacks on Dorset in 998, 1015 and 1016. In any of these a raiding party or ship's crew might have been cut off and left for local vengeance.

How, though, did these men die? Or to put it bluntly again, how does one go about cutting off fifty heads (Ridgeway), or seventy (Jomsvikings)? Most of us have a mental image of such executions: the kneeling victim, the block with a trough in it for the victim's neck. Those who have watched the television series *Wolf Hall* may know that there is another scenario, used in the execution of Anne Boleyn. Here the victim sits upright, with head held high, in less humiliating fashion, and the executioner wields a long sword. The trouble with the latter method is that it depends on the victim keeping his/her head up – and holding still without flinching, which may be difficult to do even for the bravest.

As for the first method, it depends on the executioner using an axe with a convex blade. (The long blade of a sword would be obstructed by the block itself and not make a clean cut.) In the scene with the Jomsvikings, it's stated that Thorkel Leira, the designated executioner, uses a sword. He also has assistance from slaves: 'three thralls were appointed to guard [the victims] and twist sticks in their hair'.[38] The Vikings' long hair is twisted round the sticks, and the thralls, or a thrall, holds the sticks while facing the kneeling victim and pulls his head forward. This is the basis of the Jomsviking practical joke, the man (eleventh in line) who says, 'I don't want to be led by thralls to my death.' He wants a real warrior to hold his hair and pull it right forward so that it doesn't get bloodstained. Then, as said already, he jerks his head back as the blow falls so that the man holding him loses both hands. This example of cruel humour is what starts to turn the tide of sympathy for the Jomsvikings.

All very implausible, one must say. There is also the stipulation made by Jomsviking number nine, who will not kneel and so turn his back on his executioner. He says, in the saga, 'I will not let myself be slaughtered like a sheep: I would rather face the blow. Strike straight at my face and watch carefully if I pale at all.'[39] Is this fictional posturing? Much the same story is told of St Magnus, Earl of Orkney. When he was martyred in 1118, 'The Saga of the Jarls of Orkney' says, he too refused to be executed like a thief and was instead killed by a blow to the head delivered from in front. Yet more fictional posturing? A skull from the saint's cathedral in Kirkwall has been identified as his and bears a wound that matches the saga account.[40]

What happened at the Ridgeway? The archaeologists have concluded that it was a rather 'messy' operation. There were several executioners. There were a lot of botched attempts. One unfortunate received seven blows before the job was done, and another poor soul, like Bui, had his lower

Mark Gridley's artist's impression of the Ridgeway massacre.

jaw cut off by a wild stroke; it was thrown into the mass grave, landing on his hand. There are some, but not many, signs of defensive wounds on hands and arms showing that victims had struggled. But on the whole it looks as if this real-life mass execution was much the same as the saga description. The rather grisly artist's impression on page 225 of the archaeologists's account shows a man kneeling on the edge of the pit, with one executioner's assistant holding his hands behind his back while another, with one foot on the edge of the pit, grips his long hair and pulls his head down and forward to expose the neck to the executioner, who is standing to the victim's left with a long sword. The assistants are mailed warriors, however, not thralls, which is what Jomsviking number eleven objected to.

Finally, one striking datum from the Ridgeway excavation is that while most of the killing blows were indeed delivered from behind, some seventeen (out of 112, for the average was more than two blows to each victim) were delivered from the front.[41] This must have made things significantly more difficult. Was it the case that some men insisted on facing their deaths as a point of honour – exactly like refusing the blindfold in front of the firing squad, to show you will not flinch? In which case the executioners may have agreed, perhaps out of curiosity. The archaeologists' Ridgeway picture also depicts a crowd of spectators, which in view of the very public site is extremely likely. All one can say for sure is that scenes like the mass execution of the Jomsvikings did take place. It's not hard to believe that some or most of the condemned men did their best to die well, and may have been granted the opportunity.

'Drengskapr': the unwritten rules

The topic that Jarl Eirik's career raises, though, is the concept of *drengskapr*, honourable behaviour, the behaviour appropriate to a *drengr*. How should one define this, and what is a *drengr*, exactly? *Drengr* is a 'difficult' word, comments R. I. Page. Later on he modified the judgement to 'notoriously difficult'.[42] It ill becomes one to wrangle with one's former tutor, but actually in some ways the solution seems rather simple. The problem is, as often, that the close analogue to an Old Norse word is a rather vulgar English one: the 'faculty-club' school of Viking studies has always found Viking (and English) vulgarity a problem.

The first thing one can say about *drengr* is that it has become the normal modern Danish word for 'boy', *en lille dræng*, 'a little boy'. It had a different and narrower meaning in the past. On one Swedish runestone the word means, according to Page, 'fighting-men in the (perhaps temporary) service of a lord': it was Lord Toki's *drengir* who had the runestone cut for him after his death in battle. Such men, of course, are much more likely to be young men than old ones. The word, moreover, has 'the connotations of bravery, toughness, and loyalty'.[43] One might add 'comradeship' or 'fellowship', one *drengr* to another, not just to a lord. Another runestone, from Hedeby in South Jutland, commemorates a **filaga**, a 'fellow', who was **tregR harþa kuþa**, 'a good hard *drengr*'. Page hesitates (rightly!) over the translation 'jolly good chap'.[44]

All these meanings are, however, well conveyed by the modern English word 'lad'. Once upon a time, a 'lad' was someone led by a leader: someone in service, usually armed service. It now means 'boy', the male equivalent of 'lass' (both of them implying low or lowish status). It is often used approvingly, as is *drengur* in modern Icelandic: *goður drengur* translates as 'good guy'.[45] The Jutland runestone's three words translate very readily as 'a good hard lad', someone you would want to have on your side in a fight.[46] For centuries the word has been associated with rough good-fellowship. In the medieval romance of *Havelok the Dane*, Havelock, a king's son employed as a kitchen boy, goes to join the local sports and is entered for the shot-put by his master the cook. Havelock puts the shot so far beyond everyone else's mark that the other contestants, the 'wight lads', the strong lads, give up:

> Shuldreden hi ilc oþer and lowen.
> Wolden hi namore to putting gange,
> But seyde 'We dwellen her to longe!'[47]

'They shouldered each other and laughed, / they gave up on the putting, / they said, "We're wasting our time here!"' That's the right way for a group of lads to behave: admiring prowess in others, laughing at oneself, taking things in good part.

It's true that in modern times the word (like many) has become increasingly debased, with newer connotations of drunkenness and louche behaviour, 'men behaving badly'. For all we know, that was also present among the old *drengir*. Drunkenness certainly shows up among the Jomsvikings, and Vagn Akeson's double vow, to kill a man and seduce his daughter, is frankly pretty 'laddish', even caddish. But it is quite easy to see a certain narrowly focused ethical code even among modern 'lads'. It involves what we would call sportsmanship: not taking an unfair advantage, shaking hands after the game or bout, only picking on people your own size, as well as never refusing a challenge or complaining when things don't go your way.

Surely something like this is needed to explain Jarl Eirik's generous sparing of his enemies (not unparalleled, as noted already: see Thorstein and Kerthjalfad, Chapter Six). Eirik is perhaps appreciative of the way one Jomsviking after another shows no fear. He especially admires the way Jomsviking eleven, who turns out to be Bui's son Svein, plays his prank on the executioners, and rewards him by making him a member of his own following. Note that Svein has at no point asked for mercy, unless one counts the very slight hint when he is asked how old he is: 'If I survive this year I shall be eighteen.'[48] It would have been simpler to say, 'I'm seventeen,' but the longer answer just raises the issue of possible survival. That may be as far as a *dreng* can honourably go. (Should we see Thorstein at Clontarf doing something similar, making a similar unvoiced appeal?) In any case, Eirik then overrules his grudging father Jarl Hakon to have Vagn's life spared for killing Thorkel Leira, and responds to Bjorn the Welshman's honourable refusal to accept his life unless all the others are also spared, by agreeing. One honourable or *drengiligr* gesture has to be matched by another. Even now, none of this is hard to understand.

Much of the *drengskapr* code, which *Jómsvíkinga saga* seems designed to illustrate, is in fact both familiar even now, at least at certain levels of society, and once again even sensible. Eight of Palna-Toki's laws for the Jomsvikings were listed above, and half of them would be recognized by modern armies. No one could be enlisted below the age of eighteen, and retirement age was fifty: hand-to-hand fighters who did not have to do much marching were probably effective up to that retirement age, but would not reach their peak until (one might imagine) well after eighteen. Women were not allowed inside the stronghold, but then in most early modern armies, including the British, women were not allowed into barracks. Jomsviking law was strict about prohibiting disputes among its members, but then it probably had to be in a situation where everyone had weapons to hand.

Then there are differences of emphasis. The carrying-on of inherited feuds was prohibited to Jomsvikings, but that was part of a culture in which blood feuds were normal. For the same reason, there was a requirement that comrades must be avenged – in other words, they had to be treated as if they were family members. Loot also had to be shared, the exact rule being, 'Anything of value, however big or small it was, which they won on their expeditions was to be taken to the banner; and anyone who failed to do this was to be expelled.'[49] The eighth of the Royal Navy's 35 Articles of War similarly reads:

> No person in or belonging to the fleet shall take out of any prize, or ship seized for prize, any money, plate, or goods . . . the full and entire account of the whole, without embezzlement, shall be brought in . . . upon pain that every person offending herein shall forfeit and lose his share of the capture . . .[50]

This seems to intend much the same effect as the Jomsviking rule. Similarly, the Jomsviking rule is that 'No one must speak a word of fear or show fear however hopeless things seemed' – the fifth of those executed after the Battle at Hjorungavag reminds his comrades about this. The Articles of War say much the same thing once again. Article 10 reads:

> Every flag officer, captain and commander in the fleet, who . . . shall
> not in his own person, and according to his place, encourage the
> inferior officers and men to fight courageously, shall suffer death . . .
> and if any person in the fleet shall treacherously or cowardly yield
> or cry for quarter, every person so offending . . . shall suffer death.

Articles 11 to 13 extend the rule to 'any person in the fleet', but leave a certain amount of 'wriggle room', for surrendering in a way other than the 'treacherously or cowardly' was accepted practice. But again, that is caused by the different circumstances of warfare between nation states with arrangements for taking, holding, exchanging and eventually repatriating prisoners, none of this accepted practice in the early medieval North.

One can make out a case, then, for the Jomsviking rules being no more than a formalization of accepted and even normal practice. But there are other factors in the behaviour of the saga heroes that are not so easily explained. One is the custom of *heitstrenging*.[51] This may have had a rational origin in the whole lord-and-retainer system, by which a retainer promised to stand by his lord in battle in return for support and protection. In pre-literate societies this had to be done out loud in front of witnesses, and Old English poetry often refers to the idea of the *beot*, usually translated 'boast' but derived from the earlier **behát*, 'promise'. One can see how the one turned into the other. In making a promise aloud in front of witnesses, there would be a natural tendency to go a bit further than required, to make one's own contractual obligation – for that is what it was – more generous or more striking than an ordinary one. And so a competitive element creeps in.

That is certainly present in the scene with King Svein and the Jomsvikings – Svein reminds Sigvaldi not to make a boast that is less than his own – but the whole *heitstrenging* concept seems designed *not* to be just an agreement like the *beot*, but a deliberate attempt to stir up trouble, and to do so, moreover (the Viking sense of humour strikes again), *just for fun*. There is no obligation on Svein to say anything at all, but once he has started things there is an obligation on others to follow suit or be open to the charge, not of cowardice exactly, but of not playing the game. Some of those present seem to realize that it is a set-up. Thorkel, Bui and Sigurd say in effect that they will do as much as Sigvaldi does, but no more. It is only Vagn who decides to go further, and he is rewarded for it, in the saga, by being made the hero of the execution scene. But the truth is that Sigvaldi has been outmanoeuvred, and the credit he gains for accepting the implicit challenge thrown down by Svein is cancelled by the realization that he is playing someone else's game.

Nevertheless, this sort of deliberate playing with fire seems to have been admired and entrenched in other social practices. The downmarket version of *heitstrenging* might be the Icelandic game, or social pastime, of *mann-jafnaðr*, making 'man comparisons'. In this, guests at a social occasion are encouraged to say who they think is the most distinguished person in the neighbourhood, and what his feats of prowess have been. But naming one person inevitably leads to someone else being slighted. Praise of candidate A means that supporters of candidate B will bring up old accusations about his rival, and soon the whole scene turns into something like a televised U.S. Presidential debate – among people who will react violently to gossip when they hear about it. It's impossible, actually, in a prickly, heavily armed and intensely status-conscious society, to imagine any other outcome. As with *heitstrenging*, *mannjafnaðr* was used to create dispute and violence out of nothing: that is the fun of the thing, the whole 'name of the game'.

Refusal to play it would obviously be unsporting and would ruin one's reputation. However, refusal to react can also be admirable. When Gyda says that she does not intend to waste her maidenhood on a mere petty king, King Harald's messengers urge him to teach her a lesson, by sending an army to kidnap her and bring her to him 'with disgrace' – that is, pre-sumably, to be raped and discarded instead of being given a more honourable status. But Harald refuses, and makes his own fateful *heitstrenging*. In a way, Gyda has 'done a Svein' on him by demanding that he raise his bid for her. On the other hand, and unlike Sigvaldi, Harald did have options: to use force, as his messengers advise; to say nothing and drop the matter; or accept the challenge. It's possible that the last option is what she wanted him to do all along, in which case the two parties have in a way been coop-erating to increase the prestige of both. But it takes a certain cold-blooded weighing of odds and options to be able to play this game successfully.

Cold-bloodedness, though, is also very much part of *drengskapr*, seen again and again in the love of understatement, oblique statement, refusal to react as expected. An extreme example is the mayor of Tønsberg's 'Not much news now, but it might grow into something'. This is not very far removed from the cry of 'just a flesh wound' in *Monty Python and the Holy Grail*, but the purpose of it must be to show a kind of self-decentredness. The news of invasion is important, and has to be passed on, but the loss of an arm is 'not much'. We see the same sort of reaction when Bui the Broad loses his lower jaw and says, 'The Danish woman in Bornholm won't think it so pleasant to kiss me now.' He is seeing himself from outside and (we would say) 'projecting' his own horror on to someone else.

Of course it's fiction, but fiction designed to make a point. The lack of interest in one's own fate – coupled with extreme concern for one's own prestige – is what animates the whole scene of the executions, with the many one-liners which the doomed men come out with. Thomas Bartholinus the Younger, considering this scene centuries ago, suggested that the 'cause for contempt of death among the pagan Danes' was their belief in Valhalla and a happy afterlife for those who died in battle, and the idea remained current right up to Kirk Douglas's Einar in the movie *The Vikings* (1958). But there is no sign of such a belief in 'The Saga of the Jomsvikings'. The motive for Viking stoicism is not religious belief but pride, and a belief system in which the greatest virtue is self-control.

This further relates to something that – as stated in Chapter One – has struck all readers of Norse-Icelandic literature ever since it was first rediscovered (though not everyone appreciates it). That is its very strong but cruel sense of humour. Why does Jarl Eirik let off the young man who feigns concern for his hair, only to trick Thorkel Leira into cutting his assistant's hands off? Surely, he admires the wit by which the young man has made one more score in what appeared to be an absolutely hopeless position. In the same way, he admires not only Vagn's defiant repetition of his *heitstrenging* in the face of the man he insulted, but also his refusal to admit the game is lost, and his speed in seizing even the slightest of opportunities. The scene is very like the three discussed in Chapter One: in all of them, men apparently helpless succeed in turning the tables on their enemies.

Drengskapr, in short, is not dissimilar to the gentlemanly duelling code of later European aristocrats. One significant difference is that Vikings did not have a hierarchy for duelling – there was no possibility of ducking out of a challenge because it came from someone too low in the social scale. Another is a kind of flexibility, even an awareness of irony. You could deflate a dangerous set-up by saying something bordering on cautious, like Thorkel following his brother Sigvaldi, but only as far as Sigvaldi will go. You could exploit a set-up by saying something you were ready for but which the other man was not, like King Svein vowing to invade England. You could accept a raising of the stakes and raise back again, like King Harald and Gyda. It was all more like a well-contested game of poker than a demonstration of how to stand on one's dignity. And in it, one of the critical requirements was imperturbability, or at any rate the outward appearance of fearlessness.

TEN

A Tale of Two Olafs; or,
The Tales People Tell

The last stand of Olaf Tryggvason, King of Norway, was probably the most celebrated of all Viking last stands, at any rate in the nineteenth century. The poet Longfellow, author of *The Song of Hiawatha* and 'Paul Revere's Ride', was so impressed by it that he wrote a long poem about the king's career, in 22 parts, 'The Saga of King Olaf', based on the original 'Saga of Olaf Tryggvason' from *Heimskringla*. Olaf, son of Tryggvi, is one of Snorri's main heroes, second in importance only to his namesake and successor, Olaf Haraldsson, later St Olaf, and later still 'Holy Ole', the patron saint of Norway. The deaths of both kings, at the battles of Svold and Stiklastadir respectively, are among the classics of saga narrative, and frame this chapter, which moves from the earlier Olaf to the later.

There had been sagas about King Olaf Tryggvason before, for he seems to have been one of the major inspirations of the whole idea of 'royal sagas'; and there were to be expansions and variations afterwards, notably in the great Icelandic compilation *Flateyjarbók*, whose scribes did their best to bring together absolutely everything relevant to his story and to others.[1] But for cohesion, suspense and climax, there is little to touch Snorri's account of the Battle of Svold in the history of literature. That is not to say, of course, that it can be relied on as 100 per cent historical fact.

'Ironbeard' and 'The Long Serpent': Olaf at Svold

The story Snorri tells, in the last twenty chapters or so of his 'Saga of Olaf Tryggvason' (Chs 92–113), goes like this. Olaf has effectively imposed his authority on the whole of Norway and killed or driven into exile those who opposed him, notably Jarl Eirik Hakonarson, the current holder of the Jarldom of Hladir, whose story was told in Chapter Nine. In the south of Scandinavia, however, Thyri, the sister of King Svein Forkbeard of Denmark, has been married off to King Burizlaf of Poland. She resents this on the grounds that (a) he is a heathen and she a Christian, (b) he is old, and possibly (c) he is not a Scandinavian. She accordingly runs away and finds refuge at the court of King Olaf, eventually marrying him.

But Queen Thyri, as she now is, starts to complain bitterly about her property in Poland, once part of her dowry – which one might think she had forfeited by running away. Things come to a head when King Olaf goes to the market one day in the spring and brings his wife back a large early stalk of angelica (a plant a bit like celery – greenstuff may well have been especially welcome for its vitamin content after a Norwegian winter). But Thyri, not at all grateful, says that her father King Harald Bluetooth gave better presents than stalks of angelica, and adds that he conquered Norway, while Olaf is afraid even to go south past Denmark for fear of her brother Svein. Taunting Vikings with cowardice always works, and Olaf calls his fleet together to sail south for his wife's alleged inheritance with sixty warships, including the famous *Long Serpent*, the largest dragon ship ever built in the Viking era.

This is rash indeed, for he has several deadly enemies on the way, and even if he gets through the Baltic, he still has to make it back. One enemy is King Svein. He might have passed over his sister's desertion of the marriage he arranged for her, but his own wife is Queen Sigrid the Haughty. She had previously been married to the king of the Swedes, but once widowed, some say as a result of her witchcraft, she made strong advances, Snorri says, first to King Harald *Grenski*, petty king of Grenland in south Norway, and burned him and his men to death in her own hall when her advances were rejected. She then tried her charms on King Olaf, and matters were going well until Olaf said that she would have to be baptized and become a Christian, which she refused. Olaf called her a 'heathen bitch' and slapped her in the face with his glove. One does not need Sigrid's witch-wife powers to see that her reply, though as usual understated – 'That could well cost you your life' – is all too likely.[2] After this incident, Sigrid married King Svein. Just as Queen Thyri accuses Olaf of cowardice over her dowry, so Queen Sigrid eggs on Svein to avenge the insult of having his sister marry without his permission.

Sigrid, furthermore, had a son by her first husband, and he is now King Olaf of Sweden. He is quite ready to join his stepfather Svein against King Olaf of Norway, kings of Sweden and Norway being almost permanently at odds over their border territories. And then there is the exiled Jarl Eirik, victor over the Jomsvikings, son of Jarl Hakon (who met an ignominious death at the hands of his slave Kark). Eirik has a grudge over the death of his father, and in any case, like all the Hladir jarls, no intention of submitting to rule from what is now Oslo. These three, then, the Danish King

Svein, Swedish King Olaf and Norwegian Jarl Eirik, form the coalition against the Norwegian King Olaf. Rather surprisingly, King Burizlaf does not join the coalition and agrees to the settlement of Thyri's affairs.

The deaths of heroes require either a fatal miscalculation or a traitor, and in this case Snorri opts for a traitor: Jarl Sigvaldi, still the leader of the surviving Jomsvikings, is now acting for King Svein. One of several fishy elements in Snorri's story is that Sigvaldi's motives are not clear. One might have thought he would have no reason to help out Jarl Eirik, who had defeated and indeed humiliated him at Hjorungavag some years before. But Snorri's story is that once Olaf has finished his negotiations with King Burizlaf down in the eastern Baltic, Sigvaldi, with his eleven ships, agrees to pilot King Olaf out through the sandbanks, but leads him into a trap off the island of Svold – which, if it ever existed (sandbank islands are often washed away), was presumably off what is now the large German island of Rügen.

The leaders of the coalition see Olaf's ships coming as they make their way back to Norway, and as part of the build-up of suspense Snorri has the Swedish and Danish kings identify one ship after another as the *Long Serpent*.[3] Jarl Eirik repeatedly corrects them: the first one they pick belongs to Eindridi of Grimsar; the second one belongs to Erling Skjalgsson; a third is not the *Long* but the *Short Serpent*. When they finally see the *Long Serpent*, King Svein says he means to have it for himself, but Eirik says, though not to the king's face, that the Danes will never manage to take it on their own.

The compliment is returned when King Olaf sees the enemy coalition rowing towards him. He asks who leads the central ships and is told it is King Svein. Olaf comments, 'I am not afraid of those cowards. There's no courage in Danes.' He asks who is on the right and is told it is the Swedes. He again comments contemptuously that they would do better to stay at home 'licking their sacrificial bowls' – he means, like the heathens they are. But whose are the large ships on the left? He is told, 'There is Jarl Eirik Hakonarson,' and Olaf replies, 'He will think it's right to settle matters with us, and we can expect a fierce battle from this force. They are Norwegians, like us.'

The clash is preceded by a short argument about tactics. In sea fights the two sides characteristically nuzzle into each other prow to prow, like front-row forwards in rugby packing down. Olaf's marshal Ulf the Red points out that since the *Long Serpent* is longer than any of its supporters, its prow will stick out further and expose the ship to attack all along its forward gunwales. Olaf replies that he did not know he had a forecastle-man – a *stafnbúi*, one whose action station is at the prow – who was *bæði rauðan ok ragan*, 'both red and cowardly'. Calling someone *ragr* is one of the insults which, under old Norwegian law, excuse a man from a charge of murder, and Ulf replies with a slightly more veiled accusation of cowardice, at which the king starts to aim an arrow at him, but is told to point his bow somewhere more useful. The scene suggests Olaf is at once ready for a fight and perhaps a bit rattled.

The fight then starts, with everyone joining in except Jarl Sigvaldi, who just hovers on the edges with his eleven ships. The Danes and Swedes are soon driven off by Olaf's picked men, but Jarl Eirik brings his ship *Ironbeard*, with its armoured prow, up against the left-hand ship of Olaf's line and starts to work his way along, killing the crews or making them retreat to the ship on their right and cutting each ship adrift as it is cleared. Danes and Swedes crowd in to replace his casualties, and in the end only the *Long Serpent* is left, with *Ironbeard* grappled alongside.

The final turning point of the battle, King Olaf's last chance of avoiding defeat, centres in the accounts of both Snorri and Longfellow on one of Olaf's retainers, Einar *Þambarskelfir*. Snorri says, 'He shot the hardest with a bow of any man.' Snorri had said in an earlier chapter that Einar was allowed in as an exception to the rule that no picked man must be under twenty or over sixty years old, since he was only eighteen; but because of his youth he was kept back in the section by the mast, not at the prow where the fighting was normally likely to concentrate.[4] It must be the remark about his age that made Longfellow give a rather strange description of him. It makes him look for all the world like Orlando Bloom playing Legolas in Peter Jackson's *Lord of the Rings* movies:

> Einar Tambarskelver, bare
> To the winds his golden hair,
>   By the mainmast stood;
> Graceful was his form, and slender,
> And his eyes were deep and tender
> As a woman's in the splendour
>   Of her maidenhood.

Whatever his looks, the saga says he started shooting deliberately at Jarl Eirik. His first shot hit the rudder over the jarl's head and sank in to the socket. The second passed between his side and his arm and went right through the headboard behind him. The jarl then turned to one of his own men, Finn, and told him to shoot the big man in the waist of the ship. Finn's arrow missed its target but broke Einar's bow just as he was drawing it for a third shot (which might well have been fatal). Olaf asked, in Snorri's succinct style, 'What was it snapped there so loud?' and Einar replied, 'Norway from your grasp, king.' Or in Longfellow's words:

> 'What was that?' said Olaf, standing
>   On the quarter-deck.
> 'Something heard I like the stranding
>   Of a shattered wreck'.
> Einar then, the arrow taking
>   From the loosened string,
> Answered, 'That was Norway breaking
>   From thy hand, O King!'

Olaf tells Einar to try with his own bow, but when Einar draws it he pulls the arrowhead back beyond the bowstave. Throwing the bow down in disgust, he says, 'Too weak, too weak, the supreme ruler's bow' and joins the fight with sword and shield. Or, in Longfellow's increasingly overwrought version:

> 'Olaf! For so great a Kämper
>   Are thy bows too weak!'
>
> Then with smile of joy defiant
>   On his beardless lip,
> Scaled he, light and self-reliant,
>   Eric's dragon-ship.
> Loose his golden locks were flowing,
>   Bright his armor gleamed;
> Like Saint Michael overthrowing
>   Lucifer he seemed.[5]

Nevertheless, though the defence goes on, that is that as regards the result. Jarl Eirik manages to board, and is driven off, but his men swarm aboard again, while others cluster round the *Long Serpent* in small boats to kill or capture those who try to swim for it. In the end King Olaf, like Bui the Broad at Hjorungavag before him, jumps overboard along with his marshal Kolbjorn, who looks like him and is dressed very similarly. Kolbjorn is pulled out and taken to Jarl Eirik in the belief that he is the king, but is recognized and spared. No one ever sees Olaf again.

He was, however, a famous swimmer. Snorri notes that once the battle was won, Jarl Sigvaldi brought his ships over to join in, but one of them, containing his wife Astrid, daughter of Burizlaf, rowed away and returned to the land of the Wends. Astrid had been a friend of Olaf's in the past, and some suggested that Olaf might have pulled off his mail underwater, swum to Astrid's ship and got away. This seems unlikely, most of all because he was never heard of again. It's a rumour that often springs up when the body of a leader is not found, or not securely identified.[6] The saga account ends with the three coalition leaders dividing Norway between them.

Snorri's is a fine story, outstandingly well told, and there is no doubt at least that there was such a battle and that the end of it went much as Snorri says. Several elements in it are, however, open to doubt or clearly wrong.

To begin with, King Olaf's contemptuous remarks about Danes and Swedes look like the kind of neighbourly slurs that one can hear from Scandinavians even now. The king's and the jarl's complementary indications of respect for each other – 'King Svein will never take [the *Long Serpent*] with the Danes alone', but Jarl Eirik's men 'are Norwegians like us' – are two sides of the same coin. Icelanders like Snorri, deeply involved with the Norwegian kings and claiming Norwegian ancestry themselves, would readily repeat or recreate Norwegian prejudices.

It was further noted long ago that the whole build-up of the coalition leaders watching the oncoming Norwegian fleet, and repeatedly guessing wrong until the real *Long Serpent* appears, was borrowed from a much earlier account of a king of the Lombards watching the approach of Charlemagne.[7] A more disconcerting surprise for modern admirers has nothing to do with Snorri. What does 'Thambarskelfir' mean? This was taken by Samuel Laing, the first translator of *Heimskringla*, in 1844, to be 'shaker of the bow-string', and *skelfa* does indeed mean 'to make something shake'. *Þömb*, however (genitive singular form *þambar*), means 'belly' or 'paunch', so that the nickname might best be translated 'wobble-belly'[8] – not suitable for Longfellow's girlishly slim figure at all. One might reflect that a large fat man is more likely than some teenage stripling to be able to handle a bow with a draw-weight even beyond that of the famously powerful king. Maybe Snorri made the same mistake as Laing and invented the entire bow-and-arrow story to match his understanding of the nickname, as he seems to have done with his account of the legendary King Hugleikr (see Chapter Two).

Another name open to more than doubt is that of the battle's site, the island of Svold. It does not exist now. Did it ever? Adam of Bremen, who wrote his *History of the Archbishops of Hamburg* in the 1070s, just within living memory of the event itself, and 150 years or more earlier than Snorri, is quite clear that Olaf was not turning back from the southern Baltic when the battle took place, but sailing south from Norway. And he was ambushed in the obvious place to ambush someone: in the Øresund, the narrows between Denmark and Sweden where the modern road and rail bridge spans the gap. So why did Snorri and his predecessors bring in the name Svold? Svend Ellehøj works the story back from Snorri to an earlier saga written by a monk called Odd Snorrason, from him to a Norwegian monk called Theodoricus a few years earlier, about 1180, and from him to a skaldic poem still earlier. Skaldic poems, with their complicated grammar, obsession with sound-patterning and reliance on circumlocutory and allusive 'kennings', are, as Ellehøj temperately says, 'very easily misunderstood'.[9] In this case he suggests that a string of misunderstandings mean that 'Svold' is a ghost name and the whole trip to Burizlaf is invented.

A final area of suspicion must be the motivations of all concerned. What made Olaf set out on his rash voyage? The nagging of his wife, Thyri. What made Svein decide to attack? The nagging of *his* wife, Sigrid. Sigrid in particular looks as if she has been demonized. One might well conclude that the clash between Olaf and his enemies took place for more prosaic reasons. King Svein of Denmark certainly had territorial designs on Norway, and England as well. Kings of Sweden traditionally did their best to ensure that they did not have a strong, united kingdom next to them, and did their best also to snatch off what territory they could. Jarl Eirik was clearly part of the resistance to forced unification. Snorri's history, as has been said, is about unification and Christianization, and those who oppose one are taken to oppose the other as well.

But the real motive for the whole brilliantly told Last Stand sequence is surely obvious. It is one of these stories created to massage national pride after a serious defeat, or bungle, like the Charge of the Light Brigade, or (after the disaster at Isandhlwana in the Anglo-Zulu War) the stand at Rorke's Drift. 'We lost, yes. But we were outnumbered/betrayed/poorly led (fill in as required or as imagination serves). It was a moral victory!'

The odd thing is that in his youth Olaf had been on the *winning* side in just such a battle, and it was his English opponents who constructed their own very effective and persistent self-justifying legend, which I discuss below.

Acquiring Viking charisma

The Battle of Svold was a defining moment for Icelandic tradition, and although Snorri Sturluson himself might not have agreed – his 'Saga of St Olaf' is almost three times as long as his 'Saga of Olaf Tryggvason' – it was the earlier King Olaf who became an anchor point for medieval saga writers, and for the oral tales that must have formed some part of the material they had available to them (the 'immanent saga', to use Gísli Sigurðsson's useful phrase). Icelanders readily claimed to have had relatives who fought at Svold. Gunnar of Hlidarendi, the great warrior and champion of 'Njal's Saga', was said to have had a brother called Orm Woodnose 'who fell with King Olaf on the *Long Serpent*', and the same claim was made of other Icelanders.

Iceland was a republic, though. Most of its small independent landowners had no wish to be taken over and taxed by Norwegian kings, while their country's origin myth, very possibly with a core of truth inside it, was that the first settlers had come to the country to escape from the tyranny of nation-forming kings like Harald Fairhair. As said in the previous chapter, Icelanders had played a dramatic role fighting for the Hladir jarls at Hjorungavag, with Vigfus, son of Killer-Glum, braining one of the Jomsviking berserkers and Thorleif Cross-eye stunning Vagn Akeson himself with an oaken club. There were, accordingly, those who preferred to claim connection with the winning side at the Battle of Svold: Egil Skallagrimsson's grandson Skuli was said to have been a *stafnbúi* there, but one who fought for Jarl Eirik on *Ironbeard*, not for King Olaf on the *Long Serpent*. Similar claims were made for other Icelanders, while 'The Story of Orm Storolfsson' (another descendant of Ketil Hæng, and like him a troll killer) takes a neutral attitude. According to this, Orm was not present at Svold, but had the lack of tact to say later, at Jarl Eirik's court, that if he had been on the *Long Serpent* it would not have been taken so easily – not that it *was* taken easily, as all agree. Eirik tells him to prove it by defending a ship against superior numbers, and Orm does so. The story is very unlikely to have any real basis, being the kind of self-aggrandisement characteristic of the Icelandic cultural insecurity, but it shows first a romantic tendency to side with King Olaf, together with an acknowledgement of Eirik's reputation for fair dealing, which is one aspect of *drengskapr*.

One may wonder quite why Olaf Tryggvason acquired the reputation he did. His reign was short, lasting only about five years. It was not particularly successful, and he was out-manoeuvred in the end by the Hladir jarls. Yet in the collected sagas of Icelanders he is mentioned nearly ninety times, and nineteen times again in the collected sagas of old times, or legendary sagas: all this in addition to his own saga in Snorri's *Heimskringla*, and a very much expanded saga in the massive collection of the *Flateyjarbók*, with a whole complicated tradition of earlier sagas devoted to him in addition.

Something Olaf is repeatedly praised for is his physical abilities. Snorri says of him:

[He] used to walk along the oars over the side while his men were rowing on *Ormrinn* [the *Long Serpent*], and he used to juggle with three daggers, so there was always one in the air, and every time caught them by the handle. He fought equally well with either hand, and threw two spears at once.[10]

Snorri goes on, 'He was the most cheerful of men and liked games' – though of course the Viking idea of 'a game' is not everyone's. (Their idea of fun is captured in the *Vikings* film, where Kirk Douglas as Einar duplicates the walk-along-moving-oars feat quite well.)

Olaf, then, was deft and physically formidable. It may have contributed to the survival legend attached to him – jumping overboard fully armoured and swimming away underwater – that he was a famous swimmer. We have two accounts of a visit made to Norway by Kjartan, son of Olaf the Peacock, the hero of *Laxdæla saga*, 'The Saga of the People of Laxardal', in which Kjartan also goes out in search of some fun. It is a fine day at Nidaros (now Trondheim), so the visitors see people from the town going off for a swim in the river Nid and decide to join them. Once there, they notice that one of the townspeople is 'by far the best'. They are competing at something, but what is the game? It is clearly not racing over a hundred metres, for when Kjartan asks his cousin Bolli whether he'd like to try to take the townsman on, Bolli refuses, and Kjartan makes a veiled accusation of timidity and says he will do it. Having said that, he immediately swims over to the townsman, ducks him and holds him underwater. When he lets go, the townsman pulls him under in his turn, '[holding] him under so long that Kjartan felt enough was enough' – that is, allowing for Viking understatement, until he is close to drowning. After which, of course, they both drag each other down, and this time 'they were under much longer. Kjartan was far from certain what the outcome would be.'[11] The game, in fact, is trying to half- but not quite drown one's opponent, it being a point of honour for the winner to fish the loser out and revive him. Once they have given up and tacitly agreed a draw, the two men swim to the shore. Kjartan says who he is, and after some verbal fencing, the other swimmer turns out, of course, to be King Olaf.

Much the same story is told in *Kristni saga*, while in 'The Saga of Hall-fred the Troublesome Poet' there is a tale of an anonymous man, who later proves to be the king, swimming out and retrieving an anchor cable for an Icelandic ship being driven on shore.[12] One might sum up by saying that the impression given is that Olaf was an autocrat, not just an aristo-crat. He derived his authority not from rank or descent, but from personal strength and decisiveness. This is why he did not bother with bodyguards or stand on his dignity. He didn't have to ask for respect, knowing he would get it anyway.

Was he even an aristocrat? He was accepted as the great-grandson of King Harald Fairhair, his father being Tryggvi, son of Olaf Elf of Geirstad and grandson of Harald Fairhair. Tryggvi was killed by his cousins, the sons of Eirik Blood-axe, in the murderous family feuding that followed the death of old King Harald, and – Snorri's story goes – Tryggvi's widow and her young child were forced to flee, knowing that Tryggvi's cousins were set on making a clean sweep and leaving no competitors. In their flight they were captured and enslaved in the non-Norse lands of the southern Baltic, until Olaf was one day recognized, as a child, by a relative of his mother, who bought Olaf free once more, and eventually his mother too. Olaf, still only aged nine, then distinguished himself by recognizing the slave owner who had killed his foster-father Thorolf Lousebeard and immediately killing him with an axe – a feat that led to his talents being further recognized by Baltic royalty, who supported and encouraged him until he could branch out on his own.

The whole story is obviously dubious. The child forced to flee into hiding by jealous relatives has been a stock theme from the New Testament up to C. S. Lewis's *Prince Caspian*, while the child who shows his nerve and breeding by an early act of vengeance or retaliation is a familiar figure from Icelandic saga. This is not to say that such things did not happen, but the incident of his being recognized by a passing uncle is even less likely. The Norse were impressed by bloodlines and family resemblance, but how many even of them could actually pick out from a crowd a nephew whom they had never seen before? What the legend of Olaf's early life seems to say is that an adventurer from the southern Baltic appeared on the Norse scene with a story of his ancestry that was mostly or entirely self-authenticated. Though this then raises the question: what really gave Olaf, king-to-be, his start?

Physical qualities, certainly. Snorri perhaps supplied another part of the answer when he went on from Olaf's dagger-juggling, oar-hopping and sense of fun to say:

> [He] was surpassing all men in valour in battles, the fiercest of all men when he was angry, torturing his enemies horribly, burning some in fires, having some torn to pieces by savage dogs, maiming some or having them thrown over high cliffs. As a result his friends were very fond of him, while his enemies were afraid of him.[13]

Snorri gives more graphic details of Olaf's imaginative and sometimes semi-humorous ways of dealing with opposition. But a further, and maybe the most important, reason for Olaf's continuing fame in later tradition is obvious, though to our way of thinking it raises a conflict with his cruelty: he was the first successful Norwegian royal missionary. The Icelanders later gave him credit for imposing Christianity on six lands: Norway, Iceland, Greenland, Orkney, Shetland and the Faroe Islands. A string of sagas gives details, with the conversion of Iceland naturally given special prominence.

Olaf was not the first king of Norway to be a Christian, nor the first to try to convert his subjects, for Christianity (we are not sure why) was popular in the later Viking era among Scandinavian kings. One may remember the boast of King Harald Bluetooth's runic inscription a whole generation earlier: 'This Harald is the one who conquered all Denmark and Norway also and made the Danes Christian.' At about the same time, King Hakon the Good, the most successful of Harald Fairhair's sons, who drove out his half-brother Eirik Blood-axe and ruled Norway for almost thirty years (934–61), is said to have made determined efforts to convert his subjects. What stopped him was the issue of sacrifice. Rulers were expected to make sacrifices to the pagan gods for good harvests, good fishing and prosperity, and people were clearly concerned that failure to make such sacrifices would bring bad luck. But that would bring a Christian king into conflict with the First Commandment, 'Thou shalt have no other gods before me.'

Hakon, who had been brought up as a Christian in England, allegedly as the foster-son of King Athelstan (whom even the Vikings called *inn sigrsæli*, the Victorious), could not solve the problem. His pagan backer Sigurd, the current Hladir jarl, did his best, trying to reduce the requirements to a mere token – no need to sacrifice a horse, but perhaps eat a piece of horse liver? No deal. Alright then, hold the kettle with horse meat broth in it and inhale some of the steam? In the end Hakon agreed to do the last, but would not actually touch the kettle, putting a linen cloth over the handle. In the same way he drank a ceremonial toast from the pagans' beaker, but made the sign of the cross over it first – Sigurd quick-wittedly told everyone he was making the sign of Thor's hammer. However, as Snorri says, 'neither side was well pleased.'[14]

Olaf Tryggvason faced much the same kind of opposition as King Hakon, from much the same people, if a couple of generations later. His way of dealing with it, however, was markedly different. Asked by (as usual) the stubborn inhabitants of Trondheim to follow King Hakon's example and join them in sacrifice, he agreed, but said human sacrifice would be best and that those chosen should be the noblest, not the lowliest. He then named a dozen prominent pagans as suitable victims to ensure good harvests and peace, and prepared to seize them by force.[15] Resistance promptly collapsed, and when he was later asked to attend the pagan temple (which may have been the jarls' family shrine for Thorgerd, as well as for the more familiar Æsir deities), he smashed the idols and killed the pagans' leader on the temple doorstep. He had pagan priests burned, or drowned on skerries. He took hostages to back up his demands that the Icelanders and others should convert. Faced with one obstinate pagan, he pegged him out and put a basin full of live coals on his stomach until his stomach burst. Resisted by another, he wedged his mouth open, put a stalk of angelica down his throat and dropped an adder down it, encouraging the snake on with a hot iron.[16] This last piece of missionary activity looks unlikely in practice – it would have to be a rather small snake to crawl down a narrow tube, if it could crawl at all – but later writers were at any rate sure that Olaf very much meant what he said about everyone getting baptized.

Olaf and Byrhtnoth: what made the difference at Maldon?

One has to go back from these folk tale developments to the historical question of what gave Olaf his start. And, moreover, of what stimulated his long-term project, of not just being king of the whole of Norway but making Norway and all its Western Ocean colonies Christian countries. Here one must consider what little is known about Olaf's early career, after his appearance from the Baltic and before he returned to carry out his designs on Norway.

Snorri's story is that after his first wife, Geira, died, Olaf took to raiding, first on the European mainland and then in the British Isles. He harried Northumberland and Scotland and the Hebrides and the Isle of Man and Ireland and Wales and Cumberland, ending up on the Isles of Scilly in the far southwest, where he was converted to Christianity by a hermit with the gift of prophecy; after which he married the sister of Olaf *Kvaran* (which seems to mean 'sandal'), king of Dublin and great-grand-son of Ivar. None of this sounds likely. Olaf's battles are just a list, with no more detail than given above. The story of the hermit, like the account of the kings watching out for the *Long Serpent*, is borrowed from a Latin source, this time the *Dialogues* of St Gregory the Great.[17] Olaf *Kvaran* died in 980, which is too early for Olaf Tryggvason. And Snorri then switches to the Jomsviking story, coming back to Olaf only when the latter has landed at Vik and become king in Norway. Snorri clearly knew nothing reliable about Olaf's early career.

For once, though, there is mention of him in a source from outside Norway, the *Anglo-Saxon Chronicle* – a good source, because it was (in different locations) often written up year by year, so providing contemporary evidence. Two manuscripts of this (E and F) state that 'in this year [994] Olaf and Swein [Svein Forkbeard] came to London town with ninety-four ships, and made a determined attack on the town.'[18] They got a bloody nose from the Londoners, and recoiled to raid generally in the less well-defended parts of southern England, until the English king Ethelred decided to pay them off with 16,000 pounds – close on 6 tonnes – of silver, even if they were troy or Roman pounds. In return, Olaf (but not Svein) promised that he would never attack England again, and – the *Chronicle* adds with a touch of surprise – 'he kept to it too'. Svein, by contrast, continued his attacks on England, which ended with his son Knut, or King Canute, succeeding Ethelred's son Edmund Ironside as King of England.

More interesting as regards Olaf, however, is the statement, made in only one manuscript of the *Chronicle* (a different one), that three years earlier (though the manuscript gets the date wrong),

> Olaf came with ninety-three ships to Folkestone and raided round about it, and then went from there to Sandwich, and so from there to Ipswich, and overran all that, and so to Maldon. And ealdorman Byrhtnoth came against him there with his army, and fought with them; and [the Vikings] killed the ealdorman there and had possession of the battlefield.[19]

This earlier battle, fought on 10 August 991, was significant on a large scale because it was the first time the English king, advised by his archbishop, made the disastrous error of paying Vikings to go away, this time 10,000 pounds of silver.[20] This of course only made them keener (usually) to come back, and the amounts paid got bigger and bigger, from the 16,000 pounds only three years later up to the 48,000 pounds paid in 1012, and more than 80,000 in 1018. The battle has, however, become far more famous than many larger affairs because of the accidental preservation of a large part of an Anglo-Saxon poem about it, *The Battle of Maldon*, since read and studied by many thousands of British and American students.

Furthermore, while Olaf's last battle at Svold cannot be located within several hundred miles, the site and the tactical circumstances of this earlier battle can be traced to the yard, and dated almost to the hour. We have five sources of information about it: (1) the poem just mentioned, which was probably written soon after the event by someone who had at least talked to survivors; (2) the *Liber Eliensis*, a much more hagiographical account written much later to celebrate the deeds of Byrhtnoth, the English leader, who had been a major benefactor of Ely Cathedral, where his headless body still lies. This gives the exact date of the battle; (3) the *Life of St*

Oswald, Archbishop of York, who died the following year; and (4) and (5) three manuscripts of the *Anglo-Saxon Chronicle*, A, E and F. E and F give the correct year, 991, but say only that 'This year Ipswich was raided, and very soon after that Ealdorman Byrhtnoth was killed at Maldon.' Manuscript A, however, brings Olaf into the story as quoted above.

The Anglo-Saxon poem gives an impressively detailed account of what happened. The Vikings camped, it says, on an island in the river Blackwater (its name then was the Panta). The English army, which consisted of the Essex militia, faced them across the river, but neither side could get at each other except by *flánes flyht*, 'flight of arrow', and by shouting 'across the cold water'. The Vikings offered to take payment to go away, but Byrhtnoth (in the Old English poem) contemptuously and sarcastically refused, saying all they would get from him, 'Ethelred's earl', was point and edge.[21]

But this was at high tide, when the incoming sea met the outflowing river, so that *lucon lagustréamas*, 'the streams of water locked'. As the tide ebbed, however, a narrow *bricg*, or causeway, was revealed, and the Vikings attempted to force their way across it. The attempt was easily repelled, and the Vikings then got crafty, to the disgust of the Anglo-Saxon poet. They asked free passage across the causeway, to fight it out on level ground. Byrhtnoth agreed, but his militia was not up to the match. He was killed fighting in the forefront, and many of his men took to flight.

His motive for letting them cross has provoked one of the most stultifying debates in Anglo-Saxon studies, set off, one has to confess, by J.R.R. Tolkien.[22] The poet says Byrhtnoth agreed to the Viking appeal *for his ofermóde*, and clearly regards this as a disastrous decision. But what does *ofermód* mean? How critical is it, or was it? Does it mean 'diabolical pride', sinful as well as mistaken (which is what Tolkien suggested, a suggestion eagerly lapped up by critics always ready to hunt the moral)? Or could it just be 'over-confidence'? A simple if unpopular explanation is that the Vikings appealed to Byrhtnoth's sense of *drengskapr*, shared by Anglo-Saxons even if we do not know their word for it, and he could not resist the appeal.

What attracted the attention of commentators as soon as the poem was rediscovered, however – well before Tolkien – was the fact that some of Byrhtnoth's *heorþwerod*, his 'hearth band' or household followers, refused to flee or surrender, but fought over the body of their leader until all were killed. The Roman historian Tacitus had noted nearly nine hundred years earlier that Germanic warriors regarded it as a great disgrace to survive a battle in which their lord was killed, unless they could avenge him. The *Battle of Maldon* poem suggests that not much had changed – though again it has been claimed that this is just a literary motif, not real at all.[23] Whether that is the case or not, one can at least be sure that the poem fits very well with real-world geography. The island on which the Vikings camped was Northey Island, some 3 km (2 mi.) southeast of the town of Maldon. The causeway is still there, passable at low tide. And the information about the change of the tide tells us the battle must have been fought in late afternoon.[24]

Byrhtnoth himself, like several of the English warriors named in the poem, was a well-attested and well-connected historical figure. The *Life of St Oswald* adds that he was immensely tall and white-haired, perhaps sixty years old when he was killed. The poem confirms the last detail, calling him *har*, 'hoary' or 'grey-haired'. His height seemed to be confirmed by Victorian excavators who opened his tomb in Ely Cathedral and deduced from his bones that he was 6 ft 9 in (205 cm) tall, though measurement was difficult because he had no head, this being replaced in the tomb by a ball of wax (compare the penis replacement given to the Viking warrior at Repton, see Chapter Four). The estimate is now generally revised down, but Byrhtnoth was probably tall even by modern standards.[25]

A question that has been much disputed – though not usually framed as bluntly as this – is, how did the English come to lose? To any English historian there is something unnatural about Englishmen being defeated on their own soil by foreigners of any description, even those with the next-of-kin status accorded to Scandinavians (that defeat at Hastings still rankles). Tolkien put the blame squarely on Byrhtnoth: he should not have given the Vikings free passage across the causeway. But who knows? Byrhtnoth may have calculated that he would have to fight the Vikings sometime, or surrender tamely, and that he would never have a better opportunity. Tolkien also suggested (in his playlet *The Homecoming of Beorhtnoth Beorhthelm's Son*) that the English were outnumbered. The *Liber Eliensis* also says this, but it looks like a standard excuse for a defeat and is highly unlikely. English defeats over the subsequent generation were often attributed to poor leadership, but there may have been a deeper cause: the increasing stratification of Anglo-Saxon society.

In the old northern theory of social classes, expressed in the Norse mythic poem *Rígspula*, 'The List of Rig',[26] there were three classes for men: thrall, carl and jarl, or in English, slave, churl (*ceorl*) and earl (*eorl*). The two higher grades might be translated as freeman and noble. But the carl/churl or freeman grade was, initially, perfectly respectable. Freemen carried weapons; an early king of Mercia was called Ceorl; kings of Francia were called Karl, Charles or even Charlemagne. During the recorded Anglo-Saxon period, however, the word sank in esteem. An *unorne ceorl* or 'simple churl' fights and dies alongside his betters in the poem of *Maldon*, but he gets only two lines of speech and figures perhaps as a token of national unity. By contrast, the rank of *eorl* had gone up in the world. An ealdorman traditionally commanded the levy or militia of a shire, as Byrhtnoth does that of Essex. But counties had started to be grouped, and some ealdormen, under the influence of the similar Norse word and rank of jarl, were beginning to be earls, not just of single counties but of whole provinces like East Anglia or Mercia. Byrhtnoth calls himself an *eorl*. But a widening gap between the rank-and-file and a hereditary officer class does not make for what the soldiers call 'unit cohesion', or loyalty under stress.

Archbishop Wulfstan, writing his *Sermo Lupi ad Anglos* just a few years later, was well aware that for the lowest slave class of Anglo-Saxon England, it might look like a good deal to turn *from cristendóm tó wícinge*, from being a Christian to being a (heathen) Viking. A thrall might end up fighting the thane his former master, Wulfstan fretted, and winning as well, and even worse, not having to pay the regular compensation![27] Maybe, if a sturdy thrall might chance his luck and see if the Vikings felt like taking on recruits, an overtaxed churl might decide against fighting to the death for his landlord. This was a weakness the Vikings, with their notoriously flat social structure and careers open to (warlike) talents, did not have. They had more to gain than many or most of the men they faced.

One wonders, finally, what the battle meant to Olaf. Viking leaders, and Anglo-Saxon leaders, habitually fought in front, so if Olaf was present he may have been among those who tried to force the bridge; it may have been his idea to appeal to Byrhtnoth's sense of fair play, or *drengskapr*; one would expect him to be present at the critical point of the battle and make for Byrhtnoth's personal standard – round which, as the modern Swedish novelist Frans Bengtsson wrote in his rather contrarian account of the battle, 'there was little elbow-room for men of small stature'.[28] The Old English poem credits Byrhtnoth with killing three enemies in hand-to-hand fighting, until a fourth 'crippled the earl's arm. Then the gold-hilted sword fell to the earth'.[29] (The eighteenth-century antiquarians who exhumed Byrhtnoth's body noted that his collarbone was cut through by axe or sword, which of course would immediately make his arm drop and his grip loosen.) All this could have given Olaf a good deal of the most valuable currency for an ambitious Viking leader: warlike reputation.

But it may well have been the aftermath of the battle that most impressed Olaf and provided him with the next most valuable currency for a leader: money, and a reputation for getting it. After the battle at Maldon, as the *Anglo-Saxon Chronicle*'s manuscript E declares, the Vikings were bought off with 10,000 pounds of silver, the first time the English used the disastrous tactic of paying them to go away. How many Vikings were there to share it? Here one can make a calculation. A Viking longship might carry a crew of forty men (the Gokstad ship rowed 32 oars, the *Long Serpent* notoriously 120). If forty was the average, Olaf's fleet of 93 could have carried nearly four thousand men. But forty may be a high estimate, and towards the end of a campaigning season Viking ships were probably not all fully manned: 2,500 might be more likely. If Olaf had 2,500 men in his army, and if the payment was shared out evenly, then every member of the Viking rank and file would have received 4 pounds of silver, nearly 1,000 silver pennies. What this would mean to a landless Danish or Norwegian younger son is hard to calculate. It would, for instance, be two years' stipend for a rich and senior English ecclesiastic. It would certainly be more money than an ordinary man was ever likely to own, or even see.

Of course, the money no doubt wasn't shared out evenly. If Olaf got the one-eighth of prize money an English admiral of the nineteenth century was entitled to, he would have had 300,000 pennies, and it would take a dozen men to carry them – all very useful when it came to fitting out fleets and attracting followers. Furthermore, the calculation above takes no account of the loot gathered on all the raids before the Vikings ever got to Maldon: money, provisions, valuables, church relics and books, and of course slaves, for use or for ransom. Clearly the English thought 10,000 pounds was less than they would lose if the looting went on. But King Ethelred had lost sight of the principle his ancestor King Alfred had grasped a hundred years before. Vikings did not fight for fun, but for profit. They did not have to be beaten decisively, just shown a poor cost–benefit ratio, at which point they would go somewhere else. Bringing them money without putting them to the trouble of gathering it was short-sighted, as Chronicler E noted even then.

One turns back to the three questions raised at the beginning of this section. What gave Olaf his start? Success, glory and profit on his raids of 991 and 994 (10,000 pounds the first time, split between Svein and Olaf and their men, 16,000 the second time, plus the take on a long spell of raiding over four English counties).

What set him on the project of becoming king of all Norway? One might say that Norwegians had been trying to achieve this, with little success, ever since Harald Fairhair. But Olaf may well have been impressed by one thing he saw during his expeditions to England: the ability of the English king to raise very large amounts of money in tax. If that was what a centralized kingdom could do, then surely that was the way to go.

And why add to the project of kingship the determination to make the whole of Norway Christian, a project that was quite certainly going to be resisted? Snorri Sturluson's story of the hermit on the Isles of Scilly who converted Olaf by a display of prophetic powers is borrowed, and phoney too. One cannot, of course, discount the possibility that Olaf's conversion came from a genuine religious impulse. He may have thought (correctly) that Christianity was the wave of the future in the northern lands, and decided to join it. But he may also have realized that the controlling and tax-gathering and coin-minting powers of English and Frankish kings were very much assisted by the existence of a literate state bureaucracy, at this date entirely dependent on clerics. Reading and writing were still largely a monopoly of the Church, and kings needed that skill. But they still needed their skalds as well, composing without the assistance of pen and paper, their poems passed on as they had been for centuries, without the aid of books.

Olaf I and Olaf II: two kings compared

Snorri Sturluson's 'Saga of St Olaf', in *Heimskringla*, is almost three times as long as his 'Saga of Olaf Tryggvason', and even that is exceeded by the 'Greatest Saga of St Olaf', put together by the compilers of *Flateyjarbók*. St Olaf, or Olaf Haraldsson, also known as Olaf the Stout, is also mentioned even more often than his earlier namesake in the pages of the sagas of Icelanders. Nevertheless, he doesn't seem to have made quite the same impression. Most of the references to him are chronological: such and such an event took place so many years 'after the fall of King Olaf', and so on. The outlines of both kings' careers are similar as well, including their missionary activities and right up to the hero-tales of their deaths. There are, however, two significant differences.

One is that the later King Olaf was much better served by skalds. The reputation of great men was fixed and ensured by their skalds, and we know the names of many of them and sometimes have substantial stretches of their poem. These must have been passed on by word of mouth for some considerable time before they were eventually written down, often by being incorporated into sagas, or into handbooks of skaldic technique like Snorri's own *Skáldskaparmál*. The extraordinarily complex rules of skaldic verse meant that poems were less likely to be corrupted in transmission, simply because (unlike the poems in simpler metre of the Eddas or of Old English poets) copyists did not know how to alter them successfully. Sometimes also, as in a case to be mentioned, the rules meant that only one word would fit.

As a result, memory of poet and patron often survived together. Harald Fairhair's court skald was Thjodolf of Hvin, who composed the *Ynglingatal*, or 'Tally of the Ynglings', while it was Thorbjorn Horn-cleaver who composed the *Haraldskvæthi*, a biography-cum-elegy of the great king. Similar poems were composed for King Eirik Blood-axe (the anonymous *Eiríksmál*) and for King Hakon the Good (*Hákonarmál*, by Eyvind the Plagiarist). Eyvind, like Thjodolf, also transferred to the patronage of the Hladir jarls, for whom he composed the *Haleygjatal*, an account of their ancestry in Halogaland, modelled on *Ynglingatal* as *Hákonarmál* was modelled on *Eiríksmál*. Einar Skalaglamm, one of Jarl Hakon's skalds, got his nickname 'Tinkling-scales' because, just as the great battle of Hjorungavag was about to start, he threatened to change sides and had to be bought off with the present of a set of scales that made tinkling noises and could also foretell the future.[30] He repaid the gift with the poem *Vellekla*, 'Gold Shortage', though the stanzas in this about the Jomsviking battle are considered dubious, and Jarl Hakon, guessing it would contain an appeal for money, said he didn't want to hear it. Hakon's son Jarl Eirik, the victor at Hjorungavag and at Svold, was served by the Icelander Gunnlaug Serpent-tongue, who has a famous saga of his own; and by Thord Kolbeinsson, who composed *Eiríksdrapa* and also *Belgskakadrapa*, about the treacherous death of Hakon and the escape of Eirik.

Olaf Tryggvason was not as well-provided with poets as were his enemies, perhaps because skalds initially were not sure how to turn their art, strongly linked with heathen myth, to the service of Christian kings. A generation later, by contrast, Olaf Haraldsson (St Olaf) readily attracted and kept the services of several poets. According to his saga, he asked that three of them should fight in the front line in his last battle, so that they could take account of and later memorialize the king's deeds – if, that is, they survived (which none of them did). Gizur Goldbrow and Thorfinn Mouth were killed at his side, and – as will be told later – Thormod *Kolbrúnarskáld* survived only briefly, if more memorably. A fourth poet, however, Sighvat Thordarson, missed the battle and lived to write extensively about his patron. As a result, St Olaf's death in battle has become inextricably linked with his poets, and especially with Thormod Dark-brow's Poet.

The other difference between the two King Olafs is that the second Olaf, for a while, had an easier time. Between the Battle of Svold in 1000, when Olaf Tryggvason died, and 1016, when Olaf Haraldsson took over Norway, the attention of the northern world was elsewhere, on Svein Forkbeard's attempted conquest of England. While that war went on, Olaf had only more limited domestic opposition in Norway to confront.

In other respects the early career of Olaf II was quite like that of Olaf I. Olaf II was the son of Harald *Grenski*, but his father, a great-grandson of Harald Fairhair, had been burned to death by Sigrid the Haughty (as mentioned earlier). He was then brought up by his mother and a stepfather, Sigurd Sow, another petty king of Hringariki, who was nicknamed 'Sow' because, says Snorri, 'he was a very enthusiastic farmer ... [who] frequently went himself to see to his fields and meadows, or animals'.[31] In other words, he ploughed and pushed up the earth, like a sow looking for truffles, creating wealth himself instead of going out and stealing other people's as a proper king should. Olaf Haraldsson showed his ancestry by ignoring this bad example and going to sea at (according to Snorri) the age of twelve, which would be in about 1007. Sighvat Thordarson's *Vikingavísur* record Olaf's early raids and battles, giving 'a good generalized picture of a gifted young viking working his way up in the profession'.[32]

Then, like other ambitious warriors, he became embroiled in the war going on for control of England between King Ethelred and King Svein. Snorri, basing himself on poems by the skalds Sighvat and Ottar, says Olaf sided with King Ethelred and helped the English king to reconquer London from an occupying force of Danes in 1013. The skalds say that Olaf 'broke London Bridge's towers ... broke the oaken English Bridge of London', with Snorri elaborating on this by saying that he moored his ships to the supporting piles and then rowed downstream until the bridge gave way.[33] The important events for Olaf II may have been that, first, King Svein called the Hladir jarl Eirik out of Norway to assist him, and then Svein himself died. Olaf, having presumably accumulated ships, men, money and prestige, sailed north to take advantage of the relative power vacuum in Norway.

His story after that follows the same general lines as his predecessors. On arrival in Norway he was lucky enough to capture Jarl Eirik's son Hakon, releasing him on condition that he left the country. Olaf also defeated and killed Hakon's brother Jarl Svein, and so broke the power of the Hladir jarls, though not quite for good. Like his great-great-grandfather Harald Fairhair, he made his way round Norway defeating petty kings and making them submit. One was blinded and kept at his court as a warning to others, a policy that proved dangerous. Olaf also continued to try to enforce Christianity on a generally reluctant population, smashing the temple and Thor-image of Gudbrand of the Dales as Olaf Tryggvason had done with the temple of Thorgerd Holgabrud twenty years or more earlier.

The version of Christianity being offered seems to have had little to do with concepts like charity or humility, and least of all forgiveness. Olaf was famous instead for strict adherence to the letter of the law. There is a tale, told by Snorri, of how, in exile in Sweden near the end of his life, Olaf was idly whittling a stick one Sunday. His page, noticing this, and aware of the Fourth Commandment, said very carefully, 'Tomorrow is Monday, lord.' Which means, 'Today is Sunday,' which further means, beneath two layers of indirectness, 'and you are sinning by breaking a commandment'. Olaf collected the shavings he had whittled and burned them on his open palm as a penance – and also a demonstration of the Viking virtue of stoicism.[34] But naturally, all these activities created grudges and buried resentments, and Olaf also became embroiled in the long-standing problem of keeping control of the profitable northern trade in furs, feathers and walrus ivory, for every time the concession was granted to one man, others felt deprived, all of them likely to resist and murder royal officials, starting a new cycle of retaliation and revenge.

More important, though, was the fact that the Danes had not given up on attempts to annex Norway, and Svein's son King Knut, with English and Danish resources behind him, was the most formidable enemy the northern world had ever known. In (probably) 1026 Olaf sailed to challenge him, being joined by King Onund of Sweden, and the three Scandinavian kings clashed at the Holy River on the eastern shore of Skåne, now (but not then) the southernmost province of Sweden. Snorri offers a tale of a successful ruse that wrecks many of Knut's ships, but behind the Norwegian/Icelandic bluster, it seems that Knut had the better of things. Olaf had to abandon his ships and made his way back by land, across Sweden. It must have been a major blow to his prestige, especially as Knut then sailed north, attempting to re-establish Jarl Hakon, and more significantly making contact with new Norwegian power brokers, the archer Einar Wobble-belly now among them. In a letter written to the English people the following year, Knut called himself, with justice, 'King of the whole of England, and Denmark, and Norway, and part of Sweden'.

Knut did not manage to catch Olaf, and the plan to re-establish Jarl Hakon failed when Hakon drowned in the Pentland Firth. But Norway remained ungovernable and Olaf was driven over the mountains into Sweden, and then into a further exile in Russia. When he came back, with those loyal to him and some Swedish support, he did so once again over the mountains of the Keel, and he directed his march, naturally enough, against the long-term focus of resistance to kings, Christians and central authority, the stubborn heathen farmers of the Trondheim district. There the heathens and the Christians clashed at Stiklastadir on (probably) 29 July 1030. Here Olaf's fate is inextricably bound up with that of the most famous of his poets, Thormod *Kolbrúnarskáld*, Dark-brow's Poet.

Olaf and his skalds at Stiklastadir

We have three main accounts of Olaf's last stand. One comes near the end of Snorri's 'Saga of St Olaf' in Heimskringla. There is a longer version at the end of *Fóstbrœðra saga*, which ought to mean 'The Saga of the Foster-brothers', though in fact the two heroes of the saga were not fostered together but rather took an oath of brotherhood. (The saga is regularly retitled 'The Saga of the Sworn Brothers'.) There is a still longer account at the end of the version of that saga contained in *Flateyjarbók*, whose compilers regularly opted for more popular and, we would say, more super-stitious stories than the upper-class Snorri.[35] All three versions, however, tell much the same tale in outline.

The two heroes of 'The Saga of the Sworn Brothers' are two young men who grow up together in Isafjord in Iceland. They are distinctly dis-similar types, and one wonders how they became so close: perhaps there was not much choice of companionship in their male age group round Isafjord. Thormod is of only average size and strength, but quick-witted and eventually a gifted skald and composer of love poems. Thorgeir is unusually big and strong, but comes closer to being what we would call a psychopath than any other saga hero, including even troll descendants like Egil. He 'was not much of a ladies' man', saying that 'it was demeaning to his strength to stoop to women.' The saga writer comments twice on Thorgeir's heart – once after his killers have performed a primitive autopsy on him – saying that it is small and hard, so that (like Hogni's in the Eddic poem 'The Lay of Atli', see Chapter One) it never quaked with fear.[36]

Thorgeir's first killing, at the age of fifteen, is properly motivated, for he is taking vengeance for his father, killed in a dispute over a borrowed horse, and, being of undistinguished family, there is no one more senior than Thorgeir to take up the quarrel. Other killings are given one justi-fication after another, but *Flateyjarbók* records a story which the author of the 'Sworn Brothers' preferred to leave out. In it, Thorgeir beheads a nameless shepherd who has done nothing at all provocative apart from standing with his neck stuck out. Asked why he did it by those who had to pay the compensation – Thorgeir, naturally, never has any money – all he can say is, 'I couldn't resist the temptation. He stood so well poised for the blow.'[37] Thorgeir visits Norway and makes contact with King Olaf, even (allegedly) doing one killing for him as a service, but the king notes that Thorgeir does not look like a lucky person, and indeed he is eventually killed in another revenge feud.

Before then, though, the sworn brothers have parted company. One day, Thorgeir asks Thormod who he thought would win if the two of them were ever to fight, and Thormod says immediately, and sensibly, 'this question of yours will break up our companionship.'[38] He knows that once crazy Thorgeir has got a killing in his head, he will eventually act it out. Nevertheless, Thormod later follows Thorgeir's killers to Greenland and kills them there. In one case, both Thormod and his victim fall off a cliff into the sea, and Thormod, losing the grapple, pulls down the other's breeches so he can't swim and Thormod can drown him. By this time, Thormod had gained a reputation as a poet, especially for his verses in praise of one Thorbjorg *Kolbrún*, or 'Dark-brow', though Thormod then unchivalrously reworks the verses so they can be presented to another lady, Thordis.

Thormod's career picks up when he too becomes a more welcome follower of King Olaf, and Thormod follows the king in his last exile, and in his return over the mountains to challenge the army of the *bœndur*, the farmers, or peasants, or yeomen, but in any case the recalcitrant heathens of the Trøndelag and west Norway.

The account of their last day starts, according to both *Heimskringla* and the longer version of 'Sworn Brothers' found in *Flateyjarbók*, with the king getting little sleep until late on in the short midsummer night of the north, and waking up at dawn. Thinking it is too early to wake his men, he asks Thormod to kill time with some poetry. With remarkable lack of tact Thormod sits up and recites the poem *Bjarkamál*. This was not one of Thormod's own compositions, which is perhaps what the king really wanted; it is not in skaldic but in Eddic style; it is called 'The Old Lay of Bjarki'; and it commemorates events which by 1030 were almost five hundred years old. The tactlessness of Thormod's decision comes from the fact that while it is indeed a 'wake-up' poem – it begins 'Wake, now wake' – and it is addressed to sleeping warriors, it is also a kind of suicide poem. Those who are woken in the poem will die that day defending their King Hrolf against overwhelming numbers, and what Thormod means is that the men he is waking will suffer the same fate and must die with the same courage. It's not what a modern morale expert would recommend at all.

But of course, to those imbued with a hero ethic, it's just the thing. The listeners call the poem *Húskarlahvöt*, the 'Whetting of the House-carls', and the king, perhaps deferring to popular opinion, gives Thormod a gold ring. Continuing his rather gloomy morale-booster routine, Thormod says (to which I add 'decoding' comment),

> We have a good king, though it is hard to see now how long-lived the king will be [he means the king will die in battle today]. This is my prayer, king, that you do not let us two be parted, either alive or dead [i.e. I intend to die with you].[39]

In all three versions of the scene, the king agrees, but in 'The Saga of the Sworn Brothers' the exchange is made a slightly tense one. Thormod asks the king to promise 'that we shall be resting in the same place tonight' (alive or dead, it's implied), and Olaf replies, 'I don't know whether it is within my power to decide, but if it is, then tonight you shall go where I go.'[40] What the king has left unspoken is that following the king into death will be up to Thormod; but actions speak louder than words. Though, as it happens, this is given a different and more sinister meaning later on in the scene.

When the battle starts, Thormod tucks his tunic up in front but lets it hang behind: he means to go forward, not back. He carries no shield but wields his axe with both hands until it is broken, and then carries on fighting with a sword after the king himself has fallen – cut down, according to Snorri's account in *Heimskringla*, by three battle wounds: an axe blow to the left thigh, a spear-thrust through the belly from beneath his armour, and a final sword blow to the neck. But even after the king's death, and Thormod's participation in the final counter-attack led by the king's cousin Dag Hringsson, Thormod is still alive, with only minor wounds.

The longer *Flateyjarbók* version of the 'Sworn Brothers' says that Thormod then gives the advice to use false fires, which allows Dag and his survivors to get away, but he refuses to go with them and prays to the king to keep his promise and not forsake him. In the shorter version of the saga he says bitterly, echoing the exchange between him and the king before the battle, 'Since I shall not be resting in the same place as the king tonight, living seems worse than dying.'[41] In both versions an arrow comes immediately from nowhere and bites deep – and Thormod is pleased. He thinks it is the dead king who has sent it, with a remarkably un-Christian miracle. So it *was* within the king's power, after all, to see that Thormod accompanied him into death.

A Viking dressing station

The story then switches to how the king's men bear their wounds, and once more there are three versions of this, of differing length. To start with I follow the version given in the shorter text of 'The Saga of the Sworn Brothers'.[42]

This says, as all three accounts do, that Thormod makes his way to a kind of casualty clearing station, where a woman is boiling water to wash wounds. Casualties from both sides are being treated together, and the woman asks Thormod which side he was on. He replies with a skaldic stanza. The woman asks him if he wants his wounds bandaged, but he says,

'The only wounds I have need no binding.' She asks him who fought best alongside the king, and how the king fought, and Thormod does a skald's job by replying with two complex impromptu verses of praise for Olaf and three royal followers. But then there are two strange events, which cast some light on Viking Age wound surgery.

In the first, Thormod clashes with one of the *bœndur*, who comes into the barn where the casualties are being treated with the intention, seemingly – and very much against the ideal of *drengskapr* – of taunting the king's men who are wounded. The barn was full of badly wounded men, we are told, 'and from their gaping wounds issued that terrible sound that comes with such deep cuts to the flesh'. The Trondheim *bóndi* hears this and says scornfully that it's no wonder the king lost if 'the men in here can hardly bear their wounds without screaming'. He goes on to call them 'weaklings'. Thormod asks him if his own wound seems a bad one, but when the *bóndi* comes up to look at it, Thormod hits him with his axe. When the man screams and groans, Thormod taunts him with hypocrisy: '[the men here] cannot help the sounds their wounds make. But you moan and wail over one small injury.'

The other two versions we have add byplay to this, but the central point of the story is the noise of wounds. Thormod clearly wants to make a distinction between noise that is involuntary, and therefore not blameable, and actually crying out with pain, which is. But what is the involuntary noise that comes from 'gaping wounds' or 'deep cuts'? Perhaps the saga is referring to something that must have been familiar on and after Viking Age battlefields, the noise of 'sucking chest wounds'. If the chest cavity is penetrated and the wounded man keeps on breathing, air rushes in and out as the lungs expand and contract, creating a snoring or bubbling noise. This, surely, is what the insolent *bóndi* mistakes for moaning.

In pre-modern conditions, furthermore, penetrating wounds to the chest, and even more certainly the abdomen, were usually fatal. If the gut had been pierced, no one was likely without anaesthetics to try to sew it up, and a pierced gut meant release of the contents into the abdominal cavity, followed by infection and death. But how can one tell if the gut has been pierced? The nurse who talks to Thormod is sure he has been wounded because he looks so pale; she makes him take off his tunic and sees the arrow in his side, but cannot see where the arrowhead has gone. In the long *Flateyjarbók* version she has been boiling onions in a pot (Snorri says garlic) and making a kind of porridge, and asks Thormod to eat some. What she will do then is sniff the wound. If a smell of garlic or onions comes out, that means the man's gut has been pierced and he will die. Thormod refuses the porridge, saying – though he seems to have missed the point, which is that the brew is diagnostic, not curative – 'I have nothing that herbs will cure.'[43] In all versions, though, he tells the woman to cut down into the wound and pull the arrow head out. When she cannot, he takes the pincers and pulls the arrow out himself, and looks at what is caught on its barbs: his heart fibres, some red and some white. 'Well has the king nourished us,' he says. 'There is still fat around my heart-strings.' Snorri, with his royalist sympathies, has those as Thormod's last words, still praising his king's generosity. Both other versions, however, have him die speaking one more verse of a poem, in the strict *dróttkvætt* metre. They go (and you have to see the original to get the point of the end of the story):

Emkak rauðr, en rjóðum	I am not red, yet the slim
ræðr grönn kona manni.	woman has a man unwounded.
Jarn stendr fast et forna	The ancient iron stands fast
fenstígi mér benja.	in my marsh of wounds.
Þat veldr mér, en mæra	That makes me pale now,
marglóðar nú tróða,	wearer of gold wave-fire,
djúp ok danskra vápna	the deep track at Dagshrid
Dagshríðar spor . . .	of Danish weapons . . .[44]

Thormod dies without finishing his last line. However, the rules of grammar and metre mean there are few possibilities. The missing word had to be two syllables long; it had to be a half-rhyme with *tróða*, two lines above; and it had to be a verb. The teenage Harald Sigurdsson was standing by – later he would become King Harald *Harðráði*, or Hard-counsel – and he completed the verse for Thormod, saying the word had to be *svíða*, 'cause pain'.

Much in the story of Stiklastadir has to be discounted. The claim that there was an eclipse of the sun during the battle, as if marking the king's fall, is a month wrong for the accepted date, 29 July 1030, and is probably a later addition. There can have been few bystanders to see the strike of the miraculous arrow, and in the stories we have, Thormod does not tell anyone about it. The byplay with the contemptuous *bóndi* looks like another attempt to claim a 'moral victory' after a bad defeat, like the Old English *Battle of Maldon* poem. And so on. Nevertheless, the picture of rough-and-ready treatment with hot water and onion porridge, and the detail about sucking chest wounds, are realistic if not real.

Thormod's devotion to King Olaf finally gets as close to sentimentality as Old Norse can manage, but is characteristically held back both by Thormod's own snarls at Sighvat the skald, absent from the battle, and by Olaf's own downplayed and even sarcastic reactions. Most of all, the scene of Thormod's death and Olaf's last stand bears witness to the continuing power of heroic story – in this case the story of King Hrolf and his champions – if not on the day itself, then for those who crafted and heard the story in later centuries.

Thormod, finally, combines the Viking virtues of independence verging on insubordination, refusal to show pain and, along with the king's housecarls, taking certain defeat and death as motivation rather than discouragement. It is the classic Ragnarok ethic, but felt by living men, not gods and dead champions.

ELEVEN

A Tale of Two Haralds:
Viking Endgame

The Viking Age may or may not have begun on 8 June 793, but it is generally agreed that it ended on 25 September 1066. On that day, at the Battle of Stamford Bridge, the giant king of the Norwegians, Harald *inn harðráði*, or Harald Hard-counsel,[1] who had begun his long, warlike career at Stiklastadir many years before, was taken by surprise by the arrival of the king of England, his near-namesake Harold Godwinsson. After a bitter struggle, fought out on foot for the most part with swords, spears and axes, he was killed 'striking out with both hands',[2] until brought down by a spear or an arrow in the throat. His army arrived in England in three hundred ships, and the survivors – according to Snorri Sturluson, who normally maximizes Norwegian successes – were allowed to go home in 24.

Was that really the end of an era? It is certainly true that although there were later threats and demonstrations against England by Scandinavian rulers, none of them tried seriously to take the country over ever again. Nevertheless that real end may have come just three weeks later, on 14 October, when Harold Godwinsson, having taken the survivors of his army, plus all the extra forces he could raise, by forced march from Yorkshire to Sussex, gave battle to William of Normandy. Like his Norwegian namesake, he lost the battle, the kingdom and his life.

One could argue that William's invasion was in effect another triumph for a Viking. His Normans were so-called because they were in origin Northmen, and William himself was the direct descendant of *Göngu-Hrólfr*, or Ganger-Rolf, or (as the TV series likes to call him) Rollo. It's assumed that by William's time the Normans had become totally Christianized and Frenchified, but there are reasons for doubting that, like the Sangüesa sculptures. Just the same, the contrast between Stamford Bridge and Hastings makes the point that things had changed. In fact they had been changing for a long time, to such an extent that one might say, in the end, that the word 'Viking' no longer meant anything. And that was the real end of the Viking Age.

A changed situation: the game of thrones

The main stages in Viking activity have been discussed already. First it was summer raiding, the original meaning of *fara í víkingum*, 'to go a-viking'. Then there was seizing bases; overwintering; setting up a system of slave-taking and protection money; taking over townships, like Jorvik, or creating them, like Dublin. And eventually, turning into landowners, like Halfdan's men in Northumbria and Ganger-Hrolf's in Normandy; all traced out, as remarked already, in the TV series in much compressed form.

Somewhere along the line, though, at least in Scandinavia and the British Isles, raiding and fighting between ethnic groups (English, Irish, Danish, Norwegian, Welsh, Scottish) escalated into something like a war between nations. The slow but mostly successful takeover of most of England by the descendants of Alfred – fighting it out with the descendants of Ivar Ragnarsson – was thrown into reverse by the involvement of kings of a newly united Denmark capable of mounting assaults by national fleets, Svein Forkbeard and his son Knut the Great. The deal Knut made with Ethelred *Unræd's*[3] much more formidable son Edmund Ironside was that they should share England, but whichever survived, the other would inherit the whole. Edmund died – one of many suspiciously convenient deaths in eleventh-century politics – and by this time the reward of Viking activity was not cash, or even land, but control: it had become a 'game of thrones'.

This was clearly what both Harald *Harðráði* and William the Conqueror (or *Vilhjálmr Bastarðr*, as Norse sources call him) were aiming at. There was still a difference between them, which one might call old-era/new-era. Of the three contenders to the English throne in 1066, Harald was the only one with no legitimate argument at all. His claim boiled down to something like, 'Previous kings of Norway were kings of England' (a highly dubious claim in itself), 'so I can be too.' Harold Godwinsson was not much better, viewed dynastically. He was the brother-in-law of King Edward the Confessor, Edward being the half-brother (by a Norman mother) of Edmund Ironside. But of English royal blood, descended from Alfred the Great and before him from Woden, Harold had not a drop. His claim, shakily evidenced, is that Edward wanted him to be king, and he was at least half-English, though significantly unpopular in much of the country. William's claim was no better, if not much worse. He too had not a drop of the old royal blood. His grandfather was the brother of King Edward's Norman mother, so Edward and William's father were first cousins. The person with the best dynastic claim to the throne was Edgar Ætheling, grandson of Edmund Ironside. But he was still a boy.

The difference between William and his rivals nevertheless shows up in the care he took over Edgar's position. It must have been a temptation to get rid of a focus for English resistance and rebellion by arranging for Edgar to have an accident, like other eleventh-century royals. But William and his descendants were remarkably lenient with Edgar, who died peacefully aged seventy or more. William's claim was that he was the true king, appointed by the previous king, not a usurper (Harold Godwinsson), nor a smash-and-grabber (Harald *Harðráði*). His claim was ratified by the pope; he carried a papal banner; his men had penances imposed on them even for the men they killed in battle at Hastings. William was illegitimate personally, but legitimate dynastically. He was operating under the law of nations. He might concede that it was a pity he had to enforce his claim by battle, but that was not his choice.

He was, then, in no sense a 'Viking', and Hastings was not a Viking victory, even if it looked like one. And it didn't even look like one, for while Stamford Bridge was decided by two armies of heavy infantry wielding axe, sword and spear, at Hastings the old era met the new Norman weapon system of archers and heavy cavalry. The result went the same way, both at Hastings in 1066 and at Dyrrhachium in 1081. Europe had changed, even militarily. If the Norwegian Harald had won at Stamford Bridge, William's Normans would have beaten him just the same.

A final point about the tangled situation in 1066, and the way the meaning of 'Viking' had been eroded, is this. The Viking Wars in England had lasted almost three hundred years, and had been very evenly contested – more so than the final victory of Christianity makes them look, with hindsight. During that time the two sides had grown much more like each other. Christian kings had learned to professionalize their armies. Relying on a call-up of thanes, with half-armed shire levies to back them, had worked in the past but had not worked for Byrhtnoth at Maldon. Kings increasingly paid long-service professionals to act as housecarls, and both English and Scandinavian housecarls were now armed with the long-handled axe, still called the 'Danish axe' centuries later. This had originally been a poor-man's weapon, much less expensive in metal, man-hours and charcoal for smelting than the aristocratic sword. But it delivered a heavier blow. As helmets and armour became more common, so the axe became the normal weapon for Anglo-Saxon infantrymen as well as Danes and Norse.

In the same way, as regards religion, pagans had become Christian, true. Though historians do not like to admit it, there had been a good deal of conversion the other way, apostasy among the *Gall-Goídil* (see Chapter Six) but also among Anglo-Saxons in the north. The concerns of Archbishop Wulfstan of York, around the year 1000, have already been mentioned: Christian Anglo-Saxons clubbing together to buy sex slaves, just like the pagans, and Christian slaves ungratefully running away to join the Vikings. Good for the slave, one may well say. One wonders when Viking armies started replacing their casualties by strong ex-Christian runaways on probation, and, as remarked above, quite how many Thor-worshipping 'Ragnars' and 'Eiriks' of the tenth and eleventh centuries had been baptized as Edward or Ælfric.

Meanwhile, at the top level of society, everyone was intermarried anyway, Danes, Norwegians, English and Normans. Earl Godwin, the power behind Edward's throne and father of Harold, was pure English, from Sussex, but he married a Danish noblewoman, Gyda, whose hus-band's sister had married Knut. As also remarked already, the names they gave their sons are revealing. The eldest was Svein, a Danish name that could readily be repronounced as English Swein. He disgraced himself by an act of *ódrengskapr* or unwarriorly conduct and was formally pronounced *níðingr*, a man without honour, by the whole army – he murdered his cousin Beorn (an English name, but again almost identical with the Danish Bjorn) while he was bound and helpless.[4] Next was Harold, whose name is only a spelling variant of *Haraldr*, and third was Tosti, just the normal Norse short form of Thorstein. Perhaps to make up for him, their next three boys all had very English names: Gyrth, Leofwine and Wulfnoth. One wonders what languages they all spoke at home.

Ethnic sentiment was clearly still strong in England – the *Chronicle* notes that in the stand-off between King Edward and Earl Godwin in 1052, the two armies refused to fight, 'because there was little else of any great value except English men on either side',[5] so the leaders had to make peace. The sentiment had not stopped Harold Godwinsson that same year from raiding Somerset and Devon after being sent into exile – it is unlikely that he got much support from the southwest of the country at Hastings. Or from the north of England, still bearing a grudge over the imposition on them of Tosti, Harold's brother, who had in any case turned traitor. Just as in modern politics, elites who have ceased worrying about popular support are likely to realize their mistake only when popular sup-port suddenly becomes necessary. One imagines that in late 1066 all over England, shire levies were marching towards Hastings – but slowly, with a trickle of desertions every night, and a lot of quiet grumbling among the churls, where the thanes couldn't hear, about whether the unknown William Bastard of Normandy was any worse than the home-grown bastards they already knew about.

In any case, perhaps the man who bled the life out of Anglo-Saxon England was Macbeth. His defeat by Earl Siward of Northumbria on Seven

Sleepers' Day, 25 July 1054, was, according to Shakespeare, a walk-over, with just the one significant casualty, Siward's son, Young Siward. Shakespeare was, of course, wrong. It was a hard-fought battle with heavy casualties on the English side as well as the Scottish. Earl Siward comes over even in Shakespeare as a figure from the heroic past, unmoved even by the death of his son: 'Had he his wounds before? . . . Why then, God's soldier be he. And so his knell is knolled' (Act 5, Scene 8), while in legend he was also said to be the son of a bear, just like Bodvar Bjarki from Chapter Two. Nevertheless, he seems to have adapted well to the new situation in England and to have carefully cemented his position as regards the four notoriously hostile and uncooperative ethnic groups of northern England. He himself controlled the Danes of York, he married into the family of the English rulers of Bamburgh – from whom, incidentally, Bernard Cornwell of *The Last Kingdom* claims to be descended – and through them he acquired relations by marriage among the Britons of Cumbria and the Hiberno-Norse settlers of the northwest.

But Macbeth killed almost a whole generation of potential leaders, including Siward's son Osbeorn, his sister's son Siward, and Dolfin (or Dolgfin, a Norse name), son of Thorfin of Allerdale. The plan for ethnic unity failed. Siward died, leaving only his underage son Waltheof to succeed him. The power vacancy meant he was replaced as earl of Northumbria only by Tosti Godwinsson, and the north of England returned to its default setting of bitter internal feud and division. This laid them open to the attack by Harald *Harðráði* and would be terminated only by the iron hand of the Conqueror, and the execution of Waltheof in 1076.

All things considered, then, it is no surprise that Harald *Harðráði* failed in that last attempt to bring England under Scandinavian rule by Viking-style attack. Things had changed in Britain, and in Western Europe more generally. It may not have been so obvious in Scandinavia, and especially in Norway, where raiding and dynastic warfare continued as it had done for centuries. Harald, though, was a throwback. Certainly he deserves the title often given him of 'Last of the Vikings'. His career was a Viking one *par excellence*. He himself had qualities that would have been admired by Ragnar Hairy-breeches, Egil Skallagrimsson or the Jomsvikings: great size and strength, ruthlessness extending to cruelty, marked avarice, and love of poetry, both as critic and as practitioner. He died like a Viking, too, not just 'striking out with both hands' but also exchanging sardonic remarks – not easy to understand or evaluate, but certainly with that characteristic mean streak so prized in Viking legend. To his life and death I now turn.

Harald the Varangian: blinding an Emperor

Harald was the son of Sigurd Sow, a petty king of the Uplands in Norway. As mentioned already, Sigurd's derisive nickname was given him because he was a peaceful man who preferred ploughing to raiding. Harald's mother, Asta, had previously been married to Harald *Grenski*, allegedly burned to death by Sigrid the Haughty, her son by him being King Olaf, who died at Stiklastadir. Harald Sigurdsson had even less going for him in terms of ancestry than his older half-brother. Both had to fight their own way to the top.

According to Snorri Sturluson, Harald who would become *Harðráði* showed signs of promise at an early age. When King Olaf Haraldsson paid his young half-brothers a visit, Olaf pulled faces at Harald and his two elder brothers by Sigurd, and the elder two burst into tears, but Harald remained defiant. When they were asked what they wanted, the elder two said corn and cattle (taking after their peaceable father), but Harald said, 'Housecarls', enough to 'eat up at one meal my brother Halfdan's cows'.[6] Such stories are readily invented, but Harald began to make a better-authenticated name by joining his half-brother Olaf Haraldsson and fighting for him, aged fifteen, at Stiklastadir. As recounted already, he is said to have been present at the death of Thormod the skald and to have finished his poem for him. If the story is true, he was presumably at the casualty dressing station where the wounded of both sides were being treated. The winners seem to have let the defeated be, as was likely to happen in battles between Norwegians.

Just the same, in the 'game of thrones' an exception might well have been made for the half-brother of a defeated king, and Harald went into hiding in the great forest on the Swedish–Norwegian border. Recovered from his wounds, he was being guided into Sweden by a farmer's son when he composed what is claimed to be his first surviving poem. Only four lines long, it fits the context very well, and is worth quoting:

Nú lætk skóg af skógi	Now from wood to wood
skreiðask litils heiðar.	I slink, rated little.
Hverr veit, nema ek verða	Who knows, but I may be
víða frægr of síðir?	better-famed later.[7]

One should note the technical skill. Lines one and two alliterate on *sk-*, lines three and four on *v-*. There are two alliterating stresses in each odd-numbered line, one on the first syllable of each even-numbered one. So far that is simply the old basic metre of *fornyrðislag*, the metre of Eddic poetry and Old English as well. But in Harald's four-liner, even-numbered lines also have internal rhyme: *skreið-* and *heið-* in line two, *við-* and *síð-* in line four. Lines two and four also end with a half-rhyme on the penultimate syllable, *heið-* and *síð-*. These tricks of sound are not optional. They are part of the chosen metre, and tricky metres are a major part of the skald's equipment. Of course, a technically skilled poem could still be a dull one, and Harald was prepared to concede that, even if it was a poem praising himself, as happened on one occasion (mentioned below). But you had to get the technique right even to be considered as a skald, and Harald did so.

Eric Christiansen dismisses the poem as 'late' (which is true), 'inauthentic' (which is an opinion) and applicable to anyone who became great after early adversity (though it fits Harald's situation very well).[8] The poem seems to me particularly interesting because it shows, as often with Norse poetry, a certain complexity of emotion. It starts almost with self-pity. But the poem is bracketed by the words for 'now' and 'later', and this redefines self-pity as awareness of a current bad situation, coupled with a sense that this can change – if the speaker can change it. It becomes almost a brag, not self-pity but (in very unfortunate circumstances) determination, ambition, self-confidence. Its 'I'll show them', chip-on-the-shoulder resentment and touchiness mark Harald all through his career.

Harald then followed the route taken by both the famous Olafs before him, into the Scandinavians' Wild East, to the court of Jarizleif, otherwise Yaroslav the Wise, Grand Prince of Novgorod and Kiev. Part-Scandinavian by descent, Yaroslav welcomed Harald, to whom he may have had some faint family connection. But even as a teenager Harald was unusually tall, unusually strong, and must have been skilful with his weapons: the kind of man any warlord would be happy to recruit. Quite how tall he was cannot now be known. Many Norse and Anglo-Saxon heroes are said to have been unusually big men, Byrhtnoth of Maldon estimated at 6 ft 9 in (205 cm) by early exhumers, Earl Siward of Northumbria at 6 ft 7 in (200 cm). These estimates are usually revised down – Byrhtnoth now a more modest 6 ft (183 cm), while no one has ever believed Thomas Walker's wild estimate of 9 ft (275 cm) for the man in the Repton cenotaph. But Harald certainly cut an impressive figure, even among the other Vikings. He is said to have commented of his rival Harold Godwinsson, when he saw him at Stamford Bridge, 'What a little man,' and Harold was another six-footer. He had to make his own way, but his physique gave him, literally, a head start.

Harald stayed with Yaroslav for some time, gaining reputation, and then continued on – a natural career progression – to join the Byzantine emperor's famous Varangian Guard. At this point we get a cross-bearing on the saga accounts, for Byzantium was a literate society with its own historians writing things down as they happened, rather than hundreds of years later like Snorri and the Icelandic saga writers. In Byzantium, Harald became steadily more prominent, and some of his doings even have definite dates on them. Ever since the reign of Basil II (975–1025) the Varangians had been an elite corps within the Byzantine army, for obvious reasons. They cost nothing to recruit or train, bringing their own weapons with them; they tended not to be involved with Byzantine politics; they were reliable if paid – and they were well-paid: 40 gold solidi a year for a regular Varangian, 44 for those promoted to be members of the emperor's guard.

Harald seems to have started off as a marine in the Byzantine fleet, cruising against Thracian and Arab pirates then raiding into the Aegean Sea. He served also in the Near East and may have visited the Holy Land and Jerusalem on escort duty in 1036. Byzantine accounts, however, bring him to prominence in the expeditionary force sent by Emperor Michael IV to reconquer Sicily from the Arabs, 1038–41.[9] The saga accounts are vague about where anything happened, but they do report Harald as in alliance with one Gyrgir, and this must be Georgios Maniakes, the most famous Byzantine commander of the age, another self-made man, another giant physically, with a notoriously terrible temper.

Unsurprisingly, he and Harald seem not to have got on. Snorri reports that on one occasion the Varangians on the march got to their destination first and promptly bagged the best campsite for themselves. Maniakes, turning up later, told them to move, but Harald refused. It looked like things would come to blows, but eventually it was decided that the two men should draw lots. Maniakes marked his lot, and Harald asked to see it so that he could mark his a different way. The lot was then drawn, and the man who drew it held it up. Harald took it, threw it into the sea and said, 'That was my lot that was drawn.' Challenged, Harald told Maniakes to look at the lot left in the bag, so he could see it had Maniakes's mark.[10] The point of the story is that Harald must have made the same mark as Maniakes, so that whichever was drawn, there would be a lot with Maniakes's mark left in the bag.

It seems unlikely this would have fooled a wily Byzantine, and the other exploits credited to Harald during this campaign – capturing cities by tunnelling, using firebirds, shamming death (the old coffin to get into a walled city trick) – sound more like Robin Hood stories than fact. The campaign as a whole was an expensive failure, but Harald seems to have come out of it with increased reputation and also very substantial personal profits. After another campaign in Bulgaria, Emperor Michael gave him the title Manglavites, which meant he walked before the emperor in procession, and the rank of Spatharocandidatus, only sixth of the fourteen ranks of Byzantine court officials, but a distinction for a foreigner. Harald also joined the guard-Varangians, quartered in the palace, with a 10 per cent pay rise, which by that time he could hardly have noticed.

He then became involved in Byzantine politics, which brings him even more fully into the light of history. In brief, Michael IV died in 1041. The Empress Zoë was persuaded to adopt as heir a relatively unknown person who became Michael V. He stood down the Varangians, while Maniakes got some of his own back by accusing Harald of murder, spying for Yaroslav and embezzling war loot instead of turning it in to the Imperial fisc – all charges very likely true, especially the last. Harald was jailed, but was soon released when Michael turned against his patroness and came out the loser in bloody street fighting. He and his uncle Constantine fled to take sanctuary in a monastery, but were dragged from the altar and handed over to Harald, at the head of the surviving Varangians. Harald then gouged out their eyes. Blinding was sometimes preferred by the Byzantines as it made certain that no one so mutilated could ever aspire to the throne again, while it did not incur the guilt of murder. This event too was remembered by Harald's later praise poets, Thjodolf Arnarson and Thorarin Skeggjason, and Snorri at least asks himself whether it's true. Did Harald really personally put out the eyes of the Emperor of the Greeks? He says that if it was an invention, the poets could have picked a less improbable story. In any case, 'this was the account brought back by Harald himself and the men who were with him.'[11] The next Emperor, Zoë's new husband, Constantine Monomachus IX (r. 1042–54), restored the Varangians to their old position, made Harald commander and gave him the job of purging the corps, by execution, of those who had proved unreliable or joined the wrong side.

Harald then decided to cash in his winnings and get out, and for this he had good reason, despite his fame, wealth and position. Byzantine politics, as he well knew, was horribly fickle. He had private information that his former employer Yaroslav was planning an attack on Byzantium. He also knew that his old rival and enemy Maniakes was in rebellion in Italy. He had no wish to fight either of them. But how could he slip away, and, even more important, how could he slip away with the enormous treasure he had accumulated, some of which he had already managed to bank with Yaroslav, but which was still (says Snorri) 'so immense that no one in northern Europe had ever seen the like of it in one man's possession before'?[12] Snorri notes also that it was Byzantine custom to allow the Varangians to strip the Imperial Palace every time an emperor died, and Harald had had his share of the palace-stripping three times in his career. It took twelve strong men to carry all his profits, getting on for a ton, then, of gold and silver. Snorri spices up the story with a tale of elopement with a Byzantine princess, and jealousy from the Empress Zoë, aged 65, who wanted to marry the handsome Varangian herself. None of this is likely, but it is possible that Snorri's tale of breaking a boom across the Bosphorus in order to escape could be true. Harald, anyway, did escape. He missed Yaroslav's great four-hundred-ship raid on Byzantium, which was fortunate for him, as the Russian armada (as it had been a hundred years before) was destroyed by 'Greek fire', the Byzantines' secret-weapon flame-throwers. But he could not be blamed by Yaroslav for the failure, or by Constantine for not preventing the attack. He arrived in Kiev fantastically rich and famous, the most eligible bachelor in the northern world, and accordingly was soon married to Yaroslav's daughter Elizabeth – who some ten years before had refused him, then only a teenager.

'Hard-counsel' Harald, half-king in Norway

It may be this rejection that Harald is still remembering and complaining about in the *Gamanvísur*, a poem of six stanzas attributed to him. In this he claims, rather like Ragnar in *Krákumál*, to have fought in Sicily, to have fought against the Tronds (this must be Stiklastadir, where he claims to have left a young king dead), to have steered a boat through storms, to be proficient at riding, swimming, skating, rowing and throwing the javelin, and to be widely travelled and famous for courage; but the refrain to each stanza says, *Þó lætr Gerðr í Gǫrðum / gollhrings við mér skolla*, 'And yet the lady of the gold ring in Russia holds herself aloof from me'.[13] Later on Elizabeth (or Ellisif), would be replaced by a Norwegian wife called Thora, though both women were still alive in 1066.

In 1045, now thirty years old, Harald returned to the North. He had made the right decision to stay out of the way for the fifteen years after Stiklastadir. There was no resisting the power of Knut the Great, but when Knut died in 1035 the Norwegians once again declared independence from Denmark and accepted as king, by acclamation, St Olaf's son Magnus, Harald's half-nephew. How could Harald now reinsert himself into Norwegian politics? From the long account in the anonymous saga compilation *Morkinskinna* one can make out the broad outlines of the situation facing Harald, and his not-altogether-successful strategies for coping with them.[14]

First among the recurrent strains and stresses was the relationship between Harald and King Magnus. Harald was the half-brother of Magnus's sainted father King Olaf, and – as Magnus's counsellors pointed out to him – it would be 'a tragedy' for such close relatives to be at odds.[15]

They were arguably flying in the face of reality there, for the tensions between half-brothers, and sworn brothers, blood-brothers, foster-brothers and brothers-in-law were a staple of heroic legend and then of family saga. (It might be said that the question, 'who counts as your brother?' was one of the vital themes of story and of real-life politics.) Family loyalty and prudence made an uneasy mix with jealousy and ambition.

It did not help Harald's position that Magnus was a successful king, remembered as Magnus the Good, largely because he seems to have learned the virtue of moderation and was even capable of taking criticism, a rare quality in a Viking king. In a famous scene, the poet Sighvat, who had been one of the skalds of King Olaf, recited to Magnus, in front of a large audience, his *Bersǫglisvísur* or 'Plain-spoken verses', which told him in effect that his policies were mistaken, 'your troops are tired of plunder; people are angry, king'.[16] The author of *Morkinskinna* thought that this incident changed Magnus's character and was what made him into Magnus the Good.

Even so, and even for Magnus, stresses remained. Over the North in the 1040s there still hung the shadows of two great kings, Knut the Great and Olaf the Saint. Magnus could not help remembering the death of his father at Stiklastadir, killed by men who remained among the great magnates with whom he had to deal. He asked one of them, Kalf Arnason, to show him the place where his father died at Stiklastadir. Kalf showed him the exact spot, and Magnus then asked where he, Kalf, had been at that moment. Kalf pointed to the spot. 'Your axe might have reached my father then,' said Magnus. Kalf denied it (according to Snorri's slightly different account), but he took the hint anyway and fled. *Morkinskinna* reports that he had readied his longship and stowed his goods for a fast getaway as soon as Magnus proposed the battlefield tour.[17] So there was unfinished business for Magnus, and though the policies of prudence and moderation counselled letting bygones be bygones, the vendetta ethic of his society would not let him forget it.

Meanwhile, though Knut had died in 1035 and the Norwegians had very promptly thrown off their allegiance to the crown of Denmark, Denmark remained a threat to Norway, and vice versa. Knut's own sons were soon off the board as a result of events in England, but no king of Denmark could resist the urge to recreate Knut's empire, and kings of Norway could well reflect that what was sauce for the Danish goose might well be sauce for the Norwegian gander. Magnus, then, was always at risk of taking on a war on two fronts from his power base in southeast Norway. To the north and west he had the people who had caused so much grief to successive kings of Norway: the independent, conservative, still largely pagan farmers and magnates who had followed the jarls of Hladir and who controlled the northern luxury trade. Magnus was lucky that Jarl Hakon Eiriksson, son of the victor at Svold and Hjorungavag, had drowned off Scotland, so that the Tronds had no obvious hereditary leader – but he knew they could soon find others. At the same time, Denmark had found a new king in Knut's nephew Svein Estridsson, who was furthermore first cousin to the man who would become King Harold of England.

One way of simplifying the whirl of confused events in the northern world in the 1040s and 1050s is to see Magnus balancing his two threats from north and south, with increasing concentration on the running battle between Norway and Denmark. Harald, meanwhile, was some-where on the balance point between the two main competitors, King Magnus and King Svein. He had no secure power base himself. He had been out of the country too long, and his father was only Sigurd Sow – of whom nothing more is ever heard. To begin with, he threw in with Svein, and they made a joint compact to conquer Denmark and Norway, starting (from a base in Sweden) with Denmark. Things did not go too well, Svein made a very veiled accusation that Harald was hanging back from fighting his kinsman Magnus, the two snapped at each other just like relatives at a family funeral, and Svein followed up (allegedly) with an attempt at assassination.

One thing that Harald by all accounts did have at this time – apart from the very considerable effect of his personal prestige – was money, the loot from Byzantium. The deal eventually brokered with King Magnus was a straight swap. Magnus would share his realm with his uncle Harald, and the two kings would pool their resources: in Harald's case, immense, in Magnus's, nothing. Even this deal nearly broke down on old memories. Harald poured out all his treasure on an oxhide and asked what Magnus had to show. All gone on war expenses, replied Magnus, 'I have no more gold in my possession than this one bracelet.' Harald replied, in the round-about manner that usually spells trouble in the sagas, that's not much, 'and yet there are some who would doubt your claim even to this bracelet'. It was given to me by my father, Holy King Olaf, says Magnus. True, replied Harald, laughing (a bad sign): 'your father gave you this bracelet after he had taken it from my father [Sigurd Sow] for some trifling reason . . . it was not an easy time for minor kings in Norway when your father was at the height of his power.'[18]

The next spat between the two men was a replay of the incident with Maniakes while Harald was with the Varangians. Magnus had stipulated carefully, when he gave Harald rights and title to half the kingdom, that while they shared equally, he was to take precedence whenever they were together. The middle seat of three, the king's berth in harbour. But one day when they were sailing together, Harald arrived first at the destination and tied up in the king's berth. When he saw, however, that Magnus was ready to fight for it, he cut his cables and moved. Later he said, loftily, that he would just consider Magnus's behaviour 'a mark of youth'. Magnus replied, in effect and, one feels, very accurately, that he knew if you gave Harald an inch he'd take a yard. 'It is also an old custom that it is the wiser man who must always give way,' Harald said (if one can believe the saga), and stalked off.[19]

But Magnus died in 1047, in unexplained circumstances – as so often seemed to happen after joint-rule arrangements – and Harald eventually made peace with Svein Estridsson on the rather obvious basis that one should be king of Denmark and the other of Norway. The 'war on two fronts' may have pushed Harald into this agreement, for in the fifteen years after Magnus's death a main antagonist had been Einar Wobble-belly, standing up once more for farmers' rights against royal taxation and oppression, with all the prestige of a survivor of Svold and a victor at Stiklastadir behind him. Harald murdered him treacherously, and his son Eindridi, but the feud was taken up by a more distant relative, and the 'game of thrones' went on: murders, divided loyalties, changing sides.

Perhaps, in the end, Harald's attack on England was motivated as much by a desire to unify his awkward countrymen by finding an external enemy as by the highly dubious claim to be restoring the empire of Knut. It was presumably during his almost twenty years of rule in Norway that Harald gained his hard-to-translate nickname: the Tyrannical, the Ruthless? Going along with this, there can be no doubt about Harald's personal courage – which of course comes more easily to someone who is bigger and stronger than anyone he is likely to meet. Cruelty was also a common (but not invariable) part of a hero's job description. Gouging someone's eyes out was all in a day's work for Harald, even if the victim was begging for mercy, like unfortunate Emperor Michael. But even Holy King Olaf was liable to torture people to death if, for instance, they were slower than he wished about converting to Christianity.

Harald was also unscrupulous, though this did not necessarily count as *ódrengskapr*, un-warrior-like behaviour. Most Viking warriors (if they survived a few years) had probably absorbed the advice of the god Odin in the poem *Hávamál* (Words of the High One): if you mix with warriors you soon find out that 'no one is the boldest of all', or to put it another way, there's always someone who is as tough as you are.[20] So take advantage when you can. Harald did not challenge old Einar Wobble-belly and his son face to face, since for one thing they had five hundred backers. He killed them from ambush in a closed room, leaving the five hundred supporters leaderless and unsure what to do. (Einar should have remembered the very first stanza of Odin's advice in 'The Words of the High One':

> All doorways,   before you go in,
>   look around,
>   spy around.
> Because it cannot be told   where your enemies
>   sit in the hall before you.)

Harald was brave, cruel, unscrupulous, and notorious even in his own time for gold-greediness: unattractive qualities to us, but potentially admirable in a more ruthless age.

The world's most intimidating literary critic

Digging a little deeper, some more unlikely qualities show up. As already suggested, Harald's poems could indicate that he had something of a chip on his shoulder. His four-liner as he crept through the woods of Sweden, unknown, disregarded and with no prospects except what he could make for himself, carries a sense of 'I'll show them.' His *Gamanvísur* combines a strong sense of his own merits – look at all the things I'm good at! – with a resentful awareness that the girl still turned him down. The sagas about Harald, written with the benefit of 150 years of hindsight, give him a career trajectory of continuous ascent. Still, one wonders what it was like for a teenager to turn up at the court of Kiev, no doubt with no money, no relatives, and a claim to be a king's son (a very unimportant king's son) and a dead king's brother (well, half-brother). Slights and rejections received at an early age, it is said, sting more. They may have created the touchiness about status and precedence that shows up in the two stories about Maniakes and the camping ground and Magnus and the king's mooring berth.

Finally, and unexpectedly – so unexpectedly it sounds as if it might be true tradition – there was one thing Harald could be fair-minded about, and that was poetry, which he seems to have taken very seriously. We first see him at the casualty clearing station finishing, entirely correctly, the missing word of Thormod the skald's death poem. Concern for poetry is also said to have overruled even his determination always to be top dog. *Morkinskinna* says that a poet called Arnor 'Jarls' Poet' arrived when Magnus and Harald were together and announced that he had a poem for each of them. 'Which of us will hear his poem first?' asked Harald, characteristically, and was told, Magnus – because he's young, and young men are impatient. (Subtext: don't worry, nothing to do with status.) Arnor then starts to recite his praise poem, but when he says 'every king is far inferior to you,' Harald tells him to praise Magnus but not speak ill of other kings (subtext: me). As the poem goes on, Harald again reacts derisively, but then listens to Arnor's second praise poem, which is about himself. Someone then asked him which he thought was the better poem, perhaps expecting him to continue his criticism of the one about Magnus. But he said, 'Mine will soon be forgotten . . . but the poem composed about king Magnus will be recited as long as the North is peopled.' He was in fact an honest reviewer who did not just shout for his own side.[21]

He was also a critical one. In another incident, which involved an impromptu poetry competition between Harald, Thjodolf Arnarson the skald (much of whose poetry about Harald survives) and an unknown fisherman, Harald disqualified Thjodolf, the professional's, stanza – because, he said, in line four Thjodolf used *gröm* and *skömm-* as internal rhymes, 'and that is not a true rhyme'. (There was a slight pronunciation difference between the single and the double *m*.) Thjodolf sulked, but the fisherman revealed himself to be a skilled poet and a veteran of Stiklastadir who had fought on the right side, and was taken into Harald's retinue.[22]

Even at Stamford Bridge Harald is said to have been critiquing poetry, in this case his own – though once again one wonders who survived to tell the story. The whole course of events on that day could be – much of it certainly was – Snorri's invention. Still, some of Harald's poems are likely to be genuine, and his reputation for judging poetry fairly is an unlikely quality to invent. There is no harm in accepting that in this one area at least, he was capable of stepping outside himself. His love for poets was tough love, but it was genuine.

Stamford Bridge: Vikings end as they began

In several ways, Harald looks like a repeat of Ivar Ragnarsson. The Ragnarssons had a raven banner, which prophesied victory or defeat by whether its wings spread or drooped. Harald too had a famous banner, *Landeyða*, or Land-waster.[23] His victory at York on 20 September 1066 came two hundred years almost to the day after the Ragnarssons' victory there. Harald's motivation was not so very different from the blatant aggression of the Ragnarssons. He had no real claim to the throne of England, and any hope of reviving the empire of Knut must have been a frail one. Possibly Harald's motivation was simply heroic. He had been a successful warrior for more than thirty years, and success in war was by far the major theme for the skalds he admired so much; once he had suppressed internal dissent and made his deal with the Danes under Svein, where else was he to exercise his talents?

He must also have scented an opportunity, brought to him by Harold Godwinsson's brother Tosti. All through Edward the Confessor's reign (1042–66) there had been a long struggle, sometimes breaking out into open warfare, between the Godwin family and the other magnates of England, notably Siward of Northumbria and Leofric of Mercia, with King Edward holding an uneasy balance. The seizure of the throne by Harold Godwinsson in 1066 was only the last stage in a string of takeovers by the Godwin family, who increasingly used the whole kingdom as a kind of board to play their power game on. Room had to be found for all the brothers. Since 1056, Harold had ruled the south. His brother Gyrth got East Anglia; Leofwine had a smaller earldom carved out of the East Midlands, at the expense of Earl Leofric. After Siward died, the fateful decision was made to put aside Siward's son Waltheof, and any other northern candidates there may have been, and award Northumbria to Harold's brother Tosti.

This was, naturally, resented by the northerners, and after several years of increasing turmoil for Tosti – who had no relatives in the area, no network of supporters or connections, and who was accused of being overbearing – the Northumbrians rose against him, massacred his two-hundred-strong bodyguard and chased Tosti off to refuge in Flanders. Normal Godwinsson practice would have been to reinstate him, or to find him another earldom elsewhere, but the rebellious northerners marched south, met Tosti's brother Harold, and made it clear they wanted a non-Godwinsson. Rather oddly, they did not pick one of their own – though Northumbrians were notorious for not cooperating, even with each other – but picked a man from the only other magnate family, Morcar, grandson of Earl Leofric, aided by his brother Edwin.

Harald of Norway's opportunity came because Tosti refused to accept the situation and wait for a change. He was, as noted above, first cousin to King Svein of Denmark, and his first call was on him, to see if Svein would get him his earldom back. Svein turned him down flat, and Tosti left, having made veiled accusations of cowardice. He moved on to Harald, who was also cautious, remarking, says Snorri, that 'the English are not entirely to be trusted.' Tosti pointed out that King Magnus had had a claim to both England and Denmark, implying that the claim ought to pass to his successor, Harald. If Magnus had a right to England, Harald asked, why didn't he take it? In reply, Tosti asked him why he, Harald, had not conquered Denmark.[24]

This was very close to being insulting, but sailing close to the wind seems to have been a good idea in discussions with Viking leaders: it meant you had at least got their attention, and anything like a dare was hard for them to resist. Harald indeed flared up and told Tosti he had no need to brag about his Danish relations. But Tosti then told him the answer to his own question. Harald had not conquered Denmark because the people resisted him. And Magnus had not tried to enforce his claim on England because he knew the people there would resist him. But now, he said, the situation is different. I can bring 'the majority of the chieftains in England' over to your side. England, he concluded, will be a lot easier for you, with me on your side, than Denmark ever was.

One can imagine several answers to that argument, notably, if you're so popular, how come you've been chased out? But whatever the bait was, Harald took it. The omens were bad. People had warning visions, and Harald himself had a warning dream from his half-brother St Olaf, though such portents are often invented after a disaster is known to have happened. *Morkinskinna* goes further and says that some people declared that England now had an army of *þingamenn*, the professional retinues which English kings and earls had got used to supporting. Any one of them, it was said, 'was worth no less than two of the best Norwegians among King Harald's champions'.[25] This turned out not to be true, as even the *Anglo-Saxon Chronicle* was to admit, but in any case it was a red rag to a bull.

One difference between Harald's career and those of his Viking predecessors is that we know much more about his movements. In the case of Harald we can often place events to the day and follow his marches on a map. Harald took his fleet up the river Humber, where he made rendezvous with Tosti and his band of Flemish mercenaries or adventurers, and then rowed up its tributary the Ouse. Edwin and Morcar fell back before him, taking their ships up the river Wharfe, perhaps hoping that Harald would continue along the Ouse to York, so enabling them to come downstream to the Ouse and take him from the rear. But Harald halted at Riccall, below the junction of the two rivers, so it was the earls' fleet that was now blocked. He and Tosti disembarked with their men, left a strong guard on the ships – they would be important later – and set off for York, 15 km (9 mi.) away. The two armies clashed at Fulford, just outside York, on 20 September, and the Norwegians won what seems to have been an easy victory, though both Edwin and Morcar got away. York surrendered on the 24th, and many agreed to join Harald in his march south against Harold Godwinsson – as Tosti had claimed they would, though the motive was more likely hostility to southerners, or lurking Scandinavian ethnic loyalty, than any liking for Tosti.

But, in the words of the old joke about the vet trying to blow a worm-powder down a sick bear's throat, the bear blew first. We do not know how much warning Harold Godwinsson had of Harald *Harðráði*'s invasion. He had been crowned king only on 6 January. He had been waiting in the south for the threatened invasion from Normandy all summer, and he knew it was imminent; William in fact landed on 28 September. But Harold must have started his forced march north well before the battle at Fulford, perhaps as soon as he heard that Harald was in the Humber. His counter-march from York to Hastings after the Battle of Stamford Bridge, 360 km (225 mi.) as the crow flies, took him just over two weeks (26 September to 13 October), and that was regarded as unusually fast, so he must have started with his army from the south coast not long after the start of September, at latest. On 24 September, the day York surrendered, he was approaching York, with his *þingamenn* (housecarls) at full strength – which they would not be at Hastings three weeks later.

On 25 September, the Norwegian Harald was taken off guard. He had arranged to receive hostages and provisions at Stamford Bridge, on the river Derwent about 13 km (8 mi.) east of York and rather further from Riccall to the south. A part of his army was still at Riccall with the ships. The Scandinavian sources add that it was a hot day and Harald's men had left their heavy equipment, shields, helmets and armour back at the ships. This sounds like the kind of excuse often manufactured after a smashing defeat. Any sensible Viking would once again remember the advice given by the god Odin, this time in stanza 38 of *Hávamál*, 'The Words of the High One':

> From his weapons   on the road,
>   no man should go a foot,
> because it's not known   when a man on the road
>   might have need of his spear.

Which goes double for foragers in hostile territory.

There is general acceptance, though, that Harold Godwinsson's speed took his namesake unawares. He had not even halted in York, but gone straight through, and no one seems to have ridden on ahead to give early warning. The first thing the Norwegians knew about it was a cloud of dust and the glitter of sun on weapons, which 'sparkled like a field of broken ice'.[26] Tosti wanted to fall back to the ships – though there was no clear route – but Harald sent off riders to Riccall, telling his men there to come immediately to his aid, raised his banner and stood on the defensive on the west bank of the Derwent, with the river behind him.

Icelandic sources – the anonymous manuscripts *Morkinskinna* and *Fagrskinna*, and Snorri Sturluson's *Heimskringla*, which drew on both of them – then give stirring accounts of the battle itself.[27] The trouble is that they are known to be quite certainly invented in detail later on, drawing on genuine accounts of thirteenth-century battles. The main anachronism is that the Icelanders represent the English army as fighting from horseback and being held off by Norwegian pike formations. Professor Shaun Hughes of Purdue has traced the details back to accounts of the battle of Bouvines in 1214, just a few years before *Morkinskinna* and the others were compiled.[28]

The only contemporary account is, as often, that in the *Anglo-Saxon Chronicle*, and that says little more than that it was a very hard fight which lasted a long time – except for one manuscript. This adds that when the Vikings retreated across the river Derwent, after King Harald was dead,

> There was one of the Norwegians who withstood the English so they could not cross the bridge nor gain victory. Then one Englishman shot with an arrow but it was to no avail, and then another came under the bridge and stabbed him through under the mail-coat. Then Harold, king of the English, came over the bridge and his army along with him, and there made a great slaughter of both Norwegians and Flemings.[29]

This is both detailed and somewhat discreditable to the English, who are clearly thought not to have fought fair, which makes it the more likely to be a true incident (now commemorated in the Swordsman pub at Stamford Bridge).

It still raises questions. If one man could hold the bridge, it must have been a narrow one. How long would it take for either a fleeing or a pursuing army to cross a narrow bridge? Perhaps what happened is that after the battle was decided, on the west bank of the Derwent, a relatively small number of survivors retreated over the bridge onto the east bank, the last of them holding the English off to give the others a chance to either keep running or else reform on the east bank. The Scandinavian accounts insist that late in the day one Eystein led reinforcements up from Riccall to prolong the fight, but after what must have been a 10-mile forced march, on a hot day, in armour, some could hardly stand and some stripped off their mail. Snorri notes glumly, 'Nearly all the leading Norwegians were killed there.'[30]

The most interesting part of the Icelandic accounts, however, which once again demonstrates the love of mordant conversation and famous last words so typical of Viking death scenes, is the exchanges before the battle between the leaders. It is only right that the Viking era should come to an end with words of grim defiance, spiced with ambiguity and containing the vital mean streak. This is how they go.[31]

As the two armies prepare for battle, Harald's horse stumbles and throws him. He gets up, saying quickly, 'A fall is good fortune.' But Harold Godwinsson, watching, asks who that man was, and when they tell him, comments, 'He is a stately and splendid man, but it looks as though his luck (*hamingja*) may have run out.' Sensitivity to *hamingja* – sometimes seen as a family possession, sometimes concentrated in an heirloom like an inherited weapon – was an important part of the saga hero's equipment, and the belief in luck is still pretty current. Wise people know when their luck has changed, or run out, just as they know to 'back their luck' when it's in.

A group of riders then go up to the Norwegian line and call for Earl Tosti (ex-Earl, to be accurate). Tosti asks what they want and is told by one of them that his brother Harold offers him a third of the kingdom – presumably if he would change sides, though one cannot see how he could safely manage that with Harald *Harðráði* standing right by him. Tosti, in a difficult position between brother and partner, asks what the offer is for Harald. Harold Godwinsson – for he is the spokesman, though acting incognito – replies, '[The king] did say something about how much of England he would grant him: King Harald will have seven foot of sod, or as much more as he needs because he is taller than other men.' The first half is studiedly insulting, presented as something of no great importance. The second half is a flat refusal, and a threat – as much land as it takes to bury him – pretending with further insult to be a concession. Tosti refuses, saying that to desert Harald now would not be honourable.

Norwegian Harald himself seems to have appreciated the sardonic nature of the spokesman's words, for he asks, after the emissaries have retreated, 'Who was that well-spoken man?' He is told it was the king himself. Harald replies – this is the mean streak coming out – 'That was too long hidden from me, because they were close enough to our forces so that my namesake would not have lived to report the death of our men.' He means, of course, that if Tosti had not concealed the presence of his brother, Harald would have killed him before he could get away. Indirect speech is, however, still the rule. He does not reproach Tosti except very obliquely. He appreciates that Tosti has done one honourable thing in refusing his brother's offer, and another honourable thing in concealing his identity. Tosti had a duty to both Harolds; he has respected both. Tosti says he would rather have his brother kill him than the other way around.

Harald ends the exchange by remarking – a kind of counterbalance to what Harold said about him when his horse threw him – 'That was a small man, lads, and yet he stood haughtily in his stirrups.' This also combines a slightly patronising first half with a reluctantly respectful second half.

Everyone concerned, one has to say, has given a demonstration of *drengskapr*. Harold takes a risk – a big risk, from what Harald says about him not getting away so easily – but he trusts his brother not to betray him. Tosti repays that trust, but also refuses to desert his partner. Harald accepts Tosti's ambiguous position, in a way admits he was right not to betray his brother, even if that may be the death of all of them, and notes Harold's courage as well. All put, as usual, indirectly and in few words. That is how Vikings are supposed to talk. (They would never have been able to handle committee meetings.)

It's only right that Harald's last words should be about poetry, viewed critically. Both Snorri and *Morkinskinna* quote the same lines:

Fram gǫngum vér í fylkingu	Forward we go in formation
brynjulausir und blár eggjar:	Without armour against blue-steel edges
hjalmar skina hefkat mína.	Helmets shine. I don't have mine.
nú liggr skrúð várt at skipum niðri.	Now our gear lies down with the ships.[32]

Both versions comment that Harald had a famous mail-coat, which reached down below his knees and which had never been pierced. But then Harald abandons the faint hint of feeling sorry for himself and says, that was not a good poem, I shall make a better one. And he comes out with a more complex stanza:

Krjúpum vér fyr vápna,	We creep because of weapons,
valteigs, brǫkun eigi,	of the falcon-field, the crash, not,
svá bauð Hildr, at hjaldri,	so commanded Hild, in battle,
haldorð, í bug skjaldar:	faithful, into the hollow of shields.
hátt bað mik, þars mœttusk,	High she bade me, where they meet,
menskorð bera forðum	the necklace-pole, to bear, earlier,
Hlakkar íss ok hausar,	Hlokk's ice and skulls,
hjalmstofn í gný malma.	The helmet-prop in the clash of swords.[33]

Or, unwinding the syntax: 'Faithful Hild [the valkyrie] commanded that we should not creep into the hollow of shields in battle because of the crash of weapons. The woman [necklace-pole] bade me earlier to bear my head [helmet-prop] high where sword [the ice of Hlokk the valkyrie] meets skulls in the clash of swords.' One might paraphrase this by a cry from a much-later battlefield, 'Heads up, lads, and show 'em your cap-badges.'[34]

So why is the second one a better poem? It is more defiant. It sounds for a moment as if he is saying, 'let's cringe behind our shields,' until the meaning is reversed at the end of line two by the word *eigi*, 'not'. It moves from negative to positive. But probably Harald, critical snob that he was, really preferred the much more complex metre of *dróttkvætt*, with its internal rhyme, its half-rhyme, both at set places, and its alliteration, also on compulsory syllables, to the older Eddic metre of *fornyrðislag*, which has only alliteration linking its half-lines: the basic or rock-bottom style of all old Germanic poetry.

Harald then died like a hero, for he now

> fell into such a fury of battle that he rushed forward ahead of his troops, striking out with both hands. Neither helmets nor coats of mail could withstand him, and everyone in his path gave way before him.[35]

His charge was nevertheless the death of him, for he took an arrow – *Morkinskinna* says a spear – in the throat. Harold offered quarter to Tosti and the survivors but, as Arnor the 'Jarls' Poet' declares, they refused it, choosing in traditional style to die with their lord 'rather than beg for mercy'.[36] Eystein arrived from the ships only in time to add to the death toll.

And that was the end of the last of the Vikings, at least as later ages in far-off Iceland would remember it, or reimagine it: arrogant, unlucky, self-possessed to the last, accepting fate with wry defiance. Harald did not die laughing, or commending himself to Odin like Ragnar, but he died without showing fear or weakness. His four-liner, even if he rejected it (and no matter who may have written it subsequently), has the flat note of a good death song: 'Helmets shine. I don't have mine'. Even *brynjulausir*, armourless, we'll go forward to meet the blue-steel edges. Just a hint of the rueful – perhaps that's allowed. But bad luck is all in the game. A hero has to know how to lose, but it doesn't make him what we call a loser.

TWELVE

Viking Aftermath: The Nine Grins of Skarphedin Njalsson

In Old Norse/Icelandic, literary history and real history are oddly out of line as regards dates. The heroic poems of the *Edda* deal with events far in the past, like the death of Gunnar/Gundaharius in the fifth century and the death of Iormunrekk/Ermanaricus in the fourth. The poem 'Battle of the Goths and Huns' memorializes events even further back, when the Huns made their first appearance from the Asian steppe.

By contrast, skaldic poems only celebrate kings from the ninth century onwards. But the poems celebrating kings like Harald Fairhair are accepted as contemporary with the kings, while no one can be sure when the Eddic poems were composed. In the form we have them, they could easily have been created later, not earlier, than the skaldic productions. They were *thought* to be old, though. The scribe of the Codex Regius calls the last poem in it *Hamðismál in forno*, 'The Old Lay of Hamdir', and the same adjective is used for 'The Old Lay of Bjarki'.

Much the same contradictions apply to the sagas. It would be convenient to think that the sagas of old times, like 'The Saga of the Volsungs' or 'The Saga of King Hrolf', which cover events from the fifth and sixth centuries, were written first; with the sagas of Icelanders coming next, being mostly set in the period around the conversion of Iceland in 1000; then the kings' sagas taking the sequence up to kings still alive when the sagas were being written, like King Sverrir, who died in 1202; and finally the 'sagas of the Sturlungs, which describe events (such as the murder of Snorri Sturluson) within living and personal memory of the authors.

But it doesn't work like that. The first sagas to be written seem to have been the kings' sagas, with Sverrir's one of the earliest. Some of the sagas of old times were written very late, notably 'The Saga of King Hrolf' from the fifteenth century. On the other hand, the legends on which these were based, legends of King Hrolf and the sons of Ragnar and the Volsungs, were certainly known long before, well-enough known for Saxo round about 1200 to garble and misunderstand them. Sorting out an exact chronology is not possible.

Having said that, one thing remains clear enough, which is that the men writing the great sagas of Icelanders, mostly in the period 1220–90, and looking back on their own Heroic Age, two to three hundred years before, not only knew the great legends themselves but assumed that their ancestors did too – while Snorri was taking care early on in that great creative period to ensure that knowledge of the great myths also did not die out. The pagan myths and the heroic legends, in short, remained a living presence within literature, and very likely in thirteenth-century reality as well. So much so that they could be transposed into a reality very different from that of their first compositions.

Toe and heel: remembering Volund

Of all the forty-plus sagas of Icelanders, the most problematic and controversial is 'The Saga of Hrafnkel, Priest of Frey'.[1] One may well think that this is not because it is all that hard to understand. It's because the point it makes is once again thoroughly unwelcome to the modern liberal mindset. The fact is that its hero Hrafnkel is not just a killer – all saga heroes are that – but one who admits himself that his killing was wrong; one who is moreover arrogant, overbearing and arguably lacking in *drengskapr*. Just the same, he is the hero. He has a quality that the wise ones in the saga recognize, and it's part of the make-up of a proper hero, not the sort who star in video games. Not to beat about the bush: it's self-control. Not just taking it, but taking it without reacting. And not just keeping a poker face, but making plans behind it. Not showing anything – until the moment comes.

The point is dramatized in three linked scenes. The first is one which everyone has flagged as odd, the scene of Thorgeir's toe. Hrafnkel, for religious reasons, has sworn to be the death of any man but himself who rides the stallion Freyfaxi, which he has part-dedicated to the god Frey. A poor shepherd called Einar rides the stallion in an emergency, and Hrafnkel, despite being well aware that Einar's intentions were good, kills him. He is perfectly prepared to pay compensation for his death to Einar's father, and at a very high rate – essentially lifetime care – because he admits he did wrong. But Einar's father, Thorbjorn, insists out of pride that he wants his day in court and to be treated like an equal. Hrafnkel finds this *hlægiligr*, laughable. Thorbjorn's attempt to bring the case to the Althing or Assembly gets nowhere – a poor man like him needs backers, and no one wants to take on Hrafnkel. Thorbjorn's nephew Sam, who has been pressured into taking responsibility for the lawsuit by accusations of cowardice, tells his uncle he's a fool, and Thorbjorn – this is very bad – breaks down and cries.[2]

The situation is saved by the appearance of a stranger, Thorkel, just back from Miklagard. He says they must get his brother Thorgeir to help, and explains how to do it. Thorgeir is in bed with a big boil on his foot, which has just burst. (Icelanders' diet made them very prone to boils, often mentioned in the sagas.) He is asleep in his shelter with his foot sticking out. Let old Thorbjorn go to the shelter, stumble and grab the sore toe. Is that a good idea? wonders Sam. But they do it, and Thorgeir reacts with predictable anger. Thorkel then steps in and says, semi-proverbially, 'For many people, things go worse than they intend.' Of course, in this case Thorbjorn acted perfectly deliberately. But what Thorkel means should be clear enough. It's natural that Thorgeir should react angrily when someone grabs his sore toe. It's just as natural for old Thorbjorn to react ill-advisedly when someone kills his son. He did it out of *nauðsyn*, necessity.[3]

The point is arguable, as the saga will later show, but Thorgeir accepts it. He and his men take over the Althing, block Hrafnkel from even getting into court, and Sam has Hrafnkel declared an outlaw. So far so good, but for this to count it has to be reaffirmed right away, and at Hrafnkel's own home – not so easy. Sam has just laid himself open to a serious counter-stroke as soon as he too goes home. Thorgeir says they must strike first.

They get to Hrafnkel's home in Jokulsdal, unseen, just after Hrafnkel does, and rush the place at dawn, dragging Hrafnkel out of bed. (As Odin remarked, in 'The Words of the High One' again, this time stanza 58: 'He must rise early, who wants to have / another man's life or money ... a sleeping man rarely wins.') Hrafnkel then has his outlaw status confirmed, and Sam offers him a choice: death for him and his men, or forfeiture of his farm and property and leaving the district. Hrafnkel opts for life and shame in this, the second of the three linked scenes. Thorgeir and Thorkel go home – which is a long way away – and leave Sam to take charge.

Things stay quiet for six years. Then something happens which everyone except Hrafnkel has failed to foresee, in the third linked scene. Sam's brother Eyvind comes home from successful travels abroad. He, with five men and a boy, heads for his brother's new property. On the way he rides past the farmstead which Hrafnkel has spent six years building up. Taunted by a washerwoman for his failure to take vengeance – what she says is an accusation of impotence as well as cowardice, 'Every man grows soft as he grows old'[4] – Hrafnkel collects his men, rides after Eyvind, who is too proud to flee, attacks him eighteen to six (the boy goes for help) and kills them all. Then he collects further forces and comes down on Sam's farmstead the next dawn, before Sam is ready, catches *him* in his bed and offers him the same choice he was previously given: death or poverty. Sam makes the same choice as Hrafnkel.

The next year, Sam goes to see if Thorkel and Thorgeir will help him again, but Thorgeir says no. His point is clear enough. Thorgeir is honour-bound to protect Sam if he wants to come and live nearby, but Hrafnkel has shown who is the better man.

Therein is the rub for modern critics.[5] What is meant by 'better'? Morally better? No. More of an opportunist, maybe? That depends on what one thinks about the washerwoman scene. Are we meant to think that Hrafnkel had given up on vengeance until he was taunted? Or was he biding his time all along, because he knew that Eyvind, missing for years, was the danger man of Sam's family, who would always be a risk unless he was taken out? The clue to this lies in the scene in which Hrafnkel is surprised and dispossessed, six years before the killing of Eyvind. It contains something really gratuitous.

The saga says that Sam and his backers, after they've caught Hrafnkel in his bed, take him and his men out into the yard, tie their hands, cut holes through the men's 'hough sinews' (*á hásínum*), thread a rope through and string them up upside down, so that the blood runs into their eyes. Are 'hough sinews' the hamstrings, behind the knee, or the sinews behind the heel?[6] Either way, it's a mutilation, potentially disabling.

The point is this. Hrafnkel endures the pain, just like Volund when he was hamstrung. More than that, and again like Volund, he endures years of shame and humiliation. What the washerwoman incident points out is that for years people have been saying things like that about Hrafnkel: he's old, he's crippled, he's lost his nerve. Like Volund, Hrafnkel lets people think he's beat, finished, off the board. But all the time, and once again like Volund, he is meditating a vengeance no one else sees coming.

What Hrafnkel has, then, is self-control, the ability not to lash out like a thrall or like old Thorbjorn, in spite of his physical pain and public humili-ation. In a way, the 'hough sinew' scene demonstrates the opposite of the 'sore toe' scene. It's natural for Thorbjorn to lash out in his grief, and for Thorgeir to snarl angrily when his toe is yanked. Natural, yes, but – despite what Thorkel says after he has set up his little drama – *not necessary*. People often say they had to do something, pleading *nauðsyn*, necessity, when what they mean is they can't control themselves. Hrafnkel shows some people *can* control themselves. That's part of the mindset essential for a hero.

Was the Volund story in the mind of the author of the *Saga of Hrafnkel*? It's the hough sinews that make the connection. The saga appears very realistic, especially the local geography, which is so important for tactics – the 'horse lanes' where Sam's men hide their horses before their dawn attack, the road over the moor where Eyvind could have got away[7] – but the mutilation scene seems like pure fiction. Stringing men up by their heels or their knees? The tendons would tear out. The scene is there to make a point, which is to make the connection with another famous hamstringing and by doing so to show that Hrafnkel is acting the same way. He too had in mind 'a cunning thing'.

Words about virginity: remembering Brynhild

Vital to the whole Nibelung story, as said in Chapter Three, is the scene of the 'quarrel of the queens', in which Gudrun and Brynhild exchange words that lead to the murder of Sigurd, words in which Brynhild, one way or another – each ancient version being somehow different – is told she has had sex with and lost her virginity to a man who is not her husband. We find the same scene at the core of 'Gisli Sursson's Saga'.

It has been moved sharply downmarket, however. Here we have not queens arguing over precedence, but Icelandic housewives bickering in a farmyard, initially about making a shirt. In the saga there are four men involved and two women, related as shown:

Thorgrim = Thordis Asgerd = Thorkel Gisli = Aud Vestein

Thorkel and Gisli are brothers, and their sister is Thordis (who is not involved in the critical situation). Thordis is married to Thorgrim, Thorkel is married to Asgerd, Gisli is married to Aud, and Aud's brother is Vestein. The back-story is that the four men have tried to cement their (allegedly shaky) relationship by going through a ceremony of blood-brotherhood. All goes well until the last moment of the ceremony: there's a handshake all round, but then Thorgrim pulls his hand back. He's prepared to be blood-brother to his brothers-in-law Thorkel and Gisli, but not to Gisli's brother-in-law Vestein. Refusing to shake hands with someone is still offensive, and the whole ceremony has thus made matters worse.

A quarrel over just this sort of issue animates, for instance, the Eddic poem 'The Lay of Hamdir' – is a half-brother's half-sister your sister, even if there is no blood relationship? – but one may wonder if that was all that lay behind Thorgrim's refusal. The next critical scene takes place in the brothers' farmyard.[8] Everyone is out making hay except Thorkel, who is flagged as lazy. But his wife Asgerd and Gisli's wife Aud, who are sitting sewing after breakfast, do not notice him lying down. Their conversation then goes like this. I paraphrase it, numbering the short speeches, quoting the exact words at one critical point. Then I comment on them, using the same numbers.

1) ASGERD: Will you cut out a shirt for Thorkel for me?

2) AUD: Why me? You wouldn't ask me if the shirt was for my brother Vestein.

3) ASGERD: That's another matter; and I shall feel like that for a while.

4) AUD: I've known for a long time. Let's not talk about it.

5) ASGERD: So what if I like Vestein? And you saw a lot of Thorgrim before you married Gisli.

6) AUD: That's OK, because 'I was never unfaithful to Gisli and have therefore brought no disgrace upon him.' And now we really will stop.

It's too late. Thorkel has heard, and he is angry, prophesying death as a result. But what has he understood?

1) Cutting out shirts is a wife's job. If Asgerd will not do it for Thorkel, that implies that she has no feelings for him. [She should not have said this.]

2) Which is what Aud infers. She goes on to say: but you do have feelings still for Vestein, which means you have had such feelings before. [She should not have said this either.]

3) Asgerd tries to change the subject, but admits that the feelings are still there. [No need to say that either.]

4) Aud says, we'd better stop now. [Quite right.]

5) But Asgerd decides she has been insulted and answers back. She's saying: you're no better than me, you have no right to talk.

6) Aud here really does say the unlucky words, because she implies first that she *did* have something to do with Thorgrim, and second that she's still better than Asgerd, because that was pre-nuptial – which implies that whatever Asgerd has done is post-nuptial.

What have the two women done? Bluntly, Aud has had a pre-nuptial affair with Thorgrim, and Asgerd has had a pre- and post-nuptial affair with Vestein. Even more bluntly, neither woman was a virgin on marriage, and their husbands were not their 'first men'. In the 'quarrel of the queens', this is what Gudrun tells Brynhild. When Gunnar finds out, he has Sigurd killed. In the saga, the next things that happen are, first, Thorkel and Asgerd move out to live with Thorgrim close by, and next, Vestein is killed.

This, however, creates what may be the only 'whodunnit' in the whole saga corpus, where killings are all but invariably announced. Vestein is killed by night, in bed in Gisli's house, contributing further famous last words to the set, just: 'Struck there!'[9] No one sees the killer. It has long been assumed that it must have been Thorgrim, mainly because in retaliation Gisli goes and kills Thorgrim by night in the same way. But Thorkel is the man with the sexual jealousy against Vestein. So why would Gisli kill the wrong man? Because he has grounds for sexual jealousy against Thorgrim? Or, possibly, because (full) brothers can't kill each other, but someone has to be killed.[10]

There are other enigmas in the story, notably why these early relationships were broken off. (There's a case for saying that Vestein, who must have been the head of his family, was the one who forbade his sister's marriage with Thorgrim.)[11] But the parallels between the Nibelung story and the Gisli saga story are clear, though not perfect. Vestein parallels Sigurd. Thorkel parallels Gunnar. Asgerd is a kind of Brynhild: she started the female contest for dominance. Aud is a kind of Gudrun: she blurted out the accusation about Vestein. Both scenes are all about sexual jealousy, and betrayal, in a society where a respectable woman is supposed to have only one sexual partner and where husbands whose brides are not virgins are shamed. In both cases the killings blow up out of what seems a trivial conversation.

Did the author of the saga intend the Nibelung parallel to be noted? He certainly knew about the Nibelungs, for Gisli is made to compare his sister Thordis with Gudrun, unfavourably, in a stanza of verse.[12] We might be more certain about the farmyard scene if he had used in it a loaded word like *frumverr*, 'first man', used by the authors of both 'The Saga of the Volsungs' and 'Thidrek's Saga' in the 'quarrel of the queens' scene. Still, there is a point in drawing the parallel, in showing how farmers' wives can behave like queens. The same emotions are involved. And the scene makes a point whichever work it's in. To put it proverbially once more, 'least said, soonest mended', and furthermore, do not always try to have the last word. There is a time to stop talking. Careless talk – or any kind of talk, even quite careful talk – can cost lives.

(Nearly) not showing it: remembering the Ragnarssons

Viking heroes and heroines are supposed to hide their feelings. We know this was not just a literary motif, for Adam of Bremen back in the eleventh century commented on it as a fact: 'tears and complaints and other signs of remorse ... the Danes so loathe that no-one is allowed to weep either for his sins or for the dear departed'.[13] Or for anything else. About the worst thing you can say about a grown man is that, like old Thorbjorn in 'The Saga of Hrafnkel', *hann grætr*, he weeps (or in Scottish, 'he greets'). At the same time, there are some signs of inner emotion that are not under conscious control, and it is a motif – mentioned three times already – that deep passion is betrayed by teeth-grinding (Volund), cheek flushing (Brynhild) or over-controlling (the sons of Ragnar, in their different ways).

The final scene is the classic case, and we know it was already part of the legend by 1200, when Saxo retells it. There is a close analogue to it in the longest of the sagas of Icelanders, 'Njal's Saga'.[14] The back story to this scene – the whole back-story is too long to tell – is that the wife of Njal and the wife of his great friend Gunnar of Hlidarendi have fallen out over a very small issue of precedence. Bergthora, Njal's wife, asked Hallgerd, Gunnar's wife, to move down one on a bench to make space for her new daughter-in-law, Thorhalla. It's Bergthora's home and she is the hostess, so most people would take that as reasonable. Hallgerd, however, who has been flagged all along as beautiful – her nickname is *Langbrók*, 'long-breeches' or in effect 'long-legs' – but spoiled and touchy, takes offence, the more so because her husband Gunnar does not back her up.

Since Gunnar (a great champion) will not fight for her, Hallgerd sends her overseer Kol to kill a servant of Bergthora's. Gunnar pays Njal 12 ounces of silver as compensation for the servant, accepting that his wife is in the wrong. Bergthora, however, sends one of her servants, Atli, to kill Kol. Njal gives Gunnar the same 12 ounces back, in the same bag, unopened (he knew what would happen). The killings ratchet up. Atli is killed by Brynjolf, Brynjolf is killed by Thord, each man now paid for at 100 ounces. Then Hallgerd sends a pair called Sigmund and Skjold (two more famous heroic names, like Atli) to kill Thord. Thord, however, though the son of a slave, is the foster-father of the Njalssons. This time, Njal accepts 200 ounces from the apologetic Gunnar. He asks his sons to respect the settlement, and they agree – on condition. There must be no more provocation.

But there is – not deeds this time, but even worse, words. Hallgerd invents a new nickname for Njal, who cannot grow a beard: *inn skegglausi*, 'the Beardless'. Since Njal is also well known for the strange habit (to Icelanders) of spreading dung on his fields to enrich the poor Icelandic soil, she says they will call his sons *taðskegglingar*, literally 'shit-beardlings'. She gets Sigmund, Thord's killer, to make a poem about it, all of which is of course repeated to Bergthora.[15] She tells her husband and her sons about it. Even Gunnar was enraged, she says. How about them?

This is taunting, or 'egging', from the Norse verb *eggja*, 'to put an edge on, to sharpen'. In some circumstances this is right and proper. The house-carls of King Olaf voted Thormod's recitation of 'The Lay of Bjarki' just the thing to encourage the troops and called it *Húskarlahvöt*, the 'whetting of the housecarls'. Being 'egged' or 'edged' or 'whetted' by one's female relatives – a very common scene in the sagas of Icelanders – is another matter, because it is in fact an accusation of cowardice. It sets up a kind of dilemma, rather well seen (it must be coincidence) in Shakespeare's Danish play, *Hamlet*. There Hamlet says, as he ponders over whether to take revenge, 'Rightly to be great / Is not to stir without great argument'. Understood. 'But greatly to find quarrel in a straw / When honour's at the stake' (Act 4, Scene 4). No wonder he can't make up his mind!

This, then, is the Njalssons' situation as their mother lays into them.[16] Skarphedin, the eldest, refuses to be provoked. 'We're not like women, that we become furious over everything.' (It's a masculine quality to keep your cool.) What about Gunnar? says Bergthora. *He* flew into a rage on your behalf (unspoken, and no one calls *him* unmasculine), 'If you don't set this to rights, you will never avenge any shame.' Skarphedin replies, 'The old lady enjoys all this.' He seems to be saying, all this is just a joke. There's also something disrespectful about calling his mother 'the old lady', *kerlin-ginn* – in Scots it would be 'the auld carline'. It implies, 'no need to take any notice of her'.

But *he doesn't mean it!* He may be trying to sound unflappable, but the autonomic nervous system gives him away, like with Ivar Ragnarsson. Sweat breaks out on his forehead. Red flecks appear on his cheeks. His brother Grim bites his lip. Only his brother Helgi manages not to change expression. The next thing that happens is that that night, the brothers go out fully armed, to look for sheep, they tell their father, or fish for salmon. He knows they are going to break his agreement with Gunnar by killing Sigmund and Skjold, which they do.

The parallel between the Njalssons and the Ragnarssons is a close one. Four brothers in the one case, three in the other. They all try to look unaf-fected; six out of seven betray themselves. Anyone who knew the earlier legend – and we know it had been in circulation for many years already by the time 'Njal's Saga' was written – would surely have recognized the simi-larities. But there is one difference. After Skarphedin says, 'The old lady enjoys all this,' the saga author adds *ok glotti við*, 'and [he] grinned'. This becomes Skarphedin's trademark.

Note that the verb is *glotta*. It has been borrowed into English, like many Norse words, as 'to gloat'. Gloating, of course, is not grinning. It is an expression of triumph, of delight in someone else's discomfiture: it's what Volund does, hanging in the sky, to Nidud. That is not yet appropriate for the scene between Skarphedin and Bergthora – he might in the end gloat over Sigmund, or Hallgerd, but not over his mother, and in any case there is nothing yet to gloat over. But he's not smiling, either, even if he appears to speak jokingly. The question arises: what's the difference between a grin and a smile?

The nine grins of Skarphedin Njalsson

Smiles are friendly. Grins can be friendly: they can indicate genuine or perhaps surprised amusement. But they can also be cheeky. Or nasty. They can mean, 'You can't touch me.' They may mean, 'I know something you don't.' You can deny that they mean anything at all. (The British Army has a special offence called 'dumb insolence'; grinning when rebuked by your sergeant would definitely be dumb insolence, because it could mean anything.) Some grins, however, can in context be understood, and there is a fairly clear one earlier on in 'Njal's Saga' (at the end of Chapter 16).

What has happened here is that Hallgerd Long-legs has provoked her first husband into striking her, for which he is killed by her foster-father, Thjostolf, a stereotypical aggressive Hebridean. She then married again, seemingly to Thjostolf's displeasure, but this time happily for her. Nevertheless, Thjostolf makes trouble between the couple – there is an element of sexual jealousy there, one can deduce – and her new husband also slaps her. Hallgerd categorically forbids Thjostolf to do anything about it. He says nothing, but walks away, grinning (*glotti við*). This grin surely means, 'I won't say anything, but we'll see about that.'

Thjostolf does indeed kill husband number two, and announces the fact to Hallgerd, who laughs. With surprise? Not this time from pleasure, for the next thing she does is send Thjostolf for shelter to her uncle Hrut, a hard man not at all frightened of Hebrideans and who furthermore does not like his niece. As soon as Hrut twigs that Hallgerd did not order the killing, Hrut, with nothing further said, kills Thjostolf. The saga author makes no comment on what underlies the sequence of events, but one can readily guess that Hallgerd has decided to get rid of her foster-father, who has become a liability. Thjostolf's grin was nevertheless surely 'dumb insolence'. He had no intention of obeying Hallgerd. The amusement comes, as it often does, from the contrast between what he knows is going to happen and what Hallgerd has just told him she wants to happen. It is a disobedient grin.

The next person to grin in the saga is Skarphedin, who will grin nine times in all. The first time is after the killing of Njal's servant Svart, ordered by Hallgerd. Gunnar pays Njal twelve ounces as compensation, and one day Njal shows his son the purse with the money in it. "'It may turn out to be useful,' said Skarphedin, and grinned.'[17] It is obvious what is going to happen, for Bergthora has already said that they will keep the money to pay for Hallgerd's overseer Kol when she has him killed, and she has already hired a new man (Atli) to do the job. Skarphedin grins, then, because he recognizes why Njal has kept the money separate: the joke is they all know what it's for, but are pretending not to. Skarphedin's second grin is when the killing of Kol is announced. It's all working out as predicted, but how far will it go now?

The third grin is when their mother taunts him and his brothers, as detailed above, and after the 'shit-beardlings' insult has been repeated. It's obvious – indeed it's the whole point of the scene – that he is repressing some powerful emotion and cannot quite keep from showing it. As with the Ragnarssons, it must be rage, determination to take revenge. But (as Hrafnkel showed) lashing out right away is not the way to go, and this is too serious for mere words. (There is a strong feeling in northern culture generally that fighting is for men, while 'flyting', exchanging insults, is for women, though the rule or convention is very frequently broken.) What are we meant to think about the grin? Once again, Skarphedin knows something. He knows his mother's taunting is quite unnecessary; he and his brothers were bound to take revenge for the killing and the insults anyway. So what she thinks about them – that they are peaceniks or cowards – is quite wrong. Not that that makes her insults to them easier to bear, though he pretends to take it all in fun. But she'll find out, just as Hallgerd did with Thjostolf.

The killings arranged by the two women ratchet up until there are six of them and have reached the 200 ounces level in compensation, Gunnar and Njal swapping their money back and forth. Then matters start to involve people more important than servants or wanderers. After becoming involved in another set of quarrels, Gunnar is killed in his own home after a brave defence in which Hallgerd refuses to give him her hair to replace his broken bowstring – another ancient legendary motif. Subsequently, the Njalssons exchange a string of insults with Hallgerd, now a widow, who repeats the slurs 'beardless' and 'shit-beardlings' to their faces. The Njalssons decide to take it out on all the men present, including her new son-in-law, Thrain ('Thra-in', not 'Thrane'), even though he did not associate himself with what was said. This leads to one of the great bravado scenes of saga literature, all the more powerful for being set in a spot that must have been well known to the original audience (it still is), and in peculiarly Icelandic conditions: near the Arctic Circle in winter.[18]

Thrain and seven others are riding along the Markar river when the four Njalssons plus their friend Kari come to intercept them, from the other side of the river. It's too deep to be forded, but there is an ice floe across it, and Thrain's party dismount and take up their position opposite this natural bridge. As the others run along the river towards the bridge, Skarphedin falls back to tie his shoelace. Then he takes a running jump across the river, lands on the sheet ice the other side of it, and slides along the smooth ice down-slope as fast as a bird. As he skims past the other group he hits Thrain on the head with his axe 'Battle-Troll' so hard that he splits the skull down to the jaw and Thrain's back teeth fall out on the ice. Someone throws a shield in his path to trip him, but Skarphedin hurdles it and flashes on to the ice bridge as Kari and his brothers cross it. In the melee that follows, the Njalsson party kill three others besides Thrain, and spare four.

So far so good, one might say. But part of the compensation assessed for the killings is that Njal agrees to adopt Thrain's son Hoskuld. More than adopting him, he furthers his career by finagling him a *goðorð*, or chieftaincy – a distinction never possessed either by Njal or by his own sons – and favouring him in every way. The great mystery of the saga is why the Njalssons eventually kill Hoskuld, without provocation, an act very much against the wishes of their father and one condemned by the whole community, in which Hoskuld was universally popular. The saga author puts the blame on an Iago figure called Mord Valgardsson, who tells lies to both sides about what the others are planning or saying, but this seems an inadequate explanation on its own. Should we think the Njalssons simply cannot believe that their adopted brother has forgotten the killing of his father and must be planning revenge? Are they jealous over their father's evident favouritism?[19]

Whatever the reason – and there is perhaps another one, suggest-sed below – the Njalssons, Kari and Mord ambush Hoskuld while he is sowing corn and kill him five against one, without provocation and without Hoskuld offering resistance. The deed is not only criminal, it is *ódrengiligr*, the exact opposite of the killing of Thrain.

The whole neighbourhood is horrified, Njal included, and if the Njalssons are to escape outlawry and exile from Iceland it is vital that they have support from the power brokers at the Althing. This is where Skarphedin starts to grin again. He and his two brothers, along with Kari, two cousins and a brother-in-law, are led round the booths of the great men of Iceland by Asgrim, Helgi Njalsson's father-in-law. Skarphedin makes a striking impression, which the saga describes carefully. He is dressed in blue and silver, his hair combed back and tied with a silk headband. He carries a small round shield and his axe 'Battle-Troll'. Despite his imposing appearance, he keeps to his assigned place, fifth in line, and lets Asgrim do the talking to the chieftains.[20]

All the chieftains pick him out. Who is that man, they say, fifth in line, describing him variously as 'with a pale and luckless look', 'troll-like', 'fierce and striking', 'as if he had come out of a sea cliff' (meaning, is a troll), 'luckless' and 'with a wicked and luckless look'. As soon as the chieftains pinpoint him, Skarphedin replies savagely to all of them: Skapti is a coward, Snorri the Priest has never avenged his father, Haf let his sister be kidnapped, Gudmund the Powerful has had tales told about him. Again and again he is said to be grinning. Snorri asks, who is that man 'grinning with his teeth'?[21] When Asgrim tells Skarphedin, after his fourth back-answer, to keep quiet, '[he] grinned'. He doesn't obey. When Thorkel Bully, a descendant of Ketil Hæng, with a great reputation for killing monsters, picks out Skarphedin like the others, Skarphedin sneers at him and accuses him of eating 'mare's arse' (an accusation of bestiality, perhaps, or perversion?). Thorkel draws his sword on him and boasts of the men he has killed for it and with it: 'This is the sword I got in Sweden ...'. But Skarphedin bursts past the others, 'grinning' once again, his axe raised, and says, 'This is the axe I had in hand when I leapt twelve ells over the Markar river and killed Thrain Sigfusson with eight men standing by and no-one laid hand on me.' He tells Thorkel to sheathe his sword and sit down, or else die, and Thorkel does so, backing down for the only time in his life.[22]

Three grins, then: for Snorri, for Asgrim, for Thorkel. Two more once a settlement has been reached. Compensation is set at 600 ounces, more than even Njal can pay and fifty times what was paid for the first killings. Even the judges have to contribute, for the sake of peace and harmony in the district. Judgement is pronounced. Njal thanks all concerned. Skarphedin stands by in silence, grinning. Njal asks his sons not to spoil things in any way. Skarphedin strokes his brow and grins. The money is actually piled up, waiting for Hoskuld's father-in-law Flosi to take it, when Njal for some reason adds a silk cloak to the pile, presumably as a sweetener. Flosi asks who put the cloak there. When no one answers, Flosi laughs (a bad sign) and says, don't you dare to tell me? (Bad idea.) Skarphedin says, who do you think? (Another bad idea.) Flosi says, it must have been 'Beardless', you can't tell if he's a man or a woman.

The fat is now in the fire, and Skarphedin snatches the cloak back and throws Flosi a pair of trousers, saying he'll need them. Why would I need them? asks Flosi (very bad idea, as giving Skarphedin an opportunity). Skarphedin says, because Flosi is the bride of the Svinafell-troll, who uses him like a woman every ninth night – an accusation, like being *ragr*, unmanly, specifically forbidden by law. The pile of money is immediately rejected. Only blood vengeance will do now.[23]

One has to ask – the saga author, by his deliberate repetitions, clearly intended everyone in his audience to ask – what is going on in Skarphedin's mind? *Why is he grinning?* Saga authors never give answers to questions like that, and one can only answer from one's own experience. There must be an element of anger. Snorri says in particular that Skarphedin is not only grinning, but showing his teeth (*glottir við tönn*), with his axe shouldered. Skarphedin hates the humiliation of asking people for help. When after the Thorkel fiasco Asgrim says, let's go back to our booths, Skarphedin agrees, saying 'back to our booth after begging in vain'.

And the grin when he's told to keep quiet by Asgrim? That's surely a 'dumb insolence' grin, meaning 'I'll make my own mind up about that.' The grin when he confronts Thorkel is one of triumphant hostility, what the Germans call *Gegeneinanderlachen*, laughing at, not laughing with. He grins at his father the same way he grinned at Asgrim: I won't defy you, father, but let's just wait and see. And just before, when everyone is in agreement and Njal is thanking everyone like a modern college president on valediction day, the grin means, 'whatever anyone says, this is not going to work. I know better.'

Enigmas remain. What sets Flosi off as regards the silk cloak? Is it a woman's garment? Not necessarily, though that suggestion seems to be behind the accusation that Njal isn't a proper man. Why doesn't Njal say something conciliatory? Is he taken aback? One conclusion we are surely meant to arrive at is that Skarphedin does not *want* an agreement, a reconciliation. And why not?

The enigma is still there in the climactic scene of the whole saga, the burning of Njal's farmstead, with Njal, his wife, his sons and his grand-son.[24] Njal, here, the consummate fixer, makes a seriously bad decision when he rejects Skarphedin's suggestion that they fight it out with the Burners in the open, and instead says they should stay inside the house. Look how much trouble they had killing Gunnar in his farmstead, he says. Skarphedin says, those were men of honour; these people know they have to kill us all, and they will use fire. Njal says, now you are disrespecting me, and Skarphedin gives in, casually: 'I'm ready to please [my father] by burning in the house with him, for I'm not afraid to face my death.' He remains nonchalant as his father and mother and little Thord retire to die in their bed, and refuses a chance to break out with Kari, but responds with violent humour when Gunnar Lambason – whose life he had spared by the Markar – accuses him again of weeping. He has kept one of Thrain's molars which fell out on the ice, presumably as a trophy, and he throws this up at Gunnar to gouge his eye out.

Then the beams fall in and he is trapped, though the Burners can hear him singing. The saga quotes it, and it could be the best death song of all, but unfortunately no one has been able entirely to understand it. This is appropriate, for no one can understand the forensics of Skarphedin's death, either. He was found propped upright against the wall, but his legs were burned off below the knee. He had bitten his lip (to keep from crying out?) and buried his axe head in the beam (perhaps to prevent the metal losing its temper). Most surprisingly, the excavators agree that he had branded himself front and back with a cross. No one feels fear of his body (is that because they do not think his ghost will walk?). About all this there is a feeling that Skarphedin has died willingly, refusing to try to escape. The branding suggests that he has accepted his guilt and is punishing himself – though he never had any intention of being punished by anyone else, or of being taunted, or of dying other than upright, like a man, like a Jomsviking.

The rage of Thorhall the lawyer

One goes back to the killing of Hoskuld, apparently so poorly motivated. It should be remembered that the saga was probably written about 1280, though the events described took place not long after 1000. It ought to be regarded, accordingly, as a historical novel, and Skarphedin is just as much an invented character as Tess of the d'Urbervilles or Heathcliff from *Wuthering Heights*. Or almost as much, for Skarphedin was a real person, and the basic events of the saga seem really to have happened. Stories about them must have circulated in the area, and among the descendants of the people concerned, all the time between 1000 and 1280. As remarked already, Gísli Sigurðsson of the University of Iceland has recently demonstrated how consistent the sagas are about people and events, corroborating each other in detail, even when we have two versions of the same event told by opposing factions: no contradiction, only bias. In the case of Skarphedin specifically, Gisli argues that confirmatory information known from other sagas was not included by the author of 'Njál's Saga' because he was confident his audience would already know it.[25]

Furthermore, the saga author could reasonably assume that most things back in 1000 were not very far different from 1280 – with the notable exception of political rule, for by 1280 Iceland had lost its independence to the king of Norway, after the forty years of bitter feuding among powerful families that claimed the life of Snorri Sturluson. But legends known in 1280 could be assumed, in spite of the tangled chronology of saga writing mentioned at the start of this chapter, to have been known also in 1000. The allusions to Volund in 'Hrafnkel's Saga', to the Nibelungs in 'Gisli's Saga', to the Ragnarssons in 'Njal's Saga' and also to Hogni's hard heart in the autopsy performed on Thorgeir of the 'Sworn-Brothers' Saga': these seemed at least plausible in the period in which the sagas were set. Nor, one might note, was it just stories that provided continuity. An important event in 'Gisli's Saga' is the reforging of the shards of a broken sword into a spear, given the name *Grásíða*, 'Greyflank'. A spear with that name, alleged to be the same spear, was used in a feud in 1221 and again in battle in 1238.[26] Other heirlooms may still have been in circulation, with tales attached to them.

What effect did these heroic tales have on the people who heard and told them, in Iceland, even in the tiny community of Greenland, in circumstances very different from the great movements of peoples of the Migration Period in the fifth and sixth centuries and from the great raids and battles of the Viking Age? In the year 1000 (as saga authors were well aware), the real Skarphedin could have known men who had gained glory and profit in Miklagard, like the Thorkel who rescues old Thorbjorn; or men who had fought at Hjorungavag, like Vigfus Glumsson, who brained Aslak Bald-patch with an anvil; men who had taken Danegeld from Ethelred in England; men who would eventually fight at Clontarf. Putting it bluntly, horizons much wider than a few Icelandic moors and valleys must have been familiar – as must large amounts of money. Compare the 600 ounces of silver (50 Roman pounds?) that all but bankrupts the district to pay for Hoskuld with the takes documented from Francia, England, Spain and Byzantium – 7,000 pounds from Paris; 10,000 pounds, 16,000 pounds, 24,000 pounds, 36,000 pounds and eventually 83,000 pounds from England between 991 and 1018; 90,000 gold dinars from Pamplona; and silver from Miklagard allegedly by the ton. This all gained by men who 'travelled far, *drengiligir*, like bold men'. How might the comparison have felt to a man like Skarphedin, who by all accounts could have stood in line with the best of Vikings?

The short answer to that question is, of course, 'frustrating'! Being kept at home by the old man, subject to his authority, feeling life slipping uneventfully away ... One could add that a further frustration or restriction was imposed just by Icelandic society. The sagas of Icelanders are all about feuds and killings, but, as argued by Jesse Byock,[27] their *real* subject is peace-making, making deals – what Njal does. The hero of the saga is not a warrior but a fixer. How especially frustrating to a warrior who does not *want* to be a fixer, who cannot help comparing himself with those heroes of old the Ragnarssons, who suppressed their feelings, Ragnar himself dying by torment; men who sang death-songs, if not in the flames then dying slow and hard. Perhaps the reason for the strange and discreditable killing of Hoskuld – and the saga demands that we find *some* reason for the event from the clues we are given – is that Skarphedin is tired of deals and negotiations and being held back. His real talents have no scope, except now and then and momentarily (the killings of Sigmund, Skjold and Thrain). People keep on holding him back. That's why his outbursts are so furious, threatening Thorkel Bully – all of his great deeds took place far away without witnesses! – making literally unforgivable accusations against Flosi.

There is even a counterpart to this in the saga, which rubs in the point about the contrast between what we could call 'Viking' behaviour and 'back-home Icelandic' behaviour. After the burning, the Burners are, naturally, charged at the Althing with multiple homicide. No one disputes what happened, but the legal chicanery goes on and on. The Burners fix things so that it can be argued that the charges have been brought in the wrong court, so that a counter-charge of improper procedure can be laid at Iceland's Fifth or higher court. Jurors are disqualified for their relationship to the pleader, then reinstated because the important thing is their relationship to the plaintiff, disqualified again for not being householders, and reinstated because they own milch animals. And so on and on and on. (It might be noted that Icelandic law had not been written down; it all depended on whose memory was best, the vital person being the sole paid official in the republic, the lawspeaker, whose job was to recite the whole law over a period of three successive Althings.) But in the end, the charge against the Burners is declared invalid, because the verdict was given by 42 jurors, not 36, meaning those who brought the charges can themselves be sentenced to outlawry.

This news is brought to Thorhall, the chief legal adviser of those seeking to avenge the burning and who is laid up in bed with a leg swollen from boils. When he hears what's happened, he is

> so upset that he could not speak a word. He sprang out of his bed and with both hands seized his spear, Skarphedin's gift, and drove it into his leg. Flesh and the core of the boil clung to the spear, for he cut the boil right out of his leg, and a gush of blood and a flow of pus poured like a stream across the floor.[28]

With that, he strides out to the law court so fast that no one can keep up with him, encounters one of the Burners and immediately strikes him dead with the spear Skarphedin gave him. Both sides instantly attack each other, taking the opportunity to settle personal scores. But after this sudden outbreak, Icelandic reality reasserts itself. Snorri the Priest (a heathen priest) does what he had said he would. When he reckons the avengers have killed as many men as they can afford to pay compensation for (careful calculation again by another leading fixer), he brings in his men and breaks up the fight. The next morning, they are back at the Lögberg, the Law Rock at the site of the Althing, wheeling and dealing. Significantly, the one man who won't accept any deal is the professional Viking, Kari. He will pursue his own vendetta in Iceland and in Orkney, until, much later, he too is reconciled with Flosi.

The blood and pus spurting out of the lawyer Thorhall's hideously swollen leg are like the insults pouring out of Skarphedin's mouth: driven by internal pressure, kept back too long. The question of whether they're going to settle this like lawyers or like men is, one might say, what has been bugging Skarphedin all along – and not just him, but Hallgerd Long-legs, too. Would Brynhild have accepted being asked to move down one? In Skarphedin's case it was not just his father's restraint he was chafing under. It was the whole peace-making system of Icelandic law, which coexisted only uneasily with a powerful and living tradition of violence, decision and heroic action, of never backing down from a dare, threat or challenge. It's that tension, between Viking ethos and real-world compromise, that makes the sagas.

The Viking Age: all made up?

In an extreme view, there never was a 'Viking' ethos. It's merely an early medieval imaginary, something all made up by writers in the thirteenth century and later, looking back nostalgically to a Heroic Age that never existed, very like the Wild West of John Wayne and Clint Eastwood. 'The Saga of King Hrolf', 'The Saga of the Volsungs', 'Ragnar's Saga', the blood-eagle story, 'Egil's Saga', 'The Song of the Pennants', 'The Saga of the Jomsvikings' and all the sagas of the Norwegian kings – all made up, famous last words, last stands, death songs and all.

Some of it surely was made up, as stated several times earlier. But against that extreme view there is the evidence of the skaldic poems; the scraps of unmistakably ancient material in Eddic poems, like the ones from 'The Saga of King Heidrek'; the conviction that poems like 'The Lay of Bjarki' and 'The Lay of Hamdir' really were old; the evidence of runestones and sculpture; the corroborating evidence of chroniclers from Britain and Ireland, France and Spain, Greece and the Muslim world; sometimes the suggestive but inscrutable evidence of archaeology; and not least (when it comes to chronology) the annoying, verbose, garbled retellings of Saxo, dubious in every way except their date. Can consistency like that, stories and poems and accounts in many languages, in all kinds of genres, by scores if not hundreds of authors, just have no basis in reality? Can it have been arrived at by some kind of unspoken agreement or collusion?

And, most convincing of all, there is the unique mindset revealed in scene after scene and story after story, enigmatic, sometimes on the surface contradictory, wary but cheerful, fatalistic but pragmatic, self-critical but self-sufficient. Could such a mindset have been just an individual invention? Or the bedrock of a culture? To quote Shakespeare, admittedly on an entirely different subject, and slightly adapted for the occasion:

> But all [the stories that they tell] told over,
> And all their minds transfigured so together,
> More witnesseth than fancy's images
> And grows to something of great constancy . . .[29]

Not everyone does or will admire what I have called 'the Viking spirit', in full awareness that much of it was written by people who weren't Vikings: cruel, hard-hearted, 'distasteful', so often marked by Bad Sense of Humour – the Vikings were guilty as charged.

It's distinctive, though. There's too much of it, from too many directions, to believe that it's just a literary fantasy best ignored, or airbrushed into respectability. To finish the Shakespeare quotation above,

> . . . But, howsoever, strange and admirable.

APPENDIX A:
On Poetry: Types, Texts, Translations

A great deal of Old Norse / Icelandic poetry has survived. It is normally divided into two categories, Eddic and skaldic. The word 'Eddic' is mysterious. When Snorri Sturluson wrote his guide to aspiring poets about 1230, he, or perhaps his copiers, decided to call it *Edda*. This is a word for 'great-grandmother', so perhaps 'old wives' tales'. But there is another word, *kredda*, derived from the Latin *credo*, 'I believe'. If *kredda* was coined to mean 'creed', could *edda* have been coined from the Latin *edo*, 'I compose', to mean 'composition'? Either way, Snorri's *Edda* is in three parts, in reverse order *Hattatal*, a guide to poetic metre; *Skáldskaparmál*, a guide to poetic diction; and *Gylfaginning*, a long and amusing account of Norse myth – without knowledge of which a traditional Norse poet could not function.

Since Snorri repeatedly quoted from mythical poems such as *Vǫlundarkviða*, when the famous manuscript of these and other poems was discovered by Bishop Brynjólfur Sveinsson early in the 1640s, that collection of poems became known as the *Elder Edda*, the *Poetic Edda* or *Sæmund's Edda* (Bishop Brynjolf thought his ancestor Sæmund the Wise had compiled it), while the manuscript, donated to the king of Denmark, became the Codex Regius, the 'King's Book'. The Codex Regius poems are similar in style; similar enough for other poems found elsewhere – notably the mythical poems *Rígspula* and *Grottasǫngr* and the heroic poem *Hlǫðskviða* – to be accepted as 'Eddic'. In brief, Eddic poems were composed in relatively simple metres like *fornyrðislag* or 'old-word' metre, essentially the same as the metre of Old English, Old Saxon and Old High German poetry: four-stress lines, divided into two half-lines, linked by alliteration, a basic rule being that the fourth stress must *not* alliterate. Eddic poetry, however, unlike Old English and the others, is composed in stanzas, usually of three or four lines. Eddic poetry is also remarkably direct and relatively simple, with an effect – which no one can fail to notice – of terrible force and compression.

A standard edition remains the German one of Gustav Neckel updated by Hans Kuhn (2 vols, Heidelberg, 1962–8). This contains 'the poems of the Codex Regius together with related documents', the latter consisting of the three Eddic poems mentioned above, plus three more found in other manuscripts or extracted, like *Hlǫðskviða*, from sagas. Two dozen others, some mere fragments but including the death songs of Hjalmar, Hildibrand and Arrow-Odd, and *Bjarkamál*, were edited as the *Eddica minora* by Andreas Heusler and Wilhelm Ranisch (Dortmund, 1903).

There are no comparable English editions. Ursula Dronke began the task with an edition of four Eddic 'Heroic Poems', including *Atlakviða*, in 1969, a second volume of five 'Mythological Poems', including *Rígspula* and *Vǫlundarkviða*, in

1997, and a third of four 'Mythological Poems' in 2011 (all from Oxford), but excellent as these are, they cover less than half of the whole. Appreciation of the poems as poems has remained oddly neglected, though Tolkien wrote a stirring essay on the subject, published in his Eddic recreation *The Legend of Sigurd and Gudrún*, ed. Christopher Tolkien (London, 2009), pp. 16–32, and there are now two collections of essays, *The Poetic Edda: Essays on Old Norse Mythology*, and *Revisiting the Poetic Edda: Essays on Old Norse Heroic Legend*, both ed. Paul Acker and Carolyne Larrington (New York and London, 2002, 2013).

Many have, however, taken up the challenge of translating the Eddic corpus, or much of it, into English. The most distinguished translation has to be that by W. H. Auden, assisted by the scholar Paul B. Taylor, *Norse Poems* (London, 1982). It contains 41, including the late but traditional *Solarljóð*. (My rave review of it from 1982 can be found under my name on www.academia.edu.) A more modern and more convenient translation, of 35 poems, is the one by the distinguished scholar Carolyne Larrington (Oxford, 1996, revd 2014). Also recent is Jackson Crawford's *The Poetic Edda* (Indianapolis, IN, 2015), this time containing 34 poems; in an appendix Crawford also offers the poem *Hávamál*, 'The Words of the High One', a poem of advice supposedly given by Odin, rendered into modern terms as 'The Cowboy Havamal'. It goes really well (like so much of Old Norse) into what one might call 'vulgar English', as in this version of stanza one:

> Use yer eyes,
> And never walk blind.
> There ain't no tellin'
> Where there's someone waitin'
> To put one over on you.

Other translations often used include Lee Hollander (Austin, TX, 1962) – good notes, archaic in diction – and Patricia Terry, *Poems of the Elder Edda* (Philadelphia, PA, 1990).

The other main category of Old Norse / Icelandic poetry is skaldic poetry. This is different in many respects. First, unlike Eddic poetry, it is not anonymous: the poems often come with names attached to them. Sometimes the attributions have been challenged – did Snorri record, or make up, some of the poetry said to be by Egil Skallagrimsson or Harald *Harðráði*? The many poems ascribed to named skalds like Thjodolf of Hvin, Einar Tinkling-scales and Eyvind the Plagiarist are usually taken to be genuinely the product of the men named (often named by Snorri).

Second, and notoriously, skaldic poetry is much more complicated. The metrical rules are much stricter. Whereas Eddic poetry is mostly in *fornyrðislag*, or *málaháttr* (which is not much different), or in *ljóðaháttr* (two half-lines followed by a longer one), about 85 per cent of skaldic poetry is in *dróttkvætt*, 'court metre', of which there is a sample on p. 261. The metre is difficult, with its rules about rhyme, half-rhyme, internal rhyme and syllable-counting. The diction, with its contorted and often mythological circumlocutions, adds another layer of difficulty; as Snorri noted, if you don't know the pagan myths, you can't understand the poems, which is why, in a Christian society, he had to retell the myths. Probably the biggest obstacle to understanding the poems is, however, the syntax. Words never come in normal prose order. The first thing editors of the poems do is untangle the words so they look like sentences.

Skaldic poetry has, accordingly, found few admirers in the modern world – until recently. There is currently a scholarly project reaching completion to re-edit them all: 'Skaldic Poetry of the Scandinavian Middle Ages', directed by Margaret Clunies Ross. Several volumes have now been prepared and published, and they are repeatedly cited in the notes below, but the results are also readily available at www.abdn.ac.uk/skaldic. Poetic translations are not readily available, and perhaps never will be, but studies include Roberta Frank, *Old Norse Court Poetry: The Dróttkvætt Stanza* (Ithaca, NY, 1978), and Russell Poole, *Viking Poems of War and Peace* (Toronto, 1991).

Nevertheless, skaldic and Eddic poetry are not totally divided, and there is a relatively fruitful area of overlap. It has been suggested, for instance, that the Eddic *Atlakviða* and skaldic *Hrafnsmál* are similar enough in diction to have been composed (not written) by the same man, Thorbjorn Horn-cleaver. This area of overlap was well picked out (if long ago) by Nora Kershaw (later Nora K. Chadwick). Her *Anglo-Saxon and Norse Poems* (Cambridge, 1922) includes a number of texts and translations of skaldic poems cited in this volume: *Hrafnsmál* (about Harald Fairhair), 'The Battle of Hafsfjord' (Harald's major victory; it may be part of the poem just mentioned, also known as *Haraldskvæði*), *Eiríksmál* (about Eirik Blood-axe, its author not known), *Hákonarmál* (about Hakon the Good, by Eyvind the Plagiarist), *Darraðarljóð* (anonymous) and *Sonatorrek* (by Egil Skallagrimsson).

Even from this list one can see that the main job of skalds was praising the deeds of their patrons and employers, living or dead. In most cases they do not tell stories so much as allude to them. There may, then, be a lot of information in there, as in Ragnar's list of battles in *Krákumál*, but it is hard to dig out, and in some cases (despite Snorri's assurance that no one would dare to invent such stories, see p. 19) may be completely fictional. One can also concede that some skaldic poems come over as strikingly personal, such as Egil's poems. These latter, as an exception to the general lack of critical appreciation, have been well studied in articles by John Hines, Carolyne Larrington, and Joseph Harris, all of which appear in the References to Chapter Five.

Finally, much skaldic poetry – another obstacle to appreciation – consists of *lausavísur*, 'loose verses' or scraps, quoted here and there in sagas to make a point or an allusion. Sometimes, stanzas can cautiously be fitted together, as is the case with the various parts (?) of Thorbjorn's *Haraldskvæði*. But *lausavísur*, detached from context, are especially hard to read. Even native speakers may have had trouble understanding skaldic diction: see pp. 99 and 242 for important disputed cases.

APPENDIX B:
On Sagas: Types, Texts, Translations

Sagas are conventionally divided into a number of different types, as issued for instance in the small and handy sets put out by Íslendingasagnaútgafan: twelve volumes of *Íslendinga sögur*, 'Sagas of Icelanders' and a thirteenth volume, of indexes; four volumes of *Fornaldarsögur*, 'Sagas of Old Times'; three volumes of *Konunga sögur*, 'Kings' Sagas'; three volumes of *Sturlunga saga*, 'Saga of the Sturlungs'; and other sets, including *Riddara sögur*, 'Knights' Sagas', derived from French romance, and *Biskupa sögur*, 'Bishops' Sagas'. The volumes of the 'kings' sagas' do not, however, include the massive sixteen-saga set written by Snorri Sturluson and known as *Heimskringla*, and there are large or even larger compilations in the manuscripts known as *Morkinskinna* ('rotten parchment'), *Fagrskinna* ('fine parchment') and *Flateyjarbók*, 'The Book of Flatey'. Translations of the first two are noted in the References to Chapter Eleven. Some sagas, moreover, resist categorization, like *Jómsvíkinga saga*, 'Saga of the Jomsvikings' (see References to Chapter Nine) or the legendary *Þiðreks saga af Bern*, 'Saga of Thidrik of Verona' (see References to Chapter Three).

Availability of translations goes with popularity and reputation – and of course vice versa. Throughout this work I have used the five-volume set of *The Complete Sagas of Icelanders* (CSI), done by many translators, with the general editor Viðar Hreinsson, from Leifur Eiríksson Publishing in Reykjavik (1997). Ten of the best of these are conveniently collected in a Penguin edition, *The Sagas of Icelanders: A Selection*, ed. Örnolfur Thorsson (London, 2000), along with the excellent short story about *drengskapr* 'Thorstein Staff-struck'. There is a second selection made by Diana Whaley, *Sagas of the Warrior-poets* (London, 2002). Several sagas from the CSI collection have also been issued separately, including Robert Cook's translation of the longest, *Njal's Saga* (London, 2001), which is not in the Örnolfur Thorsson collection.

Many readers will, however, own copies of older and also excellent translations – too many of them and too often reprinted for all of them to be detailed here – and it is for their convenience that I have added chapter numbers to page numbers in the References. The six most famous sagas are *Njal's Saga* and *Laxdæla Saga*, both translated by Magnus Magnusson and Hermann Pálsson (Harmondsworth, 1960 and 1969 respectively); *Eyrbyggja Saga*, trans. Pálsson and Paul Edwards (Harmondsworth, 1972); *Egil's Saga*, trans. Bernard Scudder (London, 2002); *The Saga of Gisli*, trans. George Johnston (London, 1963); and *Grettir's Saga*, trans. Jesse Byock (Oxford, 2009). Gwyn Jones's translation of *Eirik the Red and Other Icelandic Sagas* (Oxford, 1961) contains, besides the title story, 'Hrafnkel, the Priest of Frey', 'King Hrolf and his Champions', and other sagas and stories, including 'Thorstein Staff-struck'.

Of the kings' sagas, as said in the headnote to the References, except in Chapter Eleven I have used the translation of Snorri's *Heimskringla* by Alison Finlay and Anthony Faulkes in three volumes (London, 2011, 2014, 2016), all three very generously put online by the Viking Society and available at http://vsnrweb-publications. org.uk. There is an old but complete translation of *Heimskringla* by Lee Hollander (Austin, TX, 1964), and another of *Morkinskinna* by Theodore Andersson and Kari Ellen Gade (Ithaca, NY, 2000).

The most popular of the 'sagas of old times' is the *Saga of the Volsungs*, translated several times, notably by Jesse Byock, under that title (Berkeley, CA, 1990). There is an outstanding text and translation of *The Saga of King Heidrek the Wise* by Christopher Tolkien (1960, reissued London, 2010), and one of the anomalous *Saga of the Jomsvikings* by Norman Blake (Edinburgh, 1962). For a complete bibliography of the 'sagas of old times', including such other translations as there are, see http://fasnl.ku.dk/bibl.aspx.

There are, furthermore, detailed studies of all these categories in Rory McTurk, ed., *A Companion to Old Norse-Icelandic Literature and Culture* (Malden, MA, and Oxford, 2005). Information about individual sagas, and much else, can be gained from *Medieval Scandinavia: An Encyclopedia*, ed. Phillip Pulsiano (New York, 1993).

APPENDIX C:
Snorri Sturluson

Snorri Sturluson is the most significant figure in the history of Old Norse / Icelandic literature and mythology. His life is detailed in Nancy M. Brown's biography *Song of the Vikings* (New York, 2012). This is a misleading title – publishers like Vikings in titles, though scholars don't like having them in their books! Snorri was in no sense a Viking but rather was a prominent politician in Iceland in the years leading up to the island's loss of independence to the Norwegian throne. Snorri is himself a major figure in one of the 'sagas of the Sturlungs', *Íslendinga saga* or 'The Saga of the Icelanders', written by Snorri's nephew Sturla Þórðarson (the younger).

Briefly, Snorri, born in 1178/9, was the son of Sturla Þórðarson (the elder), who gave his name to the Sturlung Age. Family connections, adoption into another powerful family and a judicious marriage gave Snorri a rapid start in politics, such that he became lawspeaker of Iceland (1215–18 and 1222–31), and the richest man in the country. Like other Icelanders, Snorri aimed at success on a wider stage by going to Norway – Nancy Brown suggests that he intended to become the king's skald – and is thought to have promised the king's regent, Jarl Skuli, that he would bring the island under Norwegian rule. The jarl, however, fell out with the young King Hakon; Snorri's other nephew Sturla Sighvatsson lost the Battle of Orlygstaðir (1238), the greatest battle ever fought on Icelandic soil; and eventually Snorri was murdered in his own cellar by his sons-in-law on 22 September 1241. The most recent account of this is Ármann Jakobsson, 'Views to a Kill: Sturla Þórðarson and the Murder in the Cellar', *Saga-book of the Viking Society*, XXXIX (2015), pp. 5–20. Note that the SBVS is also now available online, at www.vsnr.org/saga-book.

Snorri is important to the present day, however, for his writings. Without them our knowledge of Old Norse/Icelandic poetry and mythology would be far weaker, and we would be without the most extensive account of the Norwegian kings from prehistoric times to Snorri's own lifetime (*Heimskringla*). As mentioned in Appendix A, Snorri decided, perhaps some time in the relatively peaceful 1220s, that aspiring poets needed guides to metre, diction and mythology and produced for them what is now known as his *Prose Edda*. We have two outstanding translations of this, by Anthony Faulkes (London, 1987) and by Jesse Byock (London, 2005). The first section in particular, with its twenty or so stories of the Norse gods, has been inspirational either directly or through the many paraphrases and children's versions of it. Three recent rewritings by authors who trace its effect back to their childhood are A. S. Byatt, *Ragnarok* (London, 2011), Joanne Harris, *The Gospel of Loki* (New York, 2014), and Neil Gaiman, *Norse Mythology* (London,

2017). And then there are the movies and the Marvel comic books. For a full account of the phenomenon, see Martin Arnold, *Thor: Myth to Marvel* (London and New York, 2011).

Heimskringla has meanwhile been familiar to the general public since the version made of it by Samuel Laing in 1844, often and still republished in the Everyman series. (Laing knew no Old Norse: he worked from a Norwegian translation, see Andrew Wawn, *The Vikings and the Victorians*, Cambridge, 2000, Ch. 4). It has also been argued that Snorri was the author of 'The Saga of Egil Skallagrimsson' (see Chapter Five and Appendix B), one of the best and longest of the 'sagas of Icelanders'. Snorri was descended from Egil, and his Reykjaholt chieftaincy included Egil's home. If one takes all three of these works together, they amount to well over a thousand pages of modern print, perhaps as much as 500,000 words. Remembering that all this was written by hand, without electric light, with nothing like library resources, it is an astonishing achievement in terms of mere quantity. When one thinks also of the difficulties of research, planning and organization – and the astonishingly high level of literary art displayed – this must be one of the, if not the, greatest bodies of work produced by a single author in the whole European Middle Ages. And he had time for politics as well, even if his career ended disastrously . . .

References

In the References I use abbreviations for five substantial bodies of work:

ASC   The *Anglo-Saxon Chronicle* in its variant forms is quoted as ASC from the multi-manuscript translation by Michael Swanton, *The Anglo-Saxon Chronicles* (London, 1996).

CSI   Sagas of Icelanders are quoted from the collective translation project *The Complete Sagas of Icelanders* (CSI), crediting individual translators.

Hskr.   Snorri Sturluson's sequence of sixteen kings' sagas, *Heimskringla*, is quoted, except in Chapter Eleven, from the ongoing translation by Alison Finlay and Anthony Faulkes (abbrev. *Hskr.*), also now online at www.vsnrweb-publications.org.uk.

N&K   Eddic poems are quoted from the edition by Gustav Neckel, revised by Hans Kuhn (abbreviated as N&K), with my own translations, unless otherwise indicated.

SPSMA   Skaldic poems are quoted, if available, from the ongoing and collective editing project 'Skaldic Poetry of the Scandinavian Middle Ages' (SPSMA), now online at http://skaldic.abdn.ac.uk, crediting individual editors.

Other poems and sagas are referenced separately. See the appendices for further details of the first four works listed above.

Preface

1 The letters ǫ and ö represent approximately the vowel sound in 'work'.
2 The letter ð or Đ represents the hard 'th', as in 'then'; þ/Þ represents the soft 'th', as in 'thin'.

Introduction

1 For which see Snorri's *Prose Edda*, translated as *Edda* by Anthony Faulkes (London, 1987), p. 21, 'all those who fall in battle are [Odin's] adopted sons.'

There are of course other surviving references to Valhalla, but Snorri's account has become the definitive one.

2 P. G. Foote and D. M. Wilson, *The Viking Achievement* (Oxford, 1970).

3 Eric Christiansen, *The Norsemen in the Viking Age* (Oxford, 2002).

4 According to the press release put out by Princeton University Press. Authors, of course, are not responsible for what publishers and publicists write.

5 Forty years ago, Professor J. M. Wallace-Hadrill Sr asked, in his lecture *The Vikings in Francia* (Reading, 1975), p. 5, whether we should conclude from recent writings that the Vikings were 'little more than groups of long-haired tourists who occasionally roughed up the natives'. He too was exaggerating, but the attitude we both indicate remains common. Thus Anthony Faulkes concludes his study of 'The Viking Mind, or, In Pursuit of the Vikings', in *Saga-book of the Viking Society*, xxxi (2007), pp. 46–83, with his personal image of 'the Viking': he does sound awfully like 'Mr Nice Guy'. Rightly does Faulkes comment that we bring our ideologies with us.

6 Respectively Alfred Smyth, *King Alfred the Great* (Oxford and New York, 1995), p. 129, Patrick Wormald, 'Viking Studies: Whence and Whither?', in *The Vikings*, ed. R. T. Farrell (London, 1982), pp. 128–53 (p. 153), and again Alfred Smyth, *Warlords and Holy Men* (Edinburgh, 1989), p. 142, quoted without demur by Edward James in 'The Northern World in the Dark Ages, AD 400–900', in *The Oxford Illustrated History of Medieval Europe*, ed. G. Holmes (Oxford, 1988), pp. 63–114 (p. 110).

7 As said in the headnote above, all quotations from Snorri's sixteen-saga cycle *Heimskringla* (up to the end of 'The Saga of St Olaf') are taken from the translation by Alison Finlay and Anthony Faulkes. For this quotation, see *Hskr.* vol. i, p. 4.

8 There is a good account of the events leading up to Snorri's death in Nancy Brown's inaccurately titled biography of Snorri, *Song of the Vikings* (New York, 2012), pp. 173–9; and a more detailed one by Ármann Jakobsson, 'Views to a Kill: Sturla Þórðarson and the Murder in the Cellar', *Saga-book of the Viking Society*, xxxix (2015), pp. 5–20.

9 R. I. Page, ed. and trans., *Chronicles of the Vikings: Records, Memorials and Myths* (London, 1995), pp. 7, 30.

10 As with the excavations at Mosfell in connection with *Egils saga*, see Jesse Byock, 'The Mosfell Archaeological Project: Archaeology, Sagas and History', in *Viking Archaeology in Iceland: Mosfell Archaeology Project*, ed. Davide Zori and Jesse Byock (Turnhout, 2014), pp. 27–44. See also Jesse Byock and Davide Zori, 'Viking Archaeology, Sagas, and Interdisciplinary Research in Iceland's Mosfell Valley', *Backdirt* (2013), pp. 124–41, available at www.viking.ucla.edu/mosfell_project.

11 Page, ed., *Chronicles of the Vikings*, pp. 25, 12.

PART I

1 The Viking Mindset: Three Case Studies

1 See Appendix A for discussion of the term 'Eddic' and for a list of full translations, several of them of outstanding quality themselves.

2 See the account in Snorri Sturluson, *Edda*, trans. Anthony Faulkes (London, 1987), pp. 52–5.

3 Ibid., pp. 21, 31–4.

4 The historical basis of the legend is discussed in Ursula Dronke, ed. and trans., *The Poetic Edda*, vol. 1: *Heroic Poems* (Oxford, 1969), pp. 29–36.

5 All translations of Eddic poems, unless otherwise indicated, are my own, based on Gustav Neckel, ed., revd Hans Kuhn, *Edda: die Lieder des Codex Regius*, 2 vols (Heidelberg, 1962–8). Quotations are referenced by poem title and stanza number, as in that edition: here *Atlakviða* 23.

6 N&K, *Atlakviða*, 24.

7 Ibid., 25.

8 Ibid., 27.

9 W. H. Auden and Paul B. Taylor, *Norse Poems* (London, 1981), p. 120.

10 N&K, *Atlakviða*, 31.

11 I forbear from giving citations here: the attitude is general, the adjectives vary.

12 N&K, *Vǫlundarkviða*, 17.

13 Ibid., 17.

14 Ibid., 20.

15 Notably in the Old English poem 'Deor'. The fate of Beaduhild (Bodvild) is one of the five 'fates worse than death' that the narrator lists, before saying that they all passed over. The birth and adventures of the child of rape who became a hero, Widia (variously spelled), form part of 'The Saga of Thidrek of Verona'.

16 N&K, *Vǫlundarkviða*, 37.

17 Ibid., 41.

18 Snorri, *Edda*, trans. Faulkes, p. 38.

19 A new edition of *Krákumál* is in preparation for SPSMA by Rory McTurk, but meanwhile I use the older edition, of Finnur Jónsson (Copenhagen, 1929), available at www.heimskringla.no/wiki.krákumál, accessed 20 February 2017.

20 Guðbrandur Vigfusson and F. York Powell, *Corpus Poeticum Boreale* (Oxford, 1883), p. 345.

21 Ibid., p. 350.

22 Saxo Grammaticus, *History of the Danes*, trans. Peter Fisher, ed. Hilda Ellis Davidson, 2 vols (Cambridge 1979), vol. 1, p. 291.

23 See John McKinnell, 'The Context of *Vǫlundarkviða*', *Saga-book of the Viking Society*, XXIII (1990–91), pp. 1–27.

24 The development of the legend has been studied in detail by Elizabeth A. Rowe, *Vikings in the West: The Legend of Ragnarr Loðbrók and His Sons* (Vienna, 2014).

25 See N. F. Blake, ed. and trans., *The Saga of the Jomsvikings* (Edinburgh, 1962), p. 27 (ch. 33), and Rory McTurk, trans., 'The Saga of Droplaug's Sons', in CSI, vol. IV, pp. 355–78 (p. 369).

2 Hygelac and Hrolf: False Dawn for the Vikings

1 ASC, MSS E and F for 793, pp. 56, 57.

2 Dorothy Whitelock, ed. and trans., *English Historical Documents*, vol. I (London, 1969), p. 776.

3 Alan Binns, 'The Viking Century in East Yorkshire', *East Yorkshire Local History Society*, EYLH series 15 (York, 1963), p. 7. Binns notes that the correct date is given by Simeon of Durham.

4 ASC, MS A for 787 (error for 789), p. 54.

5 Alistair Campbell, ed., *The Chronicle of Æthelweard* (London, 1962), p. 27. Æthelweard was ealdorman of the southwestern counties of England in the late tenth century.

6 Gregory of Tours, *The History of the Franks*, trans. Lewis Thorpe (Harmondsworth, 1974), pp. 163–4.

7 The intrusive *l* in 'Chloch-' was probably caused by Gregory's familiarity with names like Chlodomer, Chlodovald and Chlodvig.

8 For the *Liber historiae francorum* entry, see R. W. Chambers, *Beowulf: An Introduction*, 3rd edn, with Supplement by C. L. Wrenn (Cambridge, 1959), p. 3.

9 For the *Liber monstrorum* entry, see ibid., p. 4.

10 As argued in many contributions to Leonard Neidorf, ed., *The Dating of Beowulf: A Reassessment* (Woodbridge, Suffolk, 2014).

11 *Beowulf*, ll. 2506–8. All translations from the poem are mine.

12 Ibid., l. 2684.

13 Ibid., ll. 3021–7.

14 See Shippey, '*Hrólfs saga kraka* and the Legend of Lejre', in *Making History: Essays on the Fornaldarsögur*, ed. Martin Arnold and Alison Finlay (Exeter, 2010), pp. 17–32.

15 See Jesse Byock, trans., *The Saga of King Hrolf Kraki* (London, 1998). All quotations are from this translation, unless indicated otherwise.

16 In J.R.R. Tolkien, *Beowulf: A Translation and Commentary, Together with Sellic Spell*, ed. Christopher Tolkien (London, 2014), pp. 355–413.

17 *Hskr.*, vol. 1, p. 24.

18 Thus Snorri Sturluson knew the Swedish King Ottar was called 'Vendil-crow', and to explain it invented a story about him being killed in Vendil, Denmark. But there is a Vendil in North Sweden as well: Ottar chose to be buried there, and Vendil-crow is a rude term for people from Swedish Vendil. See Chambers, *Beowulf: An Introduction*, pp. 343–4.

19 Byock, trans., *Saga of King Hrolf*, p. 67, and Snorri Sturluson, *Edda*, trans. Anthony Faulkes (London, 1987), p. 112.

20 Gwyn Jones, *A History of the Vikings* (London, 1968), p. 47. Detailed reports of the excavations at Lejre up to the time of publication – they have continued since – along with discussion of their relationships with legend, are to be found in John D. Niles, ed., *Beowulf and Lejre* (Tempe, AZ, 2007).

21 Byock, trans., *Saga of King Hrolf*, pp. 62–3.

22 Saxo Grammaticus, *History of the Danes*, ed. Hilda Ellis Davidson, trans. Peter Fisher, 2 vols (Cambridge, 1979), vol. 1, pp. 63–4.

23 Sven Aggesen, 'Lex Castrensis', in *The Works of Sven Aggesen*, ed. and trans. Eric Christiansen (London, 1992), pp. 31–43 (p. 35); and for St Alphege, ASC, MS E for 1012, p. 142.

24 Byock renders it as 'Everyone . . . can be fooled by scheming', *Saga of King Hrolf*, p. 72. Gwyn Jones, in his translation of the saga in *Eirik the Red and Other Icelandic Sagas* (Oxford, 1980), p. 309, has 'One cannot keep track of everything.'

25 Siegfried Sassoon, 'Blighters', at www.allpoetry.com, accessed 15 June 2016.

26 There is a similar reaction recorded from the Vietnam War; see Michael Herr's *Dispatches* (New York, 1980), p. 179. The girl there in the Peanuts sweatshirt had done nothing offensive – except not understanding.

27 *Bjarkamál* has not yet been re-edited for SPSMA and is quoted here from E. V. Gordon, ed., *An Introduction to Old Norse*, 2nd edn, revd A. R. Taylor (Oxford, 1962), pp. 124–5. Saxo, who seems to have known the entire poem, very annoyingly gives just a paraphrase of it in his usual verbose and high-flown Latin: see Saxo, *History of the Danes*, trans. Fisher, vol. 1, pp. 56–63 – the

great Danish scholar Axel Olrik was so provoked by the loss of the poem that he rewrote it in Danish as near as he could to the original, based on Saxo.

28 Her speech, lines 1169–87, is a masterpiece of indirection – so much so that the point of it was missed by critics for many years.

29 R. W. Chambers, ed., *Widsith: A Study in Old English Heroic Legend* [1912] (New York, 1965), ll. 45–9.

30 For Hrothmund, see Sam Newton, *The Origins of Beowulf and the Pre-Viking Kingdom of East Anglia* (Cambridge, 1993), pp. 103–4. For Hyglac and Biu-uulf in the 'Northumbrian *Liber Vitae*', see Shippey, 'Names in *Beowulf* and Anglo-Saxon England', in *The Dating of Beowulf*, ed. Leonard Neidorf (Cambridge, 2014), pp. 58–79 (pp. 60–61).

31 Bede uses the phrase *in Getlingum* in his *Historia ecclesiastica*, Book 11, Ch. 14; see the translation by Leo Sherley-Price, revd R. E. Latham (Harmondsworth, 1968), p. 164.

32 Frands Herschend quoted in Giorgio Ausenda, 'Current Issues and Future Directions in the Study of the Scandinavians: Summary of Participants' Discussions and Comments', in *The Scandinavians*, ed. Judith Jesch (Wood-bridge, Suffolk, 2002), pp. 321–52 (p. 333).

33 For Nydam, Hjortspring and Illerup see respectively Birge Storgaard, Lone Gebauer Thomsen and Lars Jørgensen, *The Spoils of Victory: The North in the Shadow of the Roman Empire* (Copenhagen, 2003), Klaus Randsborg, *Hjortspring: Warfare and Sacrifice in Early Europe* (Aarhus, 1995), and Jørgen Ilkjær, *Illerup Ådal: Archaeology as a Magic Mirror* (Højbjerg, 2000).

34 Tacitus, *On Britain and Germany*, trans. H. Mattingly (Harmondsworth, 1948), p. 14.

35 Orosius, *Seven Books of History against the Pagans*, trans. A. T. Fear (Liverpool, 2010), pp. 234–5 (Book 5, Ch. 15: 5–6).

36 See 'Egil and Asmund', in *Seven Viking Romances*, trans. Hermann Pálsson and Paul Edwards (London, 1985), pp. 228–57 (p. 239).

37 See 'The Gundestrup Cauldron', https://britishmuseum.tumblr.com, accessed 28 October 2015.

38 John Haywood, *Dark Age Naval Power: A Re-assessment of Frankish and Anglo-Saxon Seafaring Activity* (London and New York, 1991), pp. 76–7.

39 Edwin and Joyce Gifford, *Anglo-Saxon Sailing Ships* (Woodbridge, Suffolk, 2002), pp. 3–4.

40 Ibid., p. 23.

41 Haywood, *Naval Power*, pp. 91–2.

42 The best account of the horns is Hans Frede Nielsen, *Guldhornsinskriften fra Gallehus: Runer, sprog ok politik* (Odense, 2002).

43 Lotte Hedeager, *Iron-Age Societies: From Tribe to State in Northern Europe, 500 BC to AD 700*, trans. John Hines (London, 1992), pp. 66–81 (p. 69).

44 Martin Rundkvist, *Meadhalls of the Eastern Geats: Elite Settlements and Political Geography, AD 375–1000 in Östergötland, Sweden* (Stockholm, 2011), p. 46.

45 Ibid., p. 39.

3 Volsungs and Nibelungs: Avenging Female Furies

1 Gisli's wife Aud breaks the nose of the man trying to bribe her to reveal Gisli's whereabouts with the 1.7-kg (60-oz) bag of silver he offers her, in Chapter 32 of Martin S. Regal, trans., 'Gisli Sursson's Saga', in *CSI*, vol. 11, pp. 1–48 (p. 41); in Robert Cook, trans., 'Njal's Saga', in *CSI*, vol. 111, pp. 1–220, Hallgerd

'High-breeches' or 'Long-legs' arranges, condones or is responsible for the killing of three husbands.

2 For translations of the five ancient versions, all discussed below, see Carolyne Larrington, trans., *The Poetic Edda* (Oxford 1996, revd edn 2014); Snorri Sturluson, *Edda*, trans. Anthony Faulkes (London, 1995); Jesse Byock, trans., *The Saga of the Volsungs* (Berkeley and Los Angeles, CA, 1990); A. T. Hatto, trans., *The Nibelungenlied*, revd edn (London, 1969); Edward Haymes, trans., *The Saga of Thidrek of Bern* (New York, 1988).

3 For Sigurd carvings, see Byock, *Saga of the Volsungs*, pp. 5–7, but also (for the examples in northern Spain) Andrew Breeze, '*Beowulf* 875–902 and the Sculptures at Sangüesa, Spain', *Notes and Queries*, n.s., XXXVIII (March 1991), pp. 2–13.

4 The *Lex Burgundionum* of King Gundobad, drawn up before 516, mentions the king's ancestors Gibicham, Gundomarem, Gislaharium and Gundaharium. The first, third and fourth of these are the Giuki, Gislhere and Gunnar (also Gunther, Guthere) of Norse and German legend. See R. W. Chambers, ed., *Widsith: A Study in Old English Heroic Legend* [1912] (New York, 1965), p. 63.

5 *Beowulf*, l. 877.

6 For Kalkriese, see www.livius.org/te-tg/teutoburg/teutoburg02.html [and five successive parts], accessed 15 June 2016.

7 *Beowulf*, l. 887.

8 Ibid., l. 889.

9 *Eiríksmál* is said to have been commissioned by Eirik's widow, the sorceress-queen Gunnhild, and describes his entry into Valhalla. See the edition by R. D. Fulk, in Diana Whaley, ed., *Poetry from the Kings' Sagas*, vol. 1: *From Mythical Times to c. 1035* (Turnhout, 2013), Part II, pp. 1003–13: also available on the SPSMA website.

10 Another alleged inspiration for Brynhild is the Frankish queen Brunhild (c. 543–c. 613). She too had a husband murdered and attempted to take vengeance for him until in the end she was executed herself (by being trampled, or pulled apart, by horses). The resemblance is not close.

11 As detailed in both Byock, trans., *The Saga of the Volsungs*, pp. 57–9 (Ch. 14), and Snorri, *Edda*, trans. Faulkes, pp. 99–100.

12 For the Sewerby burial, see Robin Fleming, *Britain after Rome: The Fall and Rise, 400 to 1070* (London, 2010), pp. 347–9. Fleming sees this as a punishment burial rather than a sacrifice.

13 Byock, trans., *The Saga of the Volsungs*. All citations of the saga are from this translation, here p. 40 (Ch. 5).

14 Ibid., p. 47 (Ch. 8).

15 'Njal's Saga', trans. Cook, in *CSI*, vol. III, p. 156 (Ch. 129).

16 Ibid.

17 Notably the burning of Flugumýri on 22 October 1253, in which about 25 people died. *Njal's Saga* was written about thirty years later, but stories about Njal must have persisted since his own lifetime almost three hundred years before.

18 Byock, trans., *Saga of the Volsungs*, p. 51 (Ch. 10).

19 Snorri, *Edda*, trans. Faulkes, p. 103.

20 Hatto, trans., *Nibelungenlied*, pp. 113–15.

21 Ibid., pp. 92, 298–9.

22 Byock, trans., *Saga of the Volsungs*, p. 82 (Ch. 30).

23 Guðni Jónsson, ed., *Þiðreks saga af Bern*, 2 vols (Reykjavik, 1984), vol. II, pp. 466–8 (Ch. 343), my translation.

24 N&K, *Sigurðarqviða in scamma*, 30.
25 Byock, trans., *Saga of the Volsungs*, p. 92 (Ch. 33).
26 Keneva Kunz, trans., 'The Saga of the People of Laxardal', in *CSI*, vol. IV, pp. 1–120 (p. 119).
27 See Ursula Dronke, ed. and trans., *The Poetic Edda*, vol. 1: *Heroic Poems* (Oxford 1969), pp. 161–242, for edition, translation and commentary on this difficult poem. An interpretation of it is given by Shippey, 'Speech and the Unspoken in *Hamthismal*', in *Prosody and Poetics: Essays in Honor of Constance Hieatt*, ed. T. J. Toswell (Toronto, 1995), pp. 180–96.
28 N&K, *Hamðismál*, 8. My italics.
29 Ibid., 10.
30 Dronke, ed. and trans., *Poetic Edda*, vol. 1, p. 32.
31 Ibid., pp. 32–3.

4 Ragnar and the Ragnarssons: Snakebite and Success

1 I borrow the phrase from Bruce Lincoln's intriguing study of another legendary hero of the ninth century, *Between History and Myth: Stories of Harald Fairhair and the Founding of the State* (Chicago, IL, 2014).
2 Guðbrandur Vigfússon and F. York Powell, eds, *Corpus Poeticum Boreale* (Oxford, 1883), pp. 339–53.
3 For Hughes and Turner, along with other anticipators of Ragnar, see Shippey, '"The Death-song of Ragnar Lodbrog": A Study in Sensibilities', in *Medievalism in the Modern World: Essays in Honour of Leslie Workman*, ed. Richard Utz and Tom Shippey (Turnhout, 1999), pp. 155–72.
4 Vigfússon and Powell, eds, *Corpus Poeticum*, p. 343.
5 E. V. Gordon, *An Introduction to Old Norse*, 2nd edn, revd A. R. Taylor (Oxford, 1962), pp. lxix–lxxi.
6 My emphasis. The poem has not yet been edited for the SPSMA project, and I have used the Finnur Jónsson edition from 1912, available at www.heimskringla.no/wiki/krákumál/, accessed 28 July 2017. (The line about the young widow is only in the even older edition by Vigfússon and Powell, *Corpus Poeticum*, p. 343.)
7 Anne Heinrichs, 'Krákumál', in *Medieval Scandinavia: An Encyclopedia*, ed. Phillip Pulsiano (New York and London, 1993), pp. 368–9 (p. 368).
8 *Krákumál*, from Finnur Jónsson edition.
9 Joseph Harris, 'Beowulf's Last Words', *Speculum*, LXVII (1992), pp. 1–32.
10 Quoted in Guðni Jónsson, ed., *Sturlunga saga*, 3 vols (Reykvavik, 1951), vol. II, p. 352. The late date means that Thorir's poem could well have been recorded by someone actually present.
11 Christopher Tolkien, ed. and trans., *The Saga of King Heidrek the Wise* [1960] (London, 2010), p. 9.
12 N&K, *Hamðismál*, 28, 30.
13 'Le Coeur de Hialmar' is one of Leconte de Lisle's *Poèmes barbares* (1862).
14 *Beowulf*, l. 2816.
15 See Michael Swanwick, 'A Changeling Returns', in *Meditations on Middleearth*, ed. Karen Haber (New York, 2001), pp. 33–46 (p. 45).
16 J.R.R. Tolkien, *The Monsters and the Critics and Other Essays*, ed. Christopher Tolkien (London, 1997), p. 21.
17 Early scholars, keen to make English sound as much like Old Norse as possible, preferred northern 'breeks' because it sounded like -*brók*.

18 For the translators, and Lord Chesterfield, see Shippey, "'The Death-song of Ragnar Lodbrog'".

19 Rory McTurk, *Studies in 'Ragnars saga Loðbrókar' and its Major Scandinavian Analogues* (Oxford, 1991), pp. 53–61.

20 Saxo Grammaticus, *History of the Danes*, trans. Peter Fisher, 2 vols (Cambridge, 1979), vol. I, pp. 281–92. *Ragnars saga* and the *Þáttr af Ragnars sonum* are in Guðni Jónsson, ed., *Fornaldarsögur Norðurlanda*, 4 vols (Reykjavik, 1959), vol. I, pp. 219–85 and 287–303, respectively. Both are translated by Ben Waggoner, *The Sagas of Ragnar Lodbrok* (New Haven, CT, 2009).

21 Attention was focused on Ragnar and his sons by Alfred P. Smyth, *Scandinavian Kings in the British Isles* (Oxford, 1977). His views and methods were heavily criticized, notably by Donnchadh Ó Corráin, in 'High-kings, Vikings and Other Kings', *Irish Historical Studies*, XXI (1978), pp. 283–333, but have been taken up and to some extent accepted by Clare Downham, *Viking Kings of Britain and Ireland: The Dynasty of Ívarr to AD 1014* (Edinburgh, 2007).

22 Adam of Bremen, *Gesta Hammaburgensis ecclesiae pontificum*, trans. Francis J. Tschan (New York, 1959), p. 37.

23 The development of the Ragnar legend is studied extensively by Elizabeth A. Rowe, *Vikings in the West: The Legend of Ragnarr Loðbrók and His Sons* (Vienna, 2014).

24 ASC, MSS A and E, pp. 74–7.

25 Ibid., p. 77.

26 Ibid., note 14.

27 Alfred P. Smyth, *Scandinavian York and Dublin*, 2 vols (Dublin, 1975), vol. I, pp. 16–18, and *Scandinavian Kings*, p. 169. Clare Downham, *Viking Kings*, pp. 1–23, accepts the Ímair/Ívar identification while withholding judgement on the Ragnarsson/'Boneless' legends.

28 Elizabeth Ashman Rowe, *Vikings in the West*, pp. 14–35.

29 Gwyn Jones, *A History of the Vikings* (London, 1968), p. 212.

30 Rowe, *Vikings in the West*, p. 32. She rejects, however, the idea that there ever was an actual person called *Loðbrók*, or that the attacker of Paris could have been the father of Irish Ímair, p. 134.

31 Ibid., pp. 165–6.

32 ASC, for 867 [correctly 866], MSS A and E, pp. 68–9.

33 Smyth, *Scandinavian Kings*, pp. 98–9.

34 Ibid., pp. 96–7.

35 Adam of Bremen, *Gesta Hammaburgensis*, p. 37.

36 'The Tale of Ragnar's Sons', in Guðni Jónsson, ed., *Fornaldarsögur Norðurlanda*, vol. I, p. 298 (Ch. 3).

37 *Hskr.*, vol. I, p. 76; Hermann Pálsson and Paul Edwards, trans., *Orkneyinga saga* (Harmondsworth, 1981), p. 30 (Ch. 8).

38 Saxo, *History of the Danes*, vol. I, p. 292.

39 Ed. Matthew Townend in *Poetry from the Kings' Sagas*, vol. I: *From Mythical Times to c. 1035*, ed. Diana Whaley (Turnhout, 2012), pp. 649–63 (here 651), also available on the SPSMA website.

40 Rory McTurk has suggested that the word *ari*, eagle, could just be a kenning or traditional substitute for 'sword', as is the more common word for eagle, *örn*. See McTurk, 'The Household of "Ragnarr loðbrók"', in *Familia and Household in the Medieval Atlantic World*, ed. Benjamin T. Hudson (Tempe, AZ, 2011), pp. 11–18 (pp. 17–18), and further McTurk, *Studies in 'Ragnars Saga'* (1991), p. 230.

41 The blood-eagle issue has been much disputed, see Roberta Frank, 'Viking Atrocity and Skaldic Verse', *English Historical Review*, XCIX (1984), pp. 332–43, and 'The Blood-eagle again', *Saga-book of the Viking Society*, XXII (1986–9), pp. 287–9. She disbelieves the whole story, but was replied to by Bjarni Einarsson, 'De Normannorum Atrocitate: or, The Execution of Royalty by the Aquiline Method', *Saga-book of the Viking Society*, XXII (1986–9), pp. 79–82, and 'The Blood-eagle Once More: Two Notes', *Saga-book of the Viking Society*, XXIII (1990–93), pp. 80–83.

42 The rune stone is one of those commemorating the failed Yngvar expedition (see Chapter Eight). It is translated by R. I. Page, *Chronicles of the Vikings* (London, 1995), p. 89, though Page prefers 'Like men' for *drengiligr* (see further Chapter Nine). There is a picture and transcription of the stone in the Wikipedia entry for 'Ingvar Runestones'.

43 'Egil and Asmund', in Hermann Pálsson and Paul Edwards, trans., *Seven Viking Romances* (London, 1985), p. 239 (Ch. 8).

44 For Abbo's *Passio sancti Eadmundi*, see Michael Winterbottom, ed., *Three Lives of English Saints* (Toronto, 1972), pp. 65–87. For Ælfric's 'King Edmund', see W. W. Skeat, ed., *Ælfric's Lives of Saints*, EETS OS 114 (1900), vol. II, pp. 314–33.

45 ASC, for 870 [correctly 869], MSS A and E, pp. 70–71.

46 James H. Todd, ed. and trans., *Cogadh Gaedhel re Gallaibh/The War of the Gaedhil with the Gaill* [1867] (Cambridge, 2012), p. 23.

47 Judy Quinn, trans., 'The Saga of the People of Eyri' (*Eyrbyggja saga*), in CSI, vol. V, p. 138.

48 Anders Winroth, *The Age of the Vikings* (Princeton, NJ, 2014), p. 37.

49 See articles cited in n. 41 above.

50 A few miles from where I live. It was recorded as *Stokes sancti Edwoldi* more than three centuries later.

51 ASC, for 874 [correctly 873], MSS A and E, pp. 72–3. The Wessex compilers of the *Anglo-Saxon Chronicle* had a vested interest in proclaiming Mercia a lapsed state, with the Wessex kings as the only true English monarchs and natural inheritors.

52 See Alex Woolf, 'View from the West: An Irish Perspective on West Saxon Dynastic Practice', in *Edward the Elder, 899–924*, ed. N. J. Higham and D. H. Hill (London, 2001), pp. 89–101. Woolf suggests that Æthelred was the son of Burgred and Alfred's sister Æthelswith, as well as being married to Alfred's daughter Æthelflæd. Cousin marriage was frequent in the West Saxon dynasty.

53 ASC, for 876 [correctly 875], MSS A and E, pp. 74–5.

54 'The Tale of Ragnar's Sons', in Guðni Jónsson, ed., *Fornaldarsögur Norður-landa*, vol. I, p. 300 (Ch. 4).

55 Peter G. Foote and David M. Wilson, *The Viking Achievement: The Society and Culture of Early Medieval Scandinavia* (London, 1970).

56 Walker's account is given in Martin Biddle and Birthe Kjølbye-Biddle, 'Repton and the "Great Heathen Army", 873–4', in *Vikings and the Danelaw: Proceedings of the Thirteenth Viking Congress* [held August 1997], ed. James Graham-Campbell (Oxford, 2001), pp. 45–96, 67.

57 Martin Biddle and Birthe Kjølbye-Biddle, 'Repton and the Vikings', *Antiquity*, LXVI (1992), pp. 36–51 (p. 67); and Biddle and Kjølbye-Biddle, 'Repton and the "Great Heathen Army"', p. 78.

58 Robin Fleming, *Britain after Rome: The Fall and Rise, 400 to 1070* (London, 2010), p. 231.

59 'The Tale of Ragnar's Sons', p. 300 (Ch. 4); see Smyth, *Scandinavian Kings*, pp. 234–5.

60 'Ragnar's saga', in Guðni Jónsson, ed., *Fornaldarsögur Norðurlanda*, vol. 1, p. 238.

61 See 'The Viking Kings: Ivar the Boneless', www.englishmonarchs.co.uk/vikings_6.html, accessed 14 June 2016.

62 Detailed at length in Downham, *Viking Kings*.

63 Nora K. Chadwick, 'The Monsters and *Beowulf*', in *The Anglo-Saxons: Studies Presented to Bruce Dickins*, ed. Peter Clemoes (Cambridge, 1959), pp. 171–203 (p. 179).

64 Adam, *Gesta Hammaburgensis*, p. 37; Abbo, *Passio sancti Eadmundi*, in Winterbottom, ed., *Three Lives of English Saints*, p. 74; Florence, *Chronicon*, ed. Benjamin Thorpe, 2 vols (London, 1848), vol. 1, p. 82.

65 Smyth, *Scandinavian Kings*, p. 239.

5 Egil the Ugly and King Blood-axe: Poetry and the Psychopath

1 All quotations are from Bernard Scudder, trans., 'Egil's Saga', in CSI, vol. 1, pp. 1–177, here p. 100 (Ch. 55). I have adapted this passage slightly, to avoid repetition, though the repetition is in the original.

2 Saying it should be considered as a historical novel does not mean it *is* a historical novel, however, a point made by Joseph Harris, 'Saga as Historical Novel', in his collection *Speak Useful Words or Say Nothing* (Ithaca, NY, 2008), pp. 227–60.

3 Scudder, trans., 'Egil's Saga', p. 114 (Ch. 59).

4 I would like to say that this comparison was made in a class I taught at Saint Louis University, by an undergraduate studying aerospace engineering, Joseph Yurgil. It seems to me extremely apt.

5 First asserted by A. Walsh, *Scandinavian Relations with Ireland during the Viking Period* (Dublin, 1922), p. 16.

6 They are in succession the sagas of Ketil Hæng, Grim Shaggy-cheek, Arrow-Odd and An Bow-Bender, and then the story of Orm Storolfsson. All have been translated by Ben Waggoner, *The Hrafnista Sagas* (New Haven, CT, 2012), and the longest of them, 'The Saga of Arrow-Odd', is in Hermann Pálsson and Paul Edwards, trans., *Seven Viking Romances* (London, 1985), pp. 25–137.

7 Jesse Byock, 'Egil's Bones', *Scientific American*, CCLXXII/1 (January 1995), pp. 82–7.

8 Scudder, trans., 'Egil's Saga', p. 177 (Ch. 89).

9 Byock, 'Egil's Bones', p. 84.

10 It takes its name from its first words, which also show its ambitious nature: *Kringla heimsins*, meaning 'The circle of the world'.

11 The legends surrounding Harald Fairhair are probed in Bruce Lincoln, *Between History and Myth: Stories of Harald Fairhair and the Founding of the State* (Chicago, IL, 2014).

12 Scudder, trans., 'Egil's Saga', p. 56 (Ch. 22).

13 Ibid., p. 92 (Ch. 49).

14 Ibid.

15 ASC, MS A for 937, pp. 107–9.

16 Scudder, trans., 'Egil's Saga', pp. 96–9 (Chs 53–4).

17 ASC, p. 112.

18 By Clare Downham, 'Eirik Blood-Axe – Axed?', *Medieval Scandinavia*, XIV (2004), pp. 51–77.

19 ASC, p. 113, note 14.

20 *Eiríksmál*, ed. and trans. R. D. Fulk, in *Poetry from the Kings' Sagas*, vol. 1: *From Mythical Times to c. 1035*, ed. Diana Whaley (Turnhout, 2012), Part 11, pp. 1003–13, also available on the SPSMA website.

21 Ibid., Odin's final speech.

22 Scudder, trans., 'Egil's Saga', p. 116 (Ch. 60).

23 Alan Binns, 'The Navigation of Viking Ships round the British Isles in Old English and Old Norse Sources', in *Fifth Viking Congress*, ed. Bjarni Niclasen (Torshavn, 1965), pp. 103–17.

24 Ibid., p. 115.

25 Scudder, trans., 'Egil's Saga', p. 118 (Ch. 60).

26 Robert Cook, trans., 'Njal's Saga', in *CSI*, vol. 111, p. 11 (Ch. 7).

27 Though little read, they take up the greater part, pp. 59–220, of Snorri Sturluson, *Edda*, trans. Anthony Faulkes (London, 1987).

28 Egil's poems are quoted from the edition of *Egils saga Skalla-Grímssonar* in Guðni Jónsson, ed., *Íslendinga sögur*, 13 vols (Reykjavik, 1968), vol. 11, pp. 1–312, here pp. 191–2. Translations are mine.

29 Scudder, trans., 'Egil's Saga', p. 124 (Ch. 62).

30 John Hines, 'Egill's *Höfuðlausn* in Time and Place', *Saga-Book of the Viking Society*, XXIV (1994–7), pp. 83–104 (p. 83).

31 To give just one example, the *Saga of Asmund, Killer of Champions* contains a death song that must be that of the hero Hildebrand, henchman of the Gothic king Theodoric the Great and a character in the extended Gudrun story. But while there is a character called Hildebrand in the saga, he can't be the same man. The saga author has fitted an older poem not quite neatly enough into his own saga. No one knows what its ancestor might have been, but it was not made up for the occasion. (It too ends uncomplainingly: 'Now shall I lie / without hope of life, / wounded by the sword / which swells my sore'). See Alison Finlay, trans., 'The Saga of Ásmundr, Killer of Champions', in *Making History: Essays on the 'Fornaldarsögur'*, ed. Martin Arnold and Alison Finlay (Exeter, 2010), pp. 19–39.

32 There is an appreciative study of two of them by Carolyne Larrington, 'Egill's Longer Poems: *Arinbjarnarkviða* and *Sonatorrek*', in *Introductory Essays on 'Egils saga' and 'Njáls saga'*, ed. John Hines and Desmond Slay (London, 1992), pp. 49–63.

33 Scudder, trans., 'Egil's Saga', p. 101.

34 As proposed by Joseph Harris, 'A Nativist Approach to *Beowulf*: The Case of Germanic Elegy', in *Companion to Old English Poetry*, ed. Henk Aertsen and Rolf Bremmer (Amsterdam, 1994), pp. 45–62 (p. 52).

35 Scudder, trans., 'Egil's Saga', p. 149 (Ch. 79). Egil's foiled attempt at suicide occupies this long chapter, pp. 149–51, which also contains the poem *Sonatorrek*, pp. 151–6.

36 Harris, 'Sacrifice and Guilt in *Sonatorrek*', in *Studien zum Altgermanischen: Festschrift für Heinrich Beck*, ed. Heiko Uecker (Berlin and New York, 1994), pp. 173–96 (p. 174).

37 Jónsson, ed., *Íslendinga sögur*, vol. 11, p. 267.

38 Harris, 'Sacrifice and Guilt', p. 173.

39 See merriamwebster.com/dictionary/psychopath, accessed 5 March 2017.

40 See www.merriam-webster.com/dictionary/sociopath, accessed 5 March 2017.

41 Hines, 'Egill's *Höfuðlausn*', p. 98.

42 A point made powerfully in Neil S. Price, *The Viking Way: Religion and War in Late Iron Age Scandinavia* (Uppsala, 2002) is that Scandinavian society had more contact with and similarity to the shamanic cultures of the sub-Arctic

than is commonly accepted. See also Eleanor R. Barraclough, *Beyond the Northlands: Viking Voyages and the Old Norse Sagas* (Oxford, 2017), pp. 47–92.

PART II: MOVING TO THE BIGGER PICTURE

1 Donnchadh Ó Corráin, 'Ireland, Wales, Man and the Hebrides', in *The Oxford Illustrated History of the Vikings*, ed. Peter Sawyer (Oxford, 1997), pp. 83–109, p. 95.

6 Weaving the Web of War: The Road to Clontarf

1 James H. Todd, ed. and trans., *Cogadh Gaedhel re Gallaibh/The War of the Gaedhil with the Gaill* [London, 1867] (Cambridge, 2012), p. 15.
2 See Clare Downham, *Viking Kings of Britain and Ireland: The Dynasty of Ívarr to AD 1014* (Edinburgh, 2007) pp. 12–15, and for discussion of 'Dark' and 'Fair' foreigners, also Downham, 'Viking Identities in Ireland: It's Not All Black and White', *Medieval Dublin*, XI (2011), pp. 185–201.
3 See references in n. 27 to Chapter Four.
4 For the career of Halvdan, see Downham, *Viking Kings*, pp. 68–71.
5 Downham, 'Viking Identities', p. 200.
6 Todd, ed. and trans., *Cogadh Gaedhel*, p. 39.
7 Ibid., pp. 41, 43.
8 ASC, MS A for 897, p. 89.
9 Duald MacFirbis, ed., *Annals of Ireland: Three Fragments* (Dublin, 1860), p. 139.
10 A classic case is Thjostolf, foster-father of Hallgerd Long-legs in *Njal's Saga*, where he figures in Chapters Nine to Seventeen. Unusually, he is given no patronymic, as if no one knew who his father was. Hallgerd uses him to kill both her first and second husbands, but then disposes of him, no compensation being paid or asked for.
11 Quoted here from Downham, 'The Good, the Bad, and the Ugly: Portrayals of Vikings in "The Fragmentary Annals of Ireland"', *Medieval Chronicle*, III (2005), pp. 28–40 (pp. 31–2).
12 ASC, MSS A and E for 897, pp. 74–5. For the significant error in MS E, see ASC, note 14 on p. 75.
13 Todd, ed. and trans., *Cogadh Gaedhel*, pp. 9, 13.
14 Most recently expressed by Sara M. Pons-Sanz, 'Whom did Al-Ghazal Meet? An exchange of Embassies between the Arabs from Al-Andalus and the Vikings', *Saga-book of the Viking Society*, XXVIII (2004), pp. 5–28. She revives an earlier theory that the account was based on the story of a quite different embassy to Byzantium, which has, however, since been lost.
15 It is translated and commented on by W.E.D. Allen, 'The Poet and the Spae-Wife', *Saga-book of the Viking Society*, XV/3 (1960), pp. vii–102.
16 Ibid., p. 20.
17 Ibid., p. 23.
18 Alfred P. Smyth, *Scandinavian Kings in the British Isles* (Oxford, 1977), pp. 98–100.
19 The argument takes up an entire chapter, ibid., pp. 83–100. The attractive part of it is the suggestion that Saxo's apparently meaningless account of Ragnar's struggles with the Galli, usually translated 'British' or 'Welsh', rests on an old misreading of the Irish word *gaill*, meaning 'foreigners', and in this context the 'old foreigners' or Hiberno-Norse. Ragnar, then, died fighting for power in Ireland, was avenged there by his son Ivar, while the story was later relocated to York by Danish inhabitants of the Danelaw.

20 Todd, ed. and trans., *Cogadh Gaedhel*, p. 23.

21 Smyth, *Scandinavian Kings*, pp. 101–18.

22 *Hskr.*, vol. 1, p. 46.

23 See Robert Ferguson, *The Hammer and the Cross: A New History of the Vikings* (London, 2009), pp. 8–9.

24 For what follows, see Downham, *Viking Kings*, pp. 17–23, and for the continuation of the Irish story through to 1014, on to p. 62.

25 See Smyth, *Scandinavian Kings*, pp. 143–57.

26 Ibid., p. 153.

27 Ibid., pp. 166–7.

28 Robert Cook, trans., 'Njal's Saga', in *csi*, vol. III, pp. 1–220, here p. 211 (Ch. 155).

29 Todd, ed. and trans., *Cogadh Gaedhel*, p. 179. The battle description runs from pp. 159–211.

30 Ibid., pp. 203, 205.

31 Cook, trans., 'Njal's Saga', p. 214 (Ch. 157). After several of his banner-bearers had been called, and others refused to carry it, the earl tore it off his pole and wrapped it round himself, but was killed also.

32 John Hines, 'Egill's *Höfuðlausn* in Time and Place', *Saga-book of the Viking Society*, XXIV (1994–97), pp. 83–104, here p. 93.

33 Cook, trans., 'Njal's Saga', pp. 214–15 (Ch. 157).

34 See Joseph Harris, 'Female Divinities, Fate, and Fiction', in *History and Literature: Essays in Honor of Karl S. Guthke*, ed. William Collins Donahue and Scott Denham (Tübingen, 2000), pp. 221–9.

35 Milton, 'Lycidas', ll. 75–6.

36 For which see Nora Kershaw [later Nora K. Chadwick], trans., *Anglo-Saxon and Norse Poems* (Cambridge, 1922), pp. 119–20, and further Russell Poole, '*Darraðarljoð*: A Viking Victory over the Irish', in Poole, *Viking Poems of War and Peace: A Study in Skaldic Narrative* (Toronto, 1991), pp. 116–56 (pp. 131–6).

37 Neil S. Price, *The Viking Way: Religion and War in Late Iron Age Scandinavia* (Uppsala, 2002), pp. 393–4.

38 All quotations are from the text and translation of the poem in Poole, '*Darraðarljoð*: A Viking Victory', pp. 116–18.

39 Price, *The Viking Way*, pp. 336–41.

40 Kershaw, *Anglo-Saxon and Norse Poems*, pp. 116–17.

41 Note C at the end of Walter Scott, *The Pirate* (1822).

42 Todd, ed. and trans., *Cogadh*, p. 203.

43 Cook, trans., 'Njals Saga', p. 214 (Ch. 157).

44 Ibid.

45 Ibid.

46 Anthony Maxwell, trans., 'The Tale of Thorstein Staff-struck', in *csi*, vol. IV, pp. 335–40; also in Gwyn Jones, trans., *Eirik the Red and Other Icelandic Sagas* (Oxford, 1961), pp. 78–88.

47 Bernard Scudder, trans., *Egil's Saga* (London, 2002), p. 167 (Ch. 84).

48 Thorstein seems not to have learned from his lucky escape. According to the short tale 'Thorstein Sidu-Hallsson's Dream', trans. Anthony Maxwell, in *csi*, vol. IV, pp. 463–4, Thorstein was eventually killed by an Irish slave of royal blood whom he had had castrated. Thorstein is warned in his dreams by three women, who seem to be *dísir*, family protectors.

49 For which see 'The Origins of the Icelanders', at www.arnastofnun.is/page/history_and_language, accessed 1 August 2017.

7 Two Big Winners: The Road to Normandy

1 Hermann Pálsson and Paul Edwards, trans., *Orkneyinga saga* (Harmondsworth, 1981), p. 1.

2 The Battle of Dyrrhachium was fought in what is now Albania on 18 October 1081, between the Byzantine emperor Alexius I Komnenos and Robert Guiscard, 'the Weasel'. The latter was a Norman adventurer who had moved into southern Italy and steadily extended his power. Dyrrhachium was quite like Hastings, in that the Varangians were initially successful and chased what appeared to be a broken Norman detachment, but were then pinned down and wiped out.

3 Andrew Breeze, 'Beowulf 875–902 and the Sculptures at Sangüesa, Spain', *Notes and Queries*, XXXVIII (March 1991), pp. 2–13.

4 See Mindy MacLeod and Bernard Mees, *Runic Amulets and Magic Objects* (Woodbridge, Suffolk, 2006), pp. 30–31.

5 Wace, *Roman de Rou*, ed. Hugo Andresen (Heilbronn, 1879), l. 3915, with the reading 'Toirie'. Wace certainly knew the name Tur as that of a pagan god.

6 Hermann Pálsson and Paul Edwards, trans., *Göngu-Hrolfs saga* (Edinburgh, 1980).

7 Investigations conducted by Danish archaeologists in an attempt to retrieve DNA, and so settle the issue of Hrolf's own ancestry. The news was passed on to me by Jesse Byock, but I am not aware as yet of any definitive publication.

8 For which see Dudo of St Quentin, *Historia Normannorum*, ed. and trans. Eric Christiansen (Woodbridge, Suffolk, 1998), and William of Jumièges (and continuators), *Gesta Normannorum Ducum / The Deeds of the Norman Dukes*, ed. and trans. Elisabeth M. C. van Houts, 2 vols (Oxford, 1992).

9 William, *Gesta Normannorum*, p. 10 (Lotrocus), p. 16 (*pedagogus*), p. 19 (human blood).

10 Ibid., p. 18 note 3.

11 ASC, MS E for 1011, p. 141, my emphasis.

12 Dudo, *Historia Normannorum*, pp. 18–20, and William, *Gesta Normannorum*, pp. 22–7.

13 For what follows, see Jón Stefánsson, 'The Vikings in Spain: From Arabic (Moorish) and Spanish Sources', *Saga-book of the Viking Society*, VI (1909–10), pp. 31–46.

14 The 'assault on Francia, 856–92' is well described by Neil Price, 'The Vikings in Brittany', *Saga-book of the Viking Society*, XXII/6 (1989), pp. 319–440, see pp. 346–55.

15 Dudo, *Historia Normannorum*, p. 35.

16 Ibid., p. xv.

17 Ibid., p. 36.

18 Ibid., pp. 36–7, William, *Gesta Normannorum*, p. 27 (for the grant of Chartres), p. 55 (for the conversation).

19 Ibid., pp. 36–7.

20 Ibid., p. 37.

21 Ibid.

22 Ibid., p. 16.

23 Ibid., p. 63.

24 Ibid., p. 57.

25 Dudo, *Historia Normannorum*, p. 49.

26 Ibid., p. 49. The poem 'The Private of the Buffs', by Sir Francis Hastings Doyle, was one of the popular classics of imperial race pride; available at www.bartleby.com, accessed 7 March 2017.

27 For which see Simon Keynes and Michael Lapidge, *Alfred the Great* (Harmondsworth, 1983), pp. 193–4.

28 For this and what follows, see ASC, MS A for 893–897 [correctly 892–896], pp. 84–9, commented on by Shippey, 'A Missing Army: Some Doubts about the Alfredian Chronicle', *In Geardagum*, IV (1982), pp. 41–55 (revised and reprinted in *Anglo-Saxon*, I (2008), pp. 219–38).

29 ASC, MS A for 893–897 [correctly 892–896], p. 84.

30 Ibid., with my clarifications.

31 Ibid., pp. 85–6, for this quotation and those above.

32 Ibid., p. 86.

33 The event is mentioned as an inspirational one by Bernard Cornwell, who grew up near Benfleet, in a note at the end of *The Burning Land* (London, 2009), fifth of 'The Saxon Stories', begun with *The Last Kingdom* (London, 2004). History is, as I remark with reference to the massacres in Chapter Nine, sometimes very close to us.

34 ASC, pp. 86–7.

35 Ibid., p. 88.

36 Ibid., pp. 74–5.

37 Gregory's Minster: for the inscription, see www.ling.upenn.edu/~kroch/scand/kirkdale.html, accessed 24 June 2016. The reading ÆT ILCVM TIDE is often instanced as a case of linguistic simplification (or 'creolization'), for *tíd*, 'time', is feminine in all Germanic languages. So it ought to be *ÆT ILCRE TIDE. Personal observation, however, convinces me that TIDE should be read TANE, 'line', which makes good sense for a sundial and makes ILCVM correct grammatically.

38 For all names mentioned, see Victor E. Watts, *The Cambridge Dictionary of English Place-names* (Cambridge, 2004).

39 For the creole disputes, see John E. McWhorter, 'What Happened to English?' in McWhorter, *Defining Creole* (New York, 2005), pp. 267–311.

40 It is the Mortain chrismal, see plate between pp. 64 and 65 of Renaud, *Les Vikings et la Normandie* (Rennes, 1989).

41 ASC, MS A for 894, p. 84.

42 Alfred was king of the West Saxons, and his mother was a Hampshire Jute. Nevertheless, in the treaty between him and King Guthrum (Keynes and Lapidge, *Alfred the Great*, pp. 171–2), he claims to be supported by the councillors of *eall Angelcynn*, 'all the English race'. This looks like a tacit claim to authority over not only Saxons and Jutes, but the Angles of Mercia and Northumbria currently under Danish rule: the beginnings of a takeover bid. See Sara Foot, 'The Making of Angelcynn: English Identity before the Norman Conquest', *Transactions of the Royal Historical Society*, n.s., VI (1996), pp. 25–49.

8 Furs and Slaves, Wealth and Death: The Road to Miklagard

1 ASC, MS E, p. 137. I have adapted this translation slightly.

2 See reference in n. 49 to Chapter Six for the largely female British/Irish element in the modern Icelandic gene pool.

3 Paul Lunde and Caroline Stone, trans., *Ibn Fadlān and the Land of Darkness: Arab Travellers in the Far North* (London, 2012), pp. 45, 46.

4 Ibid., pp. 147, 126–7, 183.

5 See further Thomas S. Norman, 'Scandinavians in European Russia', in *The Oxford Illustrated History of the Vikings*, ed. Peter Sawyer (Oxford, 1997), pp.

110–33, and also Janet Martin, *Treasure of the Land of Darkness* (Cambridge, 1986), pp. 35–40.

6   See Michael Barnes, 'Languages and Ethnic Groups', in *The Cambridge History of Scandinavia*, vol. 1: *Prehistory to 1520*, ed. Knut Helle (Cambridge, 2003), pp. 94–102.

7   Christopher Tolkien, 'The Battle of the Goths and Huns', *Saga-book of the Viking Society*, xiv (1953–7), pp. 141–63.

8   Christopher Tolkien, ed. and trans., *The Saga of King Heidrek the Wise* [1960] (London, 2010), p. 45 (the pike), p. xxiii and note (the linguistic point), p. xxv (the stone).

9   The original publication of these Gothic inscriptions, by Andrey Vinogradov, is in Russian. Of the online resources, the Wikipedia entry on 'Crimean Gothic' is as good as any.

10 The story is told in the *Annales Bertiniani* (Annals of St Bertin, 839): see Gwyn Jones, *History of the Vikings* (London, 1968), pp. 249–50.

11 Constantine vii Porphyrogenitus, *De administrando imperio*, ed. G. Moravscik, trans. R.J.H. Jenkins, revd edn (Washington, dc, 1967), pp. 57–63.

12 Ibid., p. 63.

13 A. V. Komar, 'Swords from Dnieprostroi (On the History of a Find Made in 1928)', in *Rus' in the 9th–10th Centuries: Society, State, Culture*, ed. N. A. Makaraov and A. E. Leontiev (Moscow, 2014), essay available at www.academia.edu, accessed 3 August 2017.

14 Jonathan Shepard, 'Yngvarr's Expedition to the East and a Russian Inscribed Stone Cross', *Saga-book of the Viking Society*, xxi (1982–5), pp. 22–92.

15 Constantine, *De administrando*, p. 63.

16 The stone has been lost, but R. I. Page gives a suggested text of it in *Chronicles of the Vikings* (London, 1995), p. 145, 'Sassur killed [Helgi] and did a contemptible act [*niðingsverk*]. He betrayed his fellow [*félagi*].' Page notes, 'the oath has been broken within a closed group, which is unforgivable.'

17 Transcription once again from the Wikipedia entry on 'Ingvar Runestones', my translation. Page, *Chronicles of the Vikings*, p. 89, prefers 'like men' for *drengiligr*. The word is not popular academically.

18 Andrew Jameson, private communication. See also his letter in *London Review of Books*, xxxvi/10 (22 May 2014), written in response to my review of the British Museum exhibition and book *Vikings: Life and Legend*, 'The Way of the Warrior', *London Review of Books*, xxxvi/9 (3 April 2014), and containing several interesting points. I am also grateful to Mr Jameson for sending me detailed maps of the Russian river system.

19 Samuel Hazzard Cross and Olgerd P. Sherbowitz-Wetzor, trans., *The Russian Primary Chronicle: Laurentian Text* (Cambridge, ma, 1953), pp. 59, 61. See also Martin, *Treasure*, pp. 35–60 and 110ff.

20 For the black fox-skin, see Anders Winroth, *The Age of the Vikings* (Princeton, nj, 2014), p. 113. The tenth-century historian al-Mas'udi, born in Baghdad, records an interesting experiment that explains the high valuation, see Lunde and Stone, trans., *Ibn Fadlān*, p. 161.

21 Cross and Sherbowitz-Wetzor, trans., *Russian Primary Chronicle*, pp. 59ff.

22 Ibid., p. 64.

23 Ibid., p. 72.

24 See Gwyn Jones, *A History of the Vikings* (London, 1968), pp. 261–2.

25 Cross and Sherbowitz-Wetzor, trans., *Russian Primary Chronicle*, p. 84 (eats 'jerky'), p. 88 (rallies troops), and p. 90 (cup made from skull).

26 His account is not included in Lunde and Stone, trans., *Ibn Fadlān*, but is mentioned by H. R. Ellis Davidson, *The Viking Road to Byzantium* (London, 1976), p. 127.

27 In Lunde and Stone, trans., *Ibn Fadlān*, pp. 144–6.

28 Ibid., pp. 147–52.

29 Modern historians mostly like to play down the collapse, and resist the term 'Dark Ages', for essentially political reasons: see the contrarian (and extremely amusing) account by Bryan Ward-Perkins, *The Fall of Rome and the Collapse of Civilisation* (Oxford, 2005).

30 Martin Rundkvist, '*Post festum*: Solid Gold among the Swedes from the End of the Migration Period Solidi Import to the Beginning of the Viking Raids', unpublished paper (2003). For some reason, this unpublished paper has become unavailable online (27 August 2017), but a summary is most easily reached by Googling the first four words of the title.

31 Winroth, *Age of the Vikings*, p. 124.

32 Lunde and Stone, trans., *Ibn Fadlān*, p. 183.

33 Michael McCormick, *Origins of the European Economy* (Cambridge, 2001), p. 757.

34 Ibid., p. 755 for prices.

35 Ibid., p. 776.

36 Keneva Kunz, trans., 'The Saga of the People of Laxardal', in *CSI*, vol. V, pp. 1–120, here pp. 10–11 (Ch. 12).

37 Ibid., p. 13 (Ch. 13). Myrkjartan's identity with Muircheartach was asserted by A. Walsh, *Scandinavian Relations with Ireland during the Viking Period* (Dublin, 1922), p. 16, and has often been repeated, but is no more than possible.

38 For the Gotland hoards, see Winroth, *Age of the Vikings*, pp. 99–103. Note that my disagreements with Professor Winroth (and others) are not over what they say: the information they give is usually true, valuable and part of the story. The disagreement is over what they prefer to leave out, or deny: the 'comfort-zone' issue.

39 See Martin Arnold, *The Vikings: Culture and Conquest* (London and New York, 2006), p. 115.

40 Nora K. Chadwick, *The Beginnings of Russian History: An Enquiry into Sources* (Cambridge, 1946), p. 32.

41 Cross and Sherbowitz-Wetzor, *Russian Primary Chronicle*, p. 88 (fear of disgrace), p. 91 (the 'slave's son').

42 Both edited and translated by Hermann Pálsson and Paul Edwards, *Vikings in Russia* (Edinburgh, 1989).

43 Ibid., p. 13. What sense can be drawn from the saga is probed by Robert Cook, 'Russian History, Icelandic Story, and Byzantine Strategy in *Eymundar þáttr Hringssonar*', *Viator*, XVII (1986), pp. 65–89.

44 Pálsson and Edwards, trans., *Vikings in Russia*, p. 3.

45 Ibid., pp. 41–2, for a translation of some of the runestones, and the Wikipedia entry 'Ingvar Runestones' for a translation of all of them, accessed 3 August 2017.

46 Tolkien, ed. and trans., *Saga of King Heidrek the Wise*, p. 58.

47 'Gisli Sursson's Saga', trans. Martin S. Regal, in *CSI*, vol. II, pp. 1–40, here p. 10 (Ch. 9). On this occasion I prefer my own traditional translation of a much-quoted saying.

48 Cross and Sherbowitz-Wetzor, trans., *Russian Primary Chronicle*, p. 69.

49 For 'Arrow-Odd's Saga' see Hermann Pálsson and Paul Edwards, trans., *Seven Viking Romances* (London, 1985), pp. 25–137.

50 Ibid. p. 121.

51 Chadwick, 'Appendix II', in *Beginnings of Russian History*, pp. 145–74. She suggested also, pp. 169–70, that both Oleg and Odd might be the same person as the Halogalander Ohthere, but this seems a coincidence too many.

52 My translation from the text in *Fornaldarsögur Norðurlanda*, ed. Guðni Jónsson, 4 vols (Reykjavik, 1959), vol. II, pp. 340–62, stanzas 68, 70, 71.

53 The account has been quoted many times since it was rediscovered, but a convenient translation is Lunde and Stone, trans., *Ibn Fadlān*, pp. 49–54.

54 Ibid. for all quotations in the paragraphs above: p. 49 (incessant drinking), p. 50 ('I will', and 'happily and joyfully'), p. 51 (Angel of Death), p. 52 ('Tell your master'), p. 53 ('did not know'), p. 54 (laughter).

55 Thus Winroth, *Age of the Vikings*, suggests Ibn Fadlan may have been influenced by 'racial stereotypes' (p. 97), but concedes that 'Scandinavian rituals' may have stood behind 'some and perhaps most' of what is described (p. 94). Peter Foote and David Wilson, *The Viking Achievement* (London, 1970), argue that the Rus were 'subject to foreign influences, perhaps especially from the Volga Turks' (p. 408). Lunde and Stone, in *Ibn Fadlān*, reckon they had 'incorporated practices from local cultures', p. xxiv. J. P. Schjødt, 'Ibn Fadlān's Account of a Rus Funeral: To What Extent Does it Reflect Nordic Myth?' in *Reflections on Old Norse Myths*, ed. P. Hermann et al. (Turnhout, 2007), pp. 133–48, suggests the Rus had 'acquired local Slavonic traditions' (p. 133), but notes also the connection with Saxo's Hadingus (p. 140) and concedes 'amazing similarities' with ON myth (p. 134).

56 Neil Price, 'Life and Afterlife: Dealing with the Dead in the Viking Age', video lecture, 2012, www.cornell.edu. See also reference in n. 39 to Chapter Six above.

57 In Chapter 63 of the saga in *Flateyjarbók*, of which there is no convenient modern edition. The existence of Sigrid has been doubted, and, as noted below, the compilers of *Flateyjarbók* were less sceptical than other saga writers. See also Hilda Ellis (later Hilda Ellis Davidson), *The Road to Hel* (Cambridge, 1943), pp. 50–58.

58 'Short Lay of Sigurd', in N&K, 51–2, 70.

59 For the Ballateare grave, a woman with a sliced skull, buried with a man, see pp. 118–19 of David M. Wilson, 'The Conversion of the Viking Settlers in the Isle of Man', in *Conversion and Identity in the Viking Age*, ed. Ildar Garipzanov (Turnhout, 2014), pp. 117–38. At Flakstad, three headless skeletons were found added to other graves: see Elise Naumann, 'Slaves as Burial Gifts in Viking Age Norway?', *Journal of Archaeological Science*, XLI (2014), pp. 533–40. At Trelleborg, five skeletons, four of them children, were found in a well: see Anna B. Gotfredsen et al., 'A Ritual Site with Sacrificial Wells from the Viking Age at Trelleborg, Denmark', *Danish Journal of Archaeology*, III (2104), pp. 145–63.

60 Saxo Grammaticus, *History of the Danes*, trans. Peter Fisher, 2 vols (Cambridge, 1979), vol. I, p. 31.

61 For Vikar, see ibid., p. 172. *Gautreks saga* is translated by Pálsson and Edwards as 'King Gautrek' in *Seven Viking Romances*, pp. 138–70, with King Vikar's death on p. 157.

62 Wulfstan, 'Sermo Lupi ad Anglos', in *English Historical Documents*, vol. I: *c. 500–1042*, ed. Dorothy Whitelock (London, 1969), pp. 854–9, here p. 857.

PART III: THE TALE IN THE NORTH

1 The best guide to the development of kings' sagas is Ármann Jakobsson. 'Royal Biography', in *A Companion to Old Norse-Icelandic Literature and Culture*, ed. Rory McTurk (Oxford, 2005), pp. 388–402.

2 For which see Siân Grønlie, trans., *Íslendingabók* (London, 2006), pp. 3–14, available at http://vsnrweb-publications.org.uk, accessed 3 August 2017; and Hermann Pálsson and Paul Edwards, trans., *The Book of Settlements: Landnámabók* (Winnipeg, 2007).

3 *Kálfsvísa* was quoted by Snorri in his *Skáldskaparmál*: see Snorri Sturluson, *Edda*, trans. Anthony Faulkes (London, 1987), pp. 136–7. *Dvergatal* is stanzas 9–16 of the Eddic poem *Vǫluspá*, in N&K.

4 The creation of this massive work, of which there is no English translation, is studied by Elizabeth A. Rowe, *The Development of Flateyjarbók: Iceland and the Norwegian Dynastic Crisis of 1389* (Odense, 2005).

9 The Jarls and the Jomsvikings: A Study in *Drengskapr*

1 Arngrímur Jónsson, 'Fragments of Danish History (*Skjöldunga saga*)', trans. Clarence Miller, *American Notes and Queries*, xx/3 (Summer 2007), pp. 9–33.

2 *Möðruvallabók* is the largest extant compilation of sagas of Icelanders, written down about 1350. See the entry by Stefán Karlsson in Phillip Pulsiano, ed., *Medieval Scandinavia: An Encyclopedia* (New York, 1993), pp. 426–7.

3 See Andrew Wawn, trans., 'The Saga of the People of Vatnsdal', in *CSI*, vol. I, pp. 1–66 (42–6, chs 32–4), and John Kennedy, trans., 'The Saga of Finnbogi the Mighty', in *CSI*, vol. III, pp. 221–70, (254, ch. 34). The different accounts of the incident (also mentioned in *Landnamabók*) are discussed by Gisli Sigurðsson, *The Medieval Icelandic Saga and Oral Tradition* (Cambridge, MA, 2004), pp. 309–20.

4 The Anglo-Saxon scribe writing all this down was sceptical about the whales, but he may have misunderstood what he was being told: if Ohthere/Ottar was talking about pilot whales, which used to be driven inshore and killed in a kind of battue, he could have been telling the truth. For the whole account, see Niels Lund, ed., *Two Voyagers at the Court of King Alfred: The Ventures of Ohthere and Wulfstan*, trans. Christine E. Fell (York, 1984).

5 They included Eyvind the Plagiarist, author of *Haleygjatal*, an account of the Halogaland dynasty; Einar Skalaglamm, or 'Tinkling-scales', who commemorated the battle of Hjorungavag in his poem *Vellekla*; and Hallfred Troublesome-poet, who transferred his services from the jarls to King Olaf Tryggvason (who gave him his nickname). Einar was a young friend of Egil Skallagrimsson, who in his old age liked talking to him about poetry.

6 N. F. Blake, ed. and trans., *The Saga of the Jomsvikings* (Edinburgh, 1962), p. 33 (Ch. 30).

7 As is discussed by Leszek P. Slupecki, 'Facts and Fancy in *Jómsvikinga saga*', available at www.scribd.com, accessed 2 August 2016.

8 To be found in Sven Aggesen, *The Works of Sven Aggesen*, trans. Eric Christiansen (London, 1992), pp. 31–43 (p. 31).

9 See Gwyn Jones, *A History of the Vikings* (Oxford, 1968), pp. 260–64. Doubt is cast on the barracks theory by Eric Christiansen, *The Norsemen in the Viking Age* (Oxford, 2002), pp. 84–5. He is also sceptical about the Jomsborg/Wollin equation, calling it a 'shotgun marriage between legend and archaeology', p. 83. The 'trelleborgs' nevertheless await a better explanation.

10 Well described, from several accounts, by Stéfan Einarsson, 'Old English *Beot* and Old Norse *Heitstrenging*', *Publications of the Modern Language Association*, XLIX (1934), pp. 975–93.

11 Blake, trans., 'Saga of the Jomsvikings', p. 28 (Ch. 26). The whole scene is pp. 27–9.

12 The whole complex of legends surrounding Harald Fairhair is studied by Bruce Lincoln, *Between History and Myth: Stories of Harald Fairhair and the Founding of the State* (Chicago, IL, 2014).

13 It is the skald Thorbjorn Horn-cleaver's poem *Haraldskvæði* (also known as *Hrafnsmál*, 'The Lay of the Raven'): see ed. and trans. by R. D. Fulk in *Poetry from the Kings' Sagas*, vol. 1: *From Mythical Times to c. 1035*, ed. Diana Whaley (Turnhout, 2012), Part 1, pp. 91–117, also available on the SPSMA website.

14 It is modelled on *Ynglingatal*, which is why Eyvind was called 'the Plagiarist'. It traces the ancestry of the jarls of Halogaland. See ed. and trans. by Russell Poole in *Poetry from the Kings' Sagas*, vol. 1, pp. 195–212, also available on the SPSMA website.

15 Transcription from the Wikipedia entry 'Jelling Stones', accessed 10 March 2017. The two runestones are still in place at Jellinge in Jutland, though now they are sheltered from the weather, and there is an outstanding museum next to the site.

16 *Hskr.*, vol. 1, p. 161 (the ravens; Ch. 27), p. 148 (the command; Ch. 16).

17 Blake, trans., 'Saga of the Jomsvikings', p. 31 (Ch. 28).

18 The 'wooing' is described in the Eddic poem 'The Lay of Skirnir', in N&K.

19 For this, see Nora K. Chadwick, 'Þorgerðr Hölgabrúðr and the *Trolla Þing*: a Note on Sources', in *The Early Cultures of North-west Europe*, ed. Sir Cyril Fox (Cambridge, 1950), pp. 397–417, to which this whole discussion is much indebted.

20 There is an excellent discussion of the battle involvement by female spirits of various kinds in Neil S. Price, *The Viking Way: Religion and War in Late Iron Age Scandinavia* (Uppsala, 2002), pp. 324–63.

21 There is as yet no translation of *Flateyjarbók* into English. It is an immense compilation, made for the rich farmer Jón Hákonarson by two priests, Jón Thórdarson and Magnús Thórhallsson, between 1387 and 1390: see entry by Kolbrún Haraldsdóttir in Phillip Pulsiano, ed., *Medieval Scandinavia*, pp. 197–8. In general, while it often covers similar ground to Snorri's *Heimskringla*, it adds many peripheral stories and accepts more superstitious or supernatural material. Chadwick remarks in 'Þorgerðr Hölgabrúðr', p. 416, that its 'coarseness of detail and atmosphere [in its version of a mythical story] suggests that it had its origin in stories of entertainment popular among the farming class'.

22 Chadwick, 'Þorgerðr Hölgabrúðr', pp. 405–6.

23 Blake, trans., 'Saga of the Jomsvikings', pp. 37–9 (Chs 33–4).

24 Chadwick, 'Þorgerðr Hölgabrúðr', p. 410.

25 Ibid.

26 Ibid., p. 400.

27 Following Chadwick again, ibid., pp. 414–15.

28 Blake, trans., 'Saga of the Jomsvikings', pp. 40–42 (Ch. 36).

29 See ASC, MS E for 1012, p. 142.

30 *Chronicon* of Thietmar of Merseburg, Book VII, Ch. 43, http://historyonline.chadwyck.co.uk, accessed 11 March 2017.

31 ASC, MS D for 1016, p. 152, MS E for 1004, pp. 135–6.

32 *Hskr.*, vol. II, p. 18 (Ch. 24).

33 Ibid., p. 19 (Ch. 25).

34 See A. M. Pollard et al., 'Sprouting like Cockle among the Wheat: The St Brice's Day Massacre and the Isotopic Analysis of Human Bones from sjc, Oxford', *Oxford Journal of Archaeology*, XXXI (2012), pp. 83–102 (pp. 84, 98).

35 Louise Loe et al., *'Given to the Ground': A Viking-age Mass Grave on Ridgeway Hill, Weymouth* (Dorchester and Oxford, 2014), p. 211.

36 Ibid., p. 213.

37 Ibid., p. 211.

38 Blake, trans., 'Saga of the Jomsvikings', p. 41 (Ch. 37).

39 Ibid., p. 41 (Ch. 37).

40 It has been used to make a reconstruction of his face: see Steven McKenzie, 'Face of Orkney's St Magnus Reconstructed', www.bbc.co.uk, accessed 8 February 2017. The account of his death is in Hermann Pálsson and Paul Edwards, trans., *Orkneyinga saga* (Harmondsworth, 1981), pp. 94–5 (Ch. 50).

41 Loe, *'Given to the Ground'*, pp. 72ff.

42 R. I. Page, *Chronicles of the Vikings* (London, 1995), pp. 90, 167.

43 Ibid., p. 106.

44 Ibid., p. 167.

45 Pointed out to me by Andrew Wawn.

46 Page actually uses the phrase 'very tough lad' in translating the word on another runestone: Page, *Chronicles*, p. 87.

47 G. V. Smithers, ed., *Havelok* (Oxford, 1987), ll. 1057–9.

48 Blake, trans., 'Saga of the Jomsvikings', p. 42 (Ch. 37).

49 Ibid., pp. 17–18 (Ch. 16).

50 For the Royal Navy's Articles of War (1757), see www.hmsrichmond.org/rnarticles.htm, accessed 21 February 2017.

51 For which see again Stefán Einarsson, 'Old English *Beot* and Old Norse *Heitstrenging*'.

10 A Tale of Two Olafs; or, The Tales People Tell

1 See once again Ármann Jákobsson, 'Royal Biography', in *A Companion to Old Norse-Icelandic Literature and Culture*, ed. Rory McTurk (Oxford and Malden, MA, 2005), pp. 388–402.

2 'The Saga of Olaf Tryggvason', in *Hskr.*, vol. I, p. 193 (Ch. 61): 'heathen bitch' is my translation of *hundheiðna*.

3 Ibid., pp. 220–21 (Ch. 101) for the 'approach' scene, pp. 219–31 (Chs 100–112) for the account of the entire battle.

4 Ibid., pp. 226–7 (Ch. 108) for Einar and the bow.

5 It was published as 'The Musician's Tale' in Henry W. Longfellow, *Tales of a Wayside Inn* (1863).

6 For instance, Frederick Barbarossa, and (after Flodden Field) James IV of Scotland.

7 The story is imitated from the *Annales de gestis Caroli magni*, by an anonymous monk of Saint Gall, who describes Desiderius, King of the Lombards, watching the approach of Charlemagne's army: see Gwyn Jones, *The Legendary History of Olaf Tryggvason*, W. P. Ker memorial lecture 22 (Glasgow, 1968), p. 20.

8 The point was memorably made by Jones, ibid., who translates the nickname more briskly as 'Wobble-guts'.

9 Svend Ellehøj, 'The Location of the Fall of Olaf Tryggvason', in *Proceedings of the Third Viking Congress*, ed. Kristjan Eldjarn (Reykjavik, 1958), pp. 63–73.

10 'The Saga of Olaf Tryggvason', in *Hskr.*, vol. I, p. 208 (Ch. 85).

11 Keneva Kunz, trans., 'The Saga of the People of Laxardal', in *CSI*, vol. v, pp. 1–120 (p. 59).

12 For *Kristni saga* see Siân Grønlie, trans., *Íslendingabók* (London, 2006), available at http://vsnrweb-publications.org.uk. 'The Saga of Hallfred' is in *CSI*, vol. I, pp. 225–53.

13 'The Saga of Olaf Tryggvason', in *Hskr.*, vol. I, p. 208 (Ch. 85).

14 'The Saga of Hakon the Good', in *Hskr.*, vol. I, p. 101 (Ch. 17).

15 'The Saga of Olaf Tryggvason', in *Hskr.*, vol. I, pp. 196–7 (Chs 65–7).

16 Ibid., p. 198 (Ch. 69; for destroying the idols); pp. 194–5 (Chs 62–3; for burning and drowning); pp. 201–2 (Ch. 76; for the live coals); p. 204 (Ch. 80; for the adder and the angelica).

17 The story is adapted from the conversion of Totila, King of the Goths, by St Benedict, as told in Pope Gregory's *Dialogues*: see Jones, *Legendary History*, pp. 9–10.

18 *ASC*, MSS E and F for 994, pp. 126–9.

19 Ibid., MS A for 993 [correctly 991], p. 126.

20 Ibid., MS E for 991, p. 227.

21 D. G. Scragg, ed., *The Battle of Maldon* (Manchester, 1981); this is an edition of the poem.

22 J.R.R. Tolkien, 'The Homecoming of Beorhtnoth Beorhthelm's Son', in *A Tolkien Reader* (New York, 1966), pp. 1–27.

23 Tacitus, *On Britain and Germany*, trans. H. Mattingly (Harmondsworth, 1948), p. 112. The argument about literature and reality is summarized by Joseph Harris, 'Love and Death in the *Männerbund*' [1993], reprinted in his collection *Speak Useful Words or Say Nothing* (Ithaca, NY, 2008), pp. 287–317, esp. pp. 308–10.

24 See John McN. Dodgson, 'The Site of the Battle of Maldon', in *The Battle of Maldon, AD 991*, ed. D. G. Scragg (Oxford, 1991), pp. 169–81; note that this is a collection of essays, not the edition of the poem referenced above.

25 Marilyn Deegan and Stanley Rubin, 'Byrhtnoth's Remains: A Reassessment of his Stature', in Scragg, ed., *Maldon AD 991*, pp. 289–93.

26 Edited with extensive commentary in Ursula Dronke, ed. and trans., *The Poetic Edda*, vol. II: *Mythological Poems* (Oxford, 1997), pp. 161–240.

27 Wulfstan, *Sermo Lupi ad Anglos*, in *English Historical Documents*, vol. I, ed. and trans. Dorothy Whitelock (London, 1969), p. 857.

28 Frans Bengtsson, *The Long Ships*, trans. Michael Meyer (London, 1954), p. 197.

29 Scragg, ed., *Battle of Maldon*, ll. 165–6.

30 See N. F. Blake, ed. and trans., *The Saga of the Jomsvikings* (Edinburgh, 1962), p. 33 (Ch. 30).

31 'The Saga of St Olaf', in *Hskr.*, vol. II, p. 3 (Ch. 1).

32 Gwyn Jones, *A History of the Vikings* (London, 1968), p. 375 note 1.

33 'The Saga of St Olaf', in *Hskr.*, vol. II, pp. 10–11 (Ch. 13). The chapter quotes skaldic verses by Ottar the Black and Sighvat Thordarson.

34 Ibid., p. 229 (Ch. 190).

35 For the three accounts, see ibid. (Chs 208–34), and Martin S. Regal, trans., 'The Saga of the Sworn Brothers', in *CSI*, vol. II, pp. 329–95; this latter includes the variants from *Flateyjarbók*, including the alternative ending to the battle and Thormod's death, pp. 395–403.

36 Regal, trans., 'Saga of the Sworn Brothers', p. 333 (Ch. 3; for Thorgeir's indifference to women); p. 368 (Ch. 17; for the autopsy and comment on his heart).

37 Ibid., p. 347 (Ch. 8), an addition in the *Flateyjarbók* version.

38 Ibid., p. 345 (Ch. 8), also from *Flateyjarbók*.

39 'The Saga of St Olaf', in *Hskr.*, vol. II, p. 242 (Ch. 208).

40 Regal, trans., 'Saga of the Sworn Brothers', p. 392 (Ch. 24).

41 Ibid., p. 393 (Ch. 24).

42 Ibid., pp. 393–5 (Ch. 24; for the scene in the dressing station), variant version from *Flateyjarbók* pp. 399–402 (no chapter number).

43 Ibid., p. 395. I have adapted the translation.

44 Ibid. The shorter version also gives the poem but rather misses the point by completing it, p. 395 (Ch. 24). The text of the poem is taken from the edition of *Fóstbræðra saga* in Guðni Jónsson, ed., *Íslendinga sögur*, 13 vols (Reykjavik, 1968), vol. V, p. 337.

11 Viking Endgame: A Tale of Two Haralds

1 The nickname is a difficult one. Grammatically, it is an adjective, like 'the Boneless', and dictionaries suggest both 'the Determined' (too weak?) and 'the Tyrannical' (perhaps too critical). In Viking contexts it perhaps carries a note of reluctant admiration: 'Hard-line Harald' might be a modern approximation.

2 The third volume of Alison Finlay and Anthony Faulkes's translation of *Heimskringla* had not appeared when this chapter was being written, and I used instead Magnus Magnusson and Hermann Pálsson, trans., *King Harald's Saga* (London, 1966). However, here I prefer my own translation to their 'fighting two-handed'.

3 Attempts have been made to rehabilitate Ethelred, notably Levi Roach's *Æthelred the Unready* (New Haven, CT, 2016). The Anglo-Saxon joke on his name may well have been contemporary, though not recorded until later. His nickname does not mean exactly 'unready': I would suggest 'No-idea' Ethelred, contrasting with 'Hard-line Harald' in note 1 above.

4 ASC, MSS C D and E for 1049, pp. 168–71.

5 Ibid., MS C for 1052, p. 180.

6 'Saint Olaf's Saga', in *Hskr.*, vol. II, p. 69 (Ch. 76).

7 My translation here, with text from Bjarni Aðalbjarnarson, ed., 'Haralds saga Sigurðarsonar', in *Heimskringla*, vol. III (Reykjavik, 1951), p. 69.

8 Eric Christiansen, *The Norsemen in the Viking Age* (Oxford, 2002), p. 10.

9 See Sigfús Blöndal. *The Varangians of Byzantium*, trans. and revd Benedict Benedikz (Cambridge, 2007), Ch. 4, 'King Harald', pp. 54–102.

10 Magnusson and Pálsson, trans., *King Harald's Saga*, p. 50 (Ch. 4).

11 Ibid., pp. 61–2 (Ch. 14).

12 Ibid., p. 64 (Ch. 16).

13 It is quoted in Theodore M. Andersson and Kari Ellen Gade, trans., *Morkinskinna: The Earliest Icelandic Chronicle of the Norwegian Kings, 1030–1157* (Ithaca, NY, 2000), p. 148, their text but my translation: see further n. 14 below.

14 *Morkinskinna*, meaning 'rotten vellum', is so-called because of the poor state of its cover. It was written in Iceland about 1220 and forms part of the complex tradition of 'kings' saga' writing, which includes the shorter compilation *Fagrskinna*, 'fair vellum', and Snorri's *Heimskringla*. For the former, see Alison Finlay, trans., *Fagrskinna: A Catalogue of the Kings of Norway* (Leiden, 2004). See further Ármann Jakobsson, 'Royal Biography', in *A Companion to Old Norse-Icelandic Literature and Culture*, ed. Rory McTurk (Oxford, 2005), pp. 388–402.

15 Magnusson and Pálsson, trans., *King Harald's Saga*, p. 68 (Ch. 21).

16 See Andersson and Gade, trans., *Morkinskinna*, pp. 104–9 (p. 107). Also in Kari Ellen Gade, ed., *Poetry from the Kings' Sagas*, vol. II: *From c. 1035 to c. 1300* (Turnhout, 2009), pp. 11–30, and available on the SPSMA website.

17 Andersson and Gade, trans., *Morkinskinna*, p. 103.

18 Magnusson and Pálsson, trans., *King Harald's Saga*, pp. 72–3 (Ch. 24). As is often the case, the same scene is described in Andersson and Gade, trans., *Morkinskinna*, p. 155. In what follows I use either or both.

19 Two texts as above, respectively p. 75 (Ch. 27, words quoted) and p. 156 (Ch. 14).

20 *Hávamál*, N&K, st. 64.

21 Andersson and Gade, trans., *Morkinskinna*, pp. 165–7 (Ch. 21).

22 Ibid., pp. 252–4 (Ch. 44).

23 Magnusson and Pálsson, trans., *King Harald's Saga*, p. 69 (Ch. 22).

24 Ibid., p. 137 (Ch. 79).

25 Andersson and Gade, trans., *Morkinskinna*, p. 263 (Ch. 49).

26 Magnusson and Pálsson, trans., *King Harald's Saga*, p. 147 (Ch. 87).

27 Ibid., pp. 151–4 (Chs 92–3), Andersson and Gade, trans., *Morkinskinna*, pp. 271–3 (Ch. 50).

28 See Shaun F. D. Hughes, 'The Battle of Stamford Bridge and the Battle of Bouvines', *Scandinavian Studies*, LX (1988), pp. 30–75.

29 ASC, MS C for 1066, trans. Swanton, p. 198.

30 Magnusson and Pálsson, trans., *King Harald's Saga*, p. 153 (Ch. 93).

31 Ibid., pp. 149–51 (Ch. 91), and (closely similar) Andersson and Gade, trans., *Morkinskinna*, pp. 269–70 (Ch. 50). In what follows the exact wording is from the latter.

32 The text of the poem comes from Andersson and Gade, trans., *Morkinskinna*, p. 27, my translation.

33 Ibid., p. 271, my translation again.

34 The story was told by Field Marshal Sir William Slim in his *Unofficial History* (London, 1950), short stories based on his own youthful service. During an assault in Iraq in 1917, he wrote, p. 50, that his regiment, the Warwickshires, checked before heavy Turkish fire. They were rallied by a private, 'Chuck', who called out the appeal to regimental pride (rather more rudely than I have given it). The irony, and the unexpected stroke of imagination, was that the Warwicks were wearing helmets, with no cap badges. But they knew what he meant!

35 Magnusson and Pálsson, trans., *King Harald's Saga*, p. 152 (Ch. 92). Once again, I have adapted their translation slightly.

36 Ibid., p. 153 (Ch. 92).

12 Viking Aftermath: The Nine Grins of Skarphedin Njalsson

1 Terry Gunnell, trans., 'The Saga of Hrafnkel, Frey's Godi' ['Priest of Frey'], in CSI, vol. V, pp. 261–81.

2 Ibid., p. 268.

3 Ibid., p. 270.

4 I have preferred my own translation here to Terry Gunnell's 'the older you get, the wetter you become'. What the washerwoman says is *Ergisk hverr sem eldisk*. *Eldisk* is clear, 'grows old'. The matching *ergisk*, however, contains the same root as the unforgivable insult *ragr*, and this has a strong sexual as well as moral implication: cowardly, but also unmanly, impotent. This is particularly offensive when said by a female to a male, especially as in the literal sense it is perfectly true. A good insult mingles false accusation with undeniable truth.

5 There is a brief survey of issues raised in Shippey, 'Proverbs and Proverbiousness in *Hrafnkels saga Freysgoða*', in *The Hero Recovered: Essays on Medieval Heroism*

in Honor of George Clark, ed. James Weldon and Robin Waugh (Kalamazoo, MI, 2010), pp. 127–41.

6 Gunnell, trans. 'The Saga of Hrafnkel', p. 273. Gunnell translates it as 'through the men's heels behind the tendons'.

7 See O. D. Macrae-Gibson, 'The Topography of *Hrafnkels saga*', *Saga-book of the Viking Society*, XIX/2–3 (1975–6), pp. 239–63.

8 Martin S. Regal, trans., 'Gisli Sursson's Saga', in *CSI*, vol. II, pp. 1–48 (p. 9).

9 Ibid., p. 14.

10 See Claiborne W. Thompson, '*Gísla saga*: The Identity of Vestein's Slayer', *Arkiv*, LXXXVIII (1973), pp. 85–90.

11 R. Kroesen presents a reason for thinking Vestein, as head of the family, must have forbidden his sister's marriage to Thorgrim, in 'The Enmity between Thorgrímr and Vésteinn in the *Gísla saga Súrssonar*', *Neophilologus*, LXVI (1982), pp. 386–90.

12 Regal, trans., 'Gisli Sursson's Saga', p. 23.

13 Quoted by R. I. Page, *Chronicles of the Vikings* (London, 1995), p. 42.

14 Robert Cook, trans., 'Njal's Saga', in *CSI*, vol. III, pp. 1–220.

15 Ibid., p. 52 (Ch. 44).

16 Ibid., pp. 52–3 (Ch. 44).

17 Ibid., p. 43 (Ch. 36).

18 Ibid., p. 112 (Ch. 92).

19 William Miller prefers the last explanation in his excellent book *Why is Your Axe Bloody: A Reading of Njáls saga* (Oxford, 2014), and it certainly makes sense. But it may not be the *only* explanation.

20 Cook, trans., 'Njal's Saga', pp. 140–45 (Chs 119–20).

21 I use my translation here instead of Cook's 'with a toothy sneer', to make the point that it is still the same verb being used, *glotta*, 'to grin'.

22 Cook, trans., 'Njal's Saga', p. 144 (Ch. 120).

23 Ibid., p. 148 (Ch. 123).

24 Ibid., pp. 153–9 (Chs 128–30).

25 Gísli Sigurðsson, *The Medieval Icelandic Saga and Oral Tradition: A Discourse on Method*, trans. Nicholas Jones (Cambridge, MA, 2004), p. 151.

26 See George Johnston, trans., *The Saga of Gisli*, with introductory essay by Peter Foote (London 1963), pp. 129–30.

27 The point is made by Jesse Byock, *Viking Age Iceland* (London, 2001), pp. 77–80.

28 Cook, trans., 'Njal's Saga', p. 191 (Ch. 145).

29 Shakespeare, *A Midsummer Night's Dream*, Act 5, Scene 2.

Bibliography

Further Reading

Many texts and translations are listed in the three preceding appendices, as well as important works of reference, while many others will be found in the References. For a general history of the Vikings, Gwyn Jones's *A History of the Vikings* (Oxford, 1968) remains hard to beat. Professor Jones was fully conversant with the Old Norse language, which is not always the case with historians of the period, and did not despise literary sources. More recently, Peter Sawyer has edited *The Oxford Illustrated History of the Vikings* (Oxford, 1997), which contains essays on many aspects of Viking activity. Robert Ferguson's *The Hammer and the Cross: A New History of the Vikings* (London, 2009) contains some new information, notably the revised forensics of the Gokstad burial. Anders Winroth's *The Age of the Vikings* (Princeton, NJ, 2014) likewise contains valuable details, notably of the silver hoards of Gotland. Philip Parker's *The Northmen's Fury: A History of the Viking World* (London, 2014) is written by an experienced author for a non-specialist audience. These later works, however, follow much the same narrative pattern and avoid actual Vikings as much as possible: they remain in the scholarly comfort zone. This is not the case with *The Vikings: Culture and Conquest* (New York and London, 2006) by Martin Arnold, who would have been a collaborator in this volume if not for a health issue, now thankfully resolved.

The Chronicles of the Vikings (London, 1995) by R. I. Page selects and translates a wide range of original sources, including his own speciality, runestones; this has the virtue of letting the Vikings, if Vikings they were, speak for themselves. Gruff as Professor Page always was, the major iconoclast of recent times has nevertheless been Professor Alfred Smyth, quoted repeatedly in the text. His groundbreaking and contrarian work *Scandinavian Kings in the British Isles, 850–880* (Oxford and New York, 1977), much attacked by other scholars, nevertheless enlivened debate – or, one might say, set the cat among the pigeons. It has been updated, with considerable confirmation, by Clare Downham as *Viking Kings of Britain and Ireland: The Dynasty of Ívarr to AD 1014* (Edinburgh, 2007). Downham's essays are also collected in *No Horns on their Helmet? Essays on the Insular Viking Age* (Aberdeen, 2013), soon to be available at www.academia.edu. (It needs a companion volume, *Vikings Never Joined the Faculty Club*.) Another corrective work is Elizabeth Ashman Rowe, *Vikings in the West: The Legend of Ragnarr Loðbrók and his Sons* (Vienna, 2014).

Among the many archaeological discoveries of recent years, the most dramatic include the finds at Lejre, for which see *Beowulf and Lejre*, ed. John D. Niles (Tempe, AZ, 2007), with reference to Ch. 2; the site of the Ridgeway massacre in Dorset, for which see Louise Loe et al., *'Given to the Ground': A Viking-age Mass*

Grave on Ridgeway Hill, Weymouth (Dorchester and Oxford, 2014); and the boats and weapons found in Jutland at Nydam, Hjortspring and Illerup, for which see the publications referenced in n. 33 to Chapter Two. Also visually stunning are the Viking ships found in Roskilde Fjord in Denmark, not far from Lejre. Deliberately scuttled to block entrance to the harbour during a crisis in June 1079, the five ships found show a full range of ship types, including a coastal and an ocean trader, a fishing boat and a small longship, with pride of place going to the seventy-man longship *Havhingsten*, or *Sea-stallion*, built in Ireland in 1042. These and other reconstructions (including what looks like a *monoxylon*, the Björke boat from AD 450) are on show at the Viking Ship Museum in Roskilde.

An even wider-ranging account, which takes in history, literature and archaeology all at once, is Neil Price's *The Viking Way: Religion and War in Late Iron Age Scandinavia* (Uppsala, 2002); a very striking lecture of his, available online, is also referenced in n. 56 to Chapter Eight. Literature and travel are engagingly combined in Eleanor Barraclough's *Beyond the Northlands: Viking Voyages and the Old Norse Sagas* (Oxford, 2017).

The most important re-evaluation of the whole Icelandic saga tradition is Gísli Sigurðsson's *The Medieval Icelandic Saga and Oral Tradition: A Discourse on Method*, trans. Nicholas Jones (Cambridge, MA, 2004), which (like Price's work above, and Davide Zori and Jesse Byock's Mosfell project below) makes a powerful case against fashionable scepticism. For further wide-ranging accounts, one cannot do better than read the works of Jesse Byock (who suggested the Paget's syndrome explanation for Egil Skallagrimsson): *Feud in the Icelandic Saga* (Berkeley, CA, 1982), *Medieval Iceland* (Berkeley, CA, 1988), and *Viking Age Iceland* (London, 2001). The archaeological project at Mosfell, directed by Zori and Byock, is also mentioned in n. 10 to the Introduction.

It is remarkable that a footnote on page 112 of *Viking Age Iceland* – which suggests that there is another and very much real-life way of reading the events of a feud in *Eyrbyggja saga* – stimulated the best modern retelling of a saga, Jeff Janoda's *Saga* (Chicago, IL, 2005). Byock's reinterpretation of the saga story not only assumes that events went very much as detailed in the saga, but locates them in a close study of the ground: it was all about hay and timber, two rare but vital resources. Janoda adds further plausible twists; see my rave review on www.academia.edu.

Many authors besides Janoda have moreover been stimulated to rewrite saga materials (as well as Norse myths, for which see Appendix C). Works include the science fiction author Poul Anderson's *The Broken Sword* (New York, 1954, revd 1971) and *Hrolf Kraki's Saga* (New York, 1973), Stephan Grundy's retelling of the Volsung/Nibelung legend as *Rhinegold* (1994), and Melvin Burgess's transposition of 'The Saga of the Volsungs' into science-fictional mode in *Bloodtide* (London, 1999) and *Bloodsong* (London, 2005). Anderson was thinking about rewriting the 'Hrafnistumen Sagas', mentioned in Chapter Five, not long before he died in 2001.

Finally, and returning from fiction to fact, the best thing anyone interested in Old Norse can do is get Professor Byock's course on *Viking Language* (2013). This consists of two books of graded texts and exercises, with two sets of audio recordings (downloadable via iTunes) read by a native Icelander, Ása Bjarnadóttir, in the modern pronunciation often used by scholarship. Work through these and you can read sagas, Eddas and even skaldic verse for yourself. (Yet one more rave review of this is also now under my name on www.academia.edu.)

PRIMARY TEXTS AND TRANSLATIONS

Editions of Old Norse

Edda: Die Lieder des Codex Regius, ed. Gustav Neckel and Hans Kuhn, 2 vols (Heidelberg, 1962–8)

Eddica minora, ed. Andreas Heusler and Wilhelm Ranisch (Dortmund, 1903)

Fornaldarsögur Norðurlanda, ed. Guðni Jónsson, 4 vols (Reykjavik, 1959)

An Introduction to Old Norse, ed. E. V. Gordon, 2nd edn, revd A. R. Taylor (Oxford, 1962)

Íslendinga sögur, ed. Guðni Jónsson, 13 vols (Reykjavik, 1968)

Snorri Sturluson, *Heimskringla*, ed. Bjarni Aðalbjarnarson, 3 vols (Reykjavik, 2002)

—, *Snorra Edda*, ed. Árni Björnsson (Reykjavik, 1975)

The Poetic Edda, vol. I: *Heroic Poems*, ed. and trans. Ursula Dronke (Oxford, 1969) [includes *Atlakviða* and *Atrlamál*]

—, vol. II: *Mythological Poems I* (Oxford, 1997) [includes *Vǫlundarkviða*]

—, vol. III: *Mythological Poems 2* (Oxford, 2011)

Þiðreks saga af Bern, ed. Guðni Jónsson, 2 vols (Reykjavik, 1984)

Translations from Old Norse

Eddic and skaldic poetry (see further Appendix B)

Corpus poeticum boreale: The Poetry of the Old Northern Tongue from the Earliest Times to the Thirteenth Century, ed. Guðbrandur Vigfússon and F. York Powell (Oxford, 1883) [ancient but venerable, and intended to be complete]

Kershaw, Nora [later Nora K. Chadwick], *Anglo-Saxon and Norse Poems* (Cambridge, 1922)

Norse Poems, trans. W. H. Auden and Paul B. Taylor (London, 1981) [outstanding as the work of a major modern poet. Contains most of the Eddic corpus as well as 'The Sun Song' (*Sólarljóð*), the Christian response to *Vǫluspá* (The Song of the Sybil)]

Poems of the Elder Edda, trans. Patricia Terry, revd edn (Philadelphia, PA, 1990) [complete, readable, widely used]

The Poetic Edda, trans. Jackson Crawford (Indianapolis, IN, 2015) [contains 'The Cowboy Havamal', one of the greatest of the Eddic poems, rendered very convincingly into modern American]

The Poetic Edda, trans. Carolyne Larrington (Oxford, 1996, revd 2014) [excellent, complete, accessible]

For skaldic poetry, see www.abdn.ac.uk/skaldic. This is a major project of re-editing the complete and very large corpus. This work is ongoing, but the online version helpfully gives older versions as a stopgap until the project is complete. Two volumes have so far been published as print volumes, viz.:

Whaley, Diana, ed., *Poetry from the Kings' Sagas*, vol. I: *From Mythical Times to c. 1035* (Turnhout, 2013)

Gade, Kari Ellen, ed., *Poetry from the Kings' Sagas*, vol. II: *From c. 1035 to c. 1300* (Turnhout, 2009)

See also Snorri Sturluson, *Edda*, trans. Anthony Faulkes (London, 1995). This is the *Prose Edda* (our major source for knowledge of Old Norse myth), but it contains extensive quotations from poetry, much of it not surviving elsewhere.

Kings' sagas and historical works

Arngrímur Jónsson, 'Fragments of Danish History (*Skjöldunga saga*)', trans. Clarence Miller, *American Notes and Queries*, xx/3 (Summer 2007), pp. 9–33

The Book of Settlements: Landnámabók, trans. Herman Pálsson and Paul Edwards (Winnipeg, 2007)

Fagrskinna: A Catalogue of the Kings of Norway, trans. Alison Finlay (Leiden, 2004)

Íslendingabók; Kristni saga: The Book of Icelanders; The Story of the Conversion, trans. Siân Grønlie (London, 2006) [Íslendingabók is on pp. 3–14.] Available at www.vsnrweb-publications.org.uk

King Harald's Saga, trans. Magnus Magnusson and Hermann Pálsson (Harmondsworth, 1966)

Morkinskinna: The Earliest Icelandic Chronicle of the Norwegian Kings, 1030–1157, trans. Theodore M. Andersson and Kari Ellen Gade (Ithaca, NY, 2000)

Orkneyinga saga: The Saga of the Jarls of Orkney, trans. Herman Pálsson and Paul Edwards (Harmondsworth, 1981)

Page, R. I., ed. and trans., *Chronicles of the Vikings: Records, Memorials and Myths* (London, 2000)

Snorri Sturluson, *Heimskringla: History of the Kings of Norway*, trans. Anthony Faulkes and Alison Finlay, 3 vols (London, 2011–16). The Viking Society for Northern Research and the translators have generously made this available online at www.vsnrweb-publications.org.uk. [The older version by Lee M. Hollander (Austin, TX, 1964) is adequate if old-fashioned in diction. The much older version by Samuel Laing, published by Everyman, has been extremely influential but was translated not from the original but from a modern Norwegian version, see Wawn, *The Vikings and the Victorians*, Ch. 4.]

Sagas of Icelanders

All quotations of sagas of Icelanders in this volume are taken from *The Complete Sagas of Icelanders*, general editor Viðar Hreinsson, 5 vols (Reykjavik, 1997, abbreviated here as CSI). This contains some forty full-length sagas plus close on fifty *pættir*, or short stories, by an international team of translators.

Ten sagas and seven short stories from that volume, including *Egil's Saga, Gisli's Saga, Hrafnkel's Saga* and the *Saga of the Laxdalers*, were then published by Penguin World Classics as *The Sagas of Icelanders: A Selection*, ed. Örnolfur Thorsson, Preface by Jane Smiley and Introduction by Robert Kellogg (London, 2000). Five more were reprinted in *Sagas of Warrior-Poets*, ed. Diana Whaley (London, 2002)

Older translations of the sagas, often very good ones, were published by Penguin (and others) and remain widely available. Details of the sagas used in this volume follow individually:

Egils saga, trans. Bernard Scudder, in CSI, vol. I, pp. 33–177. Also in Örnolfur Thorsson, ed., *Sagas of Icelanders*. The older translations by Hermann Pálsson and Paul Edwards (Harmondsworth, 1976), and by Christine Fell and John Lucas (London, 1985), are also highly recommended.

Eirik the Red and Other Icelandic Sagas, trans. Gwyn Jones (Oxford, 1961)

Eyrbyggja saga, trans. Hermann Pálsson and Paul Edwards, revd edn (Harmondsworth, 1989)

Gisli Sursson's Saga, trans. Martin S. Regal, in CSI, vol. II, pp. 1–48, included in Örnolfur Thorsson, ed., *Sagas of Icelanders*. Also recommended is the older translation *The Saga of Gisli*, trans. George Johnston (London, 1963)

Njal's saga, trans. Robert Cook, CSI, vol. III, pp. 1–220. The older translation by
  Magnus Magnusson and Hermann Pálsson (Harmondsworth, 1960) is also
  excellent
The Saga of Droplaug's Sons, trans. Rory McTurk, in CSI, vol. IV, pp. 355–78. Also in
  The Fljotsdale Saga and the Droplaugarsons, trans. Eleanor Howarth and Jean
  Young (London, 1990)
The Saga of Hrafnkel Frey's Godi [Hrafnkels saga], trans. Terry Gunnell, in CSI, vol.
  V, pp. 261–81. Also in Örnolfur Thorsson, ed., *Sagas of Icelanders*, and Jones,
  ed., *Eirik the Red*
The Saga of the People of Laxardal [Laxdæla saga], trans. Keneva Kunz, in CSI, vol.
  V, pp. 1–120, included in Örnolfur Thorsson, ed., *Sagas of Icelanders*. The older
  translation by Magnus Magnusson and Hermann Pálsson (Harmondsworth,
  1969) is also excellent
The Saga of the People of Vatnsdal [Vatnsdæla saga], trans. Andrew Wawn, in CSI,
  vol. IV, pp. 1–66. Also in Örnolfur Thorsson, ed., *Sagas of Icelanders*
The Saga of the Sworn-Brothers [Fóstbræðra saga], trans. Martin S. Regal, in CSI,
  vol. II, pp. 329–402 [contains variants from *Flateyjarbók*]
The Tale of Thorstein Staff-Struck, trans. George Clark, in CSI, vol. IV, pp. 335–40,
  included in Örnolfur Thorsson, ed., *Sagas of Icelanders*. Also in Jones, ed.,
  Eirik the Red
Thorstein Sidu-Hallsson's Saga, trans. Katrina C. Attwood, in CSI, vol. IV, pp. 447–59

Sagas of old times

Göngu-Hrólfs saga, trans. Hermann Pálsson and Paul Edwards (Edinburgh, 1980)
The Hrafnista Sagas, trans. Ben Waggoner (New Haven, CT, 2012) [includes *Ketils
  saga hængs*]
'The Saga of Ásmundr, Killer of Champions', trans. Alison Finlay, in *Making
  History: Essays on the Fornaldarsögur*, ed. Martin Arnold and Alison Finlay
  (Exeter, 2010), pp. 19–39
The Saga of King Heidrek the Wise, ed. and trans. Christopher Tolkien [1960]
  (London, 2010)
The Saga of King Hrolf Kraki, trans. Jesse Byock (London, 1998). Also in Jones,
  ed., *Eirik the Red*
The Saga of the Jomsvikings, ed. and trans. N. F. Blake (Edinburgh, 1962)
The Saga of Thidrek of Bern, trans. Edward Haymes (New York, 1988)
The Sagas of Ragnar Lodbrok [Ragnar's Saga and the 'Tale of Ragnar's Sons'], trans.
  Ben Waggoner (New Haven, CT, 2009)
Seven Viking Romances, trans. Hermann Pálsson and Paul Edwards
  (Harmondsworth, 1985) [includes 'Arrow-Odd', i.e. *Örvar-Odds Saga*]
The Saga of the Volsungs, trans. Jesse Byock (Berkeley, CA, 1990)
Vikings in Russia: Yngvar's Saga and Eymund's Saga, trans. Hermann Pálsson and
  Paul Edwards (Edinburgh, 1989)
For a full bibliography of *fornaldarsögur*, see http://fasnl.ku.dk/bibl.aspx

Editions and Translations from Other Languages

Abbo of Fleury, 'Passio sancti Edmundi', in *Three Lives of English Saints*, ed.
  Michael Winterbottom (Toronto, 1972), pp. 65–87
Adam of Bremen, *Gesta Hammaburgensis ecclesiae pontificum*, trans. Francis J.
  Tschan (New York, 1959)

Ælfric, 'King Edmund', in *Sweet's Anglo-Saxon Primer*, ed. Norman Davis, 9th edn (Oxford, 1957), pp. 81–91

Aggesen, Sven, *The Works of Sven Aggesen*, trans. Eric Christiansen (London, 1992)

The Anglo-Saxon Chronicles, trans. Michael Swanton (London, 2000)

The Annals of Ulster (to AD 1131), ed. and trans. Seán Mac Airt and Gearóid Mac Niocaill (Dublin, 1983)

The Annals of St Bertin (*Ninth-century Histories*, vol. I), trans. Janet L. Nelson (Manchester, 1991)

Annales Xantenses, see *Ninth-century Histories*, vol. II: *The Annals of Fulda*, trans. Timothy Reuter (Manchester, 1992)

The Battle of Maldon, ed. E. V. Gordon (London, 1937) *The Battle of Maldon*, ed. D. G. Scragg (Manchester, 1981)

Bede, *A History of the English Church and People*, trans. Leo Sherley-Price, revd R. E. Latham (Harmondsworth, 1968)

The Chronicle of Æthelweard, ed. and trans. A. Campbell (London, 1962)

Cogadh Gaedhel re Gallaibh/The War of the Gaedhil with the Gaill, trans. James H. Todd [1867] (Cambridge, 2012)

Constantine VII Porphyrogenitus, *De administrando imperio*, ed. Gy. Moravscik, trans. R.J.H. Jenkins, revd edn (Washington, DC, 1967)

Dudo of Saint-Quentin, *Historia Normannorum/The History of the Normans*, ed. and trans. Eric Christiansen (Woodbridge, Suffolk, 1998)

English Historical Documents, vol. I: *c. 500–1042*, ed. Dorothy Whitelock, 2nd edn (London, 1969)

Gregory of Tours, *The History of the Franks*, trans. Lewis Thorpe (Harmondsworth, 1974)

Havelok, ed. G. V. Smithers (Oxford, 1987)

Ibn Fadlan and the Land of Darkness: Arab Travellers in the Far North, trans. Paul Lunde and Caroline Stone (London, 2012)

Jordanes, *Gothic History*, trans. C. C. Mierow (New York, 1960)

Keynes, Simon, and Michael Lapidge, *Alfred the Great* (Harmondsworth, 1983) [contains 'The Treaty between Alfred and Guthrum' and 'The Burghal Hidage']

Liber Historiae Francorum, ed. and trans. Bernard C. Bachrach (Lawrence, KS, 1973)

Das Nibelungenlied, ed. Karl Bartsch, 18th edn, revd Helmut de Boor (Wiesbaden, 1965), trans. A.T. Hatto, revd edn (Harmondsworth, 1969)

Orosius, *Seven Books of History against the Pagans*, trans. A. T. Fear (Liverpool, 2010)

Saxo Grammaticus, *History of the Danes*, trans. Peter Fisher, ed. Hilda Ellis Davidson, 2 vols (Cambridge and Totowa, NJ, 1979)

Tacitus, *On Britain and Germany*, trans. H. Mattingly (Harmondsworth, 1948)

Three Fragments of Irish Annals, ed. Joan Newlon Radner (Dublin, 1978)

Two Voyagers at the Court of King Alfred: The Ventures of Ohthere and Wulfstan, ed. Niels Lund, trans. Christine E. Fell (York, 1984)

Van Houts, Elisabeth M. C., ed. and trans., *The Normans in Europe* (Manchester, 2000) [contains translations of many documents, including the 918 charter of Charles the Simple (25), which mentions lands granted to the Normans and Rollo]

Wace, *Roman de Rou*, ed. Hugo Andresen (Heilbronn, 1879)

William of Jumièges (and continuators), *Gesta Normannorum ducum/The Deeds of the Norman Dukes*, ed. and trans. Elisabeth M. C. van Houts, 2 vols (Oxford, 1992)

Wulfstan, *Sermo Lupi ad Anglos*, ed. Dorothy Whitelock, 3rd edn (London, 1963). Translated in *English Historical Documents*, vol. I, pp. 854–9

Some Useful Websites

For discussion of Danish weapon-dumps, see Frans-Arne Hedlund Stylegar, 'Scandinavian Armies in the Late Roman Period', 1 November 2007, http://arkeologi.blogspot.co.uk

For Gregory's Minster, see https://en.wikipedia.org/wiki/Kirkdale_sundial [but note that *ilcvm tide* should be *ilcvm tane*]

For Kalkriese, see www.livius.org/te-tg/teutoburg/teutoburg02.html [and five successive parts]

Saga-Book of the Viking Society, all issues are available at www.vsnr.org/saga-book

Many sagas are available online, in Old Norse, modern Icelandic, English and other languages, at www.sagadb.org

SECONDARY SCHOLARSHIP

Acker, Paul, and Carolyne Larrington, eds, *The Poetic Edda: Essays on Old Norse Mythology* (New York and London, 2002)

—, *Revisiting the Poetic Edda: Essays on Old Norse Heroic Legend* (New York and London, 2013)

Allen, W. E., 'The Poet and the Spae-Wife', *Saga-Book of the Viking Society*, XV/3 (1960), pp. vii–102

Andersson, Theodore M., *The Legend of Brynhild* (Ithaca, NY, 1980)

Ármann Jakobsson, 'Royal Biography', in *Companion to Old Norse*, ed. McTurk, pp. 388–402

—, 'Views to a Kill: Sturla Þórðarson and the Murder in the Cellar', *Saga-book of the Viking Society*, XXXIX (2015), pp. 5–20

Arnold, Martin, *The Vikings: Culture and Conquest* (London and New York, 2006)

Barnes, Michael, 'Languages and Ethnic Groups', in *Cambridge History*, ed. Helle, pp. 94–102

—, 'Language', in *Companion to Old Norse*, ed. McTurk, pp. 173–89

Barraclough, Eleanor R., *Beyond the Northlands: Viking Voyages and the Old Norse Sagas* (Oxford, 2017)

Bengtsson, Frans, *The Long Ships*, trans. Michael Meyer (London, 1954)

Biddle, Martin, and Birthe Kjølbye-Biddle, 'Repton and the "Great Heathen Army", 873–4', in *Vikings and the Danelaw: Proceedings of the Thirteenth Viking Congress* (August 1997), ed. James Graham-Campbell (Oxford, 2001), pp. 45–96

—, 'Repton and the Vikings', *Antiquity*, LXVI (1992), pp. 36–51

Binns, Alan, 'The Viking Century in East Yorkshire', *East Yorkshire Local History Society*, EYLH Series 15 (1963)

—, 'The Navigation of Viking Ships round the British Isles in Old English and Old Norse Sources', in *Fifth Viking Congress*, ed. Bjarni Niclasen (Torshavn, 1965), pp. 103–17

—, 'East Yorkshire in the Sagas', *East Yorkshire Local History Society*, EYLH Series 22 (1966)

Bjarni Einarsson, 'De Normannorum atrocitate: or, The Execution of Royalty by the Aquiline Method', *Saga-Book of the Viking Society*, XXII (1986–9), pp. 79–82

—, 'The Blood-eagle Once More: Two Notes', *Saga-Book of the Viking Society*, XXIII (1990–93), pp. 80–83

Breeze, Andrew, '*Beowulf* 875–902 and the Sculptures at Sangüesa, Spain', *Notes and Queries*, n.s., XXXVIII (March 1991), pp. 2–13

Brown, Nancy, *Song of the Vikings: Snorri and the Making of Norse Myths* (New York, 2012)

Byock, Jesse, 'Egil's Bones', *Scientific American*, CCLXXII/1 (January 1995), pp. 82–7

—, 'The Mosfell Archaeological Project: Archaeology, Sagas and History', in *Viking Archaeology in Iceland: Mosfell Archaeology Project*, ed. Davide Zori and Jesse Byock (Turnhout, 2014), pp. 27–44 [See also Byock and Zori, 'Viking Archaeology, Sagas, and Interdisciplinary Research in Iceland's Mosfell Valley', *Backdirt* (2013), pp. 124–41, www.viking.ucla.edu/mosfell_project/publications.html]

—, *Viking Age Iceland* (London, 2001)

Chadwick, Nora K., *The Beginnings of Russian History: An Enquiry into Sources* (Cambridge, 1946)

—, 'Þorgerðr Hölgabrúðr and the *Trolla Þing*: A Note on Sources', in *The Early Cultures of North-West Europe: Chadwick Memorial Studies*, ed. Sir Cyril Fox (Cambridge, 1950), pp. 397–417

—, 'The Monsters and *Beowulf*', in *The Anglo-Saxons: Studies Presented to Bruce Dickins*, ed. Peter Clemoes (Cambridge, 1959), pp. 171–203

Chambers, R. W., *Beowulf: An Introduction*, 3rd edn, with Supplement by C. L. Wrenn (Cambridge, 1959)

—, *Widsith: A Study in Old English Heroic Legend* [1912] (New York, 1965)

Christiansen, Eric, *The Norsemen in the Viking Age* (Oxford, 2002)

Cook, Robert, 'Russian History, Icelandic Story, and Byzantine Strategy in *Eymundar þáttr Hringssonar*', *Viator*, XVII (1986), pp. 65–89

Cornwell, Bernard, *The Burning Land* (London, 2009)

Davidson, Hilda R. Ellis, *The Viking Road to Byzantium* (London, 1976)

Deegan, Marilyn, and Stanley Rubin, 'Byrhtnoth's Remains: A Reassessment of his Stature', in *The Battle of Maldon, AD 991*, ed. Scragg, pp. 289–93

Dodgson, John McN., 'The Site of the Battle of Maldon', in *The Battle of Maldon*, ed. Scragg, pp. 17–80

Downham, Clare, 'Eirik Blood-Axe – Axed?', *Medieval Scandinavia*, XIV (2004), pp. 51–77

—, 'The Good, the Bad, and the Ugly: Portrayals of Vikings in "The Fragmentary Annals of Ireland"', *The Medieval Chronicle*, III (2005), pp. 28–40

—, *Viking Kings of Britain and Ireland: The Dynasty of Ivarr to AD 1014* (Edinburgh, 2007)

—, 'The Viking Slave Trade', *History Ireland*, XIX (2009), pp. 15–17

—, 'Viking Identities in Ireland: It's Not All Black and White', *Medieval Dublin*, XI (2011), pp. 185–201

—, 'Viking Ethnicities', *History Compass*, X/1 (2012), pp. 1–12

—, *No Horns on Their Helmets: Essays on the Insular Viking-Age* (Aberdeen, 2013)

Ellehøj, Svend, 'The Location of the Fall of Olaf Tryggvason', in *Proceedings of the Third Viking Congress*, ed. Kristjan Eldjarn (Reykjavik, 1958), pp. 63–73

Ellis, Hilda [see also Davidson, Hilda Ellis], *The Road to Hel* (Cambridge, 1943)

Faulkes, Anthony, 'The Viking Mind; or, In Pursuit of the Vikings', *Saga-Book of the Viking Society*, XXXI (2007), pp. 46–83

Ferguson, Robert, *The Hammer and the Cross: A New History of the Vikings* (London, 2009)

Fleming, Robin, *Britain after Rome: The Fall and Rise, 400 to 1070* (London, 2010)

Foot, Sara, 'The Making of Angelcynn: English Identity before the Norman Conquest', *Transactions of the Royal Historical Society*, n.s., VI (1996), pp. 25–49

Foote, Peter G., and David M. Wilson, *The Viking Achievement: The Society and Culture of Early Medieval Scandinavia* (London, 1970)

Frank, Roberta, *Old Norse Court Poetry: The Dróttkvætt Stanza* (Ithaca, NY, 1978)

—, 'Viking Atrocity and Skaldic Verse', *English Historical Review*, XCIX (1984), pp. 332–43

—, 'The Blood-eagle again', *Saga-Book of the Viking Society*, XXII (1986–9), pp. 287–9

Gifford, Edwin and Joyce, *Anglo-Saxon Sailing Ships*, 2nd edn (Woodbridge, Suffolk, 2002)

Gísli Sigurðsson, *The Medieval Icelandic Saga and Oral Tradition: A Discourse on Method*, trans. Nicholas Jones (Cambridge, MA, 2004)

Gotfredsen, Anna B., et al., 'A Ritual Site with Sacrificial Wells from the Viking Age at Trelleborg, Denmark', *Danish Journal of Archaeology*, III (2014), pp. 145–63

Graham-Campbell, James, ed., *The Cuerdale Hoard and Related Viking Age Silver and Gold in the British Museum* (London, 2011)

Harris, Joseph, 'Saga as Historical Novel', in *Structure and Meaning in Old Norse Literature*, ed. John Lindow et al. (Odense, 1984), repr. in his collection *Speak Useful Words or Say Nothing* (Ithaca, NY, 2008), pp. 227–60

—, 'Beowulf's Last Words', *Speculum*, LXVII (1992), pp. 1–32

—, 'A Nativist Approach to *Beowulf*: The Case of Germanic Elegy', in *Companion to Old English Poetry*, ed. Henk Aertsen and Rolf Bremmer (Amsterdam, 1994), pp. 45–62

—, 'Sacrifice and Guilt in *Sonatorrek*', in *Studien zum Altgermanischen: Festschrift für Heinrich Beck*, ed. Heiko Uecker (Berlin and New York, 1994), pp. 173–96

—, 'Female Divinities, Fate, and Fiction', in *History and Literature: Essays in Honor of Karl S. Guthke*, ed. William Collins Donahue and Scott Denham (Tübingen, 2000), pp. 221–9

—, 'Love and Death in the *Männerbund*', in *Heroic Poetry in the Anglo-Saxon Period: Studies in Honor of Jess B. Bessinger*, ed. Helen Damico and John Leyerle (Kalamazoo, MI, 1993), pp. 77–114, repr. in his collection *Speak Useful Words or Say Nothing* (Ithaca, NY, 2008), pp. 287–317

Haywood, John, *Dark Age Naval Power: A Re-assessment of Frankish and Anglo-Saxon Seafaring Activity* (London and New York, 1991)

Hedeager, Lotte, *Iron-Age Societies: from Tribe to State in Northern Europe, 500 BC to AD 700*, trans. John Hines (Oxford and Cambridge, MA, 1992)

Heinrichs, Anne, 'Krákumál', in *Medieval Scandinavia*, ed. Pulsiano, pp. 368–9

Helle, Knut, ed., *The Cambridge History of Scandinavia*, vol. I: *Prehistory to 1520* (Cambridge, 2003)

Herr, Michael, *Dispatches* (New York, 1980)

Herschend, Frands, quoted in Giorgio Ausenda, 'Current Issues and Future Directions in the Study of the Scandinavians: Summary of Participants' Discussions and Comments', in *The Scandinavians*, ed. Judith Jesch (Woodbridge, Suffolk, 2002), pp. 321–52

Hines, John, 'Egill's *Höfuðlausn* in Time and Place', *Saga-Book of the Viking Society*, XXIV (1994–7), pp. 83–104

—, and Desmond Slay, eds, *Introductory Essays on 'Egils saga' and 'Njáls saga'* (London, 1992)

Hughes, Shaun F. D., 'The Battle of Stamford Bridge and the Battle of Bouvines', *Scandinavian Studies*, LX (1988), pp. 30–75

Ilkjær, Jørgen, *Illerup Ådal: Archaeology as a Magic Mirror* (Højbjerg, 2000)

James, Edward, 'The Northern World in the Dark Ages, AD 400–900', in *The Oxford Illustrated History of Medieval Europe*, ed. G. Holmes (Oxford, 1988), pp. 63–114

Jameson, Andrew, Letter in *London Review of Books*, XXXVI/10 (22 May 2014)

Jón Stefánsson, 'The Vikings in Spain: from Arabic (Moorish) and Spanish Sources', *Saga-Book of the Viking Society*, VI (1909–10), pp. 31–46

Jones, Gwyn, 'The Legendary History of Ólaf Tryggvason', W. P. Ker lecture 22 (Glasgow, 1968)

—, *History of the Vikings* [1968] (London, 1973)

Kolbrún Haraldsdóttir, 'Flateyjarbók', in *Medieval Scandinavia*, ed. Pulsiano, pp. 197–8

Komar, A. V., 'Swords from Dnieprostroi (On the History of a Find Made in 1928)', available on www.academia.edu

Kroesen, R., 'The Enmity between Thorgrímr and Vésteinn in the *Gísla saga Súrssonar*', *Neophilologus*, LXVI (1982), pp. 386–90

Larrington, Carolyne, 'Egill's Longer Poems: *Arinbjarnarkviða* and *Sonatorrek*', in *Introductory Essays*, ed. Hines and Slay, pp. 49–63

Lincoln, Bruce, *Between History and Myth: Stories of Harald Fairhair and the Founding of the State* (Chicago, IL, 2014)

Loe, Louise, et al., *'Given to the Ground': A Viking-Age Mass Grave on Ridgeway Hill, Weymouth* (Dorchester and Oxford, 2014)

McCormick, Michael, *Origins of the European Economy: Communications and Commerce, AD 300 to 900* (Cambridge, 2001)

McKinnell, John, 'The Context of *Vǫlundarkviða*', *Saga-book of the Viking Society*, XXIII (1990–91), pp. 1–27

MacLeod, Mindy, and Bernard Mees, *Runic Amulets and Magic Objects* (Woodbridge, Suffolk, 2006)

McWhorter, John E., 'What Happened to English?', in McWhorter, *Defining Creole* (New York, 2005), pp. 267–311

Macrae-Gibson, O. D., 'The Topography of *Hrafnkels saga*', *Saga-book of the Viking Society*, XIX/2–3 (1975–6), pp. 239–63

Martin, Janet, *Treasure of the Land of Darkness* (Cambridge, 1986)

McTurk, Rory, *Studies in 'Ragnars saga Loðbrókar' and its Major Scandinavian Analogues*, Medium Ævum Monographs, n.s., 15 (Oxford, 1991)

—, ed., *A Companion to Old Norse-Icelandic Literature and Culture* (Oxford and Malden, MA, 2005)

—, 'The Household of Ragnarr Loðbrók', in *Familia and Household in the Medieval Atlantic World*, ed. Benjamin T. Hudson (Tempe, AZ, 2011), pp. 1–18

Miller, Clarence, 'Fragments of Danish History, Translated from Arngrimur Jonsson's *Rerum Danicarum Fragmenta* (derived from *Skjoldunga saga*)', *American Notes and Queries*, XX/3 (Summer 2007), pp. 9–22

Miller, Wiliam I., *Why is your Axe Bloody: A Reading of 'Njáls saga'* (Oxford, 2014)

Musset, L., 'Pour l'etude comparative de deux fondations: le royaume de York et le duché de Rouen', *Northern History*, X (1975), pp. 40–54

Naumann, Elise, 'Slaves as Burial Gifts in Viking Age Norway?', *Journal of Archaeological Science*, XLI (2014), pp. 533–40

Neidorf, Leonard, ed., *The Dating of Beowulf: A Reassessment* (Cambridge, 2014)

Nelson, Janet, 'The Frankish Empire', in *Oxford Illustrated History*, ed. Sawyer, pp. 19–47

Newton, Sam, *The Origins of Beowulf and the Pre-Viking Kingdom of East Anglia* (Cambridge, 1993)

Nielsen, Hans Frede, *Guldhornsinskriften fra Gallehus: Runer, sprog ok politik* (Odense, 2002)

Niles, John D., ed., *Beowulf and Lejre* (Tempe, AZ, 2007)

Norman, Thomas S., 'Scandinavians in European Russia', in *Oxford Illustrated History*, ed. Sawyer, pp. 110–33

Ó Corráin, Donnchadh, 'High Kings, Vikings, and Other Kings', *Irish Historical Studies*, XXI (1978), pp. 283–333 [review of Smyth, *Scandinavian Kings*]

—, 'Ireland, Wales, Man and the Hebrides', in *Oxford Illustrated History*, ed. Sawyer, pp. 83–109

—, 'The Vikings in Ireland', in *Vikings in Ireland*, ed. Anne-Christine Larsen (Roskilde, 2001), pp. 17–27

Parker, Philip, *The Northmen's Fury: A History of the Viking World* (London, 2014)

Pollard, A. M., et al., 'Sprouting like Cockle among the Wheat: The St Brice's Day Massacre and the Isotopic Analysis of Human Bones from sjc, Oxford', *Oxford Journal of Archaeology*, XXXI (2012), pp. 83–102

Pons-Sanz, Sara M., 'Whom did Al-Ghazal Meet? An Exchange of Embassies between the Arabs from Al-Andalus and the Vikings', *Saga-book of the Viking Society*, XXVIII (2004), pp. 5–28

Poole, Russell, '*Darraðarljóð*: A Viking Victory over the Irish', in Poole, *Viking Poems of War and Peace: A Study in Skaldic Narrative* (Toronto, 1991), pp. 16–56

Price, Neil S., 'Life and Afterlife: Dealing with the Dead in the Viking Age', video lecture, 2012, www.cornell.edu

—, *The Vikings in Brittany*, Saga-Book of the Viking Society, XXII/6, pp. 319–440

—, *The Viking Way: Religion and War in Late Iron Age Scandinavia* (Uppsala, 2002)

Pulsiano, Phillip, ed., *Medieval Scandinavia: An Encyclopedia* (New York and London, 1993)

Randsborg, Klaus, *Hjortspring: Warfare and Sacrifice in Early Europe* (Aarhus, 1995)

Renaud, Jean, *Les Vikings et la Normandie* (Tours, 1989)

—, *Rollon, Chef des Vikings* (Rennes, 2006)

—, *Vikings et noms de lieux de Normandie* (Cully, 2009)

Roach, Levi, *Æthelred the Unready* (New Haven, CT, 2016)

Rowe, Elizabeth A., *The Development of 'Flateyjarbók': Iceland and the Norwegian Dynastic Crisis of 1389* (Odense, 2005)

—, *Vikings in the West: The Legend of Ragnarr Loðbrók and his Sons* (Vienna, 2014)

Rundkvist, Martin, *Meadhalls of the Eastern Geats: Elite Settlements and Political Geography AD 375–1000 in Östergötland, Sweden* (Stockholm, 2011)

Sawyer, P. H., ed. *The Oxford Illustrated History of the Vikings* (London, 1997)

Sawyer, Peter, 'The Viking Expansion', in *Cambridge History*, ed. Helle, pp. 105–20

Schjødt, J. P., 'Ibn Fadlan's Account of a Rus Funeral: To What Extent does it Reflect Nordic Myth?', in *Reflections on Old Norse Myths*, ed. P. Herman et al. (Turnhout, 2007), pp. 133–48

Scragg, D. G., ed., *The Battle of Maldon, AD 991* (Oxford, 1991)

Shepard, Jonathan, 'Yngvarr's Expedition to the East and a Russian Inscribed Stone Cross', *Saga-Book of the Viking Society*, XXI (1982–5), pp. 22–92

Shippey, Tom, 'A Missing Army: Some Doubts about the Alfredian Chronicle', *In Geardagum*, IV (1982), pp 41–55 [revised and reprinted in *Anglo-Saxon*, I (2008), pp. 219–38]

—, 'Speech and the Unspoken in *Hamthismal*', in *Prosody and Poetics: Essays in Honor of Constance Hieatt*, ed. T. J. Toswell (Toronto, 1995), pp. 180–96

—, '"The Death-Song of Ragnar Lodbrog": A Study in Sensibilities', in *Medievalism in the Modern World: Essays in Honour of Leslie Workman*, ed. Richard Utz and Tom Shippey (Turnhout, 1999), pp. 155–72

—, '*Hrólfs saga kraka* and the Legend of Lejre', in *Making History: Essays on the Fornaldarsögur*, ed. Martin Arnold and Alison Finlay (Exeter, 2010), pp. 17–32

—, 'Proverbs and Proverbiousness in *Hrafnkels saga Freysgoða*', in *The Hero Recovered: Essays on Medieval Heroism in Honor of George Clark*, ed. James Weldon and Robin Waugh (Kalamazoo, MI, 2010), pp. 127–41

—, 'The Way of the Warrior' (review of British Museum exhibition and book *Vikings: Life and Legend*), *London Review of Books*, XXXVI/9 (3 April 2014)

—, 'Names in *Beowulf* and Anglo-Saxon England', in *Dating of Beowulf*, ed. Neidorf, pp. 58–79

Sigfús Blöndal, *The Varangians of Byzantium*, trans. and revd Benedict Benedikz (Cambridge, 2007)

Slim, Field-Marshal Sir William, *Unofficial Histories* (London, 1950)

Slupecki, Leszek P., 'Facts and Fancy in *Jómsvikinga saga*', available at www.scribd.com

Smith, A. H., *The Place-Names of the North Riding of Yorkshire*, English Place-Name Society V (Cambridge, 1928)

—, *Place-Names of the East Riding of Yorkshire*, EP-NS XIV (Cambridge, 1937)

—, *Place-Names of the West Riding*, 8 parts, EP-NS XXX–XXXVII (Cambridge, 1961–3)

Smyth, Alfred P., *Scandinavian Kings in the British Isles* (Oxford, 1977)

—, *Scandinavian York and Dublin*, 2 vols (Dublin, 1975)

—, *Warlords and Holy Men: Scotland AD 80–1000* [1984] (Edinburgh, 1989)

—, *King Alfred the Great* (Oxford and New York, 1995)

Stéfan Einarsson, 'Old English *beot* and Old Norse *heitstrenging*', *Publications of the Modern Language Society of America*, XLIX (1934), pp. 975–93

Stefán Karlsson, 'Möðruvallabók', in *Medieval Scandinavia*, ed. Pulsiano, pp. 426–7

Storgaard, Birger, Lone Gebauer Thomsen and Lars Jørgensen, *The Spoils of Victory: The North in the Shadow of the Roman Empire* (Copenhagen, 2003)

Swanwick, Michael, 'A Changeling Returns', in *Meditations on Middle-earth*, ed. Karen Haber (New York, 2001), pp. 33–46

Thompson, Claiborne W., '*Gísla Saga*: The Identity of Vestein's Slayer', *Arkiv*, LXXXVIII (1973), pp. 85–90

Tolkien, Christopher, 'The Battle of the Goths and Huns', *Saga-Book of the Viking Society*, XIV (1953–7), pp. 141–63

Tolkien, J.R.R., *The Tolkien Reader* (New York, 1966)

—, *The Monsters and the Critics and Other Essays*, ed. Christopher Tolkien (London, 1997)

—, *The Legend of Sigurd and Gudrún*, ed. Christopher Tolkien (London, 2009)

Wallace-Hadrill, J. M., *The Vikings in Francia*, Sir Frank Stenton Memorial Lecture, 1974 (Reading, 1975)

Walsh, A., *Scandinavian Relations with Ireland during the Viking Period* (Dublin, 1922)

Ward-Perkins, Bryan, *The Fall of Rome and the Collapse of Civilisation* (Oxford, 2005)

Watts, Victor E., ed., *The Cambridge Dictionary of English Place-Names* (Cambridge, 2004)

Wawn, Andrew, *The Vikings and the Victorians: Inventing the Old North in Nineteenth-century Britain* (Cambridge, 2000)

Whaley, Diana, 'Skaldic Verse', in *Companion to Old Norse*, ed. McTurk, pp. 479–502

Wilson, David M., 'The Conversion of the Viking Settlers in the Isle of Man', in *Conversion and Identity in the Viking Age*, ed. Ildar Garipzanov (Turnhout, 2014), pp. 117–38

Winroth, Anders, *The Age of the Vikings* (Princeton, NJ, 2014)

Woolf, Alex, 'View from the West: An Irish Perspective on West Saxon Dynastic Practice', in *Edward the Elder: 899–924*, ed. N. J. Higham and D. H. Hill (London and New York, 2001), pp. 89–101

Wormald, Patrick, 'Viking Studies: Whence and Whither?', in *The Vikings*, ed. R. T. Farrell (London, 1982), pp. 128–53

Acknowledgements

TEN YEARS AGO, working from home on a book like this, many miles from a university library, would have been impossible. Even now it would have been much harder without the assistance of Martin Arnold, who has repeatedly supplied me with books, photocopies and references, over and above even the claims of long friendship. Also absolutely vital has been the help of Jamie Emery, at Pius XII Library in Saint Louis University, with her colleague Shawnee Magparangalan, who looked after more interlibrary loan requests, via ILLiad, than I would have thought possible. I am most grateful too for the assistance of Andrew Wawn, who read the whole draft at a late stage, gave much advice and picked out many errors. For those that remain I am solely responsible, as I am for the views expressed, which I know are by no means shared. I am most grateful also to Rory McTurk, Jesse Byock, Rob Fulk, Matt Townend and Nelson Goering, all of whom responded generously and unconditionally to queries, all too often made late and urgently. While they too may not share my views, I hope they will not regret their part in framing them. Finally, Tor Fauskanger provided handsome and detailed maps of Norwegian battlegrounds, which we have regrettably not been able to reproduce.

Photo Acknowledgements

The author and publishers wish to express their thanks to the below sources of illustrative material and/or permission to reproduce it:

Sebastian Ballard: pp. 7, 8, 9, 10; Mark Gridley: p. 229; courtesy Nicolai Garhøj Larsen, Eyecadcher Media and Roskilde/Lejre Museum, Denmark: p. 48.

Index